CAMERA POWER

Camera Power is the first book to tackle the policy questions raised by two ongoing revolutions in recording the police: copwatching and police-worn body cameras. Drawing on original research from over two hundred jurisdictions and more than one hundred interviews – with police leaders and officers, copwatchers, community members, civil rights and civil liberties experts, industry leaders, and technologists – Mary D. Fan offers a vision of the great potential and perils of the growing deluge of audiovisual big data. In contrast to the customary portrayal of big data mining as a threat to civil liberties, *Camera Power* describes how audiovisual big data analytics can better protect civil rights and liberties and prevent violence in police encounters. With compelling stories and coverage of the most important debates over privacy, public disclosure, proof, and police regulation, this book should be read by anyone interested in how technology is reshaping the relationship with our police.

Mary D. Fan is the Henry M. Jackson Professor of Law at the University of Washington. She served as a federal prosecutor in the Southern District of California, and as an associate legal officer at a United Nations (UN) tribunal. Professor Fan was elected to the American Law Institute (ALI) in 2012 and is an Advisor to the ALI's Model Penal Code: Sexual Assault and Related Crimes Project.

Camera Power

PROOF, POLICING, PRIVACY, AND AUDIOVISUAL BIG DATA

MARY D. FAN

University of Washington

CAMBRIDGE
UNIVERSITY PRESS

CAMBRIDGE
UNIVERSITY PRESS

University Printing House, Cambridge CB2 8BS, United Kingdom

One Liberty Plaza, 20th Floor, New York, NY 10006, USA

477 Williamstown Road, Port Melbourne, VIC 3207, Australia

314–321, 3rd Floor, Plot 3, Splendor Forum, Jasola District Centre, New Delhi – 110025, India

79 Anson Road, #06–04/06, Singapore 079906

Cambridge University Press is part of the University of Cambridge.

It furthers the University's mission by disseminating knowledge in the pursuit of education, learning, and research at the highest international levels of excellence.

www.cambridge.org
Information on this title: www.cambridge.org/9781108418553
DOI: 10.1017/9781108290364

© Mary D. Fan 2019

First published 2019

Printed in the United Kingdom by TJ International Ltd. Padstow Cornwall

A catalogue record for this publication is available from the British Library.

Library of Congress Cataloging-in-Publication Data
NAMES: Fan, Mary D., 1978– author.
TITLE: Camera power : proof, policing, privacy, and audiovisual big data / Mary D. Fan, University of Washington.
DESCRIPTION: Cambridge, United Kingdom ; New York, NY : Cambridge University Press, 2019. | Includes bibliographical references and index.
IDENTIFIERS: LCCN 2018052246 | ISBN 9781108418553 (hbk : alk. paper)
SUBJECTS: LCSH: Police misconduct – United States. | Police – community relations – United States. | Video recordings – United States. | Video surveillance – United States. | Civil rights – United States.
CLASSIFICATION: LCC HV8141 .F36 2019 | DDC 363.2–dc23
LC record available at https://lccn.loc.gov/2018052246

ISBN 978-1-108-41855-3 Hardback
ISBN 978-1-108-40754-0 Paperback

For every person who just wants their beloved to come home safely.

And for Andy and Dean, always.

Contents

Figures

Tables

Acknowledgments

Expressing thanks is one of the most pleasurable tasks – but also one of the most challenging for fear of inadvertently omitting someone deeply appreciated and because it is hard to express the full strength of my gratitude. I will err on the side of brevity rather than lengthy name lists because many of your names already appear in the citations in the text. I hope you know how grateful I am to you.

Thank you to the people, named and unnamed in the pages of this book, who contributed powerful stories, deep expertise, and excellent insights. You are law enforcement officers, activists, copwatchers, community members, civil libertarians, civil rights advocates, industry leaders, and technologists. Thank you for your important work. You may not agree with each other on some of the big issues dividing our nation. But each of you from a different perspective has amazed me with your courage, vision, and crucial work. I wish each side could see what I have witnessed about how brave, hard, and crucial your work is. It has been a beautiful gift to learn from each of you and to share your time.

Many thanks to my editor, Matt Gallaway. This book exists because of your outreach. Your brilliant vision, judgment, grace, and responsiveness have guided me throughout this process. You are a writer's dream editor.

This work has benefited from presentation at many fora and from commentary by scholars and leaders in the field. Thank you to the faculty and students at the University of Alabama, UCLA, University of Colorado, University of Illinois at Urbana-Champaign, University of North Carolina, and Vanderbilt for your excellent comments and suggestions. I am especially grateful to my wonderful faculty hosts and the masterminds behind the gatherings, David Ardia, Jean-François Blanchette, Snowden Becker, Frederic M. Bloom, Jason Mazzone, Dean Jennifer Mnookin, Richard Ernest Myers II, Mary-Rose

Papandrea, Stephen Rushin, and Chris Slobogin. Thanks also to the Sousveillance Task Force of the National Association of Criminal Defense Lawyers (NACDL) for great questions, insights, and suggestions.

I want to particularly give a shout-out to three brilliant scholars and giants in my field who have inspired me, mentored me, and helped shape this project from its inception to completion with their insights: Barry Friedman, Richard Myers, and Chris Slobogin.

I also am deeply grateful and influenced by my mentors Drs. Fred Rivara and Ali Rowhani-Rahbar at the Harborview Injury Prevention and Research Center and Dr. David Hemenway and Cathy Barber at the Harvard Injury Control Center. You inspire me with your vision and dedication to violence prevention and have helped shape the soul of this project. Thank you, David and Cathy, for the wonderful daily lunches, which I miss, and the great talks as I developed this work. Thank you, Fred and Ali, for teaching me and inspiring my interest in violence prevention – and understanding when I became a hermit to finish this project.

Thanks also to advanced analytics industry leader Peter T. Parker, who read all of Chapter 4 and all the sections on audiovisual big data, machine learning, and artificial neural networks and gave extensive illuminating comments. Many thanks to Brian Sweeney, who brought an engineer's precise mind to checking facts and figures in the book. You keep me grounded and stalwartly catch me on the rock walls and beyond.

Some sections of this book draw from portions of my previously published articles. These articles include Mary D. Fan, *Privacy, Public Disclosure, Police Body Cameras: Policy Splits*, 68 ALA. L. REV. 395 (2016); Mary D. Fan, *Justice Visualized: Courts and the Body Camera Revolution*, 50 U.C. DAVIS L. REV. 897 (2017); Mary D. Fan, *Missing Police Body Camera Videos: Remedies, Evidentiary Fairness, and Automatic Activation*, 52 GA. L. REV. 57 (2017); *Hacking Qualified Immunity: Camera Power and Civil Rights Settlements*, 8 ALA. C.R. & C.L. L. REV. 51 (2017); Mary D. Fan, *Democratizing Proof: Pooling Police Body Camera and Public Cell Phone Videos*, 96 N.C. L. REV. 1639 (2018); Mary D. Fan, *Body Cameras, Big Data, and Police Accountability*, 43 L. & SOC. INQUIRY __ (2018); Mary D. Fan, *Audiovisual Analytics and Smarter Early Intervention Systems for Policing* 2018 U. ILL. L. REV. __. Many thanks to the outstanding editors at each of these publications, especially lead editors Ryan Lee Giles, Lauren Kosches, Kaitlin Melissa Phillips, Kimberly Procida, Chris Saville, Aaron Smith, Shalyn Smith, and Lee Whatling.

I am deeply grateful to the outstanding librarians of the Gallagher Law Library at the University of Washington, especially Maya Swanes, Alena Wolotira, and Cheryl Nyberg, who have been intrepid and resourceful in tracking down and amassing a library of 213 body camera policies. You have been invaluable on so many projects.

Thanks to my superb Hazelton Fellows Francesco Carriedo, Ali Gaffney, Garrett Heilman, Michelle Hur, Sophie Jin, Taryn Jones, Alyssa Nevala, Geoff Wickes, and Jake Willard. You inspired me with your enthusiasm and ideas and were stalwart, dedicated, and careful coders. Francesco and Garrett, your initiative, outreach, and intrepid ability to secure information were stellar. Michelle Hur was a particular rock star in taking on a lion's share of work and cross-checking with impeccable grace, skill, and an eagle's eye. Officer Jake Willard never ceased to amaze me with the excellence of his work and initiative in administering surveys and coding while finishing law school and also serving full time as a patrol officer with the Tacoma Police Department.

I have been blessed to work under inspirational deans. Many thanks to Dean Kellye Testy for your encouragement and leadership, which has fostered a productive environment to write this book, and to incoming Dean Mario Barnes, whose motivating check-ins (during your first weeks as dean!) spurred me to the finish line.

Thank you to Andy for the hugs and the sweet everythings that give me perspective and inspire me to slow down, at least for a little while. And thanks always to Dean, my best friend for almost half my life now and the first reader for much of my work.

Finally, thanks to my amazing students in criminal law and procedure and evidence and the outstanding law review editors who have worked on my articles over the years. You energize me with your curiosity, enthusiasm, and passions; inspire (and sometimes horrify) me with your stories; and make me so optimistic for our future. I love your fascination with innovative technology-enhanced approaches to addressing long-burning problems. I am so proud to see all that you are accomplishing in making hopes and ideas a reality in the field and in the legislature.

Introduction
Dual Revolutions in Recording the Police

Lordy, I hope there are tapes.

    – James Comey, Former Director of the Federal Bureau of Investigation (FBI)[1]

We are keeping more data on ourselves than on the public now. That's our surveillance. We are doing a lot of internal surveillance.

    – Brian Maxey, Chief Operating Officer, Seattle Police Department[2]

LIFE AND DEATH ON BODY CAMERA

It is a hot Friday night in Baltimore. People are outside to escape the brick oven heat of their homes. In the patchwork of neighborhoods that compose the city, residents talk, play, shop, visit, flirt – and sometimes call for help or scramble for cover because bullets break out.

Baltimore is one of the deadliest cities in America for the people who live in and love the city.[3] As the heat of summer 2017 hit, Baltimore was on pace to reach

---

[1] *Full Transcript and Video: James Comey's Testimony on Capitol Hill*, N.Y. TIMES (June 8, 2017), www.nytimes.com/2017/06/08/us/politics/senate-hearing-transcript.html.

[2] Throughout this book, there will be quotations and information from the more than one hundred interviews conducted for this book with police leaders and officers, community members, copwatchers, civil rights and civil liberties experts, and technologists. If a quotation is not derived from one of the interviews conducted for this book, the source is given in the footnote. As a convention, the reader can assume that quotes without secondary source attribution are from original interviews conducted for this book. This research was reviewed by the institutional review board of the Human Subjects Division (HSD) of the University of Washington (HSD study 50785).

[3] In 2015, Baltimore had the second-highest murder rate of all major US cities – eleven times the national average. Michael B. Sauter, Samuel Stebbins, & Thomas C. Frohlich, *The Most Dangerous Cities in America*, USA TODAY (Oct. 1, 2016), www.usatoday.com/story/money/business/2016/10/01/most-dangerous-cities-america/91227778/ (based on Uniform Crime Reports data for 2015). For homicide trends by city, see MATTHEW FRIEDMAN, AMES GRAWERT,

the highest per capita homicide rate in its history.[4] At the start of August 2017, community leaders and activists designated a cease-fire weekend, pleading "nobody kill anybody" for just a seventy-two-hour respite.[5] By Saturday of that cease-fire weekend, two more homicides happened.[6]

Money and violence are not evenly distributed and Baltimore is no exception. West Baltimore has families with roots many generations deep in the city, dating to the Great Migration when sharecroppers moved more northerly, drawn by steel and other industry jobs.[7] History is etched in each block, some still retaining the pride and beauty of the past and people trying to hold on. Other blocks are pocked with homes boarded, burned, and deteriorating like corpses with eyes blocked shut. Violence and the disappearance of good factory jobs have driven some people to give up homes and move from a place where even the graffiti pleads, "Stop Shooting."

Out here in the Western and its bordering Central districts, the officers and I wear bulletproof vests. The officers also wear body cameras, a new technology deployed throughout the force just this year. Over the course of the ten-hour "Charlie" shift, from late afternoon deep into the night at 3:00 AM, those cameras will record the video equivalent of several feature-length films.

Someone will be shot. A bleeding victim's friend will flag down the patrol car in an alleyway for help. Officers will search for a shooter and gun on the loose on the street where children play. Someone will be hiding in the dark as an ex-boyfriend fresh out of prison tries to break down the door. Someone will be stabbed, bleed out, and die. Repeatedly, paramedics will bear fallen community members to the University of Maryland's famous shock trauma unit, which the cops revere for its repeated miracles of reviving the dead and nearly gone.

James Cullen, Crime in 2016: Updated Analysis (Brennan Center for Justice, Dec. 20, 2016), at 3 www.brennancenter.org/sites/default/files/analysis/Crime_in_2016_Updated_Analysis .pdf; Ames Grawert & James Cullen, Crime in 2015: A Final Analysis (Brennan Center for Justice, Apr. 20, 2016), www.brennancenter.org/analysis/crime-2015-final-analysis.

[4] Luke Broadwater & Justin Fenton, *With Murders Skyrocketing in Baltimore, Feds Begin Sending Help*, Balt. Sun (May 1, 2017), www.baltimoresun.com/news/maryland/baltimore-city/bs-md-ci -atf-crime-20170501-story.html. By the end of 2017, Baltimore would report a per capita homicide rate record of 56 killings per 100,000 people for the city of 615,000 residents, a record high for the city. *2017 Sees Highest Murder Rate Ever in Shrinking Baltimore*, CBS News, Jan. 2, 2018, www.cbsnews.com/news/baltimore-homicide-murder-rate-highest-2017-crime-increase-fred die-gray-killing/.

[5] Ray Sanchez, *Second Deadly Shooting in Baltimore's "Nobody Kill Anybody" Weekend*, CNN (Aug. 6, 2017), www.cnn.com/2017/08/04/us/baltimore-ceasefire-weekend/index.html.

[6] *Id.*

[7] W. E. B. Du Bois chronicled the migration: "Negros come from country districts to small towns, then go to larger towns; eventually they drift to Norfolk, Va., or to Richmond. Next they come to Washington, and finally settle in Baltimore or Philadelphia." W. E. B. Du Bois, On Sociology and the Black Community 128 (1978).

The cameras capture all this, and people in some of their most terrifying, painful, embarrassing moments. Dying moments, crying moments, scared silent and unresponsive moments. Mixed in with everyday travails. Warring neighbors, exes, family members; hit-and-runs; and the steady drumbeat of calls about someone dealing drugs, on a residential street, in the corner store, or at the park where children play ball.

Between calls, the officers use cell phones to tag all the video with relevant metadata, such as incident time, type, and individuals involved (Figures 0.1 and 0.2). At the end of the shift, the officers upload the amassed data documenting daily life and sometimes death. The night's videos will join the rapidly growing trove of audiovisual data stored in the cloud, generating new potential and power to regulate the police, prevent the eruption of violence, and change the balance of power when it comes to proof. The massive and rapidly growing volume of audiovisual data about policing practices and daily life on the streets and in private places like homes also raises important legal questions about proof, privacy, public disclosure, data preservation, and advanced data analytics to better protect civil liberties and prevent harm.

The questions are fast-breaking and new because of the rapid uptake of police-worn body cameras. A survey of 254 police departments across the United States conducted in July 2013 found that fewer than a quarter of the responding departments used body cameras.[8] Then came the fires and protests over controversial killings in police encounters and fierce national debate over police power and use of force. West Baltimore is an emblem of the pain and national turmoil.

Just two years ago, West Baltimore burned during protests over the death of Freddie Gray, age twenty-five.[9] On April 12, 2015, Gray was walking down the street in the West Baltimore neighborhood where he grew up, and where he would die.[10] Officers said Gray spotted the police and ran, so they chased and seized him.[11]

---

[8] Police Executive Research Forum, US Dep't of Justice, Implementing a Body-Worn Camera Program: Recommendations and Lessons Learned 2 (2014), www .justice.gov/iso/opa/resources/472014912134715246869.pdf ("Although the use of body-worn cameras is undoubtedly a growing trend, over 75 percent of the respondents reported that they did not use body-worn cameras as of July 2013.").

[9] Peter Hermann, *After Rioters Burned Baltimore, Killings Pile Up Largely under the Radar,* Wash. Post (May 17, 2015), www.washingtonpost.com/local/crime/violence-has-become-pa rt-of-life-in-baltimore/2015/05/17/4909264a-f714-11e4-a13c-193b1241d51a_story.html?utm_term= .5fd20e45ee24.

[10] Freddie Gray grew up in the Sandtown-Winchester neighborhood of West Baltimore, where his fatal encounter with police occurred. Scott Shane, Nikita Stewart, & Ron Nixon, *Hard but Hopeful Home to 'Lot of Freddies,'* N.Y. Times (May 3, 2015), at A1.

[11] Kevin Rector, *The 45-Minute Mystery of Freddie Gray's Death,* Balt. Sun (Apr. 12, 2015), www .baltimoresun.com/news/maryland/freddie-gray/bs-md-gray-ticker-20150425-story.html.

FIGURE 0.1 An officer in West Baltimore tags police-worn body camera with metadata between handling calls for service.

A bystander recorded Gray calling in pain as officers pulled him into a van.[12] No citizen was along to record what happened during the ride to the police station, and officers did not have to wear body cameras back then. Somehow, during those mysterious forty-five minutes, Gray died. Today, his face is painted two stories high in a mural on the building across a street from the arrest, in remembrance and in pain. And Baltimore officers, like police officers across the nation, now are required to record most law enforcement encounters.[13]

By 2016, the Major Cities Chiefs Association and Major County Sheriffs' Association reported that 97 percent of the seventy law enforcement agencies

[12] The video can be viewed courtesy of the Baltimore Sun online at www.youtube.com/watch?v=mxbeuownxjQ

[13] *See* Baltimore Police Dep't, Pol'y 824, Body Worn Cameras (Jan. 1, 2018).

Mandatory Recording
Unless unsafe, impossible, or impractical to do so, all members (not just the primary unit) present, dispatched, or otherwise participating in any of the below listed activities must activate their BWC:
1 At the initiation of a call for service or other activity or encounter that is investigative or enforcement-related in nature . . .
6 When transporting a detainee, regardless if the transport vehicle is equipped with a Transport Vehicle Camera (TVC) System . . .

FIGURE O.2 In the Anacostia neighborhood of Washington, DC, officers link body camera video to police reports.

surveyed indicated they were going to adopt body cameras or had already done so.[14] New body camera policies require officers to record more law enforcement activities than ever before, such as stop-and-frisks, searches, and responses to calls for service.[15] The rapid proliferation of police-worn body cameras has important ramifications for police regulation and civil liberties protection – but it is only part of a larger recording revolution.

COPWATCHING, SPONTANEOUS AND ORGANIZED

To focus just on cop-worn cameras spreading across communities ranging from impoverished West Baltimore to wealthy places like the San Francisco Bay Area and New York would miss a major part of the story of police regulation by recording. Camera power radiates not just from police-worn

[14] MAJOR CITIES CHIEFS & MAJOR COUNTY SHERIFFS, SURVEY OF TECHNOLOGY NEEDS: BODY WORN CAMERAS 2 (DHS Office of Emergency Communications, Dec. 2015), https:// assets.bwbx.io/documents/users/iqjWHBFdfxIU/rvnT.EAJQwK4/vo. *See also* Mike Maciag, *Survey: Almost All Police Departments Plan to Use Body Cameras*, GOVERNING (Jan. 26, 2016), www.governing.com/topics/public-justice-safety/gov-police-body-camera-survey.html (quoting a figure of 95 percent).

[15] See Table 1.3 for a summary of the common contexts where the 213 body camera policies coded for this book require recording.

body cameras but also from the multitude of cell phones that community members carry, with the potential to record police encounters in public or in private.

People wield cameras as a form of self-protection, as protest, and as a way to address imbalances in power. You may not have the badge, the gun, the official imprimatur of the state. People may not believe you, or even bother to hear you when you cry or speak. But a video can go viral. It carries the authority of seeming documentary objectivity and the power to get the word out. And if someone dies, the camera offers an alternative viewpoint to the official story. The camera is a form of self-defense, particularly in communities of color where people live the reality behind the grim statistics that African Americans face a higher risk of stops, frisks, arrests, and death in police encounters.[16]

Like communities anywhere, people need to have someone they can call when tragedy or emergency strikes. When someone is bleeding out. When a gun and shooter is on the loose. When someone fears for her life. Even in communities with high mistrust of the police, people call the police in times of need, as evident from the stream of calls throughout the day and night. But people do not trust the officers that come.[17] That mistrust is visible the moment officers pull up. Community members – even those who called the police – often have their cell phones at the ready to record (Figure 0.3). And when something goes down, like a frisk or an arrest, a crowd will quickly gather, mobilized by Facebook Live recording. Organized copwatchers also patrol in some communities, keeping an eye on the cops and encouraging people to record in a form of self-help regulation and community engagement in policing by protest and dissent.

So the people record the cops. And the cops are now directed by new body camera rules to record almost every encounter with the public. The body cameras go with officers into homes to respond to domestic calls; into the

---

[16] The data on homicides by police are notoriously spotty, leading to efforts by major news organizations to conduct newspaper surveillance of deaths. *See, e.g., The Counted Database*, THE GUARDIAN (last updated Dec. 2016), www.theguardian.com/us-news/ng-interactive/201 5/jun/01/the-counted-police-killings-us-database (presenting searchable data on killings by the police in 2015 and 2016). For graphs of Centers for Disease Control and Prevention data on the disparities in the risk of death people face in police encounter by race, see Figures 1.1–1.2.

[17] For work on the crisis of trust in policing, particularly in disadvantaged minority communities, *see, e.g.,* Rod K. Brunson, *"Police Don't Like Black People": African-American Young Men's Accumulated Police Experiences*, 6 (1)CRIMINOLOGY & PUB. POL'Y 71–101 (2007); Jeffrey Fagan & Garth Davies, *Street Stops and Broken Windows: Terry, Race, and Disorder in New York City*, 28 FORDHAM URB. L. J. 457–504 (2000); Tracey Meares, *The Legitimacy of Police among Young African-American Men*, 92 (4)MARQUETTE L. REV. 651–656 (2009); Tom R. Tyler, *Policing in Black and White: Ethnic Group Differences in Trust and Confidence in the Police*, 8 (3)POLICE QUARTERLY 322–342 (2005).

FIGURE 0.3 A West Baltimore resident records the police talking to witnesses and searching for bullets after a shooting.

middle of the night to halt an alleged home invader; into the blind alleys and stairwells; and into many other sites and moments when a bystander with a camera may not be around.

As a Western Baltimore resident with roots three generations deep explained to me, the cameras on cops – even the ones she called to her home to keep the peace as her daughter's ex moves out – are reassuring. "Keeps from the he-said, she-said. It makes you feel better because you can see. You can see what really happened. Just go to the video."

These everyday scenes on the streets reflect the dual recording revolutions that are transforming policing, proof, and privacy in the United States. Everyone has incentive to record to contest or control the narrative. With widespread access to small portable cell phone cameras any ordinary Chris,[18] Feidin,[19] or Ramsey[20] can film the police and release a viral video shot from his point of view. As mistrust grows, and protests and riots erupt over controversial uses of force, police departments also have incentive to deploy body cameras to offer evidence beyond the officer's word, which is no longer as credited as it used to be.[21]

---

[18] Air Reserve base worker Chris LeDay played an important role in disseminating the video of the shooting of Alton Sterling to the public. Peter Holley, *"Super-fishy": Man Who Posted Video of Alton Sterling Killing Claims Employer Still Refusing to Let Him Work*, WASH. POST. (July 24, 2016), www.washingtonpost.com/news/post-nation/wp/2016/07/13/man-who-posted-v ideo-of-alton-sterling-killing-claims-he-was-targeted-by-vengeful-police/?utm_term= .2c4e3f596bee.

[19] Immigrant barber Feidin Santana recorded the shooting of Walter Scott in South Carolina. *Feidein Santana, Who Recorded Police Shooting of Walter Scott, Speaks Out*, NBC NEWS (Apr. 8, 2015), www.nbcnews.com/news/latino/feidin-santana-who-recorded-man-shot-police-officer-speaks-out-n338171.

[20] Deli worker Ramsey Orta filmed the death of Eric Garner. J. David Goodman, *Man Who Filmed Fatal Police Chokehold Is Arrested on Weapons Charges*, N.Y. TIMES (Aug. 4, 2014), at A19.

[21] Concern over possible police "testilying" has been long-standing. *See, e.g.,* Christopher Slobogin, *Testilying: Police Perjury and What to Do about It*, 67 U. COLO. L. REV. 1037–1060 (1996). But the concern is particularly salient today, with confidence in the police reaching its lowest point in

TOUTVEILLANCE

We live in an age of rapidly expanding toutveillance, where virtually every-one has the pocket-sized means to record. The French language gave us the word *surveillance*.[22] The proposition *sur*, meaning "on" or "over," implies a directionality of control where the people below are watched from over-seers in power above.[23] In contrast, the French word *tout* is a more capacious concept, meaning "all," "every," or "whole." Toutveillance is more than the top-down of surveillance. Toutveillance also is more than the bottom-up control suggested by *sousveillance*, from the French *sous*, meaning "below" or "underneath." Steven Mann used the term *sousveillance* to refer to citizens exercising bottom-up control to monitor the watchmen.[24] I would go farther.

In our toutveillance society, people and the police are recording each other from all directions, making everyone at once surveilled and surveillor. I am recording you, you are recording me, and the police are recording us too, because the people demand it. The lines of power and control radiate from all directions as people seek to document their perceptions and thus shape the narrative. This is captured by the flexible French term *tout*. The phenomenon also is captured by the recordings by the police, community members, and private and public surveillance devices increasingly interspersed throughout the landscapes of our daily lives. The growing trove of police, public, and privately generated data has great power, potential – and perils – for protecting civil liberties, police regulation, and harm prevention.

This book is about the implications of pervasive police recording for proof, privacy, big data analytics, civil rights protection, and violence prevention. Emerging policies and laws are now laying the foundation for a future that will be shaped by the rise of audiovisual big data amassing from police-worn body

twenty-two years in 2015 according to Gallup Polls. Jeffrey M. Jones, *In US, Confidence in Police Lowest in 22 Years*, GALLUP POLLS (June 19, 2015), http://news.gallup.com/poll/183704/confidence-police-lowest-years.aspx. Even at the low point, 52 percent of Americans surveyed still express "a great deal" or "quite a lot" of confidence in police. *Id.* This is a mark of how much trust and credibility officers have historically enjoyed – and why there has previously been little incentive to record rather than ask the public to rely on the officer's word.

22 For a concise and colorful history of the "very French word" surveillance, see The Vocabularist, *The Very French History of the Word "Surveillance,"* BBC MAGAZINE (July 14, 2015), www.bbc.com/news/blogs-magazine-monitor-33464368.

23 KEVIN MACNISH, THE ETHICS OF SURVEILLANCE 1 (Routledge 2018).

24 Steve Mann, *New Media and the Power Politics of Sousveillance in a Surveillance-Dominated World*, 11 (1/2)SURVEILLANCE & SOC'Y 18–34 (2013); Steve Mann, Veillance and Reciprocal Transparency: Surveillance Versus Sousveillance, AR Glass, Lifeglogging, and Wearable Computing, 2013 PROC. IEEE INT'L SYMP. ON TECH. & SOC'Y 1, 1.

cameras, bystander cell phone recordings, and other surveillance systems. Audiovisual big data analytics already is being used in criminal investigations. Video integration systems in places like Atlanta and Los Angeles can amass video and other data feeds from multiple sources for crime-predictive analytics and to track persons of interest.[25]

The next frontier is using audiovisual big data and predictive analytics for improved police regulation, civil rights and civil liberties protections, and violence prevention in law enforcement encounters. The audiovisual big data on policing practices coming from the dual revolutions in recording the police present opportunities to discover new ways to prevent harm to the public and officers using machine learning methods such as artificial neural networks. But there are major challenges, including the risk of severe privacy harms; refusals to disclose data; misleading or biased audiovisual data; and limits on the use and preservation of one of the major sources of data, body camera videos, for officer evaluation and discipline.

The book draws on more than 100 interviews with law enforcement rank-and-file officers, supervisors, community members, copwatchers, civil rights and civil liberties advocates, and technology executives and experts to explore the issues and how to address them. The book also presents the results of the coding and analyses of 213 body camera policies from jurisdictions across the nation to show the main policy approaches, splits, and coming challenges.[26] Recording by the public is a force as powerful, wild and unregulated as the will of a crowd. In contrast, the volume of police-worn body camera policies prescribing more standardized recording protocols is growing. While state legislatures are beginning to pass laws pertinent to police-worn body cameras, much of the early policy action is in the less visible realm of police department policies. Mapping the policy approaches is a foundation for debates about trade-offs between privacy, public disclosure, and regulation by transparency. The policy analyses also reveal potential obstacles to maximizing the harm prevention and police regulation power of aggregated audiovisual big data.

The goal is to provide a forward-looking account of the potential of widespread police recording and the resulting audiovisual big data to reshape criminal justice and the politics of privacy. The book focuses on the rise of police-worn body cameras and citizen recording to capture police encounters on the streets and inside homes and other private places. The pervasiveness

---

[25] For a discussion of big data analytics in police investigations, *see, e.g.,* ANDREW FERGUSON, THE RISE OF BIG DATA POLICING (2017).

[26] See the appendix for a summary of the methods of policy collection and coding and a list of the 213 jurisdictions, ordered by state.

and ease of such recordings pose important questions regarding privacy, accountability, transparency, proof, and the balance of power between officers and citizens. Technology rapidly changes but the overarching issues this book explores will pose continuing challenges and questions for communities, legislatures, and police departments.

The issues also cross borders and have comparative import. The United Kingdom, followed by the United States, are the earliest movers in widely deploying police-worn body cameras. Other nations are likely to follow. From Rio de Janeiro, Brazil, to Kingston, Jamaica, to Cape Town, South Africa, to Manila, the Philippines, police forces are exploring police-worn body cameras and other recording strategies.[27] Because of the ubiquity of cell phone cameras across the world, citizen recording of authorities is growing as a strategy of protest, resistance, and accountability seeking. The rapid spread of police recording culture and the resulting market for technological advances in utilizing the audiovisual data has important implications for the future of criminal justice, privacy, safety, and security.

This book also is about the value choices and hard trade-offs communities face. Communities and police departments are investing limited budgetary dollars in body cameras in the hopes of saving lives, preventing escalation to violence, averting riots, providing better proof, and potentially exonerating community members – and officers – from false accusations.[28] Though people

---

[27] Gráinne Perkins, *Lights, Camera, Action! Body-Worn Cameras: Challenges and Opportunities in Police Research*, 11 POLICING: A JOURNAL OF POLICY AND PRACTICE 1–5 (2017); Kim Brunhuber, Police in Crime-Ridden Rio de Janeiro Try a Cheaper Body Camera: Their Phones, CBC, Apr. 11, 2016, www.cbc.ca/news/world/brazil-crime-police-cameras-1.3527618; Monique Grange, Bunting Announces That Police Are to Start Wearing Body Cameras, JAMAICA GLEANER (Jan. 23, 2014), http://jamaica-gleaner.com/power/50696.

[28] *See, e.g.*, POLICE COMPLAINTS BD., ENHANCING POLICE ACCOUNTABILITY THROUGH AN EFFECTIVE ON-BODY CAMERA PROGRAM FOR MPD OFFICERS 3 (2014) ("The devices have the potential to enhance public safety and improve relations between police and members of the public by reducing misconduct, facilitating the resolution of incidents that arise, and improving officer training. Other potential advantages for the District government include enhancing public confidence in the criminal justice system and reducing the city's exposure to civil liability."); POLICE EXECUTIVE RESEARCH FORUM, US DEP'T OF JUSTICE, IMPLEMENTING A BODY-WORN CAMERA PROGRAM: RECOMMENDATIONS AND LESSONS LEARNED 2 (2014) ("Among police executives ... reported benefits include the following: Strengthening police accountability by documenting incidents and encounters between officers and the public[;] Preventing confrontational situations by improving officer professionalism and the behavior of people being recorded[;] Resolving officer-involved incidents and complaints by providing a more accurate record of events[;] Improving agency transparency by allowing the public to see video evidence of police activities and encounters[;] Identifying and correcting internal agency problems by revealing officers who engage in misconduct and agency-wide problems[;] Strengthening officer performance by using footage for officer training and monitoring[;] Improving evidence documentation for investigations

wielding cameras may feel protected in the way that warriors in older times felt protected by wearing a talisman into battle, actual harm prevention effects may vary. The scientific data on whether body cameras actually alter police and public behavior and reduce complaints and violence is mixed, as the book will discuss.[29] But the turn to body cameras and citizen recordings also opens other avenues of police regulation and investigation that the book will explore.

and prosecutions."); NAACP ET AL., CIVIL RIGHTS COALITION URGES NATIONAL REFORMS AND RECOMMENDATIONS TO ADDRESS POLICE ABUSE (2015), https://lawyer scommittee.org/wp-content/uploads/2015/08/Civil-Rights-Coalition-on-Police-Reform-Resou rce-Packet.pdf (urging the adoption of body cameras); Jay Stanley, *Police Body-Mounted Cameras: With Right Policies in Place, a Win for All, Version 2.0* ACLU (Oct. 2015), www .aclu.org/sites/default/files/assets/police_body-mounted_cameras-v2.pdf ("Although we at the ACLU generally take a dim view of the proliferation of surveillance cameras in American life, police on-body cameras are different because of their potential to serve as a check against the abuse of power by police officers ... Cameras have the potential to be a win-win, helping protect the public against police misconduct, and at the same time helping protect police against false accusations of abuse.").

[29]   See, e.g., David Yokum, Anita Ravishankar, & Alexander Coppock, EVALUATING THE EFFECTS OF POLICE BODY-WORN CAMERAS: A RANDOMIZED CONTROLLED TRIAL 18 (The Lab@DC, Oct. 20, 2017), http://bwc.thelab.dc.gov/TheLabDC_MPD_BWC_Workin g_Paper_10.20.17.pdf (reporting the results of a randomized controlled trial of body cameras in DC and a null finding, indicating the inability to detect a statistically significant impact of body cameras on police use of force, citizen complaints about policing activities, or judicial outcomes); Barak Ariel et al., *The Effect of Police Body-Worn Cameras on Use of Force and Citizens' Complaints against the Police: A Randomized Controlled Trial*, 31 J. QUANTITATIVE CRIMINOLOGY 509 (2015) (reporting results from a Rialto, California, trial finding that officers who did not wear body cameras had twice the incidence of uses of force compared to officers randomly selected to wear body cameras); Barak Ariel et al., *Report: Increases in Police Use of Force in the Presence of Body-Worn Cameras Are Driven by Officer Discretion: A Protocol-Based Subgroup Analysis of Ten Randomized Experiments*, 12 J. EXPERIMENTAL CRIMINOLOGY 453, 459–461 (2016) (reporting the results from the largest set of randomized controlled trials of the effectiveness of uses of body cameras and finding that uses of force jumped by 71 percent among officers who did not follow the recording protocol and instead recorded at their discretion, whereas, among officer who followed the protocol, the use of force decreased by 37 percent among body cameras wearers compared to controls); Charles M. Katz ET AL., ARIZ. STATE UNIV. CTR. FOR VIOLENCE PREVENTION AND CMTY. SAFETY, EVALUATING THE IMPACT OF OFFICER WORN BODY CAMERAS IN THE PHOENIX POLICE DEPARTMENT 33 (2014), http://publicservice.asu.edu/sites/default/files/ppd_spi_feb_20_2015_final.pdf.   (finding a 22.5 percent decline in complaints against officers in a precinct that tested body cameras during a time when complaints were rising in other precincts); MICHAEL D. WHITE, POLICE OFFICER BODY-WORN CAMERAS: ASSESSING THE EVIDENCE 17–19 (2014), http://cvpcs .asu.edu/products/police-officer-body-worn-cameras-assessing-evidence (follow "Documents" hyperlink) (finding a decline in complaints against Mesa, Arizona, police officers after the introduction of body cameras); Wesley G. Jennings et al., *Cops and Cameras: Officer Perceptions of the Use of Body-Worn Cameras in Law Enforcement*, 42 J. CRIM. JUST. 549, 550 (2014) (discussing a Mesa, Arizona, Police Department evaluation which found a 40 percent decline in complaints against officers and a 75 percent decrease in use of force incidents after the introduction of body cameras).

CHANGING THE BALANCE OF POWER OVER PROOF

Part I discusses the major cultural shift represented by the police recording revolution and the potential benefits. Once upon a time, not long ago, people who recorded the police were arrested. Progressive prosecutors struggled to convince law enforcement officers to record even a small snippet of the investigative process, the interrogation. While recording the police still carries dangers today, much has changed. Members of the public are wielding cell phone cameras as peaceful weapons of resistance. Courts increasingly are protecting the public's right to record the police. Police departments are attempting to rebuild battered public trust and protect officers and communities from fierce disputes by recording most law enforcement activities formerly shrouded in opacity and retrospective accounts. Because cell phone videos can go viral and spark riots, police departments increasingly are under intense pressure to have and release video in a race for control of the narrative.

Chapter 1 is about the body camera revolution sweeping police departments and the hopes for improved harm prevention, accountability, and better evidence propelling the shift. Chapter 2 is about copwatching, organized and otherwise, and the increasingly recognized right to record the police. Chapter 3 explores how these dual revolutions in recording the police constitute a major power shift toward democratizing the power of proof. Recordings are no magic bullet, but they can change the formerly extremely one-sided balance of power in police-said, suspect-said disputes.

With rapidly spreading uptake, body cameras have the potential to be disruptive technology in the sense of having the transformative power to shake up old ways of analyzing criminal procedure cases – and the resulting rules of deference and noninquiry. Analysis of pooled data across cases can reveal patterns and practices that may lead courts to rethink whether to address weak and blind spots in the law on issues such as pretextual stops, arrests for minor offenses; knock and announce violations; and traffic stops to secure revenue-generating fines and forfeitures.[30] Moreover, even if doctrines in the courts of law pose numerous hurdles to a formal legal remedy, videos have the power to take a case directly to the people and exert pressure to settle cases.

---

[30] Members of the Supreme Court have left open the possibility that showing a pattern and practice of violations may lead the Court to reconsider its decisions refusing to intervene in certain police practices such as knock and announce violations, or arrests for minor offenses. *See, e.g.*, Hudson v. Mich., 547 US 586, 604 (2006) (Kennedy, J., concurring); Atwater v. City of Lago Vista, 532 US 318, 353 n.25 (2001).

AUDIOVISUAL BIG DATA ANALYTICS FOR JUSTICE AND HARM PREVENTION

Aggregating audiovisual big data on everyday practices that were formerly opaque to courts and disciplinary boards can reinvigorate police oversight and early intervention systems (EIS). Analyses of the pooled big data across thousands of everyday police encounters can reveal hidden patterns and practices that can inform the work of courts, oversight bodies, and investigators. Machine learning methods such as artificial neural networks can uncover patterns that are predictive of risk for officers to avert the escalation to violence or rights violations. Technology is advancing to permit real-time steering of escalating situations, adjusting responses to facilitate deescalation and safer interactions.

Part II is about the great promise and perils of audiovisual big data and advanced analytics deploying machine learning techniques. Chapter 4 offers a vision for how audiovisual big data analytics can generate ways to better avert harm; promote officer and public wellness; and protect civil rights. Big data mining, like surveillance, is often portrayed as a Big Brotherly tool of power and a threat to privacy, civil liberties, and individual freedoms.[31] Yet the power of big data also may be deployed to protect civil rights and civil liberties and curb government power, if policies permit.

Analyses of patterns across cases can reveal issues that would otherwise be invisible at the individual case level, such as how officers' words and tones of respect may vary by the race of the community member, as a recent study using Oakland Police Department body camera data found.[32] Evolving technology and techniques can permit searches and analyses based on voice, tone, choice of language, facial scanning, and other criteria. This pattern detection power can enhance harm prevention by police departments and civil liberties protection via administrative and judicial review.

---

[31] Dana Boyd and Kate Crawford, *Critical Questions for Big Data, Information*, 15(5) COMMUNICATION & SOCIETY 662–679 (2012); TERENCE CRAIG AND MARY E. LUDLOFF, PRIVACY AND BIG DATA (Sebastopol: O'Reilly Media 2011); José van Dijck, *Datafication, Dataism and Dataveillance*, 12(2) SURVEILLANCE AND SOCIETY 197–208 (2014); Elizabeth E. Joh, *Policing by Numbers: Big Data and the Fourth Amendment*, 89 WASH. L. REV. 35–68 (2014).

[32] Rob Voigt, Nicholas P. Camp, Vinodkumar Prabhakaran, William L. Hamilton, Rebecca C. Hetey, Camilla M. Griffiths, David Jurgens, Dan Jurafsky, and Jennifer Eberhardt, *Language from Police Body Camera Footage Shows Racial Disparities in Officer Respect*, 114 (25)PROC. NAT'L ACADEMY OF SCI. 6521–6526 (2017).

RECURRENT CHALLENGES AND FRAMEWORKS
FOR THE FUTURE

While the dual recording revolutions and resulting audiovisual big data have pathbreaking potential, there are important countervailing concerns and resistance to address. Chapter 5 discusses how recordings from one perspective may be partial and misleading – yet have a truthiness that leads us to reshape our memories to conform to the video. Because big data analytics is only as good as the quality of the data used to train algorithms, it is important to be aware of how we generate our audiovisual big data and the risk of hidden biases in the information.

Chapter 6 addresses the steep privacy costs of regulation by recording and the conflicting strong public interest in disclosure of important data. Chapter 7 discusses how the principles of controlled access and privacy protection planning drawn from the health sciences can help us realize the potential of audiovisual big data to better inform violence and rights violation prevention while protecting privacy. Chapter 7 also addresses data preservation and storage issues. Chapter 8 discusses the detection and disciplinary dilemmas that communities and police departments face when officers do not record as required, or when videos reveal misconduct.

The Partiality and Potential Biases of Video Evidence and Audiovisual Data

The rise of audiovisual evidence calls for greater awareness about the limitations of recordings in revealing the truth to settle conflicts over what really happened. Audiovisual evidence may be partial, misleading, and subject to interpretive conflicts. Chapter 5 delves into the dangers of vesting too much trust in the seeming objectivity and impartiality of recordings and perceptual errors and biases. Supporters of recording the police often express hope that video footage will be unbiased and objective evidence that will help resolve partisan disputes.[33] Where there is heady faith and optimism, there are often scholars ready to give the contrary view. There is a growing body of literature dispelling the myth of the camera's objectivity

---

[33]   *See, e.g.*, Austin Police Dep't, Policy Manual, Policy 303, at 132 (May 4, 2015) ("The use of body worn digital recording (BWDR) system provides an unbiased audio/video recording of events that employees encounter."); Phila. Police Dep't, Directive 4.21 (Apr. 20, 2015) (explaining that body cameras "provide an unbiased audio and video recording of events that officers encounter").

and truth-telling power.[34] Recordings can be partisan, either intentionally or unintentionally. Our perceptions also are partisan. People from different perspectives viewing the same video may still disagree fiercely on the propriety of an officer's conduct, and the risk a suspect posed.

Camera angle and perspective can shape what story gets told.[35] How the camera is positioned, and how people are framed, can influence our perceptions of what is happening. What the camera may leave out because of its positioning also can mislead. From two-dimensional video, it is difficult to evaluate potentially important details such as distance, velocity, height, and depth. Belatedly activated cameras also can omit important parts of the story, such as a suspect raising hands and laying prone in surrender.[36] A suspect may seem to be resisting if an altercation is recorded at a tight and low angle. A higher wider perspective may reveal something altogether different – such as officers stomping on a prone suspect. We are more adept at applying our common sense to judge the credibility of witnesses, considering their motives, hesitation, and demeanor.[37] In contrast, we are more apt to view

---

[34] Mary D. Fan, *Justice Visualized: Courts and the Body Camera Revolution*, 50 U.C. DAVIS L. REV. 897, 947–953 (2017); Dan M. Kahan et al., *Whose Eyes Are You Going to Believe? Scott v. Harris and the Perils of Cognitive Illiberalism*, 122 HARV. L. REV. 837, 859, 879 (2009); Caren Myers Morrison, *Body Camera Obscura: The Semiotics of Police Video*, 54 AM. CRIM. L. REV. 791 (2017); Seth Stoughton, *Police Body-Worn Cameras*, 96 N.C. L. REV. 1363 (2018); Howard M. Wasserman, *Recording of and by the Police: The Good, the Bad, and the Ugly*, J. GENDER, RACE & JUSTICE 543, 552, 557 (2017); Michael D. White & Henry Fradella, *The Intersection of Law, Policy, and Police Body-Worn Cameras: An Exploration of Critical Issues*, 96 N.C. L.REV. 1579 (2018); Howard Wasserman, *Recording, Police Misconduct, and Judicial Procedure*, 96 N.C. L. REV. 1313 (2018).

[35] Much of the work on camera perspective on viewer perceptions has been done in the police interrogation context. *See, e.g.*, Daniel Lassiter, Shari Seidman Diamond, Heather C. Schmidt, & Jennifer K. Elek, *Evaluating Videotaped Confessions: Expertise Provides No Defense against the Camera-Perspective Effect*, 18 PSYCHOL. SCI. 224, 224–225 (2007) [hereinafter *Evaluating Videotaped Confessions*]; G. Daniel Lassiter et al., *Further Evidence of a Robust Point-of-View Bias in Videotaped Confessions*, 21 CURRENT PSYCHOL. DEVELOPMENTAL, LEARNING, PERSONALITY 265, 267 (2002) [hereinafter *Further Evidence*]; *see* G. Daniel Lassiter et al., *Attributional Complexity and the Camera Perspective Bias in Videotaped Confessions*, 27 BASIC & APPLIED SOC. PSYCHOL. 27, 28–29 (2005) [hereinafter *Attributional Complexity*].

[36] Chapter 5 delves into an example of two contrasting stories about the arrest of Derrick Prince conveyed by cameras at different angles.

[37] For a discussion on evaluating witness credibility, *see, e.g.*, Steven I. Friedland, *On Common Sense and the Evaluation of Witness Credibility*, 40 CASE W. RES. L. REV. 165, 174–177 (1990). Perceptual biases based on factors such as a person's appearance also may lead us astray. *See, e.g.*, Olin Guy Wellborn III, *Demeanor*, 76 CORNELL L. REV. 1075, 1078–1082 (1991) (discussing biases and heuristics in evaluating witness credibility). But we are more apt to see humans as partial and interested and consider their motives, while viewing cameras as impartial and objective.

the images on recordings as objective reality, transparently offering a window to judge what really happened.[38]

Finally, videos may lead to armchair jockeying that ignores the legally relevant measure of proper officer behavior. Under the law, officers are judged from the perspective of a reasonable officer facing the situation in the field, rather than from the cool remove of hindsight.[39] Stress can dramatically narrow a person's field of vision.[40] An officer's human perception and awareness of the circumstances may be more limited than all that a body-mounted machine might record. Conversely, a camera may not capture the full range of events or information known to the officer. Despite legitimate reasons for differences in camera and human perception, officers may feel pressure to conform reports and recollections to the video. This concern has led to debates over whether officers should be allowed to view recordings before memorializing their recollections in reports.[41] Fact-finders also may misjudge or discredit officer and other witness accounts that deviate from what they see on the video even though perceptions may honestly differ.

The risk of putting too much weight on video evidence does not detract from the fact that the availability of recordings is an important advance.

---

[38]   For a discussion of the perceived transparency, objectivity and impartiality of images, *see, e.g.,* NEAL FEIGENSON & CHRISTINA SPIESEL, LAW ON DISPLAY 8 (2009).

[39]   Graham v. Connor, 490 US 386, 396 (1989).

[40]   The San Diego Police Department's policy provides an important caution applicable to courts as well as officers: "BWCs [body-worn cameras] have a field of vision of either 75 degrees for the Flex or 130 degrees for the Axon. While human beings have a field of vision of 180 degrees, the human brain has a field of attention of 50–60 degrees. Under stress, this field can narrow down to a 1/2 degree. Stress also induces auditory exclusion and prevents the brain from analyzing and remembering all the stimuli that it takes in through the senses.

"Officers make decisions based on the totality of the human senses. An officer's recollection of specific details may be different from what is captured in digital evidence since BWCs only capture audio and video."

CITY OF SAN DIEGO, SAN DIEGO POLICE DEP'T PROCEDURE NO. 1.49 1, 11 (July 8, 2015).

[41]   *Compare, e.g.,* UPTURN, THE ILLUSION OF ACCURACY: HOW BODY-WORN CAMERA FOOTAGE CAN DISTORT EVIDENCE (Nov. 2017), www.teamupturn.org/reports/2017/the-illusion-of-accuracy (arguing that officers should not be allowed to view body camera footage before writing reports because viewing videos can skew perception, imbue officer accounts with inflated credibility, taint memory, and undermine procedural justice); *with* POLICE EXECUTIVE RESEARCH FORUM, US DEP'T OF JUSTICE, IMPLEMENTING A BODY-WORN CAMERA PROGRAM: RECOMMENDATIONS AND LESSONS LEARNED 29 (2014), www .justice.gov/iso/opa/resources/472014912134715246869.pdf ("Officers should be permitted to review video footage of an incident in which they were involved prior to making a statement about the incident. Reviewing footage aids officer recollection and leads to more accurate documentation of events. Real-time recording is considered best evidence and is unaffected by stress or other factors. Most police executives PERF consulted favor allowing review in these circumstances.").

Recordings can address imbalances of power in suspect-said, officer-said credibility contests. Data aggregated across recordings can offer important systemic information about patterns and practices of conduct. More data can lead to better-informed decision-making for users literate in the limitations and proper uses of the information. Pooling community member videos in an independent repository can add a fuller range of perspectives for analyses, supplementing police-generated videos. The potential benefits can be cultivated and the costs reduced by the societal choice of policies, managing expectations, and educating to spread audiovisual interpretive literacy.

Privacy Perils and Public Disclosure Controversies

One of the paramount concerns regarding pervasive recording of and by the police are privacy harms. Police officers intervene at some of the worst or most embarrassing moments of our lives. We call the police because of intimate partner violence, sexual assaults, fights, home invasions, hurt loved ones, and much more. Police see us when we are battered and bleeding, drunk and disorderly, distraught, traumatized, enraged, strung out on drugs, and worse. Now the pain, embarrassment, and low points that police see daily will be recorded – and perhaps broadcast.

When a video goes viral, it may raise public awareness and debate. But this consciousness-raising and public participation in discussing police use of force comes at a severe price to the lives – and perhaps deaths – captured on camera and the families of the people involved. Imagine being the person screaming as you or your loved one is dragged away, whether off an overbooked airplane, or from your home or car. Traumatic and painful moments replay repeatedly on the news, and are frozen in the permanent storage of the Internet, forever accessible and painful. In states with strong public disclosure laws and no exemptions for police recordings, members of the public could request such videos and post them on YouTube for public comment. This is not a hypothetical but is drawn from real-life cautionary tales that you will read in this book.

The privacy harms are demonstrably real. But the reaction in some places has been extreme. Increasingly, legislatures are enacting laws withholding body camera videos from public disclosure, or making disclosure at the discretion of law enforcement, unless compelled by a court order.[42] This

---

[42] Sophia Murguia, More States Set Privacy Restrictions on Bodycam Video, Reporters Committee for Freedom of the Press (June 29, 2016), www.rcfp.org/bro wse-media-law-resources/news/more-states-set-privacy-restrictions-bodycam-video (discussing

creates new controversies. Battles over nondisclosure or delayed disclosure of police videos are creating new grounds for mistrust. Ironically, what was meant to be groundbreaking regulation by transparency has prompted renewed concerns by community activists about police opacity.[43]

A better approach than nondisclosure is disclosure with redaction. At the time nondisclosure laws were enacted, the redaction process was expensive, laborious, and required tedious work by a human eye. Automated redaction of videos was a difficult challenge because unlike surveillance videos mounted on a fixed object, body cameras and cell phone cameras are constantly in motion.[44] In an astonishingly short time, however, companies have vastly improved automated redaction. Human intervention is still required but technology is reducing the time and labor. Laws and policies change at a glacial pace compared to technology and once enacted, are hard to dislodge from their frozen archaism. The nondisclosure issues are an example of a larger overarching issue when it comes to technology-aided police regulation. Technology is much more adaptable, fast changing, and responsive than law. Policy should not be driven by technology limitations. Rather, choose the right policy and technology will rapidly adapt.

Controlled Access and Privacy Protection Planning

The transformative vision of the recording revolution is regulation by information. Because the information is volatile and powerful, there will always be pressures to withhold, delete, and otherwise severely restrict its use and dissemination. Doing so, however, has the perverse consequences of putting exponentially more cameras into communities and on officers without the promised benefits of trust rebuilding, harm prevention, and effective oversight

legislation restricting disclosure of body camera video in New Hampshire, Minnesota, Louisiana, Missouri, and North Carolina). The Reporters Committee for Freedom of the Press has a helpful map of legislation and policies governing access to police body-worn camera videos, available here: www.rcfp.org/bodycams.

[43] For accounts of the growing disillusionment due to the nondisclosure of body camera videos, *see, e.g.,* Kimberly Kindy & Julie Tate, *Police Withhold Videos Despite Vows of Transparency,* Wash. Post (Oct. 8, 2015), www.washingtonpost.com/sf/national/2015/10/08/police-withhold-videos-despite-vows-of-transparency/?utm_term=.cf32874baf4b (quoting Chad Marlow, attorney with the American Civil Liberties Union: "If police departments and law enforcement become the sole arbiters of what video the public gets to see, body cameras will go from being a transparency and accountability tool to a surveillance and propaganda tool.").

[44] *See, e.g.,* Robinson Meyer, *What Good Is a Video You Can't See?,* The Atlantic (Apr. 26, 2015), www.theatlantic.com/technology/archive/2015/04/what-good-is-a-video-you-cant-see/391421/ (discussing the technological challenges with redaction, necessitating costly human time).

and accountability. As critics of body cameras fear, the technology will become yet another way to comprehensively surveil communities and get more damning evidence to speed guilty pleas, without the promised benefits that led civil rights, civil liberties, and community groups to join in spurring the police recording revolution.

Rather than withholding information and aggravating controversies over police opacity 2.0, Chapter 7 proposes controlled access and privacy protection planning modeled on the approaches that have advanced medical and public health research using highly private and protected health data. There are powerful privacy, victim protection, and investigative reasons to restrict the release of information – but not to withhold it altogether from responsible parties that could use the data to improve oversight, promote accountability, and protect civil rights and liberties.

Drawing on approaches time-tested in the realms of medicine and public health, which also generates information from highly private sensitive data, the controlled access approach reduces potential privacy harms while maximizing data benefits. Data disclosure is limited to those who demonstrate that their project serves public well-being or the protection of constitutional rights, and that their training and qualifications enable them to effectively conduct the analyses and implement protocols to reduce privacy harms. This maximizes the benefits while limiting the risk of harm from data disclosure and use.

Currently, when the legitimate use of force is disputed, evidence of potential patterns of harm – from rough or rude treatment to injuries, deaths, and property destruction – are most accessible to departments with the least incentive to share it. Moreover, labor laws and collective bargaining limit the ability of departments to realize the full analytical power of the data out of concern for harassing and demoralizing line-level officers.[45] Controlled access would allow data analytics to detect and prevent problematic or dangerous patterns; improve harm prevention; protect cities and their police departments from lawsuits; and inform police regulation by courts, administrative bodies, and we the people.

Audiovisual Evidence Preservation

A third cluster of pragmatic operational challenges include data storage and retention. As the volume of amassed video grows, police departments are

---

[45] Under federal labor laws, collective bargaining with the workers' union is required when the conditions imposed by management constitute a material change to the applicable labor contract secured through collective bargaining. *See* 29 USC § 158(d) (2018) (describing the obligation to bargain collectively).

learning that data storage costs far exceed the start-up costs of putting body cameras on officers. Deletion of video that is not usable in a criminal prosecution is an alluring strategy to reduce data storage costs and protect privacy. Police departments have varying retention times for body-worn video, calibrated primarily to the relevance to a criminal investigation or prosecution. But the focus on the value of data at the level of an individual prosecution misses the harm prevention and police regulation power of amassed audiovisual data from the many encounters that may never lead to an arrest, much less go to court. Chapter 7 also presents findings on the varied approaches to data retention and the insights of technologists about addressing data storage costs.

Advancing beyond Blame: Addressing Resistance, Mistakes, and Discipline Dilemmas

Another important issue likely to recur in the era of pervasive police recording is the missing video problem. There is growing controversy and concern over officers not activating their body cameras to capture audio and video at crucial moments despite recording requirements.[46] There are many legitimate reasons for nonrecording in the heat and stress of incidents in the field – but also concerns about officer resistance and subversion of requirements. Addressing failure to record is important for public safety and for rebuilding community trust and protecting justice. The first findings from the largest set of randomized controlled trials of the effectiveness of body cameras revealed that uses of force are 71 percent higher among officers who did not follow the recording protocol and instead recorded at their discretion.[47] In contrast, among officers

---

[46] E.g., Mark Berman, *What the Minneapolis Police Shooting Tells Us about the Limits of Body Cameras*, WASH. POST (July 19, 2017), http://wapo.st/2uAnJoI; Nashelly Chavez, *Rocklin Officers Who Shot Former Honor Student Didn't Turn on Body Cameras Until Later*, SACRAMENTO BEE (Mar. 3, 2017, 6:11 PM), www.sacbee.com/news/local/crime/arti cle136372438.html (did not record until after fatal shooting); Wesley Lowery, *Charlotte Officer Did Not Activate Body Camera Until After Keith Scott Had Been Shot*, WASH. POST (Sept. 26, 2016), http://wapo.st/2cwPtXn; Annie Sweeney & Jeremy Gorner, *Chicago Police: Body Camera Didn't Record Cop's Fatal Shooting of Teen in Back*, CHI. TRIB. (Aug. 2, 2016, 7:04 AM), www.chicagotribune.com/news/local/breaking/ct-chicago-police-shooting-eddie-j ohnson-met-20160801-story.html; Aliyah Frumin, *After Baton Rouge Shooting, Questions Swirl around Body Cam Failures*, NBC NEWS (July 7, 2016), www.nbcnews.com/news/us-n ews/after-baton-rouge-shooting-questions-swirl-around-body-cam-failures-n605386? cid=em1_onsite.

[47] Barak Ariel et al., *The Effect of Police Body-Worn Cameras on Use of Force and Citizens' Complaints against the Police: A Randomized Controlled Trial*, 31 J. QUANTITATIVE CRIMINOLOGY 509 (2015).

who followed the protocol, the use of force decreased by 37 percent among body cameras wearers compared to controls.[48] Adherence matters – and nonadherence by officers equipped with body cameras may be associated with perversely heightened risk. Technology must be used as directed to have a chance of working as hoped.

The disciplinary use of video, or sanctions because of failures to record, can be a difficult issue for police departments. The introduction of body cameras throughout a police force requires buy-in from line officers – and can lead to court battles and collective bargaining with the police union arguing that having to be surveilled on the job is a material change in labor conditions.[49] The analyses of 213 body camera policies found widespread silence regarding sanctions for nonrecording. Some departments also have express protections and limitations regarding the use of body camera video for officer monitoring, evaluation, and discipline.

Some state legislatures and civil rights and liberties groups have proposed sanctions at the adjudication level for failures to record, such as adverse jury instructions or disqualifying testimony from officers who do not record as required.[50] Proposals focused on sanctions during trial misses the more than

---

[48] *Id.*

[49] *See, e.g.*, Ben Conarck, *Jacksonville Sheriff, Police Union Clash over Body Camera Rules*, FLA. TIMES UNION (Jacksonville) (Feb. 8, 2017), *available at* 2017 WLNR 6684923 (reporting on a dispute between the local police union and the sheriff over whether body camera rules are subject to mandatory collective bargaining); Brian Bakst, *Maplewood Police Officers Challenge Body Camera Policy in Lawsuit*, MPR NEWS (Minn.) (Nov. 21, 2016), www.mprnews.org/story/2016/11/21/maplewood-police-officers-challenge-body-camera-policy-lawsuit (reporting on lawsuit by police officers who objected to random audits of body camera recordings and argued that such provisions must be subject to collective bargaining); Jan Ransom, *Boston Slow to Adopt Policing Innovations; Changes Stall as Unions Seek Role*, BOS. GLOBE (Sept. 5, 2016), 2016 WLNR 27007841 (reporting on a court battle between a Boston police union and Boston Police Department management over the introduction of body cameras and whether rules should be subject to collective bargaining); Harry Bruinius, *Why Police Are Pushing Back on Body Cameras*, CHRISTIAN SCI. MONITOR (Aug. 30, 2016), WLNR 26450977 (detailing lawsuits and debates involving police unions over the body camera issue); Brian Brus, *Police Union Complaint Halts Body-Cam Test Program*, J. REC. (Okla. City), June 15, 2016, 2016 WLNR 18940773 (discussing how a lawsuit by an Oklahoma City police union put the city's body camera program on hold); Andrew Blake, *Body Cameras Spark Lawsuit between Denver Cops, City Officials*, WASH. TIMES (Nov. 6, 2015), *available at* 2015 WLNR 33002278 (discussing a lawsuit by a Denver police union seeking collective bargaining over body camera rules).

[50] *See, e.g.*, H.B. 1613, 2017 Sess. (Va. 2017) (providing that an officer who fails to record using the body camera as required may still testify about the events that should have been recorded, but the court should instruct the jury to consider the failure to record "in determining the weight given to [the officer's] testimony," or if there is no jury, then the court should consider the factor in weighing the testimony); ACLU OF MASS. & SAMUELSON LAW, TECH. & PUB. POLICY CLINIC NO TAPE, NO TESTIMONY 2 (2016) [hereinafter ACLU, NO TAPE,

90 percent of criminal convictions that come from plea bargaining, never reaching the trial jury instructions phase.[51]

Moreover, playing the blame game can be dangerous, messy, and unfair. There are many reasons why officers may not record, including legitimate and understandable ones. Most members of the public do not have experience with the high-stress situations that officers enter into multiple times daily. It is important to remember that a person under stress makes mistakes and has to prioritize responsibilities. But that should not be a sweeping justification that overlooks real problems and resistance to recording. If evidence is to be excluded, it should not depend on courts wading through the swamp of individual blame and fault. Rather, it should proceed from an evidentiary fairness perspective that asks if the missing video – regardless of the reason – leads to an imbalance between sides that requires remedies such as exclusion of partial recordings, or positive inferences for the other side.

Optimally, a technological solution is far preferable to using the blunt sticks of distant penalties. Instead of entering the murky morass of deciding whether a failure to record is justifiable or subversion, it is better to automate recording and take the human factor out. Technology companies are offering solutions such as automatic recording triggered by sounds, such as gunshots; motion, such as a weapon coming out of a holster or a door opening; or even biometric markers, such as an officer's heart rate.[52] Much more work remains to be done. Here again, policy should drive technology rather than the ephemeral technology limitations of the moment shaping policy choices.

No Testimony], https://aclum.org/wp-content/uploads/2016/11/ACLU_BodyCameras_11.21 _final.pdf (proposing an instruction that "would tell the jury that, if it finds that the police unreasonably failed to create or preserve a video of a police-civilian encounter, it can devalue an officer's testimony and infer that the video would have helped the civilian. If the jury finds that the case involves bad faith, such as the outright sabotage of body cameras, then it should be instructed to disregard officer testimony altogether.").

[51]   Dep't of Justice, Bureau of Justice Statistics, Sourcebook of Criminal Justice Statistics Online tbl.5.22.2009 (2009), www.albany.edu/sourcebook/pdf/t522200 9.pdf.

[52]   *See* Laura Diaz-Zuniga, *New Bodycams Start Recording with the Draw of a Gun*, CNN (July 21, 2017, 7:11 PM), http://cnn.it/2vJNMQr (discussing automatic activation technology triggered by the removal of a weapon from its holster); Robert Maxwell, *Lakeway Police First to Use Automatic Body Cameras*, KXAN (Austin, Tex.) (June 12, 2015, 4:57 PM), http://kxan.com/20 15/06/12/lakeway-police-first-to-use-automatic-body-cameras/ (discussing recording activation triggers linked to a patrol vehicle's "lights, siren, brake system, airbag, dome light or doors"); Ryan Mason, *More than a Body Cam*, Police: The Law Enforcement Magazine (Apr. 28, 2015), www.policemag.com/channel/technology/articles/2015/04/more-than-a -body-cam.aspx (describing Utility's system, which "allows the camera to automatically activate based on policies set by the agency" and triggers such as the vehicle speeding over seventy-five miles per hour, entering into a geofenced area, or during certain types of interactions).

Doing More with Less and Technological Silver Bullet–Think

In a time when state and local government agencies are forced to do more with less, it is tempting to seek a technological silver bullet.[53] The underlying problems that give rise to tragedies, however, take long-term investments to address. Money is finite and communities need to confront the hard questions about whether to direct dollars to long-neglected areas and issues that no technology, however sexy, can fix.

One of the major challenges that can create the conditions for tragedy is that contemporary society leaves it to police officers and the criminal justice system to address social challenges that really belong in the mental health, addiction, and social work fields.[54] High-stress situations, such as responding to suicide calls and protecting battered children, can take a heavy toll on officers and potentially impair subsequent decision-making.[55] Technology and audiovisual data analytics may assist in identifying officers who have just handled stressful calls and help protect both the officer and the community by building in decompression time and sending another team to the next critical incident. But technology cannot relieve us from examining the harder deeper questions, such as why it falls to the police rather than trained mental health and addiction experts to deal with public health crises.

---

[53] *Cf.* Samuel Tanner & Michael Meyer, *Police Work and New "Security Devices": Tales from the Beat*, 46(4)SECURITY DIALOGUE 384–400 (2015) (discussing the tendency to search for technological "magic bullets" to policing challenges).

[54] *See, e.g.,* Bernard Harcourt, *Reducing Mass Incarceration: Lessons from the Deinstitutionalization of Mental Hospitals in the 1960s*, 9 (1)OHIO ST. J. CRIM. L. 53–88 (2011) (exploring how divestment in social services, such as care for the mentally ill, has intensified the policing and incarceration challenges of modern American society); Sylvester Amara Lamin, Consoler Teboh, & John Martyn Chamberlain, *Police Social Work and Community Policing*, 2 (1)COGENT SOC. SCI. 1–13 (2016) (discussing the challenges police face in addressing mental health crises and the need for experts trained in social work); Forrest Stuart, *From "Rabble Management" to "Recovery Management": Policing Homelessness in Marginal Urban Space*, 51(9)URB. STUDIES 1909–1925 (2014) (discussing the role of police in dealing with addiction among the homeless).

[55] *See, e.g.,* Barry N. Feldman, Albert J. Grudzinskas Jr., Bernice Gershenson, Jonathan C. Clayfield, & Richard P. Cody, *The Impact of Suicide Calls on the Police*, 8 (4) PSYCHIATRY ISSUE BRIEF (2011) (unpaginated) (presenting findings that "suicide calls are often critical incidents in police officers' careers and are among the highest anxiety- and stress-provoking circumstances to which police officers must respond"); John M. Violanti, Desta Fekedulegn, Tara A. Hartley, Luenda E. Charles, Michael E. Andrew, Claudia C. Ma, & Cecil M. Burchfiel, *Highly Rated and Most Frequent Stressors among Police Officers: Gender Differences*, 41(4)AM. J. CRIM. JUST. 645–662 (2016) (reporting that dealing with family disturbances and battered children are among the most commonly occurring high-stress events for officers).

Ultimately the recording revolution is here to stay and spread. In these camera-ubiquitous times, informational and evidentiary tastes are changing. People will demand video and draw inferences that support their worldviews if video is missing. The battle over control of the narrative using recording – by community members as well as the police – will not cease. The future will be recorded. The important questions are how laws and policies will shape the future of pervasive police recording and how we can manage the costs and cultivate the benefits of extreme transparency. This book and the pages that follow explore these questions.

PART I

TOUTVEILLANCE POWER AND POLICE CONTROL

Policing in the Camera Cultural Revolution

We got you on Snap, baby. We got you.[1]

PEACEFUL WEAPONS — AND SHIELDS

As dusk descends in Anacostia, the high-poverty part of Washington, DC, that visitors to the capital do not see, a call comes from dispatch. Residents are reporting seeing two armed young men. One of the suspects is wearing a red shirt and white shoes and is about eighteen to twenty-four years old. He is armed with a gun and a knife. The second young man is in black pants and black shoes. Both are reportedly black in a neighborhood that is more than 90 percent black.[2]

The two were last seen walking down a residential street. The officers shift into action from their routine patrols along the streets. Multiple units fan out to search the streets for the armed youths.

No persons bearing weapons are in sight on the residential street where callers last reported seeing the armed persons. The officers spread out to search adjacent streets. In this community with three times the poverty rate of the rest of DC, housing projects and row homes intermingle.[3] An update from

---

[1] Voice-over commentary by a person who recorded an officer tasing a University of West Georgia student. *Police Respond to Brutality Allegation*, TIMES-GEORGIAN (Apr. 16, 2017), www.youtube.com/watch?v=DbpS-J_matg.

[2] *See* Race and Ethnicity in Anacostia, Washington, District of Columbia, Statistical Atlas (last updated Apr. 22, 2015), https://statisticalatlas.com/neighborhood/District-of-Columbia/Washington/Anacostia/Race-and-Ethnicity (providing data visualizations of US Census Bureau data and reporting that Anacostia is 96.4 percent African American).

[3] Poverty rate three times the rest of DC: Claire Zippel, *DC's Black Residents Increasingly Live East of the Anacostia River*, DC FISCAL POLICY INSTITUTE (Sept. 28, 2016) , www.dcfpi.org/all/dcs-black-residents-increasingly-live-east-of-the-anacostia-river/; Andrew Giambrone, *Poverty in D.C. Is Getting Worse East of the Anacostia River, Study Finds*, WASH. CITY

dispatch sends all units to a housing project, where multiple patrol units are converging.

By the time the unit in which I am riding arrives, six young black men are spread against the wall inside the building's ground floor with their hands and legs splayed for frisks. The tension is extreme. The youths are shouting curses and invectives, particularly heaping insults on the black officers, the shorter heavier officers, and the sole female officer. The youths protest in variations of the following, as voiced by one of the teens: "What the fuck you stopping us for? We didn't do anything."

The cameras on all sides are recording as officers frisk the detained youths. Each officer wears a body camera catching the scene from his or her position. Bent with legs spread for a frisk and a hand braced against the wall, at least three of the youths have their iPhones aimed at the officers, recording from their positions.

It is a standoff by camera.

None of the searches of the six youths turns up any weapons or contraband. Puzzled, officers search the grass and shrubs near the building in case guns and knives were dropped nearby. The canvass also does not turn up weapons.

The standoff breaks. Officers release the youths from their spread-eagled positions against the wall and begin to withdraw from the scene.

Furious about the stop-and-frisk, the youths run after the retreating officers with cell phone cameras aimed and recording.

"Get the fuck out of here!"

"Are you scared? Are you scared?"

"You must have been nerds in school getting beat up and now you want to bully people."

All the frustration and pain of being perennially a suspect as a young black male in a neighborhood long designated as high crime and thus under higher suspicion pour forth.[4]

Grim-faced, recorded on multiple devices mounted on their chests and aimed at them from the shouting youths, the officers are silent in their retreat. In the patrol cars, the atmosphere is heavy and silent with words suppressed unsaid.

The body cameras do not deactivate until the encounter ends and the youths running after the cops are well out of sight.

PAPER (Sept. 29, 2016), www.washingtoncitypaper.com/news/housing-complex/blog/20835238/poverty-in-dc-is-getting-worse-east-of-the-anacostia-river-study-finds.

4   *See, e.g.,* Ill. v. Wardlow, 528 US 119, 125–126 (2000) (holding that running from the police in a high-crime area is a sufficient basis for reasonable suspicion for a stop).

On a break, when the heavy gaze of the camera is off, one of the officers who bore the heaviest brunt of taunts because she is a young, petite black woman speaks sadly, reflectively. Ever since she was a child, she wanted to be a cop because she thought cops were the people you called when you needed help. But the painful anger and mistrust she experiences daily are grinding.

"This was a culture shock. I wanted to be the police because I love helping people. You just keep telling yourself it's OK. I don't think you ever get used to it," she says.

It is a fleeting moment of vulnerability. Then another call comes and she is back on camera again, performing with inscrutable polish. She is back to saying little, holding everything inside, even with her partner, who is so well matched they often perform wordlessly but in synchrony.

In a tense encounter filled with anger and humiliation on all sides, the cameras wielded by the officers and the youths were a peaceful form of protection. Because the stop-and-frisk yielded no evidence, no court or other adjudicator is likely to review the rights and wrongs of the encounter. Absent the compulsion of a court order or structural reform settlement, there are limited data on stops-and-frisks in many jurisdictions in America.[5]

DC is special among police departments, as a relatively well-resourced agency serving a center of power and wealth. DC also is a progressive place – and one of the most Democratic cities in the nation.[6] In 2016, the DC Council mandated that the police department collect information on stops-and-frisks, including the race, gender, and age of the persons seized and searched.[7] In 2017, the American Civil Liberties Union (ACLU) submitted Freedom of Information Act (FOIA) requests to get access to the information.[8]

The six youths stopped on the ground floor of a housing project in their community likely did not have the expertise or resources to file FOIA requests

---

[5] *See, e.g.*, Paul Butler, *The System Is Working the Way It Is Supposed To: The Limits of Criminal Justice Reform*, 104 GEO. L.J. 1419, 1447 (2016) (noting limited stop-and-frisk data and collecting available information).

[6] This remains true in the Trump era. Indeed, Trump staffers apparently are finding it difficult to date in DC because the city is so Democratic and anti-Trump. *See* Eliza Relman, *Young Trump Staffers Are Complaining That They Can't Date in DC Because Everyone Hates Them*, BUSINESS INSIDER (June 22, 2018), www.businessinsider.com/trump-staffers-are-complain-th at-they-cant-date-in-dc-2018-6.

[7] Neighborhood Engagement Achieves Results (NEAR) Act, Bill 21-0360, DC City Council (passed Mar. 2016).

[8] ACLU, Press Release, Civil Rights Advocates Seek Data on Race, Gender, and Age of Persons Stopped and Searched in Washington, DC (Feb. 10, 2017), www.aclu.org/news/aclu-dc-files-foia-request-stop-and-frisk-dc-police.

for the documentation of their encounter. But the youths were creating their own record of the actions of the police. The officers wearing body cameras were doing so too. If anything went bad in this specific encounter, there would be a video, recorded from the perspective of each side. And even if nothing erupted from this specific encounter, there would still be a video documenting that this event occurred and the identities and demographics of the people involved.

The showdown by camera captures the dual recording revolutions sweeping policing. We live in an age of more mobile cameras ready to record at a moment's notice than ever before in history.[9] In communities fraught with police–citizen tension, like the Anacostia neighborhood of DC or the Western District of Baltimore, cameras act as insurance on both sides.

A patrol officer coming off a tough shift in Baltimore points to his body camera and tells me, "People think we don't like them but we don't mind them here. Because they can help. Because people are always lying. They lie, lie, lie about what went down. Now we can just point to this."

From a different perspective, CopWatch NYC and Black Lives Matter activist Elsa Waithe explains to me, "Police lie and they lie for each other." A prime example, she observes, is how a bystander cell phone recording disproved the official account regarding the killing of Walter Scott.

The talismanic power of a camera is captured by a copwatcher in West Baltimore. "We are not afraid. We will use the weapons that we have in these cameras," Kevin Moore – neighbor to Freddie Gray, who died during police transportation – explained. "I am going to make sure that every single time the police are out there doing something they have no business doing, that it is going to be recorded, it is going to be documented."[10]

THE RADICAL CULTURAL CHANGE ON RECORDING THE POLICE

The competing yet complementary perspectives capture our current cultural change on recording the police. Everyone has incentive to record and use

---

[9]   Rose Eveleth, *How Many Photographs of You Are Out There in the World?*, ATLANTIC (Nov. 2, 2015), www.theatlantic.com/technology/archive/2015/11/how-many-photographs-of-you-are-out-t here-in-the-world/413389/ [https://perma.cc/9YB8-XC33]; *When Fatal Arrests Are Caught on Camera*, TIME (July 23, 2014), http://time.com/3024396/fatal-arrests-police-camera/ [https://per ma.cc/FB7A-KZM7].

[10] Poh Si Teng & Ben Laffin, Video, *Copwatch vs. Cops: After Freddie Gray*, N.Y. TIMES (Aug. 2, 2015), www.nytimes.com/video/us/100000003824112/copwatch-v-cops-after-freddie-gr ay.html.

the video to contest or control the narrative. Community members protest their police encounters by camera. Police departments in turn have incentive to deploy body cameras to offer a competing visual depiction of everyday law enforcement activities shot from their perspective. As police departments race to adopt body cameras and community members take up cameras to record the police, such showdowns present new opportunities and challenges for police regulation, civil rights protection, and harm prevention by radical transparency.

Police discretion is often described as opaque.[11] That very opacity is an important source of police power, not just a description of how it operates. Law enforcement officers have wide discretion to use formidable power to stop, interrogate, arrest, and even kill. For most of our history, our knowledge of how and why that discretion operates is largely based on the officer's word. Suspects may try to challenge the officer's account. But who are you going to believe – a suspect or an officer of the law? Introducing another source of information – recordings of the police by the public, as well as officers – changes that balance of power.

The power shifts not just because all sides in a dispute have additional, potentially more objective evidence revealing what really happened. Indeed, Chapter 5 discusses how the seductive assumption that recordings will reveal the objective truth may prove incorrect and how recordings can mislead in some cases. Rather, pervasive recording of police encounters creates a massive new source of data that illuminate everyday encounters for which there may otherwise never be a record, or only a written summary by an officer. The rise of recording police encounters also represents a major shift in the culture of police control.

No one likes being the object of surveillance – and that includes the masters of surveillance, the police.[12] Historically, police departments resisted recording even a portion of their work – interrogations – because of concerns that videotaping would prevent suspects from talking and reveal strategies that

---

[11] *See, e.g.,* KENNETH CULP DAVIS, DISCRETIONARY JUSTICE: A PRELIMINARY INQUIRY 38–40, 52, 83 139, 144 (1969); WAYNE R. LaFAVE, ARREST: THE DECISION TO TAKE A SUSPECT INTO CUSTODY 75–82, 162–163 (Frank J. Remington ed. 1965); SAMUEL WALKER, TAMING THE SYSTEM: THE CONTROL OF DISCRETION IN CRIMINAL JUSTICE 1950–1990 21, 39–41 (1993).

[12] FRED E. INBAU, JOHN E. REID, JOSEPH P. BUCKLEY, BRIAN C. JAYNE, CRIMINAL INTERROGATION AND CONFESSIONS 45–51 (2001) (discussing resistance to recording); Richard A. Leo & Kimberly D. Richman, *Mandate the Electronic Recording of Police Interrogations,* 6 CRIMINOLOGY & PUB. POL'Y 791, 791 (2007) (noting that many police departments continue to resist recording interrogations, though electronic recording has become increasingly common).

might be unpalatable to judges and juries.[13] I know firsthand. I was one of the federal prosecutors charged with enforcing my office's requirement that our partner agencies record interrogations, or we would not take the case.

The year was 2005. My boss, the US Attorney for the Southern District of California, was a career prosecutor who believed mightily in the Supreme Court's job description:

> The United States Attorney is the representative not of an ordinary party to a controversy, but of a sovereignty whose obligation to govern impartially is as compelling as its obligation to govern at all; and whose interest, therefore, in a criminal prosecution is not that it shall win a case, but that justice shall be done.[14]

We had many cases where the agents' report stated the defendant confessed to the crime. An agent would take the stand and testify about what the defendant admitted. With little recourse in response to that damning evidence, defense attorneys would either allege that the agents threatened and intimidated the defendant into a false confession or claim that the defendant never confessed at all and the police were making it up. Defense attorneys frequently told the jury, if the defendant really confessed freely and the government had nothing to hide, then why was there no recording as proof?

A cynic about prosecutorial power — as many great scholars are[15] — would say that the prosecutors wanted agents to record confessions to get even more leverage to extract plea bargains and win at trial. The reality is both more noble and more stark. We already had a guilty rate well above the target of 92 percent[16] set by the US Department of Justice in its budget submission to

---

[13] INBAU, REID, BUCKLEY, JAYNE, *supra* note 12, at 49–51; Saul M. Kassin, Richard A. Leo, Christian M. Meissner et al., *Police Interviewing and Interrogation: A Self-Report Survey of Police Practices and Beliefs*, 31 L. & HUM. BEHAV. 381, 385 (2007).

[14] Berger v. United States, 295 US 78 (1935).

[15] The literature on the uses and abuses of prosecutorial power is vast. *See, e.g.,* ANGELA J. DAVIS, ARBITRARY JUSTICE: THE POWER OF THE AMERICAN PROSECUTOR (2007); KENNETH CULP DAVIS, DISCRETIONARY JUSTICE: A PRELIMINARY INQUIRY (1969); Albert W. Alschuler, *The Prosecutor's Role in Plea Bargaining*, 36 U. CHI. L. REV. 50, 60 (1968); Stephanos Bibas, *Plea Bargaining Outside the Shadow of Trial*, 117 HARV. L. REV. 2463, 2471–2472 (2004); Angela J. Davis, *The American Prosecutor: Independence, Power, and the Threat of Tyranny*, 86 IOWA L. REV. 393, 411–414 (2001); Tracey L. Meares, *Rewards for Good Behavior: Influencing Prosecutorial Discretion and Conduct with Financial Incentives*, 64 FORDHAM L. REV. 851, 869–870 (1995); Daniel C. Richman & William J. Stuntz, *Al Capone's Revenge: An Essay on the Political Economy of Pretextual Prosecution*, 105 COLUM. L. REV. 583, 623–624 (2005).

[16] The Justice Department's budget submission to congress for fiscal year 2008 explained, "In the criminal area, there are two primary performance measures for the USAs [US Attorneys],

Congress.[17] In fiscal year 2005, for example, the conviction rate of defendants was 99.5 percent.[18] The plea bargaining rate was 93 percent.[19] There is not much room to improve when your percentages are that high. The concern that animated the effort to get agents to record confessions was the damage done to the appearance of justice by allegations that confessions were coerced or agents were downright lying about what happened during interrogations.

Prosecutors can only advise and persuade agents to do something, not order action. Prosecutors sometimes refer to the agents with whom they work as "their" agents, showing the close camaraderie between prosecutors and agents. But investigators follow a separate chain of command. Asking nicely does not work if an agency is resistant. A hardball approach to incentivize compliance is to leverage the prosecutorial power to charge – or decline to take a case. The criteria that prosecutors use to systematically decide whether to take cases are often specified in prosecutorial guidelines.[20] The strategy the prosecutor's

including 1) terrorism convictions, and 2) criminal cases favorably resolved." US Dep't of Justice, Congressional Submission: FY 2008 Performance Budget United States Attorneys 16–18, 21 (2007). The target win rate was 92 percent. For a discussion of the pressures of prosecutorial performance measures, see Mary De Ming Fan, *Disciplining Criminal Justice: The Peril amid the Promise of Numbers*, 26 Yale L. & Pol'y Rev. 1–74 (2017).

[17] US Dep't of Justice, Program Performance Measures, Measure: Percent of Criminal Cases Favorably Resolved, *archived at* https://obamawhitehouse.archives.gov/sites/default/files/omb/assets/omb/expectmore/detail/10002208.2007.html#performanceMeasures.

[18] This figure was calculated based on the data on the numbers of defendants processed and outcomes given in US Dep't of Justice, 2005 Annual Statistical Report, *infra* note 19, at tbls. 2–2A. The numerator aggregates the numbers of defendants convicted in federal and magistrate court. The denominator aggregates the number of defendants convicted or acquitted in federal and magistrate court. The calculation is (2,589+12)/(19+2,589+12).

[19] This figure was calculated based on the data on the numbers of defendants processed and outcomes given in US Dep't of Justice, Executive Office for US Attorneys, US Attorney Annual Statistical Report, Fiscal Year 2005, tbls. 2–2A (2010). The numerator aggregates the numbers of defendants who plead guilty in federal and magistrate court, which is the number of guilty defendants minus the number of convictions after court or jury trials. The denominator aggregates the number of defendants convicted or acquitted in federal and magistrate court. The calculation is ((2,589+12)−(12+147))/(2,589+19+12).

[20] For research delving into prosecutorial guidelines, *see, e.g.,* Norman Abrams, *Internal Policy: Guiding the Exercise of Prosecutorial Discretion*, 19 UCLA L. Rev. 1, 10–18, 25–28 (1971); Mary De Ming Fan, *Disciplining Criminal Justice: The Peril amid the Promise of Numbers*, 26 Yale L. & Pol'y Rev. 1, 36–41 (2007); Marc L. Miller & Ronald F. Wright, *Black Box*, 94 Iowa L. Rev. 125, 129–132, 174–189 (2008); Michael A. Simons, *Prosecutorial Discretion and Prosecution Guidelines: A Case Study in Controlling Federalization*, 75 N.Y.U. L. Rev. 893, 956 (2000); David A. Sklansky, *Starr, Singleton, and the Prosecutor's Role*, 26 Fordham Urb. L.J. 509, 537 (1999).

office used to get agents to record interrogations was to require a videotape of any interrogation under prosecutorial guidelines for accepting cases.

The recording requirement roused concerns among partner agencies. Agents argued that recording interrogations took limited resources, disrupted the flow of interviews, and generally impeded the efficient extraction of confessions. Agents noted that a layperson might not understand what interrogators must do to get a resistant person to admit their wrongdoing. The interviewing officer might appeal to religious convictions, lie about whether a co-conspirator has implicated the suspect, or any of a variety of other tactics that may seem unsavory to the inexperienced. Our partner agencies were not alone in these concerns or in their resistance. Other agencies opposing recording of interrogations have expressed similar objections.[21]

In recent years, as more investigators have gained experience with recording suspect interviews, there has been a shift toward appreciating the benefits of recording interrogations.[22] Because of a combination of legislation, judicial and prosecutorial encouragement, and voluntary departmental action, today more than half of law enforcement agencies now record at least some interrogations, according to estimates.[23]

This pace of change on recording suspect interrogation over the decades has been glacial compared to the rapid-fire rush among law enforcement agencies to embrace a much more radical approach to police transparency – police-worn body cameras. In just the span of three painful years, the number of agencies planning to deploy body cameras has spiked from less than a quarter, according to a sample of mixed-size agencies in 2013, to 97 percent of major-city and major-county agencies by the start of 2016.[24]

---

[21]   For a discussion of law enforcement resistance and concerns regarding recording police interrogations, *see, e.g.*, Fred E. Inbau, John E. Reid, Joseph P. Buckley, Brian C. Jayne, Criminal Interrogation and Confessions 45–51 (2001); Richard A. Leo & Kimberly D. Richman, *Mandate the Electronic Recording of Police Interrogations*, 6 Criminology & Pub. Pol'y 791, 791 (2007).

[22]   Saul M. Kassin, Richard A. Leo, Christian M. Meissner et al., *Police Interviewing and Interrogation: A Self-Report Survey of Police Practices and Beliefs*, 31 L. & Hum. Behav. 381, 385 (2007).

[23]   Thomas P. Sullivan, *Recording Federal Custodial Interviews*, 45 Am. Crim. L. Rev. 1297, 1311–1312 (2008).

[24]   Police Executive Research Forum, US Dep't of Justice, Implementing a Body-Worn Camera Program: Recommendations and Lessons Learned 2 (2014), www .justice.gov/iso/opa/resources/472014912134715246869.pdf; Major Cities Chiefs & Major County Sheriffs, Survey of Technology Needs: Body Worn Cameras 2 (DHS

A VIOLENT REVOLUTION

The recording revolution, like revolutions throughout history, was born in bloodshed, turmoil, and tragedy. The galvanizing event in 2014 can be evoked with one word because it is so branded into our times – Ferguson. A previously little-known suburb of St. Louis, Missouri, Ferguson became a flashpoint in the conflagration that has long burned in America over race and policing.

The city was a former "sundown town" that banned African Americans after dusk.[25] Older community members still recall the chains and blockades on the main road from the poor, all-black suburb near Ferguson into town. A second road opened during the day for black housekeepers and nannies.[26] Tensions grew as Ferguson's demographics changed from 25 percent black in 1990 to 67 percent by 2010, concerning some city officials.[27] Among cities with at least ten thousand black residents, Ferguson has the painful distinction of being the city that has the highest proportion of "missing" black men – men between twenty-five and fifty-four who have disappeared from the community because of incarceration or early death.[28] Though Ferguson is majority black, Ferguson was policed by a force that only had four black officers among fifty white officers.[29]

The long-burning tensions erupted when Ferguson police officer Darren Wilson shot and killed eighteen-year-old Michael Brown at midday in August 2014. Wilson was white; Brown was black and unarmed. Witness accounts sharply conflicted. Did Wilson punch and then shoot Brown in the back when the teen had his hands up in surrender? Or did Wilson shoot Brown after the 6′4″ youth punched the nearly 6′4″ officer, ran, then turned to charge? No video captured the encounter.

Office of Emergency Communications, Dec. 2015), https://assets.bwbx.io/documents/users/i qiWHBFdfxIU/rvnT.EAJQwK4/vo. Unfortunately, we do not have the same selection of agencies between the 2013 and 2015 surveys conducted by two different groups. However, the proportions still give a sense of the dramatic nature of the change.

[25] US Dep't of Justice, Civil Rights Division, Investigation of the Ferguson Police Department 76 (Mar. 4, 2015), www.justice.gov/sites/default/files/opa/press-relea ses/attachments/2015/03/04/ferguson_police_department_report.pdf.

[26] *Id.*

[27] *Id.*

[28] Justin Wolfers, David Leonhardt, & Kevin Quealy, *1.5 Million Missing Black Men*, N.Y. Times (Apr. 20, 2015), at www.nytimes.com/interactive/2015/04/20/upshot/missing-black-men .html.

[29] Initial reports indicated that three out of fifty-three officers were Black, but the Ferguson police chief amended that number to four. Katie Sanders, *Ferguson Has Three Black Officers, 50 White Officers, NBC's Mitchell Claims*, PunditFact (Aug. 17, 2014), www.politifact.com/ punditfact/statements/2014/aug/17/andrea-mitchell/ferguson-police-department-has-50-white-officers-t/.

Ferguson has been termed "a watershed event in policing" by police leaders.[30] Protests over the killing drew national attention to how black men in America face a much higher risk of injury and death from police use of force and the difficulty of getting any recourse. The problem did not suddenly arise in 2014. It is just that the nation finally started paying attention.

Police use of fatal force is haunted by racial disproportionality. We lack complete and accurate data collection on killings by police.[31] The lack of data on nonfatal injuries sustained in law enforcement encounters is even more dire. A focus on deaths does not capture the full scope of harm because many injuries – even extremely serious, life-altering ones – may not result in death thanks to advances in medical care.[32] Researchers to date have been unable to study nonfatal injuries due to law enforcement, except in a few cases where scholars gained access to a particular jurisdiction's data or records.[33] Scholars have expressed grave dismay that in a free democratic society, citizens have so little access to information about the injurious use of force by their police forces.[34]

The data that exist reveal disproportionality that may be the tip of a larger iceberg. The longest-running official source of data on deaths in police

---

[30]   Sandhya Somashekhar, Wesley Lowery, Keith L. Alexander, Kimberly Kindy, & Julie Tate, *Black and Unarmed*, WASH. POST (Aug. 8, 2015), www.washingtonpost.com/sf/national/2015/08/08/black-and-unarmed/.

[31]   For a discussion of the missing data problem, *see, e.g.*, James J. Fyfe, *Too Many Missing Cases: Holes in Our Knowledge about Police Use of Force*, 4 JUST. RES. & POL'Y 87, 87–98 (2002); David A. Klinger, *On the Problems and Promise of Research on Lethal Police Violence: A Research Note*, 20 HOMICIDE STUD. 78, 78–95 (2012).

[32]   *See, e.g.*, Anthony R. Harris et al., *Murder and Medicine: The Lethality of Criminal Assault 1960–1999*, 6 HOMICIDE STUD. 128, 128–155 (2002) (discussing the impact of improvements in medical care in transforming what formerly would be murders into assaults because the victim's life is saved by trauma care).

[33]   *See, e.g.*, William A. Geller & Kevin J. Karales, *Shootings of and by Chicago Police: Uncommon Crises, Part I: Shootings by Chicago Police*, 72 J. CRIM. L. & CRIMINOLOGY 1813, 1826–64 (1981) (focusing on Chicago Police Department); James P. McElvain, *Police Officer Characteristics and the Likelihood of Using Deadly Force*, 35 CRIM. JUST. & BEHAV. 505, 510–19 (2008) (focusing on Riverside County); James P. McElvain & Augustine J. Kposowa, *Latino Officers and Their Involvement in Police Shootings*, J. CRIMINOLOGY 1, 3–7 (2014), www.hindawi.com/journals/jcrim/2014/726492/abs/. Roland G. Fryer Jr., *An Empirical Analysis of Racial Differences in Police Use of Force* (NBER Working Paper No. 22399, issued July 2016, rev'd Jan. 2018), www.nber.org/papers/w22399 (focusing on Southern California's largest sheriff's department, Austin, Dallas, Houston, New York City, Los Angeles County, and six large Florida counties).

[34]   James J. Fyfe, *Too Many Missing Cases: Holes in Our Knowledge about Police Use of Force*, 4 JUST. RES. & POL'Y 87, 87–98 (2002); David A. Klinger, *On the Problems and Promise of Research on Lethal Police Violence: A Research Note*, 20 HOMICIDE STUD. 78, 78–95 (2012).

encounters, going back to 1949, comes from state death certificate data entered into the National Vital Statistics System (NVSS).[35] Killings by the police are classified by a medical diagnostic code as deaths due to "legal intervention." This category means "injuries inflicted by the police or other law-enforcing agents, including military on duty, in the course of arresting or attempting to arrest lawbreakers, suppressing disturbances, maintaining order, and other legal action."[36]

The NVSS draws from submissions by local coroner and medical examiners offices and depends for accuracy on the varying reporting and coding practices of these offices. Criminologists and epidemiologists have long noted the vital statistics system undercounts homicides by police because of miscoding or omitting mention of police involvement in a death.[37] With the major caveat that the vital statistics data do not capture all homicides by police, Table 1.1 and Figures 1.1 and 1.2 draw on the death certificate data to give a partial picture of the racial disproportionality in deaths due to law enforcement.

Table 1.1 summarizes the incidence of deaths due to law enforcement by race from 1999 to 2016. Because risk of a law enforcement encounter varies by age, the age-adjusted rate is used for comparability across different population proportions and age distributions by race. The adjustment uses the age distribution by racial group in the year 2000. The disparity index then compares differences in the risk of death in a law enforcement encounter by calculating the ratio of age-adjusted rates by race, using the rate for the most populous group, whites, as a baseline.

Although Table 1.1 aggregates the disparity in risk over time into single summary measures, the trends in disparities have changed over time. Figure 1.1 shows trends over time, from 1999 to 2016, in the age-adjusted rates of death by racial and ethnic group. The rates are compared because

---

[35] BUREAU OF JUST. STAT., US DEP'T OF JUST. THE NATION'S TWO MEASURES OF HOMICIDE (Jill Thomas ed., 2014), www.bjs.gov/content/pub/pdf/ntmh.pdf; *Fatal Injury Reports, National, Regional, and State, 1981–2016*, CTRS. FOR DISEASE CONTROL & PREVENTION (last updated Feb. 19, 2017), https://webappa.cdc.gov/sasweb/ncipc/mortrate .html.

[36] World Health Organization. International statistical classification of diseases and related health problems – 10th revision, http://apps.who.int/classifications/icd10/browse/2010/en.

[37] *E.g.*, Lawrence W. Sherman & Robert H. Langworthy, *Measuring Homicide by Police Officers*, 70 J. CRIM. L & CRIMINOLOGY 546, 551–560 (1979); Justin M. Feldman, Sofia Gruskin, Brent A. Coull, & Nancy Krieger, *Quantifying Underreporting of Law-Enforcement Related Deaths in United States Vital Statistics and News-Media-Based Data Sources: A Capture-Recapture Analysis*, PLoS Med. 14 (10);e10002399, https://doi.org/10.1371/journal .pmed.1002399.

TABLE 1.1 *Deaths Due to Legal Intervention, by Race, 1999 to 2016, Counts and Age-Adjusted Rate per One Hundred Thousand of the Population, National Vital Statistics Data*

Race	Number of deaths	Age-adjusted rate per 100,000	Disparity index
White	5,470	0.13	Baseline
Black	2,125	0.28	2.15
Hispanic origin[38]	1,490	0.17	1.31
Am. Indian/Alaskan Native	166	0.23	1.77
Asian/Pacific Islander	171	0.05	0.38

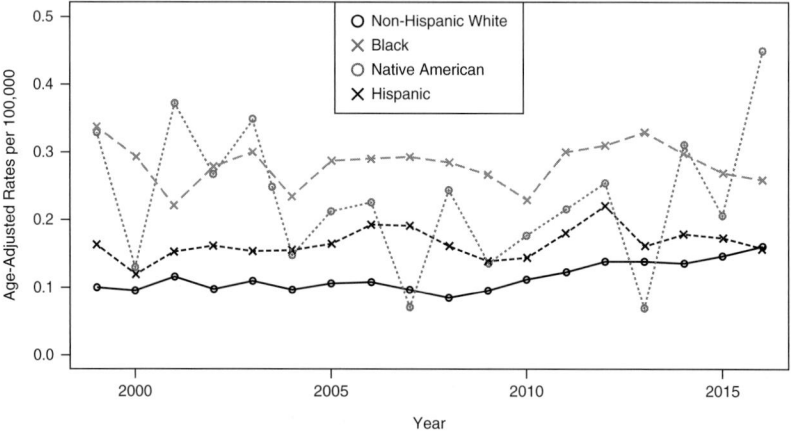

FIGURE 1.1 Longitudinal trends in the risk of death by race, 1999–2016 (age-adjusted rates per one hundred thousand of the population).

they account for the different population proportions and age distributions of each racial group. As the figure indicates, the incidence of dying in a law enforcement encounter is generally low, but highest for blacks and Native

---

[38] Hispanics are classified primarily as white (1,439), but also have been classified as Black (28), American Indian/Alaskan Native (17), and Asian/Pacific Islander (6). The rates for white, black, American Indian/Alaskan Native, and Asian Pacific/Islander include persons also classified as Hispanic. The rate for persons of Hispanic origin separately breaks out persons who were classified also as of Hispanic origin. Because of inconsistencies in recognition and classification by Hispanic ethnicity, there is likely particular underclassification of deaths by Hispanic origin, and the age-adjusted rate is therefore particularly likely to understate the actual rate by Hispanic origin.

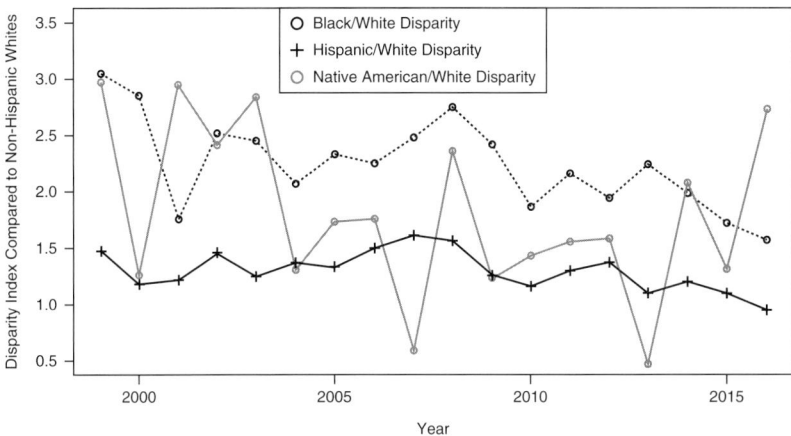

FIGURE 1.2 Racial disparities in the risk of death by race, longitudinal trends, 1999–2016 (ratios of age-adjusted rates per one hundred thousand of the population).

Americans. The trend line for Native Americans fluctuates sharply because of smaller numbers but generally shows an elevated risk compared to non-Hispanic whites. The trend line for Asians and Pacific Islanders is omitted for ease of viewing multiple trends in one figure. In general, the incidence of dying in a law enforcement encounter is higher for all minority groups captured in the data than non-Hispanic whites, except for Asians and Pacific Islanders.

Figure 1.2 compares trends over time in the racial disparity indexes, calculated by comparing the ratio of the age-adjusted rate of death due to law enforcement for each minority group compared to a baseline of non-Hispanic whites. Because Native Americans are a smaller group, the rates fluctuate more sharply from year to year. Of all the minority groups captured in the data, the rates for Asian and Pacific Islanders are the only ones lower than for non-Hispanic whites. The trend line for Asians is omitted for ease of reading the figures because the incidence figures are so low. The risk for Hispanics has fluctuated from as high as 1.6 times that of non-Hispanic whites in 2007 and 2008 to about the same as non-Hispanic whites in 2016.

The risk of death is most disproportionate for African Americans. The disproportionality in the risk of death in a police encounter during this time period was as high as three times that of non-Hispanic whites in 1999, declining to 1.6 in 2016. While there have been fluctuations from year to year, the disparity ratios have been generally declining over time for blacks and Hispanics since 2010. This is in part because, as Figure 1.1 shows, the incidence rate of whites dying in police encounters has been rising gradually in 2010.

In contrast, as Figure 1.1 shows, the incidence rate pattern for Hispanics and blacks shows an undulating pattern, rising and regressing back toward the mean in intervals. The larger structural reasons for time trends in the incidence and disparity rates of deaths in police encounters is an important question in need of further investigation. Potential hypotheses that warrant further investigation include the impact of increasing professionalization, training and diversification of police forces on the incidence of deaths in police encounters and on trends in disparity ratios.[39]

Another question the available official data raise is whether there are patterns in the underreporting of deaths in law enforcement encounter. Studies of the extent and nature of undercounting of deaths due to law enforcement in the official data are difficult to conduct due to the lack of a gold standard data set against which to compare. The FBI's Supplementary Homicide Reports collects reports by law enforcement agencies on the number of "felon[s] killed by a police" – a category that is conducive to confusion and underreporting because a person killed in a police encounter may never have been adjudicated a felon, and many street stops may involve a misdemeanor rather than felony. Beginning in 2003 and temporarily terminating in 2014 for a data collection redesign, the Bureau of Justice Statistics (BJS) collected arrest-related death records.[40] Comparisons of the FBI data and BJS data have found a substantial lack of correspondence – for example, the FBI reports counted 352 homicides by police officers in California between 2003 and 2005, whereas the BJS data set counted just 160.[41] A potentially promising data source is the National Violent Death Reporting (NVDRS) system, which does not rely on a single source, but instead combines records from medical examiners, law enforcement, and crime labs.[42] The challenge is that the NVDRS does not cover the entire United States yet.

---

[39] For calls for further investigation of the impact of increasing police professionalization and diversification on adverse outcomes such as injuries and deaths in police encounters, see David Alan Sklansky, *Not Your Father's Police Department: Making Sense of the New Demographics of Law Enforcement*, 96 J. Crim. L. & Criminology 1209, 1225 (2006); Mary D. Fan, *Violence and the Police Diversity Rationale: A Call for Research*, 2015 BYU L. Rev. 875–914.

[40] *Deaths in Custody Reporting Program*, Bureau of Just. Stat. (last visited July 29, 2018), www.bjs.gov/index.cfm?ty=tp&tid=19.

[41] David A. Klinger, *On the Problems and Promise of Research on Lethal Police Violence: A Research Note*, 20 Homicide Stud. 78, 78–95 (2012).

[42] Catherine W. Barber, Deborah Azrael, David Hemenway, Lenora M. Olson, Carrie Nie, Judy Schaechter, & Sabrina Walsh, *Suicides and Suicide Attempts Following Homicide*, 12 Homicide Stud. 285, 286–287 (2008); L. J. Paulozzi, J. Mercy, L. Frazier Jr., & J. L. Annest, *CDC's National Violent Death Reporting System: Background and Methodology*, 10 Inj. Prevention 47, 49 (2004).

A study comparing NVDRS data for sixteen states from 2005 to 2012 with those reported in FBI and vital statistics data found that the NVDRS captured 71 percent more law enforcement-related deaths than reported by vital statistics, and more than twice that in the FBI data.[43]

Following the fires of Ferguson in 2014, the *Washington Post* and the *Guardian* made major efforts to supplement the official report by collecting accounts of police killings in news media. The resulting media databases gives us a sense of the extent of underreporting in the official data. The *Washington Post*'s database reports police shootings from 2015 to the present.[44] The *Guardian*'s database reports shootings from 2015 to 2016.[45] A recent study aiming to quantify the extent of underreporting in the vital statistics system drew on the *Guardian*'s police shootings database for 2015.[46] The investigators compared the number of cases captured by both databases and by only one of them. Then using capture-recapture statistical methods, the investigators estimated the number of cases likely missed both by databases. The study concluded that the vital statistics system reported just 44.9 percent of law enforcement-related deaths in 2015, whereas the *Guardian*'s database for 2015 likely captured 93.1 percent. Underreporting was more likely to occur in lower-income counties, probably because of resource and training constraints among coroners and medical examiners in poorer places. Underreporting also more likely when the deceased was killed by another means than a gun. Because of the potential value of newspaper surveillance, the BJS in 2015 piloted a redesign of its arrest-related data-gathering to draw on open-access sources like media databases to supplement law enforcement reports.[47]

[43] Catherine Barber. Deborah Azrael, Amy Cohen, Matthew Miller, Deonza Thymes, David Enze Wang, & David Hemenway, *Homicides by Police: Comparing Counts from the National Violent Death Reporting System, Vital Statistics, and Supplementary Homicide Reports*, Am. J. Pub. Health 106(5): 922–927 (2016).

[44] *Fatal Force Police Shooting Database*, Wash. Post (last updated May 3, 2018) (last visited June 18, 2018), www.washingtonpost.com/graphics/2018/national/police-shootings-2018/?utm_term=.86363d72b957.

[45] *The Counted: People Killed by Police in the US*, The Guardian, www.theguardian.com/us-news/ng-interactive/2015/jun/01/the-counted-police-killings-us-database (last visited June 18, 2018).

[46] Justin M. Feldman, Sofia Gruskin, Brent A. Coull, Nancy Krieger, *Quantifying Underreporting of Law-Enforcement Related Deaths in United States Vital Statistics and News-Media-Based Data Sources: A Capture-Recapture Analysis*, PLoS Med. 14(10); e10002399, https://doi.org/10.1371/journal.pmed.1002399.

[47] Bureau of Justice Statistics, Arrest-Related Deaths Program Redesign Study, 2015–16: Preliminary Findings (NCJ 250112, Dec. 2016), www.bjs.gov/content/pub/pdf/ardprs1516pf_sum.pdf.

While the data varies, there is generally one overriding message: black Americans are more likely to die in a police encounter.[48] In laboratory simulations, numerous studies have shown that people are more likely to mistakenly perceive African Americans holding innocuous objects as threatening and shoot.[49] Studies also document the continuing prevalence of implicit associations of black persons with crime and danger.[50] While training and conscious attempts to deactivate implicit stereotypes can abate the risk of mistakes, even people trying their best to act in good faith are vulnerable to implicit biases, meaning stereotypes and mental shortcuts that can affect our judgment and behavior without our conscious awareness.[51] These findings in video game simulations translate to recurring tragedy and pain in real life.

As for nonfatal injuries, Harvard economist Roland G. Fryer addressed the lack of national data by assembling data from cities in Texas, counties in

---

[48]   *See, e.g.,* James W. Buehler, *Racial/Ethnic Disparities in the Use of Lethal Force by US Police, 2010–2014.* AM. J. PUB. HEALTH 107(2): 295–297 (2017) (finding that blacks had 2.8 times higher and Hispanics had 1.7 times higher mortality rates in law enforcement encounters between 2010–2014 based on vital statistics data and discussing prior findings of disparities based on other data sets).

[49]   Joshua Correll et al., *Across the Thin Blue Line: Police Officers and Racial Bias in the Decision to Shoot,* 92 J. PERSONALITY & SOC. PSYCHOL. 1006, 1015 (2007) (finding that subjects drawn from the community were more "trigger-happy" with black targets than white targets but trained officers made more accurate judgments and had less or no bias in decisions regarding whether to shoot; but all subjects showed bias in their response times); Joshua Correll et al., *The Police Officer's Dilemma: Using Ethnicity to Disambiguate Potentially Threatening Individuals,* 83 J. PERSONALITY & SOC. PSYCHOL. 1314, 1325 (2002) (using a video simulation to evaluate the impact of race on the likelihood of being shot and finding that participants faced with making quick decisions were more likely to mistakenly unarmed black persons than white persons); Anthony G. Greenwald, Mark A. Oakes, & Hunter G. Hoffman, *Targets of Discrimination: Effects of Race on Response to Weapons Holders,* 39 J. EXPERIMENTAL PSYCHOL. 399, 403–405 (2003) (finding using a virtual reality simulation that unarmed blacks were incorrectly shot at higher rates than whites and objects were held by blacks were more likely to be perceived as weapons); Ashby E. Plant & Michelle B. Peruche, *The Consequences of Race for Police Officers' Responses to Criminal Suspects,* 16 PSYCHOL. SCI. 180, 181–183 (2005) (finding that law enforcement officers tested in a simulation were more likely to shoot unarmed black suspects than white suspects but training ameliorated this effect).

[50]   Jennifer L. Eberhardt et al., *Seeing Black: Race, Crime and Visual Processing,* 87 J. PERSONALITY & SOC. PSYCHOL. 876 (2004); Anthony G. Greenwald et al., *Targets of Discrimination: Effects of Race on Responses to Weapons Holders,* 39 J. EXPERIMENTAL SOC. PSYCHOL. 399 (2003); Sheri Lynn Johnson, *Unconscious Racism and the Criminal Law,* 73 CORNELL L. REV. 1016 (1988); Jerry Kang, *Trojan Horses of Race,* 118 HARV. L. REV. 1489 (2005).

[51]   Anthony G. Greenwald & Linda Hamilton Krieger, *Implicit Bias: Scientific Foundations,* 94 CAL. L. REV. 945, 951–951 (2006); Brian A. Nosek, et al., *Harvesting Implicit Group Attitudes and Beliefs from a Demonstration Web Site,* 6 GROUP DYNAMICS: THEORY, RES. AND PRAC. 101, 102 (2002).

Florida, LA County, and New York City.[52] Fryer found that blacks are 21.2 more likely to suffer a use of force in a police encounter despite being compliant, and where no arrest is made. Surprisingly, in light of prior research on racial disparities, Fryer found that after adjusting for contextual factors, there was no statistically detectable difference by race in the likelihood of being shot by the police during an encounter. Fryer's findings could be due to factors such as incentives to report more threatening contextual factors after a fatal shooting of a minority suspect and selection bias in terms of the departments willing to share data for his study. It could also reflect the impact of heightened incentive to use restraint in shooting minority suspects because of departmental review procedures after an officer-involved shooting. More fundamentally, Fryer focused on the risk of an individual police encounter turning deadly.[53] From public health and personal safety perspectives, what matters is the overall risk of being involved in a fatal police encounter, which also includes the heightened risk that minority community members face of being stopped by the police in the first place.[54]

Hunger for a Technological Fix

In 2014, when Michael Brown died, the risk of a black male dying in a police encounter in the United States was at least twice that of a white male.[55] In Ferguson, African American community members were stopped more, searched more – though less likely to have contraband when searched – and more likely to receive multiple citations for minor offenses such as "manner of walking" from which the city would extract fine revenue.[56] Though black community members constituted 67 percent of the population, nearly

---

[52] Roland G. Fryer Jr., *An Empirical Analysis of Racial Differences in Police Use of Force* (NBER Working Paper No. 22399, issued July 2016, rev'd Jan. 2018), www.nber.org/papers/w22399 (focusing on Southern California's largest sheriff's department, Austin, Dallas, Houstin, New York City, Los Angeles County, and six large Florida counties).

[53] James W. Buehler, *Racial/Ethnic Disparities in the Use of Lethal Force by US Police, 2010–2014.* AM. J. PUB. HEALTH 107(2): 295–297 (2017).

[54] *Id.*

[55] The calculation is based on vital statistics data. The incidence rate of dying in a law enforcement encounter in 2015 was 0.55 per 100,000 for non-Hispanic black males and 0.28 for non-Hispanic white males). The data are obtainable from *Injury Prevention & Control: Data & Statistics* (WISQARS), CDC, www.cdc.gov/injury/wisqars/index.html.

[56] US DEP'T OF JUSTICE, CIVIL RIGHTS DIVISION, INVESTIGATION OF THE FERGUSON POLICE DEPARTMENT 2–4, 62–75 (Mar. 4, 2015), www.justice.gov/sites/default/files/opa/press-releases/attachments/2015/03/04/ferguson_police_department_report.pdf.

90 percent or more of arrests, police uses of force, and revenue-generating citations were against black persons.[57]

The painful imbalance of power and sense of injustice exploded when Ferguson officer Darren Wilson shot Brown and a grand jury refused to indict Wilson for the shooting. Part of the pain was not knowing what really happened. Witnesses offered polarized and dramatically divergent accounts.[58] Some witnesses said Wilson punched and shot Brown in the back even though Brown held his hands up in surrender.[59] In an account supported by some other witnesses, Wilson said Brown punched him, tried to grab his gun, and ran away but then turned to charge him when Wilson pursued him, and Wilson shot in fear for his life.[60] It was another deeply divergent painful credibility contest – with no camera recording the key events to show what had unfolded.

In the embers of the protests and pain, Michael Brown's grieving mother, Lesley McSpadden, called for police to wear body cameras.[61]

"On August 9th, there was no recorded account of my son's last moments in life," she told a Missouri Senate Committee.[62] "I still do not have closure. Please let police-worn body cameras be a voice of truth and transparency in Missouri communities."[63]

As Ferguson shows, there are many major structural and historical reasons for police–community tensions in America. The nation has long wrestled with concentrated poverty and disadvantage; historical structuring of inequality; anxieties over demographic change; and implicit and explicit biases. There are no quick fixes. But technology offers the allure of a fresh approach to painful entrenched problems.

---

[57] *Id.* at 45.
[58] *See* US Department of Justice, Report Regarding the Criminal Investigation into the Shooting Death of Michael Brown by Ferguson, Missouri Police Officer Darren Wilson 6–8 (Mar. 4, 2015) [hereinafter Brown Death Investigation Report], www.justice.gov/sites/default/files/opa/press-releases/attachments/2015/03/04/doj_report_on_shooting_of_michael_brown_1.pdf (summarizing conflicting witness accounts about what happened); Frances Robles & Michael S. Schmidt, *Shooting Accounts Differ as Holder Schedules Visit to Ferguson*, N.Y. Times (Aug. 20, 2014) at A1 (reporting on divergent witness accounts).
[59] *See* Brown Death Investigation Report, *supra* note 58, at 7–8.
[60] *Id.* at 6–8; Frances Robles & Michael S. Schmidt, *Shooting Accounts Differ as Holder Schedules Visit to Ferguson*, N.Y. Times (Aug. 20, 2014), at A1.
[61] Josh Sanburn, *The One Battle Michael Brown's Family Will Win*, Time, Nov. 24, 2014, http://time.com/3606376/police-cameras-ferguson-evidence/.
[62] Alisa Nelson, Video, *Michael Brown's Mother Testifies for Required Police Body Cameras*, Missourinet (Feb. 17, 2016), www.missourinet.com/2016/02/17/video-michael-brown-juniors-mother-testifies-for-required-police-body-cameras/.
[63] *Id.*

One of the biggest concrete reforms to emerge from the pain and protests is body cameras for police officers.[64] A national opinion poll conducted around the time of the protests found disagreements in perceptions of the police along racial lines – but agreement across racial lines supporting body cameras.[65] The hunger for a technological fix to long-burning problems brought together unusual bedfellows in support of the rapid spread of police-worn body cameras to record most law enforcement encounters.

"I've never seen anything like that in all my days of policing when virtually people from all walks of life – nine out of ten people – think it's a good idea," says Darrel Stephens, executive director of the Major Cities Chiefs Association from 2010 to 2017 and a long-serving chief of police for the Charlotte-Mecklenburg Police Department. "In fifty years of policing I've never seen technology adopted so fast."

Galvanized by the events in Ferguson, major civil rights and civil liberties groups, such as the NAACP and the Lawyers' Committee for Civil Right under Law, united to call for the required use of body cameras.[66] Even the ACLU, which has a track record of opposing surveillance and a strong concern for privacy, joined the call for putting body cameras on the police.[67] The hope uniting the traditional police watchdog groups was that body cameras would help police the police, promote greater transparency, and reduce the risk of injuries and deaths in law enforcement encounters.[68]

---

[64] Josh Sanburn, *The One Battle Michael Brown's Family Will Win*, TIME (Nov. 25, 2014), http://time.com/3606376/police-cameras-ferguson-evidence/.

[65] Max Ehrenfreund, *Blacks and Whites Agree on Body Cameras for Cops, If Little Else*, WASH. POST: WONKBLOG (Dec. 29, 2014), www.washingtonpost.com/news/wonk/wp/2014/12/29/wonkbook-blacks-and-whites-agree-on-body-cameras-for-cops-if-little-else/.

[66] *See, e.g.*, Press Release, NAACP et al., Civil Rights Coalition Urges National Reforms and Recommendations to Address Police Abuse (Sept. 24, 2015), www.naacp.org/latest/civil-rights-coalition-urges-national-reforms-and-recommendations-to-addres/ (calling for police to wear body cameras); Lawyers' Comm. for Civil Rights Under Law et al., A Unified Statement of Action to Promote Reform and Stop Police Abuse (Aug. 18, 2014), www.aclu.org/sites/default/files/assets/black_leaders_joint_statement_-_final_-_8-18.pdf [hereinafter Unified Statement], (a joint statement of multiple civil rights and civil liberties groups urging the adoption of police-worn body cameras); Mike Maciag, *Survey: Almost All Police Departments Plan to Use Body Cameras*, GOVERNING (Jan. 26, 2016), www.governing.com/topics/public-justice-safety/gov-police-body-camera-survey.html (reporting on the widespread adoption of police-worn body cameras by departments around the nation).

[67] Unified Statement, *supra* note 66; Jay Stanley, *Police Body-Mounted Cameras: With Right Policies in Place, a Win for All*, ACLU (Oct. 9, 2013), www.aclu.org/technology-and-liberty/police-body-mounted-cameras-right-policies-place-win-all.

[68] Unified Statement, *supra* note 66.

To address the crisis in trust, police departments across the nation have rushed to adopt body cameras.[69] Police chiefs who might been reluctant five years ago to adopt body cameras realized their utility in offering evidence of what happened, rebuilding trust, and reducing unfounded complaints.[70] The denouement of the US Department of Justice's investigation into the killing of Brown further underscored the benefits of recording. Seven months later, the US Department of Justice would conclude that forensic evidence was inconsistent with claims that Brown was shot in the back with his hands up in surrender.[71] But by then, police had realized that public support and trust was severely eroding.[72]

Officers are increasingly seeing body cameras as a form of protection with the potential to exonerate them.[73] Body cameras offer a powerful example of Derrick Bell's interest-convergence thesis that progress for the powerless occurs when the reform converges with the interests of the powerful.[74]

[69]   Alan Gomez, *After Ferguson, Police Rush to Buy Body Cameras*, USA TODAY (Oct. 11, 2014), www.usatoday.com/story/news/nation/2014/10/11/police-body-cameras-ferguson-privacy-con cerns/16587679/.

[70]   *E.g.*, POLICE EXECUTIVE RESEARCH FORUM, US DEP'T OF JUSTICE, IMPLEMENTING A BODY-WORN CAMERA PROGRAM: RECOMMENDATIONS AND LESSONS LEARNED 5–6 (2014), www.justice.gov/iso/opa/resources/472014912134715246869.pdf; MARA H. Gottfried, *St. Paul Police to Get Body Cameras, Explain Details at Community Meetings*, TWIN CITIES PIONEER PRESS (Dec. 17, 2015), www.twincities.com/2015/10/19/st-paul-police-to-get-body-cam eras-explain-details-at-community-meetings/ (quoting Andy Skoogman, Executive Director of Police Chiefs Association).

[71]   BROWN DEATH INVESTIGATION REPORT, *supra* note 58, at 6–8.

[72]   Sandhya Somashekhar, Wesley Lowery, Keith L. Alexander, Kimberly Kindy, Julie Tate, *Black and Unarmed*, WASH. POST (Aug. 8, 2015), www.washingtonpost.com/sf/national/2015/08/08/black XE "African Americans:Black"-and-unarmed/.

[73]   POLICE COMPLAINTS BD., ENHANCING POLICE ACCOUNTABILITY THROUGH AN EFFECTIVE ON-BODY CAMERA PROGRAM FOR MPD OFFICERS 7–8 (2014). *See also, e.g.*, AUSTIN POLICE DEP'T, AUSTIN POLICE DEPARTMENT POLICY MANUAL, Policy 303, at 125 (May 4, 2015) (stating that body-worn cameras can help protect against false allegations of misconduct); CHICAGO POLICE DEP'T, SPECIAL ORDER S03-14 (Dec. 30, 2015) (effective Jan. 1, 2016) (stating that body-worn cameras "can protect members from false accusations through the objective documentation of interactions between Department members and the public"); Doug Wyllie, *Survey: Police Officers Want Body-Worn Cameras*, POLICEONE (Oct. 23, 2012), www.policeone.com/police-products/body-cameras/articles/6017774-Survey-P olice-officers-want-body-worn-cameras/ (reporting the results of a survey, sponsored in part by a maker of body cameras, finding that 85 percent of the 785 respondents "believe that body-worn cameras reduce false claims of police misconduct, and reduce the likelihood of litigation against the agency").

[74]   Derrick A. Bell Jr., Comment, Brown v. Board of Education *and the Interest-Convergence Dilemma*, 93 HARV. L. REV. 518, 523 (1980).

Violence Prevention and Conflict Resolution

A shared hope across diverse perspectives is that body cameras will help prevent the escalation to violence in police encounters.[75] One of the most oft-invoked and earliest studies about the potential effectiveness of body cameras involves fifty-four officers of the Rialto, California, Police Department who were randomly assigned to wear body cameras or the control condition of not wearing body cameras.[76] The results indicated that officers not wearing body cameras used force about twice as often as officers wearing body cameras. The investigators were unable to detect a statistically significant between-groups effect due to the low number of complaints against either group. But a comparison of complaint volume and uses of force before and after body cameras in Rialto indicated that the volume of complaints fell by more than 90 percent, and uses of force dropped by 60 percent.[77]

Promising findings have been replicated in other police departments. A study of body cameras mounted on Phoenix Police Department officers found that complaints against officers declined by 22.5 percent even as complaints against officers in comparable precincts were rising.[78] A study of the Mesa Police Department found a 40 percent decline in complaints against officers and a 75 percent drop in use of force incidents after the introduction of body cameras.[79] A study of the Orlando Police Department found

[75] POLICE COMPLAINTS BD., *supra* note 73, at 3; POLICE EXECUTIVE RESEARCH FORUM, *supra* note 24, at 5–6; Eugene P. Ramirez, A REPORT ON BODY WORN CAMERAS, MANNING & KASS, ELLROD, RAMIREZ, TRESTER, LLP 3–4 (2014), www.bja.gov/bwc/pdfs/14-005_Report_BODY_WORN_CAMERAS.pdf [http://perma.cc/WXB2-5JHW]; Michael D. White, POLICE OFFICER BODY-WORN CAMERAS: ASSESSING THE EVIDENCE 20–22 (2014), https://ojpdiagnosticcenter.org/sites/default/files/spotlight/download/Police%20Officer%20Body-Worn%20Cameras.pdf [http://perma.cc/228K-KNB5]; Wesley G. Jennings, Lorie A. Fridell, & Mathew D. Lynch, *Cops and Cameras: Officer Perceptions of the Use of Body-Worn Cameras in Law Enforcement*, 42 J. CRIM. JUST. 549, 552 (2014).

[76] Barak Ariel, William A. Farrar, & Alex Sutherland, *The Effect of Police Body-Worn Cameras on Use of Force and Citizens' Complaints Against the Police: A Randomized Controlled Trial*, 31 J. QUANTITATIVE CRIMINOLOGY 509, 520 (2015).

[77] *Id.* at 523–524.

[78] Charles M. Katz et al., CENTER FOR VIOLENCE PREVENTION AND COMMUNITY SAFETY, ARIZONA STATE UNIVERSITY, EVALUATING THE IMPACT OF OFFICER WORN BODY CAMERAS IN THE PHOENIX POLICE DEPARTMENT 33 (2014), https://publicservice.asu.edu/sites/default/files/ppd_spi_feb_20_2015_final.pdf [http://perma.cc/96ZQ-QBQA].

[79] Michael D. White, POLICE OFFICER BODY-WORN CAMERAS: ASSESSING THE EVIDENCE 35 (2014), https://ojpdiagnosticcenter.org/sites/default/files/spotlight/download/Police%20Officer%20Body-Worn%20Cameras.pdf [http://perma.cc/228K-KNB5]; Wesley G. Jennings, Lorie A. Fridell, & Mathew D. Lynch, *Cops and Cameras: Officer Perceptions of the Use of Body-Worn Cameras in Law Enforcement*, 42 J. CRIM. JUST. 549, 552 (2014).

a statistically significant 65.4 percent reduction in external complaints against officers for officers who wore body cameras.[80]

Other findings are mixed and concerning, however. A meta-analysis of ten randomized controlled trials on the use of body cameras in six jurisdictions detected no effect on police uses of force, and an association with an increased rate of assaults against officers.[81] Randomized controlled trials are the gold standard method of getting scientific evidence because the randomization of people to the test condition – here body cameras – or the control condition – here, no body cameras – helps eliminate selection bias.[82] If the sample size is sufficiently large to permit good randomization and an even distribution of characteristics of test subjects, then we can be more confident in making causal inferences that body cameras make a difference, rather than selection biases such as more skilled and open-minded officers volunteering to use body cameras.

Aggregating results across jurisdictions and all groups of officers can mask certain dynamics that might account for surprising results. The investigators conducted subgroup analysis by officer compliance with recording requirements and identified a major factor that may be at play in the disappointing results. The investigators found that force increased by 71 percent among officers with body cameras who recorded at their discretion.[83] In contrast, among officer who followed the protocol, the use of force decreased by 37 percent among body cameras wearers compared to controls.[84]

The investigators posited several potential explanations for their finding that wearing body cameras is associated with a 14 percent increase in the rate of

80 Wesley G. Jennings, Mathew D. Lynch, & Lorie Fridell, *Evaluating the Impact of Police Officer Body-Worn Cameras (BWCs) on Response-to Resistance and Serious External Complaints: Evidence from the Orlando Police Department (OPD) Experience Utilizing a Randomized Controlled Experiment*, 43 J. Crim. Just. 480, 480 (2015).

81 Barak Ariel, Alex Sutherland, Darren Henstock, Josh Young, Paul Drover, Jayne Sykes, Simon Megicks, Ryan Henderson, *Wearing Body Cameras Increases Assaults against Officers and Does Not Reduce Police Use of Force: Results from a Global Multi-Site Experiment*, European J. Crim. 13(6): 744–755 (2016), http://journals.sagepub.com/doi/pdf/10.1177/1477370816643734.

82 Laure E. Bothwell, Jeremy A. Greene, Scott H. Podolsky, & Davis S. Jones, *Assessing the Gold Standard – Lessons from the History of RCTs*, New England J. Med. 2016: 374: 2175–2181.

83 Barak Ariel et al., *Report: Increases in Police Use of Force in the Presence of Body-Worn Cameras are Driven by Officer Discretion: A Protocol-Based Subgroup Analysis of Ten Randomized Experiments*, J. Exp. Crim. 12: 453–463 (2016), https://link.springer.com/content/pdf/10.1007%2Fs11292-016-9261-3.pdf [https://perma.cc/R7M9-PD6M] [hereinafter Ariel et al., *Report: Increases Driven by Discretion*].

84 *Id.* at 453–463.

assaults against officers. One may be atypical results from small-sample studies, which accounted for the strongest associations between increased assaults and body cameras. Removing the small-sample studies rendered the result no longer statistically significant. Another possible explanation is that officers wearing body cameras may be more willing to report assaults against them because there is documentation on camera. More concerning, other possible explanations are that recordings inflame an already tense situation, or inhibit officers from taking full command and control to deter assaults against them.[85]

Other studies of police forces in Edmonton, Canada, London, and Washington, DC also have been unable to detect a statistically significant effect on reducing use of force or complaints against officers.[86] In a study involving 2,224 officers of DC's Metropolitan Police, half the force was randomly assigned to wear body cameras while the other half did not. After running the trial for a year and a half, spanning 2015 to 2016, the investigators were unable to detect any statistically significant effect of wearing body cameras on uses of force, citizen complaints, the vigorousness of policing, or outcomes of criminal cases.[87]

While the results are disappointing, they may not be generalizable to other US police departments. The Metropolitan Police is special because DC officers keep order in the nation's capitol and have more resources and training than many other departments.[88] The police department is so progressive that it made an unprecedented voluntary request that civil rights attorneys at the US Department of Justice investigate its police practices.[89] As a result,

---

[85] Ariel et al., *supra* note 81, at 752–753.

[86] EDMONTON POLICE SERVICE, BODY WORN VIDEO: CONSIDERING THE EVIDENCE 8, 55, 62 (2015), www.edmontonpolice.ca/News/BWV.aspx [http://perma.cc/242Q-HJ9S]; Lynne Grossmith et al., POLICE, CAMERA, EVIDENCE: LONDON'S CLUSTER RANDOMISED CONTROLLED TRIAL OF BODY WORN VIDEO 13 (2015), http://whatworks .college.police.uk/Research/Documents/Police_Camera_Evidence.pdf [https://perma.cc/T7 94-AH8G].

[87] David Yokum, Anita Ravishankar, & Alexander Coppock, EVALUATING THE EFFECTS OF POLICE BODY-WORN CAMERAS: A RANDOMIZED CONTROLLED TRIAL 11, 18 (Working Paper, The Lab @ DC, Oct. 20, 2017), https://bwc.thelab.dc.gov/TheLabDC_MPD_BWC_ Working_Paper_10.20.17.pdf.

[88] *Id.* at 20.

[89] *See, e.g.,* Findings Letter from William R. Yeomans, Acting Assistant Attorney General, Civil Rights Division, US Dep't of Justice, to the Hon. Anthony Williams, Mayor of the District of Columbia, and Charles H. Ramsey, Chief of Police, Metropolitan Police Dep't (undated), www.clearinghouse.net/chDocs/public/PN-DC-0001-0002.pdf (noting the "unprecedented genesis of the investigation – at the request of the agency to be investigated"); Memorandum of Agreement between the US Dep't of Justice and the District of Columbia and the District of Columbia Metropolitan Police (June 13, 2001), www.clearinghouse.net/ chDocs/public/PN-DC-0001-0001.pdf (noting the "unprecedented request" by DC to be investigated, and the "unusual genesis of the investigation").

the DC police has implemented numerous reforms since signing a memorandum of agreement with the US Department of Justice on June 31, 2001.[90] If the baseline performance is high from the start, it is harder to detect improvements from an incremental new reform. Also fundamentally, as the Edmonton report noted, for large police agencies, it is hard to isolate the effect of any one reform.[91] DC, London, and Edmonton, Canada may simply start from different baselines and a much different room for improvement on uses of force than many other US police departments.

Another oft-expressed hope is that video evidence will provide objective unbiased evidence to resolve contested events and save us from the partiality of human memory and imbalanced credibility contests.[92] The realities of what the camera reveals and how pervasive recording changes the balance of power are more complex. As Chapter 5 will discuss, camera positioning, angle, and framing can powerfully shape viewer judgments without the viewer realizing this effect.[93] Our personal beliefs and views on authority will shade our interpretation of what we are watching. Video is no magic bullet to end fierce conflicts in interpretation[94] – but a plethora of police and public videos has the potential to provide more data to reveal hidden problems that can help address perceptual biases and provide more data for decision-making.

---

[90]   Memorandum of Agreement between the US Dep't of Justice and the District of Columbia and the District of Columbia Metropolitan Police, *supra* note 89.

[91]   EDMONTON POLICE SERVICE, *supra* note 86, at 55.

[92]   E.g., AUSTIN POLICE DEP'T, AUSTIN POLICE DEPARTMENT POLICY MANUAL, POLICY 303, at 130 (May 4, 2015) ("The use of Body Worn Camera (BWC) system provides an unbiased audio/video recording of events that employees encounter."); PHILA. POLICE DEP'T, DIRECTIVE 4.21, § 1.A.2 (Jan. 27, 2017), www.phillypolice.com/assets/directives/D4 .21-BodyWornCameras.pdf [http://perma.cc/L7S9-AGQK] (body cameras will "provide an unbiased audio and video recording of events"); SAN DIEGO POLICE DEP'T, PROC. NO. 1.49, 1 (Sept. 26, 2017), https://rcfp.org/bodycam_policies/CA/SanDiegoBWCPolicy_up date.pdf [http://perma.cc/HF7P-Z5ZR] ("Cameras provide additional documentation of police/public encounters and may be an important tool for collecting evidence and maintaining public trust.").

[93]   G. Daniel Lassiter, Shari Seidman Diamond, Heather C. Schmidt, & Jennifer K. Elek, *Evaluating Videotaped Confessions: Expertise Provides No Defense against the Camera-Perspective Effect*, 18 PSYCHOL. SCI. 224, 224–225 (2007); G. Daniel Lassiter et al., *Further Evidence of a Robust Point-of-View Bias in Videotaped Confessions*, 21 CURRENT PSYCHOL.: DEVELOPMENTAL, LEARNING, PERSONALITY 265, 267 (2002); see G. Daniel Lassiter et al., *Attributional Complexity and the Camera Perspective Bias in Videotaped Confessions*, 27 BASIC & APPLIED SOC. PSYCHOL. 27, 28–29 (2005).

[94]   The differences in views on Eric Garner's death on video illustrates that a recording is no magic bullet, as I have earlier explained. Vivian Yee & Kirk Johnson, *Body Cameras Worn by Police Officers Are No Slam Dunk, Experts Say*, N.Y. TIMES (Dec. 7, 2014), at A1.

THE FUTURE WILL BE RECORDED

There is a coming deluge of more audiovisual data on police practices than ever before in history. Coding and analysis of body camera policies from 213 jurisdictions throughout the United States[95] conducted for this book reveals widespread requirements that most law enforcement encounters previously memorialized only in summary police reports or citations – and often not at all – will be recorded.

One of the early policy debates over body cameras was how much discretion officers should have over whether to record.[96] The scale of discretion can range between a continuous recording model, with no officer discretion, to complete officer discretion. In the middle of the two extremes is a highly limited discretion model, where cameras must be on for all law enforcement encounters, or interactions with the public, and a limited-discretion model,

---

[95] In January 2018, the author and a team of librarians collected body camera policies from municipal police agencies and sheriff's offices using open-source materials supplemented by public records requests. The resulting sample had great diversity of region and city size. Major jurisdictions like New York City, with 8.5 million people, were included, but small jurisdictions, such as Kotzbue, Alaska, population 3,245, also were analyzed. For population size data, see US Census Bureau, Annual Estimates of the Resident Population for Incorporated Places of 50,000 or More, Ranked by July 1, 2016 Population: April 1, 2010 to July 1, 2016, https://factfinder.census.gov/faces/tableservices/jsf/pages/productview.xhtml. The appendix gives more details about the methods and lists the 213 jurisdictions for which we collected and coded departmental body camera policies, ordered by state. The codebook used to systematize and standardize policy coding was generated through an iterative process, based on an evaluation of the provisions. For background on policy coding, see, e.g., Charles Tremper et al., *Measuring Law for Evaluation Research*, 34 Evaluation Rev. 242, 252–255 (2010).

[96] See, e.g., Compare ACLU, A Model Act for Regulating the Use of Wearable Body Cameras by Law Enforcement 1–2 (May 2015), www.aclu.org/files/field_document/aclu_police_body_cameras_model_legislation_may_2015.pdf (providing that body cameras must be activated at the initiation of any law enforcement or investigative encounter between an officer and the public but providing exceptions for exigent circumstances and to protect privacy), *with* S.B. 5732, 64th Leg., Reg. Sess. § 3 (Wash.) (as introduced by Senate, Jan. 30, 2015) (bill requires continuous recording when officer is on duty and only deactivates if the officer goes to the bathroom or on break), *and* Josh Feit, *Seattle State Senator, ACLU Call for Tougher Body Cam Guidelines than in SPD Pilot*, Seattle Met (Feb. 9, 2015), www.seattlemet.com/articles/2015/2/9/aclu-body-cam-bill-calls-for-tougher-oversight-than-spd-version-february-2015 (discussing how S.B. 5732 requiring continuous recording is backed by the ACLU of Washington state). *See also, e.g.,* Jay Stanley, *Police Body-Mounted Cameras: With Right Policies in Place, a Win for All*, ACLU 2–3 (Mar. 2015), www.aclu.org/sites/default/files/assets/police_body-mounted_cameras-v2.pdf. ("Perhaps most importantly, policies and technology must be designed to ensure that police cannot 'edit on the fly' – i.e., choose which encounters to record with limitless discretion. If police are free to turn the cameras on and off as they please, the cameras' role in providing a check and balance against police power will shrink and they will no longer become a net benefit.")

TABLE 1.2 _Approaches to Officer Discretion over Recording, 213 Body Camera Policies_

No discretion (continuous – no discretion)	All encounters with the public (highly restricted)	Specified circumstances (limited)	At officer discretion (discretionary)	Not specified
0 (0%)	57 (27%)	149 (70%)	6 (3%)	1 (0.5%)

where cameras must be on for specified types of interactions. Even as debates continue, a consensus is appearing in the body camera policies that takes a middle-ground approach on discretion.

Table 1.2 summarizes the distribution of approaches among the 213 policies coded. The most prevalent model of police recording discretion – followed in 70 percent of the 213 jurisdictions coded – is a limited-discretion model. A limited-discretion model curtails officer discretion by requiring recording of several specified law enforcement activities, while leaving some situations up to officer discretion.[97] Of the remainder of the jurisdictions coded, 27 percent follow a highly limited discretion model. This approach requires that body cameras record during all law enforcement encounters with the public, with only limited exceptions.[98] No jurisdictions coded has adopted the extremely intrusive continuous recording model.

The next question is which types of enforcement encounters must be recorded. As summarized in Table 1.3, the majority of the 213 policies coded require officers to record stops, searches, arrests, uses of force, and officer responses to calls for service. Notably, in light of the national controversy over the death of Freddie

---

[97] _See, e.g._, Mark G. Peters & Philip K. Eure, BODY-WORN CAMERAS IN NYC: AN ASSESSMENT OF NYPD'S PILOT PROGRAM AND RECOMMENDATIONS TO PROMOTE ACCOUNTABILITY ii (2015), www.nyc.gov/html/oignypd/assets/downloads/pdf/nypd-body-camera-report.pdf (defining a limited-discretion model).

[98] _See, e.g._, CHARLOTTE-MECKLENBURG POLICE DEP'T, DIRECTIVE 400-006 (Apr. 29, 2015), www.cjin.nc.gov/infoSharing/Presentations/BWC%20Directive%20400-006.pdf ("While on duty, BWCs shall be turned on and activated to record responses to calls for service and interactions with citizens."); PHILA. POLICE DEP'T, DIRECTIVE 4.21, § 4 (Apr. 20, 2015), www.phillypolice.com/assets/directives/D4.21-BodyWornCameras.pdf ("Body-Worn Cameras shall be activated when responding to all calls for service and during all law enforcement related encounters and activities involving the general public."); PHX. POLICE DEP'T, OPERATIONS ORDER 4.49, at 2 (Apr. 2013), www.bwcscorecard.org/static/policies/2013-04%20Phoenix%20-%20BWC%20Policy.pdf ("The VIEVU PVR-LE2 camera must be activated during all investigative or enforcement contacts.").

TABLE 1.3 *Law Enforcement Activities That Must Be Recorded, 213 Body Camera Policies*

Enforcement activity	Mandatory: number (%) of departments	Discretionary: number (%) of departments	No provision: number (%) of departments
Terry stops	136 (64%)	0	77 (36%)
Traffic stops	185 (87%)	1 (0.5%)	27 (13%)
Arrests	153 (72%)	1 (0.5%)	59 (28%)
Pursuits, foot or traffic	147 (69%)	0	66 (31%)
Responding to calls for service[a]	141 (66%)	5 (2%)	63 (30%)
Searches	147 (69%)	2 (1%)	64 (30%)
Encounters that escalate or get adversarial	139 (65%)	3 (1%)	71 (33%)
Use of force	118 (55%)	2 (1%)	93 (44%)
Transporting persons in custody	106 (50%)	6 (3%)	101 (47%)
Consensual encounters	135 (63%)	7 (3%)	71 (33%)

[a] This row sums to 209 rather than 213 because four jurisdictions did not require officers to record routine calls for service.

Gray in Baltimore during transportation by the police, half of the body camera policies coded also require recording of suspect transportation.[99]

Remarkably, a majority of the departments require recording of one of the most opaque and unregulated zones of policing – consensual encounters. Consensual encounters is criminal procedure lingo for an encounter where the subject is – theoretically at least – free to leave.[100] Consensual encounters are useful for investigative purposes where there is either no basis yet for reasonable articulable suspicion to justify an investigative *Terry* stop or if it is unclear if the officer has enough basis yet for a stop.[101] Because these encounters are based on consent, they are not considered searches and seizures regulated by the Fourth Amendment, the main body of constitutional conduct rules for police. Consensual encounters also are controversial because consent often is fictional from the perspective of the person approached, and because of the risk for targeting based on hunches predicated on a person's race,

[99] See, e.g., Sheryl Gay Stolberg & Jess Bidgood, *Starkly Different Accounts of Freddie Gray's Death as Trial of Officer Begins*, N.Y. TIMES (Dec. 3, 2015), at A20 (discussing the controversy and mystery over Freddie Gray's death while being transported in custody).

[100] Florida v. Rodriguez, 469 US 1, 5–6 (1984).

[101] See, e.g., United States v. Avery, 137 F.3d 343, 352 (6th Cir. 1997) (describing the unregulated nature of consensual encounters, "which may be initiated without any objective level of suspicion").

gender, and socioeconomic status.[102] It is a remarkable shift for a majority of
departments to require recording of one of the most opaque domains of police
power unregulated by the Fourth Amendment.

The body camera revolution poses a major paradigm shift for three reasons:
systematic comprehensiveness, detail, and volume. Bystanders have sometimes captured key footage of police encounters long before this era of viral
police videos, as Chapter 2 will discuss. In an increasing number of jurisdictions, courts have access to recordings of police interrogations.[103] Patrol
vehicle dash cameras can also yield relevant footage, albeit sometimes at an
awkward distance or angle.[104] But body-worn video will cover a much wider
array of police enforcement activities than interrogations or encounters that
happen near a police vehicle.[105] Body-worn cameras can go to places police

---

[102] Janice Nadler, *No Need to Shout: Bus Sweeps and the Psychology of Coercion*, 2002 SUP. CT.
       REV. 153, 156 (2002) ("[T]he Court's Fourth Amendment consent jurisprudence is either
       based on serious errors about human behavior and judgment, or else has devolved into a legal
       fiction of the crudest sort – a mere device for attaining the desired legal consequence.");
       Margaret Raymond, *The Right to Refuse and the Obligation to Comply: Challenging the
       Gamesmanship Model of Criminal Procedure*, 54 BUFFALO L. REV. 1483, 1486 (2007) ("Police
       are free to initiate a consensual encounter with an individual for any reason or no reason,
       perhaps based on a whim or a 'hunch' that cannot be supported by specific and articulable
       facts."); Daniel J. Steinbock, *The Wrong Line between Freedom and Restraint: The Unreality,
       Obscurity, and Incivility of the Fourth Amendment Consensual Encounter Doctrine*, 38 SAN
       DIEGO L. REV. 507, 509 (2001) ("Requiring no objective indication of criminality,
       a consensual encounter can be initiated for no reason or for any reason at all, including the
       kind of inchoate hunches and suspicions disallowed even for stops, the least intrusive form of
       seizure.").
[103] *See* G. Daniel Lassiter, Patrick J. Munhall, Andrew L. Geers, Paul E. Weiland, &
       Ian M. Handley, *Accountability and the Camera Perspective Bias in Videotaped
       Confessions*, 1 ANALYSIS SOC. ISSUES & PUB. POL'Y 53, 54 (2001) (noting estimates that
       more than half of law enforcement agencies videotape some interrogations).
[104] *See, e.g.,* Lard v. State, 431 S.W.3d 249, 255, 264–265 (Ark. 2014) (holding that the trial court
       did not err in allowing the government to play dash camera footage of the defendant killing
       a police officer in a capital case); Commonwealth v. Favinger, No. 1678 MDA 2013, 2014 WL
       10987112, at *7 (Sup. Ct. Pa. 2014) (mem.) (noting that the trial court adjudicating the
       suppression motion reviewed the dash camera video to determine whether there was probable
       cause to stop the defendant for not driving in his lane but "it was very difficult to see from the
       video the distance" the defendant was traveling over the line and therefore the court relied on
       testimony).
[105] *See* Table 1.3. *See also, e.g.,* ATLANTA POLICE DEP'T POLICY MANUAL, SPECIAL ORDER
       APD.SO.14.05, at 2–3 (Sept. 1, 2014) (on file with author) (requiring recording of pedestrian
       stops, field interviews, foot pursuits, search warrant executions, victim and witness interviews
       as well as traffic-related law enforcement activities); AUSTIN POLICE DEP'T, AUSTIN
       POLICE DEPARTMENT POLICY MANUAL, POLICY 303, at 125–126 (May 4, 2015) (on file
       with author) (requiring recording of warrant service, investigatory stops, and "any contact that
       becomes adversarial in an incident that would not otherwise require recording" as well as
       traffic stops); HOUSTON POLICE DEP'T DRAFT GEN. ORDER 400-28, at 5–6 (Nov. 20, 2015)
       (on file with author) (requiring body-worn camera activation when "[a]rriving on scene to any

FIGURE 1.3 View from patrol vehicle dash camera. Courtesy Sterling Police Department.

cars cannot, such as porches, homes, on foot patrol, while executing warrants, and more. If recording policies are followed, then body camera recordings are more systematically gathered data than the happenstance of a community member at the scene and brave enough to record the police.

Body cameras record events closer up, yielding more detail than ever before captured by testimony or a dash camera. Even in stops that happen near a patrol car, a dash camera often does not capture the relevant details of what might give police probable cause for a search or arrest, or the basis for a deadly use of force. A body camera is more likely to capture what the officer saw before making a discretionary decision. Sometimes this detail can help resolve cases more quickly, clearing up questions and exonerating officers.

The detail also may mitigate concerns regarding pretextual stops and false testimony (often dubbed *testilying*) by officers. Compare the two stills in

call for service, . . . [s]elf-initiating a law enforcement activity," initiating a stop, conducting searches, during transportation after arrest, while interviewing witnesses and complainants as well as during vehicular stops and pursuits); SAN FRANCISCO POLICE DEP'T, BODY WORN CAMERAS POLICY, RECOMMENDED DRAFT, at 2–3 (Dec. 2, 2015) (on file with author) (requiring recording of detention and arrests, "consensual encounters," pedestrian stops, foot pursuits, service of search or arrest warrants, consent-based as well as suspicion-based searches, transportation of arrestees and detainees, and "[d]uring any citizen encounter that becomes hostile" as well as vehicle pursuits and traffic stops).

FIGURE 1.4 View from officer-worn body camera. Courtesy Sterling Police
Department.

Figures 1.3 and 1.4 from video of the same traffic stop.[106] The still on the left is
from the patrol vehicle dash camera. The still on the right is from the officer's
body camera. Now imagine if the officer conducting a traffic stop in the
famous Supreme Court case on pretextual stops of minority motorists,
Whren v. United States, was wearing a body camera.[107]

In *Whren,* two young black men, Michael Whren and his friend James Brown,
were driving in a DC neighborhood when two plainclothes vice officers in an
unmarked police car decided to follow them. The officers testified that they grew
suspicious when they "saw a dark Pathfinder truck with temporary license plates
and youthful occupants" in a "high drug area" stop at a stop sign for "what
seemed an unusually long time – more than 20 seconds" with "the driver looking
down into the lap of the passenger at his right."[108] The officers executed a U-turn
to tail Whren and Brown, whereupon the Pathfinder "turned suddenly to its
right, without signaling, and sped off at an 'unreasonable' speed."[109] The officers
followed until they overtook the Pathfinder when it stopped at a red light.[110]

[106] Sterling Police Department, *The Difference a Camera Can Make,* YouTube (Sept. 12, 2014),
        www.youtube.com/watch?v=ZXy17SIzpbQ.
[107] Whren v. United States, 517 US 806, 808–809 (1996).
[108] *Id.* at 808.
[109] *Id.*
[110] *Id.*

An officer approached the driver's side door, whereupon, lo and behold, "he immediately observed two large plastic bags of what appeared to be crack cocaine in petitioner Whren's hands."[111]

Why were the two large plastic bags sitting boldly in plain view in Whren's hands when Whren and Brown knew officers had been tailing them and were nervous enough to try to drive sharply away? The question has vexed scholars, who have suggested that the facts in *Whren* are an example of testilying – telling a more legally palatable tale to avoid suppression of the evidence – that the Court ignores.[112] Indeed, scholar L. Bennett Capers has observed that both of the officers involved in the stop had "been the subject of misconduct allegations, including allegations of planting evidence and providing false testimony."[113] Yet, without the defendant's testimony offering a contrary story at the suppression hearing, nor video, there is not much a court can do. As discussed in the next chapter, a defendant has formidable reasons against taking the stand to tell his side of the story lest he waive his Fifth Amendment privilege to remain silent. Even if the defendant testifies, it is harder to credit a suspect's word over that of two law enforcement officers. As the still photos above illustrate, even if the officers in Whren's case had dash camera footage, it would not tell the lawyers or the court much. We cannot see what was in Whren's lap. But the body camera footage would give the court the ability to replay the encounter and check the official story.

The much greater comprehensiveness of coverage exponentially expands the volume of video evidence relevant to cases and controversies that courts, litigants, and potentially the media and public will be able to access as a routine matter. With rapidly spreading uptake, body cameras have the potential to be disruptive technology in the sense of having the transformative power to shake up old ways of analyzing criminal justice issues and legal cases.[114] As Chapter 3 will discuss, events previously reconstructed primarily by

[111] *Id.* at 809.

[112] Tracey Maclin, *Race and the Fourth Amendment*, 51 VAND. L. REV. 333, 384 (1998) (discussing concern over police perjury in a case like *Whren*); I. Bennet Capers, *The Fourth Problem*, 49 TULSA L. REV. 431, 435 n. 34 (2013) (book review) (discussing "the improbability of the officers' version of the events and the likelihood that they in fact engaged in 'testilying'" in *Whren*).

[113] Capers, *supra*, 112, 435.

[114] *See* Clayton M. Christensen, THE INNOVATOR'S DILEMMA 7–28 (3d ed. 2003) (discussing the concept of disruptive technology in the private sector); Tom Casady, *Hidden Cost of Body Cameras*, THE DIRECTOR'S DESK (Oct. 31, 2014, 6:12 AM), http://lpd304.blogspot.com/2014/10/hidden-cost-of-body-worn-cameras.html ("In some ways, [body-worn video] is a disruptive technology: a game-changer that leap frogs vehicle-mounted systems.").

testimony will now be captured on video that offers judges, disciplinary boards, and the general public the opportunity – and temptation – to see and decide for themselves what happened. The spread of body cameras also are only part of the picture, and the police recording revolution. As the next chapter will discuss, community members increasingly are aiming cell phone cameras at the police to seize control of the story, and courts increasingly are recognizing the right to record.

2

Copwatching and the Right to Record

There's been a culture of surveillance for us and this is our culture of countersurveillance.
– Elsa Waithe, CopWatch NYC and Black Lives Matter Activist

COMMUNITY COUNTERSURVEILLANCE

A gifted comedian and writer, Elsa Waithe works multiple jobs in New York. At night, when she is not performing, she transforms.

"That's the Clark Kent. At 6:00 PM – I'm watching the cops or getting involved in a protest. People yell 'Get a job.' This is seven o'clock on a Saturday, we're supposed to be off work and yet we're working right now," Waithe says, as she readies pamphlets educating the public about the right to record the police to distribute on her CopWatch patrol.

Waithe's group CopWatch NYC emerged in 2015. Volunteers go to neighborhoods with a high number of complaints about the police to record, hold rallies, and protest. She and her fellow volunteers walk the streets of Brooklyn's poorest neighborhoods, populated by large proportions of people of color working numerous jobs to pay the rent. Sometimes the team walks their streets in uniform, a black CopWatch T-shirt. Sometimes the Copwatchers go "incog-negro, as I like to say," Waithe explains (Figure 2.1).

The volunteer copwatchers are a small force in one of the world's largest cities. They may not be on hand at the crucial moment to capture an aggressive use of force and create the viral video that broadcasts brutality to the world. A patrol may consist of watching as officers stand at a designated crime hotspot. Even if the patrol seems relatively uneventful, it can still make a difference, Waithe believes.

"When you record, 95 percent of the time you are not going to see anything. And that is a good thing. Rights violations look subtle. It is not always someone getting beaten or dying on camera," Waithe explains.

FIGURE 2.1 Copwatchers Elsa Waithe and Anthony Beckford on patrol.

In a place where the police popularized aggressive crackdowns for minor offenses and heavy patrols facilitate gentrification of neighborhoods like the one where Waithe lives, sometimes it is the minor crimes that matter the most. Civil rights advocates and scholars are increasingly paying attention to minor crimes enforcement because the resulting fines, forfeitures, and collateral consequences can be crippling for the hardest-hit and their communities.[1]

Waithe recalls witnessing an officer pulling over a person for having windows that were allegedly tinted too darkly. She recorded the officer as he wrote the ticket without testing or verifying the window tint, which she believed was

---

[1] *See, e.g.*, Am. Civil Liberties Union, In for a Penny: The Rise of America's New Debtors' Prisons *available at* www.aclu.org/report/penny-rise-americas-new-debtors-pris ons; Alicia Bannon, Mitali Nagrecha, & Rebekah Diller, Criminal Justice Debt: A Barrier to Reentry (2010), www.brennancenter.org/sites/default/files/legacy/Fees%20a nd%20Fines%20FINAL.pdf; Alexes Harris, *Drawing Blood from Stones: Legal Debt and Social Inequality in the Contemporary United States*, 115 Am. J. Soc. 1753 (2010); Wayne A. Logan & Ronald F. Wright, *Mercenary Criminal Justice*, 2014 U. Ill. L. Rev. 1175; Kevin R. Reitz, *The Economic Rehabilitation of Offenders: Recommendations of the Model Penal Code (Second)*, 99 Minn. L. Rev. 1735 (2015); Jenny Roberts, *Why Misdemeanors Matter: Defining Effective Advocacy in the Lower Criminal Courts*, 45 U.C. Davis L. Rev. 277 (2011); Symposium, *Misdemeanor Machinery: The Hidden Heart of the American Criminal Justice System*, 98 B.U. L. Rev. 669 (2018).

a legal hue. She then gave the video to the motorist so he would have it in court to contest the fine.

"Two hundred dollars can make a big difference in someone's life," she explained.

Just being visible can deter rights violations, Waithe believes. The recording may not always change the outcome of a case or secure a conviction if someone is shot. But Waithe has a greater vision.

"It's also changing the social zeitgeist," she explains. "I hear a lot of times people say I didn't know we can do this, I didn't know we could record the police. There is a lot of information out there. It is empowering people out there. Who watches the watchmen? We have the legal right to do this. To challenge the power structure and create a social movement that we are all watching. I tell people to tell the officer, 'I am watching the situation for the safety for all involved.' If the guy at the Burger King has to have a camera on him – he is making food – why not the guy who is supposed to protect and serve? If you have a camera to watch your nanny or housekeeper, why not watch the police? These are also our servants."

An organizer in two major movements, Black Lives Matter and CopWatch NYC, Waithe has been injured so badly for her protest and recording activities that she had to go to the emergency room.

"We were hanging back from the rest of the copwatch contingent and watching the police act very aggressively that day," Waithe recalls. "They were using the police vans to corral people. I was able to capture footage of the police van turning into the crowd. They were using the vans as crowd control. I was getting video of the license plates in case one of these vans run something over.

"Now we are on the Brooklyn side, near Barclays Center. This is when they were starting to kettle us. They were using the nets and dragging them across the street. That's when people started to run. I started to run too. They were ordering people on the sidewalk. I was on the sidewalk. There are a couple of videos that confirm that I was on the sidewalk.

"There was a kid and several officers jammed him against the wall. I am watching them basketball dribble his head against the wall. I say pull the camera out – I've got to record this. That's when I was shoved. It took me out. It took out the legal observer. I landed on the guardrail on the street. And it fractured the ribs.

"I thought I might have been shot or stabbed because the pain was so intense when I landed on the guardrail. I thought I was shot or stabbed or impaled when I landed on the guard rail. There was a moment when I was feeling for blood and I was holding myself on the ground and half expected my hand to be wet. You often hear from people who have been shot that they didn't hear the gunshot. I thought that might have happened."

In the chaos, someone either stepped on Waithe's head or her head hit something and she fell unconscious. She ended up at the hospital.

Waithe sued the police for those injuries and won a settlement after about a year and a half – thanks to recordings of the event by her fellow CopWatchers.

"Absolutely the video footage helped. The way we work in CopWatch is we have one person copwatching the scene and one person watching the cop-watcher. We were in standard formation – there was one person behind me still recording. The video was undeniable. I think it really helped. They didn't want to go trial with this because they knew the video was there."

Like the nation, Waithe's views have evolved greatly over the last few turbulent years. Facebook's "on this day" and timeline features remind her of who she used to be by reviving her old posts periodically – including one she wrote around the time protests erupted over the killing of Michael Brown by a Ferguson police officer in August 2014.

"I wrote, 'yeah the police are bad but there's just as much problems with black people killing each other.' I was making black-on-black crime arguments on Facebook."

Her awakening came a few months later. She was late to performing in her comedy show in Brooklyn. She was supposed to be on Franklin Street but she ended up on Franklin Avenue. They are not close. The Franklin Avenue area of the borough is a predominantly black neighborhood. The Franklin Street area is hipsterfying.

Looking up the bus map, she realized she could grab a bus across town. The club manager moved her back in the lineup. The bus hit a patch of traffic. The club owner called and asked where she was. She realized that if she jumped off the bus and ran, she could make it in time.

"I have my headphones on, hood up because it is dark and cold. I'm running. Out of nowhere, this car hops the curb, it blocks my path, and I literally run into this car on the sidewalk. I wipe out on the ground. My first thought was, 'Oh, this guy is having a car accident, why would he hop the curb?' I went up to the window to say, 'Yo, are you OK?'

"The car door flies open, hits me in the stomach, and someone jumps out of the car and is yelling at me. And then flashlights are in my face now. And I see his undercover police officer badge around his neck. Now I am starting to get worried because his hand is also on his hip. I instinctively put my hands up and knock one of my headphones out of my ear. And he is saying, 'Where are you going, what are you doing, you were running. Where are you running to?'

"When I finally gather what is going on he literally says to me, 'You are running too fast.' And I have to show him my ID. I wound up showing him on the phone that I am following directions. I showed him the flier for the show. I showed him I am on my way to a show. I tried to diffuse it with a humor – being a comedian. I said, 'Hey man if you are throwing me into the car, mind taking me to the show?'

"And he laughed, we laughed. It was not until the next day that I was talking to someone and I realized how dangerous the whole situation was. My friend said you had to show him papers to proceed. You couldn't run, just be someone jogging.

"The cop even said, 'I am making sure you are not robbing someone, running from the scene of the crime.' It hit me, had he shot me on the street, my phone could have looked like a gun to him. I realized that was really dangerous. Eric Garner and Mike Brown came out at the same time. They were like back to back. That's when it hit home. Had something happened, and I was hurt or killed, it would have been my fault by default. It would have been something like, 'why did you have your hood up, why were you running so fast?' It would have been my fault even though I was doing nothing wrong, even though I was technically going to work. That's when it all clicked for me. No amount of respectability matters, you can be in a suit you can be in your house, or someone's neighborhood. It was a very quick transition."

For dedicated copwatcher and New York state assembly candidate Anthony Beckford, the awakening was coming home after serving in the US Marine Corps.

"Someone asked 'do you want to carry a sign' and I said I wear a sign all day long," he says. "I took an oath to defend against enemies foreign and domestic. I guess I'm domestic."

Beckford believes so deeply in his work that he sometimes walks the streets of this Brooklyn neighborhood where he grew up as a one-man team, handing out pamphlets educating his community about the right to record. The hope of copwatch educators like Beckford is that education about the power to record also changes the consciousness of the people regarding power over police oversight.

"Copwatching is something we all can do in different capacities," Beckford explains. "I teach you how to recognize when you're just out on the train. The whole thing is [for] copwatching to be like everyday actions. It's not just going to a protest or going to a march. You live social justice. Hopefully as you go through your day, you question. Once you start to think about it, you want to do something about it."

THE RISE OF COPWATCHING

The probability of being recorded by someone has never been higher at any time in human history – and this includes the recording of law enforcement encounters.[2] In the United States, 91 percent of adults have cell phones.[3] Community members are increasingly aiming these cameras at the police to protest, check power, create proof, and sometimes just to satisfy their curiosity. In many prominent cases, the recordings are made by bystanders who were incidentally or fortuitously at the scene and were moved to record. Some of the recording arises from organized copwatching.

In this era of toutveillance, policing occurs in a modern-day Panopticon constructed of cameras. Before it was a famous metaphor, the Panopticon was a plan for an efficient modern prison by a father of modern deterrence theory, Jeremy Bentham.[4] As conceived by Bentham in 1791, the Panoptic prison would put prisoners in transparent cells around an opaque watchtower. The guardhouse looms above the prisoner. The prisoner never knows when the eye is on him – but it could be on him at any time. Thus vulnerable, the prisoner self-polices, behaving as if there was a guard watching him at all times to ensure compliance with the rules. The idea of control via the prospect of omnipresent observation has become an influential metaphor for the management of modern-day society.[5] In the police regulation context, panopticism for police turns the logic of control by transparency on the traditional masters of surveillance, law enforcement.[6]

---

[2] Rose Eveleth, *How Many Photographs of You Are Out There in the World?*, THE ATLANTIC (Nov. 2, 2015), www.theatlantic.com/technology/archive/2015/11/how-many-photographs-of-you-are-out-there-in-the-world/413389/; *When Fatal Arrests Are Caught on Camera*, TIME (July 23, 2014), http://time.com/3024396/fatal-arrests-police-camera/.

[3] Lee Rainie, *Cell Phone Ownership Hits 91% of Adults*, PEW RES. CTR. (June 6, 2013), www .pewresearch.org/fact-tank/2013/06/06/cell-phone-ownership-hits-91-of-adults/.

[4] Miran Božovič, *Introduction* to JEREMY BENTHAM, THE PANOPTICON WRITINGS 13–17 (Miran Božovič ed., 1995).

[5] *See, e.g.*, Michel Foucault, DISCIPLINE AND PUNISH: THE BIRTH OF THE PRISON 200–201 (Alan Sheridan trans., 1977) (extending Panopticon metaphor to one of management of modern society); THEORIZING SURVEILLANCE: THE PANOPTICON AND BEYOND 4–8, 14–17 (David Lyon ed., 2006) (extending metaphor to management of modern society); Larry Catá Backer, *Global Panopticism: States, Corporations, and the Governance Effects of Monitoring Regimes*, 15 IND. J. GLOBAL LEGAL STUD. 101, 112 (2008) (tracing modern decentralized and globalized surveillance state); Daniel J. Solove, *Privacy and Power: Computer Databases and Metaphors for Information Privacy*, 53 STAN. L. REV. 1393, 1415–1416 (2001) (tracing influence in modern governance and discourse).

[6] Mary D. Fan, *Panopticism for Police: Structural Reform Bargaining and Police Regulation by Data-Driven Surveillance*, 87 WASH. L. REV. 93, 102–103 (2012).

Shankar Narayan, a privacy proponent at the ACLU's Washington office points out there is an important distinction between government actors and private persons recording police activities. When community members record, the "narrative is unfiltered through the government lens," he says.

Barry Friedman has illuminated how democratic disengagement with police oversight contributes to controversies and crises over abuse of power.[7] Beyond more cameras aiming at police, the larger project of copwatching is cultivating a culture of public concern that can help address this democratic disengagement. Each case of crucial bystander video that hits the news, and each copwatch group that educates more people about the right to record, create further-reaching cultural cascades. Opinion leaders can spur informational and reputational cascades to spread new social norms and spur behaviors.[8] As more people record the police, the social meaning of the conduct can change from creepy to societally beneficial, even courageous.[9]

From Ferguson to Baltimore to Chicago to Boston, copwatch groups have risen up in recent years, spurred by controversies over police killings, and the spread of cell phone cameras among rich and poor.[10] The groups vary in political orientation, from progressive, to libertarian, to anarchist.[11] They also vary in activities, which may also include education and political activism as well as recording.[12]

While our present is unprecedented in the probability of being recorded, copwatching has longer historical roots predating cell phones or even clunky camcorders. Out of the ashes and turmoil of the Watts riots in 1965 came the Community Alert Patrol, founded to document police misconduct.[13] The Watts patrol members trailed police in their cars and used notebooks and pencils to document activities.[14]

The police were not pleased at being followed by activists. A patrol member spoke of police harassment to a reporter for the *Movement*, a publication of the

---

[7] *See* Barry Friedman, UNWARRANTED: POLICING WITHOUT PERMISSION xiv (2017) ("We have abdicated our most fundamental responsibility as citizens in a democracy: to be in charge of those who act in our name.").

[8] Robert C. Ellickson, *The Market for Social Norms*, 3 AM. L. & ECON. REV. 1, 10, 16, 26–27 (2001).

[9] *Cf.* Dan M. Kahan, *Social Influence, Social Meaning, and Deterrence*, 83 VA. L. REV. 349, 362–365 (1997) (discussing the snowball effect in changing social meaning).

[10] Jocelyn Simonson, *Copwatching*, 104 CAL. L. REV. 391, 411 (2016).

[11] *Id.* at 413.

[12] *Id.*

[13] Robin D. G. Kelley, *Remember What They Built, Not What They Burnt*, L.A. TIMES (Aug. 11, 2015), www.latimes.com/opinion/op-ed/la-oe-0811-kelley-watts-civil-society-20150811-story .html.

[14] Joshua Bloom & Waldo E. Martin Jr., BLACK AGAINST EMPIRE: THE HISTORY AND POLITICS OF THE BLACK PANTHER PARTY 39–40 (2013).

Student Nonviolent Coordinating Committee, commenting, "There's only one way to stop all this, and that's to get out guns and start shooting."[15]

Huey Newton of the Black Panthers read about the Watts community patrols in *Movement* and was inspired.[16] Newton drew on his legal studies and personal research of California law and concluded that the law permitted people to carry weapons in public as long as they were not concealed.[17] The law also permitted people to observe officers carrying out their duties from a reasonable distance, Newton believed.[18] And thus was born the Black Panther practice of armed patrols to police the police.[19] Copwatching Black Panthers would jump out of their cars when officers initiated an investigative stop and observe the activity from a lawful distance with their weapons on display, mirroring officer actions, drawing a gun, and ejecting cartridges when officers did so.[20]

Volunteer-based strategies such as copwatching can take fire rapidly and proliferate contagiously – but also sporadically, and sometimes flicker out until the next crisis rouses people to action. Some copwatch groups that emerged around 2014 and 2015 have gone dormant, becoming perhaps just a ghost page, floating on Facebook, until the next crisis rouses people to action. Other groups continue to patrol, powered by stalwarts such as Waithe and Beckford. The education through "Know Your Rights" trainings that these groups seed in their neighborhoods survive and propagate beyond the organized group. As Beckford explains, while conducting outreach to community members about the right to record during a patrol, "Copwatch is an uprising. Often watching the police is someone's first act of defiance." Waithe adds, "It's an act of radical love. I'm looking out for you. I don't care if you're guilty. If you're going to jail let's get you there safe tonight."

CORRECTING – OR CREATING – THE RECORD

Before cell phone cameras or YouTube, plumber George Holliday made one of the most famous viral police videos of modern times. The year was 1991.

[15] Terrence Cannon, *A Night with the Watts Community Patrol*, MOVEMENT, Aug. 1966, at 3.
[16] Bloom & Martin, *supra* note 14, at 39–40.
[17] *Id.*
[18] Lauren Grants & Stanley Nelson, Op-Docs, *Black Panthers Revisted*, N.Y. TIMES (Jan. 23, 2015), www.youtube.com/watch?v=qGZpDt6OYnI.
[19] *Id.; Policing the Police: How Black Panthers Got Their Start*, NPR FRESH AIR (Sept. 23, 2015) , www.npr.org/2015/09/23/442801731/director-chronicles-the-black-panthers-rise-new-tactics-we re-needed.
[20] Grants & Nelson, *supra* note 18; *Policing the Police: How Black Panthers Got Their Start, supra* note 19.

It was past midnight. Holliday was sleeping with his wife in their Lakeview Terrace apartment, about twenty miles outside Los Angeles, when the wail and beat of police sirens and helicopters woke him. He got onto his balcony and saw police officers beating a black man.

"Before they started hitting him, he was pretty much cooperative," Holliday later recalled.[21]

An immigrant who grew up in Argentina, Holliday said, "I was thinking, 'What did the guy do to deserve this beating?' I came from a different culture, where people would get disappeared with no due process. Police would pick people up on suspicion. I didn't expect this in the U.S."[22]

A few weeks earlier, Holliday had bought something few people had in 1991 – a home video camera that recorded VHS videos, two unwieldy relics in our times.[23] Holliday's Sony Handycam was still in the box. Grabbing it, Holliday filmed a police encounter that would leave twenty-five-year-old Rodney King with permanent brain damage, skull fractures, and broken bones and teeth.[24] The video recorded four Los Angeles Police Department (LAPD) officers stomping and slamming batons down on a man lying face-down on the ground. More than a dozen officers stood by watching and commenting as the beating continued.

Holliday was so disturbed by what he saw that he called the police station the next day to find information about the black man he saw beaten so badly. The police refused to disclose any information. So Holliday went the old-fashioned route for going viral. He called the local television station and complied with instructions to leave his tape at the station.[25]

That evening Holliday's eight-minute recording began making history. Los Angeles exploded in riots when a jury acquitted the four LAPD officers of the

---

[21] Seth Mydans, *Tape of Beating by Police Revives Charges of Racism*, N.Y. TIMES (Mar. 7, 1991), www.nytimes.com/1991/03/07/us/tape-of-beating-by-police-revives-charges-of-racism.html?pagewanted=all.

[22] Michael Goldstein, *The Other Beating*, L.A. TIMES (Feb. 19, 2006), www.latimes.com/la-tm-holidayfeb19-story.html?barc=0.

[23] Few had home video cameras in 1991, according to this retrospective interview with Holliday. *Rodney King Beating: "I Thought, I Should Film This,"* NBC LOS ANGELES CHANNEL 4 (Mar. 3, 2016), www.nbclosangeles.com/on-air/as-seen-on/Rodney-King-Attacked-by-LAPD-Officers-25-Years-Ago_Los-Angeles-371005161.html.

[24] *Id.*

[25] Juan Gonzalez, *George Holliday, the Man with the Camera Who Shot Rodney King While Police Beat Him, Got Burned Too*, N.Y. DAILY NEWS (June 20, 2012), www.nydailynews.com/news/national/george-holliday-man-camera-shot-rodney-king-police-beat-burned-article-1.1098931.

beating in a trial in state court.[26] Two of the officers were later convicted in federal court of civil rights violations.[27] The city of Los Angeles offered to admit liability.[28] A jury awarded King $3.8 million in damages in his civil suit.[29]

The fortuity of Holliday's video made all the difference for Rodney King – and for the LAPD.

The scrutiny led to a "lot of self-examination by the Los Angeles of Police Department, and a lot of changes in training," recalled then lieutenant and now LAPD police chief Charlie Beck.[30] Today, "everybody that I know is walking around with a recording device on them and that has changed the world, and changed public expectations," Chief Beck stated.[31]

While some video evidence arises from organized copwatching, in many prominent cases, the recordings are made by bystanders who were incidentally at the scene and moved to record. Bystander recordings have proved powerful supplements to police-worn body cameras in contemporary controversial cases.

Consider, for example, the fatal shooting of Alton Sterling. The two Baton Rouge police officers involved in the shooting of Alton Sterling said their body cameras fell off,[32] but two bystanders were able to capture graphic footage of the tragic encounter.[33] Sterling died after he asked a homeless man who would not stop seeking money from him to leave him alone and displayed his gun. The homeless man called 911, claiming that Sterling was "brandishing a gun." A bystander's video of the officers' subsequent shooting of Sterling, a father and CD salesman, went viral, commanding national attention.

In Charlotte, cell phone camera footage of the shooting of Keith Scott intensified pressure on the Charlotte-Mecklenburg Police Department to

---

[26] Anjuli Sastry, *When LA Erupted in Anger: A Look Back at the Rodney King Riots*, NPR (Apr. 26, 2017), www.npr.org/2017/04/26/524744989/when-la-erupted-in-anger-a-look-back-at-the-rodney-king-riots.,

[27] Seth Mydans, *Sympathetic Judge Gives Officers 2 ½ Years in Rodney King Beating*, N.Y. Times (Aug. 5, 1993), at A1.

[28] Associated Press, *Los Angeles Set to Settle with Rodney King*, N.Y. Times (Feb. 24, 1994), at 1001010.

[29] Mydans, *supra* note 27, at A14.

[30] *Id.*

[31] *Id.*

[32] *ACLU Questions Lack of Police Body Cams in Alton Sterling Shooting*, CBS News (July 6, 2016, 7:30 PM), www.cbsnews.com/news/alton-%20sterling-baton-rouge-police-shooting-aclu-questions-lack-of-body-cameras/ [http://perma.cc/9R5E-9RM6].

[33] Joshua Berlinger, Nick Valencia, & Steve Almasy, *Alton Sterling Shooting: Homeless Man Made 911 Call, Source Says*, CNN (July 8, 2016), www.cnn.com/2016/07/07/us/baton-rouge-alton-sterling-shooting/index.html [http://perma.cc/U2NH-DBFV].

release their videos of the fatal encounter.[34] The father of seven parked his car in a spot where he often waited for his kids to come home from school, a visitor's space at his apartment complex located about half a mile from the University of North Carolina, Charlotte.[35] Around 4:00 PM, Charlotte-Mecklenburg police officers arrived at the complex to execute a search warrant. The officers claimed that they saw Scott holding a gun next to his SUV then climb inside. In her cell phone recording, Scott's wife, Rakeyia Scott, repeatedly begged the officers not to shoot, saying her husband was unarmed and had a traumatic brain injury. The officers repeatedly yelled at Scott to drop a weapon. It is unclear from Mrs. Scott's cell phone recording whether Scott was holding a weapon; Scott's family says he was holding a book.

When authorities released their videos, further controversy arose over the failure to record the fatal moment by body camera.[36] The plainclothes officers who initially responded were not wearing body cameras. But a subsequent officer with a body camera who arrived at the scene did not activate the recording until after the fatal shooting.

These controversies illustrate the import of recordings by community members to supplement the record even in jurisdictions that have deployed body cameras. Recording by the public supplements police-worn body camera recordings in at least three important ways. First, the recording by a community member may be the only audiovisual evidence where no body camera video exists at all, either in a jurisdiction that has not yet deployed body cameras, or where officers did not record despite wearing body cameras.[37] Bystander videos, such as the cell phone recording made by immigrant barber Feidin Santana of the shooting of Walter Scott in North Charleston, South Carolina, can powerfully challenge and correct the official account of what happened.[38] Community

---

[34] Alan Blinder, *Charlotte Is Pressured to Release Police Video of the Fatal Encounter*, N.Y. TIMES (Sept. 23, 2016), www.nytimes.com/2016/09/24/us/keith-scott-charlotte-shooting-arrest .html [http://perma.cc/DQ7B-T7VG (dark archive)].

[35] Richard Faussett & Yamiche Alcindor, *Video by Wife of Keith Scott Shows Her Pleas to Police*, N.Y. TIMES (Sept. 23, 2016), www.nytimes.com/2016/09/24/us/charlotte-keith-scott-shooting-video.html [http://perma.cc/4ZKK-UVSD (dark archive)].

[36] Wesley Lowery, *Charlotte Officer Did Not Activate Body Camera Until after Keith Scott Had Been Shot*, WASH. POST (Sept. 26, 2016), www.washingtonpost.com/news/post-nation/wp/20 16/09/26/charlotte-officer-did-not-activate-body-camera-until-after-keith-scott-had-been-shot-2 /?utm_term=.1463a9f57580 [http://perma.cc/G2T2-Y6LQ (staff uploaded archive)].

[37] *See* Mary D. Fan, *Missing Police Body Camera Videos: Remedies, Evidentiary Fairness, and Automatic Activation*, 52 GA. L. REV. 57, 74–82 (2017) (discussing the challenges of addressing failures to record using officer-worn body cameras).

[38] Phil Hesel, *Walter Scott Death: Bystander Who Recorded Cop Shooting Speaks Out*, NBC NEWS (Apr. 9, 2015, 11:54 AM), www.nbcnews.com/storyline/walter-scott-shooting/man-who-recorded-walter-scott-being-shot-speaks-out-n338126 [https://perma.cc/2MNT-PP2Y].

member recordings can help generate an official record where none may exist, such as in a street stop-and-frisk that yields no evidence. Individually, such a stop-and-frisk may not present a legal case or controversy. In the aggregate, however, documenting such opaque street-level encounters may reveal important legally significant patterns and practices.

Second, community member videos can offer an important competing perspective. As Chapter 5 will discuss, the framing and perspective of videos can subtly shape viewer perceptions about legally important issues, such as whether an encounter was justified or a person was coerced. The framing of an encounter from the perspective of an officer's body camera, activated when an encounter begins to escalate, may miss details another camera might catch. A camera situated at a different angle, perspective, or time frame may capture the tone of the encounter before the escalation, or whether the bucking and grappling of officers shown on body camera is due to the suspect aggressively resisting or officers stomping on a prone suspect. Third, community member recording also can give officers incentive to record to capture a contested encounter from the police perspective. In the competition for public perceptions, each side is better protected by recording from that party's viewpoint.

ARRESTED FOR RECORDING THE POLICE

Once upon a time, not long ago, people who recorded their encounters with police risked arrest. Even today, there are dangers. The risks of recording the police are particularly acute in places that require the consent of all parties to a conversation for recording.[39] Sometimes dubbed "two-party consent" statutes and part of state wiretap laws, the provisions typically make it a crime to surreptitiously record a conversation unless every party to a conversation consents.[40] In contrast, federal wiretap law and state laws similar to federal wiretap law only require the consent of one party to the conversation.

---

[39]   E.g., Kelly v. Borough of Carlisle (Kelly I), 2009 WL 1230309, at *1 (M.D. Penn. 2009), *aff'd in part, vacated in part, remanded by* Kelly II, 622 F.3d 248 (3d Cir. 2010); Andy Grimm, *Woman Acquitted in Eavesdropping Case Files Lawsuit against Chicago Police*, CHI. TRIB. (Jan. 14, 2012); *Tiawanda Moore, Woman Who Recorded Cops, Acquitted of Felony Eavesdropping Charges*, HUFFINGTON POST (Aug. 25, 2011), www.huffingtonpost.com/2011/08/25/tiawanda-moore-acquitted-n_936313.html; Daniel Rowinski, *Police Fight Cellphone Recordings*, BOS. GLOBE (Jan. 12, 2010), www.boston.com/news/local/massachusetts/articles/2010/01/12/police_fight_ cellphone_recordings/.

[40]   For an overview of the laws and where the states stand on them, *see, e.g.,* REPORTERS COMMITTEE FOR FREEDOM OF THE PRESS, A STATE-BY-STATE GUIDE TO TAPING PHONE CALLS AND IN-PERSON CONVERSATIONS (Summer 2012), www.rcfp.org/rcfp/orde rs/docs/RECORDING.pdf.

There are egregious examples of prosecutions for recording the police. For example, Tiawanda Moore, age twenty-one, spent two weeks in jail and a year of her life struggling with felony charges for recording officers trying to dissuade her from filing a sexual harassment complaint.[41] Her ordeal began in July 2010 when Chicago Police Department officers responded to her home because of a domestic violence call.[42] One of the responding officers found Moore alone in her bedroom. According to Moore, the officer touched her chest and bottom, then wrote down his number on a piece of paper. He placed his number on her bed and instructed her not to tell anyone he slipped her his number.

Moore filed a complaint, which was assigned to two internal affairs officers. She showed the officers the number left on her bed. The two investigators proceeded to try to convince her to sign a letter declining to proceed with the investigation, claiming if she went to court she would not win, and that they had spoken to the offending officer and his behavior would not repeat. Moore said she wished to proceed with her complaint. Because of the pressure to drop her complaint, she activated a recording device on her Blackberry. When the officers noticed her recording, they arrested her, charging her with two counts of felony eavesdropping under Illinois law.

It took more than a year after her ordeal began with the domestic violence call for a jury to find Moore not guilty of the felony eavesdropping charges in August 2011. It took a First Amendment challenge by the ACLU and legislative action to get the provisions under which Moore was charged amended.[43]

Until 2014, Illinois wiretap law was particularly aggressive in punishing people who record the police. The statute made it a felony to record a conversation without the consent of all parties, regardless of whether the conversation was private, or whether the recording was surreptitious or openly conducted.[44] Recording the police without consent constituted a more severe

[41] Grimm, *supra* note 39; *Tiawanda Moore, Woman Who Recorded Cops, Acquitted of Felony Eavesdropping Charges, supra* note 39.

[42] Moore v. City of Chicago, Case No. 1:12-cv-00238, Memorandum Opinion and Order (N.D. Ill., Apr. 28, 2014), *available at* www.washingtonpost.com/news/volokh-conspiracy/wp-content/uploads/sites/14/2014/05/MoorevCityofChicago.pdf. The facts that follow come from the district court's memorandum of opinion in the case, in which the court discusses the undisputed facts.

[43] Pub. Act 98-1142, S.B. 1342, 98th Gen Assembly, 2014, L ST Ch. 720 § 5/14-4, *available at* 2014 Ill. Legis. Serv. P.A. 98-1142 (S.B. 1342); ACLU of Ill. v. Alvarez, 679 F.3d 583, 587–588 (2012).

[44] *See* ACLU of Ill. v. Alvarez, 679 F.3d 583, 587–588 (2012) (giving history of the Illinois wiretapping statute and the broadening after 1994 amendments to cover the recording of any conversation without the consent of all parties, regardless of whether the conversation was meant to be private); People v. Clark, 6 N.E.3d 154, 159 (Ill. 2014) (discussing 1994

felony than recording other people generally, elevated to a class 1 felony from a class 4 felony for a first-time offense.[45]

The ACLU challenged the statute, arguing that it aimed to launch a police accountability program that would record police officers in public but its videographers risked prosecution for doing so.[46] The district court dismissed the case, holding there is no First Amendment right to record officers without their consent, because no "willing speaker" was involved.[47] Reversing, the Seventh Circuit Court of Appeals held that audiovisual recordings are expressive media commonly used to convey information and foster debate and thus protected by the First Amendment freedoms of speech and press.[48] Over a dissent by Judge Posner, who discussed the important state interest in protecting civilians interacting with the police from the privacy harms of recording,[49] the Seventh Circuit issued a preliminary injunction blocking enforcement of the Illinois statute. The court ruled that there was a strong likelihood that the statute violated the First Amendment because it was so overly and unusually broad, applying to any recording of any conversation, rather than the more common prohibitions on surreptitious recording of private conversations.[50]

Even where a judge has ruled that recording the police is not a crime, people have gone to jail for recording. Consider the case of Tony Alford. For recording the police, Tony Alford was arrested, his car was towed, and he spent the night in jail – though recording the police was not a crime under state law.[51] Heading to work one November night in 1997, Alford stopped to help motorists stranded by

---

amendments that made clear "that the consent of all parties to recording a conversation is required, regardless of whether the parties intended their conversation to be private").

[45] 720 Ill. Comp. Stat. § 5/14-4(b) (2010). For historical edits, see Pub. Act 98-1142, S.B. 1342, 98th Gen Assembly, 2014, L ST Ch. 720 § 5/14–4, *available at* 2014 Ill. Legis. Serv. P.A. 98–1142 (S.B. 1342). *See also* ACLU of Ill. v. Alvarez, 679 F.3d 583, 586 (7th Cir. 2012) ("The offense is normally a class 4 felony but is elevated to a class 1 felony – with a possible prison term of four to fifteen years – if one of the recorded individuals is performing duties as a law-enforcement officer. *Id.* 5/14-4(b). Illinois does not prohibit taking silent video of police officers performing their duties in public; turning on a microphone, however, triggers class 1 felony punishment.").

[46] *Alvarez,* 679 F.3d at 586.

[47] ACLU of Ill. v. Alvarez, Civil Action No. 10 C 5235, 2011 WL 66030 (N.D. Ill. May 8, 2012), *rev'd,* 679 F.3d 583 (7th Cir. 2012).

[48] *Alvarez,* 679 F.3d at 595.

[49] *Alvarez,* 679 F.3d at,611 (Posner, J., dissenting).

[50] *Alvarez,* 679 F.3d at 607.

[51] Alford v. Haner, 333 F.3d 972, 974–975 (9th Cir. 2003), *rev'd sub nom,* Devenpeck v. Alford, 543 US 146 (2004); *see also* State v. Flora, 845 P.2d 1355, 1358 (Wash. Ct. App 1992) (holding that recording police officers performing their public duties, in this case an arrest, is not a violation of the state's privacy act because "the arrest was not entitled to be private" and the officers "could not reasonably have considered their words private").

the side of the road with a flat tire.[52] Alford helped the people jack up their car, gave them his flashlight, and then went back to his car.[53]

Meanwhile, a state trooper, who was headed in the opposite direction, saw the disabled vehicle and Alford pulling his car over to help. The trooper, Joi Haner, turned his car around and arrived at the scene as Alford was going back to his car. Alford told the trooper that the motorists had a flat tire and that he gave them the flashlight they needed to fix it. Alford then drove off. Haner checked on the stranded motorists, who told him they thought Alford was a police officer because Alford's car had wig-wag headlights, the distinctive, alternatively flashing headlights of police vehicles.

Haner became concerned that Alford was impersonating a police officer. He called his supervisor Sergeant Devenpeck and then pursued Alford, pulling him over. Haner noted that Alford's license plate was virtually undecipherable because of a tinted plate cover. He also noted that Alford had a portable police scanner, handcuffs, and an amateur radio that relayed calls from the Kitsap County Sheriff's Office. While Haner and Sgt. Devenpeck, who arrived to investigate, clearly found Alford creepy, the officers ultimately arrested Alford because he recorded their conversation. Sgt. Devenpeck informed Alford he was under arrest for allegedly illegally recording the encounter.

This was apparently not the first time Alford had recorded the police. He told the officers that he had a similar run-in with sheriff's deputies over recording. He said he carried in his glove compartment a Washington Court of Appeals opinion holding that the state's Privacy Act prohibiting recording without permission did not apply to police officers performing their public duties.[54] Refusing to examine the opinion, Sgt. Devenpeck ordered Alford transported to jail. He testified later that the arrest was based solely on his

---

[52] *Devenpeck*, 543 US at 148.

[53] The facts presented by the Ninth Circuit and the US Supreme Court differ in their sympathy to the would-be Samaritan (or fake cop) Alford, and whether he walked away after giving the motorists his flashlight, or "hurried" off after the trooper arrived at the scene. *Compare Devenpeck*, 543 US at 148 ("The stranded (motorists asked Haner if respondent was a 'cop'; they said that respondent's statements, and his flashing, wig-wag headlights, had given them that impression. They also informed Haner that as respondent hurried off he left his flashlight behind.") (citations omitted), *with Alford*, 333 F.3d at 974 ("While driving to his night job, Alford noticed a disabled car on the shoulder of a highway. The area was dark and deserted and he pulled over to offer assistance. After helping the motorists jack up their car and giving them a flashlight to use, he began walking back to his car."). The narrative that follows derives from both the Ninth Circuit and the US Supreme Court's accounts.

[54] The Court of Appeals of Washington had indeed so held that the state's Privacy Act did not apply to officers performing their public duties, such as arrests. State v. Flora, 845 P.2d 1355, 1358 (Wash. Ct. App. 1992).

belief that recording the encounter violated state law. Though the belief was mistaken and it was legal to record in Washington state, the US Supreme Court held the arrest would nonetheless be proper if the facts known to the officer would give rise to some other violation – even if a prosecutor had to post hoc propose an alternative basis to justify the arrest for a noncrime.

GROWING RECOGNITION OF THE RIGHT TO
RECORD THE POLICE

Fast-forward two decades to a late autumn evening. The setting is the same state where Devenpeck was arrested. Another police enthusiast, Tim Clemans, is out recording the police, as he often does in the bustling hours of 1:00 to 2:30 AM on Saturdays and Sundays, when the night spots in the Capitol Hill neighborhood of Seattle are hopping. Clemans explains that he started using his cell phone "as an always on bodycam" when he heard about a Google manager who was assaulted by an officer for checking on the welfare of a suspect in a police encounter. He mounts the cell phone on his chest and the video uploads to YouTube every few minutes. The cell phone is plugged into a fast-charging battery pack because he does a lot of filming of police and he has the camera always on so that he does not miss important things.

Clemans is well known to the police as the notorious requester.[55] He made public records requests to police departments across Washington state for police videos from dash cameras and body cameras.[56] Police departments like Spokane or Bellingham, without the resources to painstakingly redact or fight the broad public disclosure requests, released volumes of body camera and dash camera video, sometimes in sensitive contexts, which Clemans posted to YouTube.[57] The Seattle Police Department wrestled with how to redact sensitive information from more than 360 terabytes worth of dash camera videos, 911 call records, and other data subject to thirty broad public

---

[55] Mark Harris, *The Body Cam Hacker Who Schooled the Police*, MEDIUM: BACKCHANNEL (May 22, 2015), https://medium.com/backchannel/the-body-cam-hacker-who-schooled-the-poli ce-co46ff7f6f13 [https://perma.cc/T2M7-ZDWC]; *Seattle Police Body Camera Program Highlights Unexpected Issues*, NPR (Apr. 15, 2015, 5:36 PM), www.npr.org/2015/04/15/39993774 9/seattle-police-body-camera-program-highlights-unexpected-issues.

[56] Rachel Alexander, *Records Advocate Wants All Spokane Police Body Camera Videos*, SPOKESMAN-REV. (Jan. 13, 2016), www.spokesman.com/stories/2016/jan/13/records-advo cate-wants-all-spokane-police-body-cam/#/o [https://perma.cc/SG6G-6NXL].

[57] Mary D. Fan, *Privacy, Public Disclosure, Police Body Cameras: Policy Splits*, 68 ALA. L. REV. 395, 397–398, 433 (2016).

disclosure requests by Clemans.[58] In a savvy move, the Department hired Clemans, who then dropped his requests, only to file two hundred more when he resigned due to personality conflicts.[59]

The tale of two Washingtonians illustrates the cultural shift to regulation by radical transparency. One man gets arrested and his car towed for recording his own police encounter in public. Another man wields his camera like a roving ronin striking frustration in the hearts of organized law enforcement and posts videos on YouTube. His reward is a job with the police department. That police department, like countless others across the nation, is planning to outfit its officers with body cameras. If the department follows the approach taken by the hundreds of other departments that have deployed body cameras, officers will be required to record most law enforcement activities previously documented by an officer's report, word, or no evidence at all.

Times and public expectations are changing – and so are the legal and cultural constraints on law enforcement. Every federal circuit court to address the question has ruled that there is a First Amendment-protected right to record the police in public.[60] There also is an efflorescence of scholarship exploring the First Amendment bases for the right to record.[61] Courts recognize that recording the police serves the core First Amendment values of sharing information and spurring discourse about government officials and the appropriate use of power.[62] Courts also recognize that a community member's cell phone video

---

[58]   *Seattle Police Body Camera Program Highlights Unexpected Issues*, NPR (Apr. 15, 2015, 5:36 PM), www.npr.org/2015/04/15/399937749/seattle-police-body-camera-program-highlights-une xpected-issues [https://perma.cc/MN6Q-HZN5 (staff-uploaded archive)].

[59]   Jennifer Sullivan, *SPD Tech Officer Quits, Files 200 More Public Disclosure Requests*, SEATTLE TIMES (Oct. 29, 2015), www.seattletimes.com/seattle-news/spd-tech-officer-resign s-resumes-public-records-requests/ [https://perma.cc/W5YK-Y4G8].

[60]   *See* Fields v. City of Phila., 862 F.3d 353, 356 (3d Cir. 2017); Turner v. Lieutenant Driver, 848 F.3d 678, 688 (5th Cir. 2017); Gericke v. Begin, 753 F.3d 1, 3 (1st Cir. 2014); ACLU of Ill. v. Alvarez, 679 F.3d 583, 595 (7th Cir. 2012); Glik v. Cunniffe, 655 F.3d 78, 79 (1st Cir. 2011); Smith v. City of Cumming, 212 F.3d 1332, 1333 (11th Cir. 2000); Fordyce v. City of Seattle, 55 F.3d 436, 439 (9th Cir. 1995).

[61]   There is a rich and growing body of literature on the right to record. *See, e.g.,* Margot E. Kaminski, *Privacy and the Right to Record*, 97 B.U. L. REV. 167, 184–199 (2017) (analyzing case law on the right to record generally); Jocelyn Simonson, *Beyond Body Cameras: Defending a Robust Right to Record*, 104 GEO. L.J. 1559, 1569–1574 (2016) (arguing that filming the police is a form of First Amendment–protected speech); Howard M. Wasserman, *Police Misconduct, Video Recording, and Procedural Barriers to Rights Enforcement*, 96 N.C. L. REV. 1313 (2018) (collecting and evaluating theories of the First Amendment foundations of the right to record). *Cf.* Jane Bambauer, *Is Data Speech?*, 66 STAN L. REV. 57, 82–83 (2014) (discussing what is protectable in generating photographs).

[62]   *See, e.g.,* Glik v. Cunniffe, 655 F.3d 78, 83 (1st Cir. 2011) ("Gathering information about government officials in a form that can readily be disseminated to others serves a cardinal First Amendment interest in protecting and promoting "the free discussion of governmental

is often the first source of crucial newsworthy information and rivals or complements the media's ability to gather and broadcast information.[63] Of course the right to record the police is not absolute.[64] Like the right to protest, it is subject to reasonable time, place, and manner restrictions.[65]

THE CONTINUED RISK OF RETALIATION FOR RECORDING AND JUDICIAL PUSHBACK

Still, some officers have used wiretapping statutes or amorphous charges like obstruction or disorderly conduct to stop people from photographing or recording police activities.[66] For example, in 2010, Anthony Graber was indicted on multiple charges, including "unlawful interception of an oral communication" and possessing a device "primarily useful for the purpose of the surreptitious interception of oral communications" for recording his traffic stop and posting the video on YouTube.[67] Ultimately, a Maryland state court judge dismissed the charges, writing Graber's conduct was not a violation of the wiretapping statute.[68]

---

affairs."); Fields v. City of Phila., 862 F.3d 353, 359 (3d Cir. 2017) ("Access to information regarding public police activity is particularly important because it leads to citizen discourse on public issues, 'the highest rung of the hierarchy of First Amendment values, and is entitled to special protection.'") (quoting Snyder v. Phelps, 562 US 443, 452 (2011)).

[63]   See, e.g., Fields, 862 F.3d at 358 ("[C]itizens' gathering and disseminating 'newsworthy information [occur] with an ease that rivals that of the traditional news media.'") (quoting 2012 US Dep't of Justice Letter to the Baltimore Police Department); Glik, 655 F.3d at 84 ("The proliferation of electronic devices with video-recording capability means that many of our images of current events come from bystanders with a ready cell phone or digital camera rather than a traditional film crew, and news stories are now just as likely to be broken by a blogger at her computer as a reporter at a major newspaper.").

[64]   See, e.g., Fields., 862 F.3d at 361 ("The right to record the police is not absolute.").

[65]   Ward v. Rock against Racism, 491 US 781, 791 (1989); Kelly v. Borough of Carlisle, 622 F.3d 248, 262 (3d Cir. 2010).

[66]   See, e.g., Fields., 862 F.3d at 356 (describing case of officer who confronted Temple University student photographing officers breaking up a house party, seized and searched his cell phone, and cited him for obstructing public passageways; and case of an officer who pinned legal observer to a protest against a wall to prevent her from recording an arrest); Adkins v. Suba, 2011 WL 4443225, at *1–2 (D. Guam 2011) (considering case where officer arrested a person for using a cell phone to photograph an unattended crash site as police officers stood in the shade across the street); Joel Rose, *This Is the Police: Put Down Your Camera*, NPR (May 13, 2011), www.npr.org/2011/05/13/136171366/this-is-the-police-put-down-your-camera (chronicling several cases, including that of Khaliah Fitchette, sixteen, arrested for recording the police dealing with a collapsed man on the bus).

[67]   For a compelling account of Graber's story, see Barry Friedman, Unwarranted: Policing without Permission 308 (2017).

[68]   State v. Graber, No. 12-K-10-647, 2010 Md. Cir. Ct. LEXIS 7, at *35 (Md. Cir. Ct. Sept. 27, 2010).

"Those of us who are public officials and are entrusted with the power of the state are ultimately accountable to the public," Judge Emory Plitt ruled. "When we exercise that power in public fora, we should not expect our actions to be shielded from public observation. 'Sed quis custodiet ipsos custodes' [Who watches the watchers?]."[69]

In 2013, award-winning freelance journalist Mannie Garcia decided to record officers arresting two young Hispanic men because he was concerned the officers were using excessive force.[70] In his civil suit against the police, Garcia alleged that the officers put him in a chokehold, forcibly dragged him to the ground, and confiscated his camera. When his wife approached out of concern, an officer said, "If that fucking bitch takes one more step I am going to arrest her ass." The officers arrested Garcia for disorderly conduct and took his video card. Garcia says he never got the video card back. He was acquitted of the disorderly conduct charge.

The case so concerned the US Department of Justice that it filed a Statement of Interest in the case. "The United States is concerned that discretionary charges, such as disorderly conduct, loitering, disturbing the peace, and resisting arrest, are all too easily used to curtail expressive conduct or retaliate against individuals for exercising their First Amendment rights," wrote the attorneys for the Justice Department's Civil Rights Division.[71] "[T]he Court should not make a distinction between the public's and the media's rights to record here. The derogation of these rights erodes public confidence in our police departments, decreases the accountability of our governmental officers, and conflicts with the liberties that the Constitution was designed to uphold."[72]

Simon Glik had the temerity to use his cell phone to record an arrest on the Boston Common because he believed he saw an officer punch the arrestee.[73] After confirming that Glik's cell phone recorded audio, officers arrested him for allegedly violating the Massachusetts wiretap statute; disturbing the peace; and aiding the escape of a prisoner.[74] A municipal judge dismissed the charges, writing that the fact that "officers were unhappy they were being recorded ... does not make a lawful exercise of a First Amendment right

---

[69] *Id.*

[70] The facts as alleged by Garcia are chronicled in Garcia v. Montgomery County, Maryland, Civ. No. JFM-12-3592, 2013 WL 4539394 (D. Md. Aug. 23, 2013).

[71] Statement of Interest of the United States, Garcia v. Montgomery County, Civ. No. 8:12-cv -03952-JFM, at 1 (D. Md. Mar. 4, 2013), *available at* www.justice.gov/sites/default/files/crt/leg acy/2013/03/20/garcia_SOI_3-14-13.pdf.

[72] *Id.* at 2.

[73] Glik v. Cunniffe, 655 F.3d 78, 79 (1st Cir. 2011).

[74] *Id.* at 80.

a crime."[75] The US Court of Appeals for the First Circuit ruled that the police violated Glik's well-established First Amendment rights and were not entitled to qualified immunity.[76]

The Ninth Circuit has indicated that officers who retaliate against members of the public for recording the police with stops or arrests with no legal basis are subject to civil rights lawsuits and are not shielded by qualified immunity.[77] The Third Circuit earlier ruled that the right to record officers was not sufficiently clearly established to overcome qualified immunity.[78] But in 2017, the Third Circuit joined the "growing consensus" on First Amendment protections against retaliation for recording the police, meaning officers now should not expect qualified immunity.[79] The Fifth Circuit in 2017 recognized a First Amendment right to record but ruled the officers had qualified immunity because the right was not clearly established at the time of the officers' actions.[80] But going forward, officers are similarly on notice regarding the right to record in the Fifth Circuit.

A NEW GENERATION OF COPS ON CAMERA

A new generation of officers are also acclimatizing to doing their job on camera. Officers work in public and private spaces saturated with cell phone cameras, Facebook Live, YouTube viral videos, and surveillance cameras and sensors. Often these forms of surveillance supply evidence for law enforcement. Increasingly these proliferating forms of monitoring and tracking are directed at officers rather than the people they investigate. Whether officers began their job in Muskogee, Baltimore, Anacostia, Seattle, or Tacoma, the officers interviewed for this book report that members of the public frequently record their work.

A patrol officer with five years of experience in Washington state said he has been recorded "more times than I can count. The recordings (some) were put online." Another officer noted, "Even people who call us to come into their homes, they'll still record us." Another officer with twenty-four years of experience as both a police officer and a sheriff's deputy noted: "I have been recorded many times; it is quite common in the bar areas for people to pull out their cell phones and start recording if police respond in the area. The only

[75]   *Id.*
[76]   *Id.* at 82–85.
[77]   Adkins v. Limtiaco, 537 F. App'x 721, 721–722 (9th Cir. 2013) (mem.).
[78]   Kelly v. Borough of Carlisle, 622 F.3d 263 (3d Cir. 2010).
[79]   Fields v. City of Phila., 862 F.3d 353 (3d Cir. 2017).
[80]   Turner v. Lieutenant Driver, 848 F.3d 678, 687 (5th Cir. 2017).

time it causes a problem is when the citizen we are dealing with then feels pressured to 'perform' for the cameras. I would hope that I do my job to the best of my ability whether someone is watching or not."

An officer with several years of experience, primarily in Muskogee, Oklahoma, said he already had lots of experience being recorded by the public before he donned a body camera to self-record his activities. "If the public wants to record they can as long as they do not interfere with what is going on," he said. This is a commonly expressed sentiment among officers interviewed: "I am OK with being recorded as long as it does not interfere with my job and safety."

While there is certainly resistance to being recorded among rank-and-file officers and the unions that represent them, concerns are tempered by the realization that someone may be recording anyway – and it is better to have your own audiovisual proof. In interviews and surveys for this book, multiple law enforcement officers expressed concerns regarding the fairness and accuracy of citizen recording. Among police supporters of body cameras, one of the oft-expressed hopes is that body cameras can help exonerate officers.

An officer captured the recurring concern: "Others' recordings have been altered and edited to make the incident appear worse than it was or to make the officer appear to be in the wrong. Citizen recordings do not always show the complete interaction."

Another patrol officer with experience wearing body cameras captured an oft-voiced hope of officers and police departments that support body cameras thus: "I feel like the cameras can help police in certain instances when it is a citizen's word against the officer's word. I feel like the cameras will save officers more than hurt them."

Veteran officers who have seen a change in the culture of public recording the cops, also are coming around to the utility of body cameras. Explained a veteran Tacoma police department officer with twenty-four years of experience: "I believe that body cameras will protect officers from false and frivolous accusations, and will help with catching suspects if the officer is injured."

Of course, not all patrol officers agree that pervasive recording is a good thing. Many expressed concern for the privacy of the people they encounter, often in the worst moments of their lives. These important privacy concerns will be discussed in Chapter 6. Being recorded sometimes in public by a bystander also is different from pervasive recording by body cameras. As Chapter 8 will discuss, some powerful police unions representing line-level officers have opposed such pervasive recording by body cameras and gone to court to try to block such moves. Yet despite the concerns and barriers, police departments are responding to public demand by including provisions on the public's right to record in police department manuals, and deploying body cameras. Having that video evidence can be crucial for police departments in the fierce battle in the court of public opinion – and even forestall riots.

GOING VIRAL: THE RACE FOR PUBLIC PERCEPTIONS

In November 2017, just over a year after violent riots erupted in Charlotte, North Carolina over the police shooting of Keith Lamont Scott, law enforcement leaders, officers, legislators, and civil liberties experts gathered to discuss recording policies. The law enforcement leaders were intimately familiar with camera power. Charlotte-Mecklenburg is one of the earlier major American cities to adopt body cameras, training and equipping all patrol officers by September 2015.[81] But the officer wearing a body camera at the scene of the shooting of Scott in September 2016 did not activate his camera to capture both audio and video until after the shots were fired.[82] A father of seven, Scott died at age forty-three. Protests and riots erupted, leading the governor to declare a state of emergency.

Public demand for recordings and the volatile power of cell phone videos were major issues on the minds of the law enforcement leaders. In 2016, the North Carolina legislature enacted a new body camera law that limits release of recordings absent a petition and court order.[83] Law enforcement leaders soon learned that the petition process could hamstring them in the race for public perceptions.

"A cell phone video goes viral in forty-eight hours," explained Charlotte-Mecklenburg's City Attorney, Tom Carruthers. "People say, 'It is a clear example of disparate treatment by officers in the south.' Within seventy-two hours, a police attorney has to file a request with a court to release the police video showing the officer doing what he is supposed to do. Maybe not a perfect job, but what is right."

Explained Knightdale Chief of Police Lawrence Capps, "There may be a timeliness issue, if I have to go through the petition process, if the city is in chaos and we're sitting doing the work getting an order. Look at the speed at which a preliminary opinion on a use of force is put out there for public

---

[81]   Adam Bell, *All CMPD Patrol Officers Now Have Body Cameras*, CHARLOTTE OBSERVER (Sept. 16, 2015), www.charlotteobserver.com/news/local/crime/article35451150.html.

[82]   Wesley Lowery, *Charlotte Officer Did Not Activate Body Camera Until after Keith Scott Had Been Shot*, WASH. POST (Sept. 26, 2016), http://wapo.st/2cwPtXn.

[83]   House Bill 972, Law Enforcement Recordings, North Carolina General Assembly (2015–2016 Session) (signed by Governor, July 11, 2016).

consumption through social media. There are few guidelines these people have to follow. We've tried to streamline our processes for releasing police recordings. That is still an eternity compared to the speed at which things travel through social media. In reality, you have about ninety seconds to respond to that first social media tweet or post. It catches fire."

"Videos have often exonerated officers," said Darrel Stephens, former chief of police for Charlotte-Mecklenburg and president of the Major Cities Chiefs Association. "Quick release has helped correct the narrative in several cases."

On the other side of the country, an officer with decades of combined experience, at the Tacoma Police Department and the Pierce County Sheriff's Department, described similar pressures: "I think that the swiftness and the reach of information sent out over social media networks and other media outlets have changed society as a whole. It is so easy to send out an anonymous posting that the writer never has to defend or back up with facts, and so easy to send videos that have been timed so the entire incident cannot be viewed."

These conversations reveal the pressures that police departments face in the age of pervasive recording. The rapid pace at which viral videos get disseminated on social media can create intense pressure on police departments to respond with recordings from the officers' perspectives. Police departments also have incentive to record to address community member videos that may only give a partial potentially misleading story.

Copwatchers, civil libertarians and community members have similar concerns about the partiality of police video, creating mutually reinforcing pressures to record. As copwatcher Waithe explains, "I feel like the more cameras the better. But the officers can manipulate the body cams. They can turn it on, turn it off, put stuff in front of it. And they don't like releasing them. So we need to record as well, more videos I can control. And I can release those videos, I don't have to wait for police to release it."

Wider-spread recording by community members in turn generate heightened incentives for police departments to record and release video in a race for public perceptions. As more community members take up cameras to protest or document police actions – and more courts recognize the right to do so – police agencies have growing incentive to record from the officer's perspective and release video in the struggle for control over the narrative. Citizen and police recordings are complementary, providing more points of view and data from which to decide what happened.

3

Democratizing Proof, Taking the Case to the People

I'm going to [expletive] punch you in the face ... I don't care if you are [expletive] fourteen years old or not. I will punch you in your face, and when we go down to court, it's your word against mine, and mine wins every time.

– Principal caught on camera threatening high school student[1]

When justice removes the blindfold, vision of injustice is actually possible. Just as the veil is an obfuscation, so is the blindfold ... [B]lindness is no romantic trait.

– Imani Perry[2]

GAME-CHANGING EVIDENCE

What really happened? Did Walter try to grab the officer's Taser while attempting to flee from a traffic stop for a broken taillight, forcing the officer to shoot him, as the police reports say?[3] Or did the officer shoot Walter in the back five times when he was running away?[4]

Did Officer Jared commit sexual misconduct against the young woman he stopped for driving while intoxicated?[5] Or did the twenty-three-year-old

[1] *Principal Placed on Leave for Video of Him Threatening Student*, CBS NEWS (Dec. 1, 2016), www.cbsnews.com/news/kevin-murray-woodland-hills-principal-placed-on-leave-for-video-of-him-threatening-student/.

[2] Imani Perry, *Occupying the Universal, Embodying the Subject*, 17 LAW & LIT. 97, 116 (2005).

[3] See Alan Blinder & Manny Fernandez, *Residents Trace Police Shooting to a Crime Strategy Gone Awry*, N.Y. TIMES (Apr. 10, 2015), at A1; Mark Berman, S.C. Investigators Say They Thought Fatal Police Shooting Was Suspicious before Video Emerged, WASH. POST (Apr. 10, 2015), www.washingtonpost.com/news/post-nation/wp/2015/04/10/south-carolina-investigators-say-they-thought-fatal-police-shooting-was-suspicious-before-video-emerged/.

[4] Matt Apuzzo & Timothy Williams, *Citizen's Videos Raise Questions on Police Claims*, N.Y. TIMES (Apr. 9, 2015), at A1.

[5] Uriel J. Garcia, *Local Agencies Aim to Expand Use of Lapel Cameras*, SANTA FE NEW MEXICAN (Dec. 14, 2014), www.santafenewmexican.com/news/local_news/local-agencies-aim-to-expand-use-of-lapel-cameras/article_44abf0eb-cffe-52c0-b7e7-cf17533936f3.html.

concoct the complaint in retaliation for the DUI arrest after her attempts to talk her way out of the arrest did not succeed?[6]

Did Kenneth flee from officers trying to warn him about riding a bike without a light at night, resulting in a struggle that lead to the discovery of drugs in his pocket, as police reports say? Or did officers pull Kenneth from his bike after he did not hear them through the music on his headphones, punch him, pull his pants down, and poke their fingers into his buttocks and anus in a roving search for drugs while he cried out in pain and fear?[7]

Did Andre interfere with the capture of a runaway suspect while screaming profanities, then push and try to fight an officer?[8] Or was Andre actually a witness to the police beating up a suspect and punished by officers for speaking out against the use of force with a pretextual arrest?[9]

Did Roxanne consent to a search of her home or did police coerce her into letting them in by threatening to take away her child if she did not?[10]

Or for the *Making a Murderer* fans, did police discover or plant the murder victim Teresa's car keys in Steven's bedroom and Steven's blood in the victim's car?[11]

As officers are increasingly learning and coming to believe, video evidence can protect and exonerate against false claims.[12] In New Mexico, officer

---

[6] *New Mexico Officer Cleared of Sexual Assault by Body Camera*, KOB Channel 4 (Albuquerque, NM) (Dec. 16, 2014), www.youtube.com/watch?v=Lt4u11aI5No.

[7] Allison Ash, *Raw Video from SDPD Officer's Body Camera Shows Man's Arrest at Park*, Youtube (Jun. 17, 2015), www.youtube.com/watch?v=OvbgZFQYG18 [hereinafter Simmons Body Camera Video].

[8] Jones v. United States, 16 A.3d 966, 968–969 (D.C. Cir. 2011).

[9] *Id.* at 968.

[10] *See* Fernandez v. California, 134 S. Ct. 1126, 1143 n.5 (2014) (Ginsburg, J., dissenting) (noting conflicting accounts between police officers and the defendant's battered girlfriend over whether she consented to a search or acquiesced when threatened with removal of her child).

[11] *See* Brief of Defendant-Appellant at 8, Wisconsin v. Avery, No. 2010AP411-CR (Wis. Ct. App. June 25, 2010), 2010 WL 2691415 (recounting the defense theory that the police planted the evidence); *Making a Murderer* (Netflix 2015) (suggesting the police planted the evidence); *see also, e.g.*, Commonwealth v. Sparks, 746 N.E.2d 133, 138 (Mass. 2001) (alleging that police planted evidence found in his living quarters); Reed v. State, No. 62117, 2013 WL 3256317, at *1 (Nev. 2013) (discussing the defendant's argument that his defense counsel was deficient for not contending the search of his car was nonconsensual and that the police planted the evidence); People v. McGirt, 198 A.D.2d 101, 102 (N.Y. App. Div. 1993) (discussing defendant's claim that that the police "hassle" him every day and that on the day of his arrest, they planted evidence on him after using a ruse to get him out of his parents' apartment to search him); State v. Pogue, 17 P.3d 1272, 1275 (Wash. Ct. App. 2015) (discussing the defendant's claim that the police planted the drug evidence during a vehicle search).

[12] *See, e.g.*, Michael Blasky, *Conduct on Camera*, Univ. of Nev., Las Vegas (Mar. 11, 2015), www.unlv.edu/news/article/conduct-camera (reporting findings that officers initially skeptical of body cameras changed their views after Ferguson because they realized that wearing

Jared Frazier's body camera recording a DUI arrestee telling her friend, "How can I get this officer in trouble," through the bathroom door helped clear him of her subsequent complaint of inappropriate touching.[13] In Texas, body camera footage helped quell viral outrage over a North Texas woman's allegation that she was sexually assaulted during a DUI stop because it documented that no such assault occurred. Body camera footage helped officers of the controversy-beset Cleveland Police Department show that a fatal shooting really occurred as a last resort, after the suspect shot an officer and officers still refused to shoot, pleading with the man to get help.[14]

On the other side of the equation, video evidence, from cell phones as well as body cameras, can make justice more probable if there has been wrong-doing by some officers.

In the case of Walter Scott's fatal shooting in April 2015, the crucial evidence was a cell phone video shot by a Dominican immigrant barber on his way to work.[15] After Officer Michael T. Slager stopped Scott for driving a Mercedes-Benz with a broken taillight, the patrol dash cam recorded just a brief interaction before Scott ran away out of view of the dash camera.[16] The official police statement about the fatal shooting said that Scott ran away and Officer Slager deployed his Taser to try to stop

    a camera might help exonerate them); Doug Wyllie, *Survey: Police Officers Want Body-Worn Cameras*, POLICEONE (Oct. 23, 2012), www.policeone.com/police-products/body-cameras/a rticles/6017774-Survey-Police-officers-want-body-worn-cameras/ (reporting the results of a survey, sponsored in part by a maker of body cameras, finding that 85 percent of the 785 respondents "believe that body-worn cameras reduce false claims of police misconduct, and reduce the likelihood of litigation against the agency"). *See also, e.g.,* AUSTIN POLICE DEP'T, AUSTIN POLICE DEPARTMENT POLICY MANUAL, Policy 303, at 125 (May 4, 2015) (stating that body-worn cameras can help protect against false allegations of misconduct); CHICAGO POLICE DEP'T, SPECIAL ORDER S03-14 (Dec. 30, 2015) (effective Jan. 1, 2016) (stating that body-worn cameras "can protect members from false accusations through the objective documentation of interactions between Department members and the public").

[13]   Garcia, *supra* note 5; *New Mexico Officer Cleared of Sexual Assault by Body Camera, supra* note 6.

[14]   Henry Gass, *Cleveland Case Shows How Body Cameras Can Help Police*, CHRISTIAN SCI. MONITOR (Oct. 13, 2015), www.csmonitor.com/USA/Justice/2015/1013/Cleveland-case-shows-how-body-cameras-can-help-police.

[15]   Steve Almasy, *Feidin Santana on S.C. Shooting: I Told Them What They Did Was an Abuse*, CNN (Apr. 13, 2015), www.cnn.com/2015/04/09/us/south-carolina-witness-video/index.html; *Video of Police a Game Changer*, RICHMOND FREE PRESS (Apr. 16, 2015), http://richmond freepress.com/news/2015/apr/16/video-police-game-changer/.

[16]   Mark Berman, *Mistrial Declared in Case of South Carolina Officer Who Shot Walter Scott after Traffic Stop*, WASH. POST (Dec. 5, 2016), www.washingtonpost.com/news/post-nation/wp/2016/12/05/mistrial-declared-in-case-of-south-carolina-officer-who-shot-walter-scott-after-tr affic-stop/?noredirect=on.

him.[17] According to the police spokesman, an altercation then ensued in which Scott tried to get the Taser device and use it on Officer Slager.[18] Fearing for his life, Officer Slager used his gun and shot Scott[19]

Then the crucial video emerged. The barber, Feidin Santana, later recalled that an officer who saw him recording the crucial three-minute video told him to stop recording.[20] He refused, saying what he saw was an abuse of power, and he was a witness.[21] The officer ordered him to stay at the scene but he left.[22] Santana was initially so frightened for his life that he considered deleting the video.[23] But he mustered the courage to give the video to Scott's family.[24]

The video transformed a local shooting into national news because it contradicted the police spokesman's story offered before the recording dropped. The recording begins apparently after officer Michael T. Slager fired his Taser at Scott because electrical wires from the Taser can be seen extending from Scott's body.[25] Scott continues to run away.[26] From a distance of about fifteen to twenty feet, Slager shoots into Scott's back repeatedly as Scott runs.[27] The video also captures Officer Slager appearing to lift an object from the ground and drop that object or something else closer to Scott's body.[28] In Officer Slager's later trial, prosecutors showed the

---

[17] Christina Elmore & David MacDougall, *N. Charleston Officer Fatally Shoots Man*, POST & COURIER (Apr. 3, 2015), www.postandcourier.com/archives/n-charleston-officer-fatally-shoots-man/article_44804f9f-a733-57fc-b326-bdf95032d33c.html.

[18] *Id.*

[19] *Id.*

[20] Steve Almasy, *Feidin Santana on S.C. Shooting: I Told Them What They Did Was an Abuse*, CNN (Apr. 13, 2015), www.cnn.com/2015/04/09/us/south-carolina-witness-video/index.html.

[21] *Id.*

[22] *Id.*

[23] *Id.* Mark Berman, *S.C. Investigators Say They Thought Fatal Police Shooting Was Suspicious before Video Emerged*, WASH. POST (Apr. 10, 2015), www.washingtonpost.com/news/post-nation/wp/2015/04/10/south-carolina-investigators-say-they-thought-fatal-police-shooting-was-suspicious-before-video-emerged/?utm_term=.9f8cf7fdde4e.

[24] *Id.*

[25] *Walter Scott Death: Video Shows Fatal North Charleston Police Shooting*, N.Y. TIMES (Apr. 7, 2015), www.youtube.com/watch?v=XKQqgVlkoNQ; Michael S. Schmidt & Matt Apuzzo, *Officer Is Charged with Murder of a Black Man Shot in the Back*, N.Y. TIMES, Apr. 7, 2015, at A1, www.nytimes.com/2015/04/08/us/south-carolina-officer-is-charged-with-murder-in-black-mans-death.html.

[26] *Walter Scott Death Video*, *supra* note 25; Schmidt & Apuzzo, *supra* note 25, at A1.

[27] *Walter Scott Death Video*, *supra* note 25; Schmidt & Apuzzo, *supra* note 25, at A1.

[28] Manny Fernandez, *After Shooting, Scrutiny Turns to Second Officer*, N.Y. TIMES (Apr. 17, 2015), at A1, www.nytimes.com/2015/04/18/us/after-walter-scott-shooting-scrutiny-turns-to-2nd-officer.html.

object Officer Slager placed near Scott's body on the video was the Taser device.[29]

The video was transformative for what would otherwise be another local news item about a shooting of a black man.[30] The North Charleston Police Department fired Officer Slager after the video aired,[31] and then he was arrested.[32] The department also ordered an additional 150 body cameras so "every officer on the street" could wear one.[33] By October the same year, the police department quickly entered a civil settlement with Scott's family in which they received $6.5 million.[34]

The Walter Scott case is one of the few where prosecutors criminally charged an officer with murder and manslaughter for an on-duty shooting.[35] In the state trial, jurors came close to convicting Officer Slager for voluntary manslaughter but deadlocked without a unanimous decision.[36] Officer Slager then pleaded guilty to a federal civil rights charge in an agreement with federal prosecutors where the sentencing judge would decide whether the underlying homicide that violated Scott's civil rights was murder or voluntary manslaughter.[37] Slager ultimately received a sentence of twenty years for a homicide the sentencing judge considered murder for its "reckless, wanton, and inappropriate" nature.[38]

Kenneth Simmons survived his police encounter, which did not make the national news. But video evidence was transformative for him too. To read the police reports, his case sounds mundane – a stop for a minor infraction that turns into a small-quantity drug possession charge for having a baggie of crack cocaine.[39]

---

[29] Alan Blinder, *White Officer Who Shot Black Man Is Sentenced to 15 Years*, N.Y. TIMES (Dec. 7, 2017), at A15, www.nytimes.com/2017/12/07/us/michael-slager-sentence-walter-scott.html.

[30] *Id.*

[31] *Id.*

[32] *Id.*

[33] Ashley Fantz & Holly Yan, *South Carolina Shooting: Officer Charged and Fired*, CNN (Apr. 9, 2015), www.cnn.com/2015/04/08/us/south-carolina-officer-charged-with-murder/index.html.

[34] Richard Fausset, *Settlement Reached in Shooting by Officer*, N.Y. TIMES (Oct. 8, 2015), at A24, www.nytimes.com/2015/10/09/us/walter-scott-settlement-reached-in-south-carolina-police-shooting-case.html.

[35] Blinder, *supra* note 29, at A15.

[36] *Id.*

[37] Jaweed Kaleem, *Michael Slager, Officer Who Fatally Shot Walter Scott, Pleads Guilty in Federal Case*, L.A. TIMES (May 2, 2017), www.latimes.com/nation/la-na-michael-slager-walter-scott-2017-story.html; Blinder, *supra* note 29, at A15.

[38] Blinder, *supra* note 29, at A15.

[39] San Diego Regional Officer's Report Narrative, Incident Number 14050033181 (May 17, 2014) (hereinafter Simmons Police Report) (on file with author). *See also* CAL. HEALTH & SAFETY CODE § 11350(a) (West 2014) (prohibiting possession of a controlled substance).

Officers say they initially approached Kenneth Simmons to educate him against riding a bicycle at night without his lights on.[40] When the officers approached him, Simmons did not stop. He says he did not hear the police because he had headphones on; police reports say he fled.[41]

The police report states that when officers apprehended him, Simmons rolled around, flopped his legs, tried to kick officers, and pulled out a knife, which officers removed.[42] An officer's report then described the search that led to discovery of the baggie of crack cocaine:

> I saw Simmons grabbing towards his right pants pocket. We were able to gain control of Simmons. I grabbed Simmons [sic] right hand and started to search Simmons. When I would search his right pocket he would try rolling over so I could not search him. I was able to search his pocket and did not find any controlled substances or weapons. I search [sic] Simmons right coin pocket and discovered a clear plastic baggy with a rock like substance that I recognized as a controlled substance.[43]

At the preliminary hearing, the officers involved similarly testified as to the chase, the struggle, and the discovery of the drugs in the suspect's pocket.[44] There was no mention of pulling Simmons's pants down, exposing his buttocks and feeling inside his underwear inside the buttocks region (Figures 3.1 and 3.2).

Now view and listen to the body camera video.[45] Because a video cannot be reproduced in text, stills from the video are offered below. Like all the other stills from body camera footage presented in this article, the images are in the public domain, released to the public pursuant to public records or discovery requests, or pursuant to departmental policy.

During much of the search, Simmons's pants are pulled down and his buttocks are exposed.[46] As multiple officers involved in the search lift, turn, and search him, he is crying out, panting, and voicing fear.[47] There are

---

40 Simmons Police Report, *supra* note 39.
41 *Compare* Simmons Police Report (stating Simmons fled), *with* Notice of Motion and Motion for Production of Evidence, Simmons v. City of San Diego, Case No. 30-2015-00803397-CU-PO-CJC (Cal. Superior Ct. Feb. 8, 2016), at 1 (stating Simmons did not hear the police because he had headphones on).
42 Simmons Police Report, *supra* note 39, at 3–4.
43 *Id.* at 4.
44 People v. Simmons, Case No. SCD-256148, Preliminary Hearing and Arraignment Transcript, June 4, 2014, at 6–9.
45 Simmons Body Camera Video, *supra* note 7. The video first shows officers pulling Simmons off his bike and arresting him. The search begins at 2:35 in the video.
46 *Id.* at 2:58–6:36.
47 *Id.*

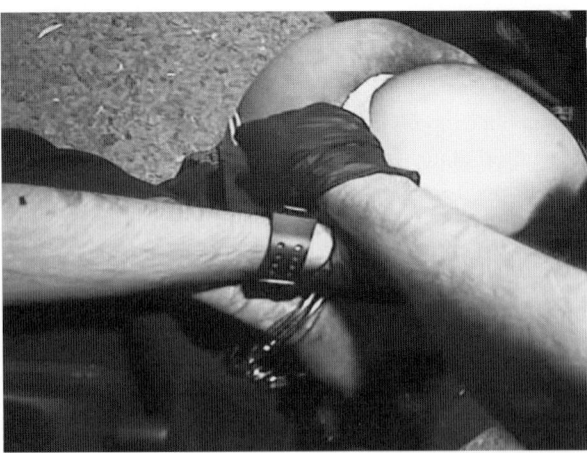

FIGURE 3.1 Still image from body camera video of the search of Kenneth Simmons showing officer's hand between Simmons's buttocks. Courtesy San Diego Police Department.

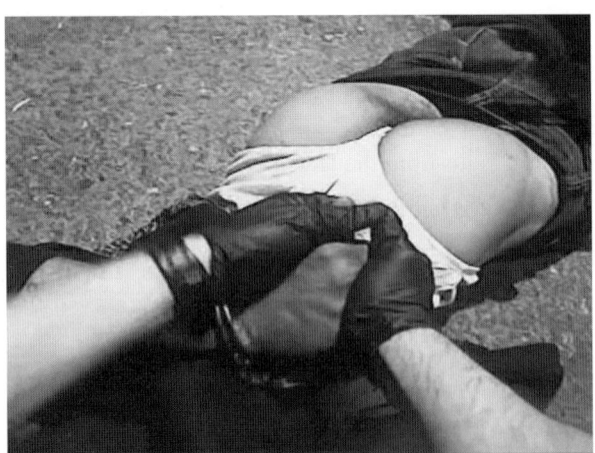

FIGURE 3.2 Still image from body camera video of the search of Kenneth Simmons showing Simmons's pants pulled down. Courtesy San Diego Police Department.

indications that he may have defecated in fear.[48] Most of the search footage is focused on Simmons's buttocks and groin region, indicating the area of focus

---

[48] *Id.* at 4:38–4:55. *See also* Simmons v. San Diego, Case No. 30-2015-00803397-CU-PO-CJC, Second Amended Complaint for Damages and Demand for Jury Trial, at 7 (Nov. 12, 2015)

by the officer wearing the camera, but later we finally see Simmons's face, swollen and bloody.[49]

The summary in the report does not capture the full experience of the search shown in the video – nor even what two stills from the video can convey. The contrast between video, testimony, and report dramatically captures how the camera can reveal far more than testimony or reports. Even a factually accurate summary of events from the officer's perception may leave out important facts. The video can be a game-changer for a defendant in a criminal case – and a plaintiff in a civil suit.

In Simmons's case, the jury acquitted him of the charges the prosecution pressed for allegedly using a deadly weapon in a fight; willfully resisting or obstructing an officer; and resisting an executive officer.[50] The jury hung on the drug possession charges, returning no conviction on the multiple charges against Simmons.[51] A jury question posed to the court during deliberations, inquiring about the legal effect if an officer "performed his duties unlawfully" suggests that disapproval of the officers' conduct played an important role in the jury's refusal to convict and the acquittals.[52]

And in Simmons's civil suit, a jury awarded him $100,000 in damages, $296,100 in attorneys' fees, and $18,500 in prejudgment costs. The total verdict against the city of San Diego for that search caught on camera: $414,600.[53]

The outcome in Andre M. Jones's case was much different. The judge ultimately convicted the twenty-two-year army veteran with no prior convictions of assaulting an officer.[54] In a bench trial, the judge listened to what the prosecutor called the "starkly different" testimonies of Jones versus the police regarding whether his arrest was false retaliation for speaking out against the police beating a suspect or justified by his shoving and obstructing an officer.[55]

As for Roxanne Rojas, the trial court and the jury did not credit her testimony that police threatened her into giving consent to a search of her apartment, whereupon police found evidence against her abusive boyfriend.[56]

[hereinafter Simmons v. San Diego, Second Amended Complaint] (alleging he partially defecated in fear).

[49] Simmons Body Camera Video, *supra* note 7, at 7:19–7:30.

[50] Simmons v. Superior Ct., 7 Cal. App. 5th 1113, 1116 (4th Dist., Div. 1, Dec. 29, 2016).

[51] *Id.*

[52] *See id.* (describing jury question).

[53] Simmons v. City of San Diego, Case No. 37-2015-00012269-CU-CR-CTL, Docket Entry 189 (Apr. 4, 2018), https://roa.sdcourt.ca.gov/roa/faces/CaseSearch.xhtml.

[54] Jones v. United States, 16 A.3d 966, 968–969 (D.C. Cir. 2011).

[55] *Id.*

[56] Fernandez v. California, 134 S. Ct. 1126, 1130, n.2 (2014); *Fernandez*, 134 S.Ct., at 1143 n.5 (Ginsburg, J., dissenting).

And – spoiler alert! – Steven Avery, featured in *Making a Murderer*, was convicted based on evidence the police found during a search of his bedroom and the murder victim's car – evidence he and the documentary suggest was planted.[57] Avery is far from alone in trying to explain away damning evidence as police fabrication – many defendants have tried and failed.[58]

Maybe the judges and juries were right to credit the testimony of the police over the conflicting claims of the defendants or the abused girlfriend. Maybe the fact-finders were wrong. We do not know. What is certain is that the credibility contests can be deeply damaging, tarnishing the police as well as the defendant, and there is a major imbalance of power in them. The defendant has formidable incentives to remain largely silent. Suspects in police encounters also face major credibility challenges even when they speak. And judges are stuck with the difficult and sometimes frustrating task of sorting between clashing accounts.

Judge Shira A. Scheindlin of the Southern District of New York offered a judge's perspective about being caught between police-said, suspect-said disputes in a case where African American and Hispanic plaintiffs alleged they were targeted for illegal stops because of their race.[59]

"[E]valuating a stop in hindsight is an imperfect procedure," wrote Judge Scheindlin.[60] "Because there is no contemporaneous recording of the stop (such as could be achieved through the use of a body-worn camera), I am relegated to finding facts based on the often conflicting testimony of eyewitnesses."[61]

Pervasive police recording can democratize power over proof, giving the people more power over the narrative of what happened and judges more data to sort between competing accounts. Videos also have the volatile power to take the case directly to the people, to create intense pressure for settlement,

---

[57]   *See* Brief of Defendant-Appellant at 8, Wisconsin v. Avery, No. 2010AP411-CR (Wis. Ct. App. June 25, 2010), 2010 WL 2691415 (recounting the defense theory that the police planted the evidence); *Making a Murderer* (Netflix 2015) (suggesting the police planted the evidence).

[58]   *See, e.g.,* Commonwealth v. Sparks, 746 N.E.2d 133, 138 (Mass. 2001) (alleging that police planted evidence found in his living quarters); Reed v. State, No. 62117, 2013 WL 3256317, at *1 (Nev. 2013) (discussing the defendant's argument that his defense counsel was deficient for not contending the search of his car was nonconsensual and that the police planted the evidence); People v. McGirt, 198 A.D.2d 101, 102 (N.Y. App. Div. 1993) (discussing defendant's claim that that the police "hassle" him every day and that on the day of his arrest, they planted evidence on him after using a ruse to get him out of his parents' apartment to search him"); State v. Pogue, 17 P.3d 1272, 1275 (Wash. Ct. App. 2015) (discussing the defendant's claim that the police planted the drug evidence during a vehicle search).

[59]   Floyd v. City of New York, 959 F. Supp. 2d 540, 562 (S.D.N.Y. 2013).

[60]   *Id.*

[61]   *Id.*

avoiding the usual daunting hurdles to bringing a suit for alleged civil rights violations. This chapter delves into each of these ways recording the police changes the balance of power on proof.

THE SIDE OF THE STORY THAT TRADITIONALLY GETS TOLD

Blind justice, or justice shaped heavily by police reports and testimony in a system where one party is often silent and both sides wage fierce credibility wars, poses the risk of being incomplete justice. One side of the story is often missing because of the myriad reasons for defendants to remain silent.

When reading constitutional criminal procedure cases, one sometimes marvels at the facts – and the information gaps between the facts. How did Michael Whren just happen to be holding two large plastic bags of cocaine boldly in plain view when the police officers he saw tailing him pulled him over and walked up to his car?[62] When Officer Lang asked Christopher Drayton "Mind if I check you?" after just arresting Drayton's travel companion and seatmate for drug trafficking, and Drayton lifted his hands eight inches from his legs, was that really consent to a search?[63] It seems that one part of the story – one whole side of the story – is missing.[64] Why?

One major reason for the seeming one-sidedness of the facts in many criminal procedure cases is that the other key party to the event – the defendant – has several formidable reasons to stay silent. A defendant who takes the stand loses the shelter of the Fifth Amendment privilege against self-incrimination and may be cross-examined by the prosecution on issues

---

[62] Whren v. United States, 517 US 806, 808–809 (1996).

[63] United States v. Drayton, 536 US 194, 199 (2002).

[64] From the filings, it appears that the testifying persons at the suppression hearings were all government agents, not the defendants. *See* Brief for Petitioner, Whren v. United States, Case No. 95-5841, at 3 (US 1996), *available at* 1996 WL 75758 (discussing the lineup of witnesses at the suppression hearing); Brief for Appellant, Brown v. United States, Case No. 99-15152-I, at 6–8 (US 1999), *available at* 1999 WL 33616942. *See also, e.g.,* Kevin R. Johnson, *The Song Remains the Same: The Story of* Whren v. United States, *in* RACE LAW STORIES 419, 428–429 (Rachel F. Moran & Devon Wayne Carbado eds., 2008) (discussing the suppression hearing generally). Scholars have also suggested that the officers' side of the story in *Whren* is improbable and needs greater scrutiny and adversarial examination. *See, e.g.,* Tracey Maclin, *Race and the Fourth Amendment*, 51 VAND. L. REV. 333, 384 (1998) (discussing concern over police perjury in a case like *Whren*); I. Bennet Capers, *The Fourth Problem*, 49 TULSA L. REV. 431, 435 n.34 (2013)(book review) (discussing "the improbability of the officers' version of the events and the likelihood that they in fact engaged in 'testilying'" in *Whren* and noting that "both officers have been the subject of misconduct allegations, including allegations of planting evidence and providing false testimony").

reasonably related to his direct testimony.[65] A decision by the defendant to testify is thus also a decision to "waive his privilege completely" and "having once cast aside the cloak of immunity he may not resume it at will, whenever cross-examination may be inconvenient or embarrassing."[66]

Deciding to speak and becoming subject to cross-examination can be more than just inconvenient or embarrassing for a defendant – it can destroy his case and credibility. A testifying defendant faces the risk of impeachment by reference to his prior convictions.[67] The testifying defendant also incurs the risk of impeachment by evidence suppressed because of a search or seizure in violation of the defendant's Fourth Amendment rights.[68] Defendant testimony at a suppression hearing also presents special challenges because prosecutors can use inconsistencies in testimony at the suppression hearing to impeach him if he testifies at trial, though suppression hearing testimony cannot be used as substantive evidence of guilt at trial.[69]

If a defendant stays silent in a criminal trial, the prosecution may not suggest that adverse inferences be drawn from that silence.[70] Indeed, a defendant is entitled to a jury instruction that no adverse inferences may be drawn from silence.[71] But if the defendant chooses to testify, "his failure to deny or explain

---

[65] *See, e.g.*, McGautha v. California, 402 US 183, 215 (1971) ("It has long been held that a defendant who takes the stand in his own behalf cannot then claim the privilege against cross-examination on matters reasonably related to the subject matter of his direct examination. It is not thought overly harsh in such situations to require that the determination whether to waive the privilege take into account the matters which may be brought out on cross-examination.") (citations omitted); Rogers v. United States, 340 US 367, 373 (1951) ("[I]f the witness himself elects to waive his privilege, as he may doubtless do, since the privilege is for his protection and not for that of other parties, and discloses his criminal connections, he is not permitted to stop, but must go on and make a full disclosure.") (quoting Brown v. Walker, 161 US 591, 597 (1896)).

[66] Grunewald v. United States, 353 US 391, 419 (1957).

[67] *See, e.g.*, Ohler v. United States, 529 US 753, 759 (2000) ("It is also generally recognized that a defendant who takes the stand in his own behalf may be impeached by proof of prior convictions or the like.") (quoting McGautha v. California, 402 US 183, 215 (1971)).

[68] United States v. Havens, 446 US 620, 628 (1980).

[69] *Compare* Simmons v. United States, 390 US 377, 394 (1968) ("[W]e find it intolerable that one constitutional right should have to be surrendered in order to assert another. We therefore hold that when a defendant testifies in support of a motion to suppress evidence on Fourth Amendment grounds, his testimony may not thereafter be admitted against him at trial on the issue of guilt unless he makes no objection."), *with, e.g.*, People v. Douglas, 136 Cal. Rptr. 358, 363 (Cal. Ct. App. 1977) ("We conclude that defendant's testimony at a suppression hearing may be used for impeachment purposes if he takes the stand at his trial and testifies in a manner inconsistent with his pretrial testimony."), *and* People v. Mahone, 614 N.Y.S.2d 409, 411 (N.Y. App. Div. 1994) ("It was not improper for the prosecutor to use inconsistencies between defendant's testimony at the suppression hearing and at trial to impeach him.").

[70] Griffin v. California, 380 US 609, 614 (1965).

[71] Carter v. Kentucky, 450 US 288 (1981).

evidence of incriminating circumstances of which he may have knowledge may be the basis of adverse inference, and the jury may be so instructed."[72]

A defendant who wants to tell his side of the story must weigh the benefits against the substantial potential costs of taking the stand.[73] The balance of costs and benefits is such that lawyers often advise defendants to not take the stand and remain silent.[74] Thus, defendant silence is prevalent throughout the criminal process, including at hearings to contest the admissibility of evidence based on claims of wrongful search or seizure. This typically means that judges dependent on traditional testimony hear one side of the story more prominently than the other.

Sometimes snippets of the defendant's voice emerge, memorialized as evidence by the government.[75] For example, the police report in Simmons's case stated that Simmons told officers: "I did not know you were the police. I had my headphones in. I never looked back. I could not hear you yelling at me. I knew that I had rocks on me. I only knew that you were the police when we were fighting."[76] What the police report states is important because it is what prosecutors, defense attorneys and officers consult to understand or recall a case from myriad others.[77] When you view the body camera video you hear that Simmons said a lot more about the search and seizure.[78] But what is memorialized is what has evidentiary value in the government's case. Thus, without cameras, even when the defendant's voice is heard, it is filtered through reports focused on memorializing statements that may serve as potential evidence.

---

[72] Raffel v. United States, 271 US, 494 (1926).

[73] *See, e.g.*, Ohler v. United States, 529 US 753, 759 (2000) ("[I]t is not thought inconsistent with the enlightened administration of criminal justice to require the defendant to weigh such pros and cons in deciding whether to testify.").

[74] For a discussion from a former defense attorney's perspective, *see, e.g.*, Alexandra Natapoff, *Speechless: The Silencing of Criminal Defendants*, 80 N.Y.U. L. Rev. 1449 (2005).

[75] *See, e.g.*, People v. Austin, No. 112721-U, 2013 WL 2302080, at * 3 (Ill. App. Ct. 2013) (noting that while the defendant's statements to the officer were not taped, videorecorded or memorialized, the "substance of the interview" was included in the police report); State v. Ingram, 774 S.E.2d 433, 437 (N.C. Ct. App. 2015) (reporting that the defendant's statements while in the hospital after he shot at officers and officers shot him were recorded in the police report); Sambolin v. State, 387 S.W.2d 817, 819 (Tenn. 1965) (noting that the defendants' oral admissions were made a part of the police report and discussing the admissibility of the statements against the defendants).

[76] Simmons Police Report, *supra* note 39, at 5.

[77] Consider this compelling account: "And for the defender, the flow of cases is endless; a limitless stream of files. A dozen or so clean, raw files appear on their desks in the morning, at most containing a police report and the defendant's application for indigent defense. Into court they come, stack of files in hand, yelling to determine if their clients have even shown up. 'Is there a Mr. Firmen here? Is Ms. Nonce in court?'" John B. Mitchell, *Redefining the Sixth Amendment*, 67 S. Cal. L. Rev. 1215, 1240–1241 (1994).

[78] Simmons Body Camera Video, *supra* note 7, at 2:35–6:36.

DAMAGING CREDIBILITY CONTESTS, MALLEABLE MEMORY

Another challenge of the traditional reliance on testimony and reports is the ugly credibility contests that often ensue if the defendant does dispute officer accounts. Neither side emerges unscathed – defendants are often assumed to be lying criminals with serious credibility problems.[79] The police are impugned as liars, evidence planters, and abusers of power.[80] The innocent are stained along with the culpable, including officers as well as defendants. Courts are also burdened, awash in deeply partisan and divergent stories in which both sides are smeared.[81] When these credibility contests play out before juries or the larger public, the attempts to impugn each side can tarnish the criminal justice system as well.

The credibility contest is an uneven one. Stories proffered by defendants are more likely to be discounted; indeed defendants were historically deemed unqualified to testify under oath.[82] Claiming the officer is lying is a risky move because it risks alienating the fact-finder.[83] Moreover, judges are keenly aware of the consequences of suggesting that the officer is a liar, which can end a career by rendering the officer unusable as a witness.[84] There are powerful institutional pressures against making such a finding.[85]

---

[79] *See, e.g.,* Donald A. Dripps, *The Constitutional Status of the Reasonable Doubt Rule,* 75 CALIF. L. REV. 1665, 1695 (1987)(discussing the credibility difficulties defendants face).

[80] *See, e.g.,* Fernandez v. Cal., 134 S. Ct. 1126, 1143 n.5 (2014) (Ginsburg, J., dissenting) (noting the account of the defendant's battered girlfriend that police coerced her into letting them into the house by threatening to take her child away); Jones v. United States, 16 A.3d 966, 968–969 (D.C. 2011) (discussing defendant's allegation that the police arrested him and roughed him up because he witnessed them beating a suspect and tried to speak up); Comm. v. Sparks, 746 N.E.2d 133, 138 (Mass. 2001) (discussing the defendant's allegation that police planted the evidence found during the search of his home); People v. McGirt, 198 N.Y.2d 101, 102 (N.Y. Sup. Ct. App. Div. 1993) (discussing defendant's claim that that the planted evidence on him after using a ruse to get him out of his parents' apartment to search him); State v. Pogue, 17 P.3d 1272, 1275 (Wash. Ct. App. 2015) (noting the defendant's claim that the police planted the drug evidence during a vehicle search).

[81] *See, e.g.,* Thompson v. Keohane, 516 US 99, 118 (1995) (noting that "the trial judge will often have to weigh conflicting accounts of what transpired").

[82] Portuondo v. Agard, 529 US 61, 66 (2000).

[83] *See, e.g.,* John B. Mitchell, *Narrative and Client-Centered Representation: What Is a True Believer to Do When His Two Favorite Theories Collide?,* 6 CLINICAL L. REV. 85, 116 (1999) (discussing how defendants face risks when telling stories that clash with the schemata harbored by jurors).

[84] *See* Morgan Cloud, *Judges, "Testilying," and the Constitution,* 69 S. CAL. L. REV. 1341, 1352 (1996); Christopher Slobogin, *Testilying: Police Perjury and What to Do about It,* 67 U. COLO. L. REV. 1037, 1043–1047 (1996).

[85] Slobogin, *supra* note 84, at 1043–1047.

Of course, many officers and people caught up in police encounters are trying their best to tell what happened in good faith. Mistakes may arise in recalling perceptions in the stress and heat of heat of the moment, among people trying their best to reconstruct what happened.[86] A large body of important work has illuminated how our memory is not as trustworthy a record as we believe, even when we are trying earnestly to tell the truth.[87] While much of the evidence is in the context of the accuracy of eyewitness identification, the insights about memory apply to other testimonial contexts.[88] Despite the common perception that we are better at remembering situations "burned into our memory" because they occurred in high-stress situations, the scientific evidence indicates that high stress actually negatively impacts memory.[89] When emotional arousal is intense, performance on memory tasks significantly decreases in accuracy.[90] Responding to stressful

---

[86] *See, e.g.,* Atwater v. City of Lago Vista, 532 US 318, 347 (2001) ("Often enough, the Fourth Amendment has to be applied on the spur (and in the heat) of the moment"). *See also, e.g.,* Gen. Order. 4.09.03, Woodland Police Department, at 4.09.03-1 (effective Sept. 1, 2004, rev'd Oct. 14, 2009), *available at* www.cityofwoodland.org/gov/depts/police/secure/order%20man ual.pdf ("The arresting officer is responsible for the completion and submission for approval of all arrest reports before the end of his/her shift."); Terry A. Beehr, Lana Ivanitskaya, Katherine Glaser, Dmitry Erofeev, & Kris Canali, *Working in a Violent Environment: The Accuracy of Police Officers' Reports about Shooting Incidents,* 77 J. Occupational & Organizational Psych. 217, 230, 232 (2004)(discussing the impact of stress on event recall by officers and the implications for police reports and testimony).

[87] *See, e.g.,* Brian L. Cutler & Steven D. Penrod, Mistaken Identification: The Eyewitness, Psychology and the Law 68 (1995) (reporting that more than two thousand studies have been performed illuminating the problems with memory, perception, and eyewitness identification); Elizabeth F. Loftus, Eyewitness Testimony 52–133 (1996) (discussing seminal studies and memory processes); Elizabeth F. Loftus, *Make-Believe Memories,* 58 Am. Psychol. 867, 868–871 (2003)(reviewing findings on faulty eyewitness memory).

[88] *Cf.* Jack B. Weinstein, *Eyewitness Testimony,* 81 Colum. L. Rev. 441, 442–443 (1981)(book review) (discussing insights from eyewitness memory studies for other evidentiary contexts).

[89] *See, e.g.,* Loftus, *supra* note 87, at 33; Kenneth A. Deffenbacher et al., *A Meta-Analytic Review of the Effects of High Stress on Eyewitness Memory,* 28 L. & Human Behav. 687, 699 (2004); Charles A. Morgan III et al., *Accuracy of Eyewitness Memory for Persons Encountered during Exposure to Highly Intense Stress,* 27 Int'l J. L. & Psychiatry 265, 265–267 (2004); Richard S. Schmechel, Timothy P. O'Toole, Catherine Easterly, & Elizabeth F. Loftus, *Beyond the Ken? Testing Jurors' Understanding of Eyewitness Reliability,* 46 Jurimetrics J. 177, 179 (2006); *see also, e.g.,* Jennifer Thompson-Cannino, Ronald Cotton, Erin Torneo, Picking Cotton: Our Memoir of Injustice and Redemption 15–20 (2010) (describing attempt to memorize every detail of assailant and certitude of identification that proved wrong).

[90] Loftus, *supra* note 87, at 33 (discussing seminal studies and memory processes); Kenneth A. Deffenbacher et al., *A Meta-Analytic Review of the Effects of High Stress on Eyewitness Memory,* 28 L. & Human Behav. 687, 699 (2004).

situations divides our attention and reduces our capacity to process and remember events.[91]

Whether stressed or not, humans are also vulnerable to confirmation bias, the cognitive tendency to ignore facts that are inconsistent with our hypotheses or beliefs and focus on details that support them.[92] If one suspects someone is guilty of a crime, one is more likely to focus on information supporting that suspicion and overlook information that would disconfirm the view.[93] Confirmation bias is not limited to police officers, of course – it is a human cognitive tendency common to lay and professional persons.[94] For example, commentators have noted that judges also display confirmation bias, tending to find errors harmless or not depending on whether the court believes a defendant is guilty.[95]

We reason from schemata, mental categories for how situations will play out based on our experiences and beliefs.[96] If someone or some situation resembles one previously experienced, these schemata shape our expectancies and our perceptions to confirm our beliefs.[97] In ambiguous situations where information is missing, schemata fill in the gaps, leading people to believe or perceive based on past experiences and beliefs.[98] To translate in terms of

---

[91]   Sven-Ake Christianson, *Emotional Stress and Eyewitness Memory: A Critical Review*, 112 PSYCHOL. BULL. 284, 284–304 (1992); Maria S. Zaragoza & Sean M. Lane, *Processing Resources and Eyewitness Suggestibility*, 3 LEGAL & CRIMINOLOGICAL PSYCHOL. 305, 307–310 (1998).

[92]   Thomas Gilovich, HOW WE KNOW WHAT ISN'T SO: THE FALLIBILITY OF HUMAN REASON IN EVERYDAY LIFE 33 (1991); Raymond S. Nickerson, *Confirmation Bias: A Ubiquitous Phenomenon in Many Guises*, 2 REV. GEN. PSYCHOL. 175, 198–199 (1998).

[93]   For a discussion and examples in the criminal context, *see, e.g.*, Keith A. Findley & Michael S. Scott, *The Multiple Dimensions of Tunnel Vision in Criminal Cases*, WISCONSIN L. REV. 291, 296–316 (2006).

[94]   See Anna Harvey & Michael J. Woodruff, *Confirmation Bias in the United States Supreme Court Judicial Database*, 29 J. L., ECON. & ORG., 414, 421–428 (2011); Friedrich James, *Primary Error Detection and Minimization (PEDMIN) Strategies in Social Cognition: A Reinterpretation of Confirmation Bias Phenomena*, 100 PSYCHOL. REV. 298, 298 (1993); Raymond S. Nickerson, *Confirmation Bias: A Ubiquitous Phenomenon in Many Guises*, 2 REV. GEN'L PSYCHOL. 175, 175–218 (1998); Matthew Rabin & Joel L. Schrag, *First Impressions Matter: A Model of Confirmatory Bias*, 114 QUARTERLY J. ECON. 37, 41–48 (1999).

[95]   Harry T. Edwards, *To Err Is Human, but Not Always Harmless: When Should Legal Error Be Tolerated?*, 70 N.Y.U. L. REV. 1167, 1187 (1995); Keith A. Findley & Michael S. Scott, *The Multiple Dimensions of Tunnel Vision in Criminal Cases*, WISCONSIN L. REV. 291, 349–352 (2006).

[96]   See D. Michael Risinger et al., *The Daubert/Kumho Implications of Observer Effects in Forensic Science: Hidden Problems of Expectation and Suggestion*, 90 CALIF. L. REV. 1, 14 (2002).

[97]   *Id.*

[98]   *Id.*

operations in the field, an officer may reason: I've caught a lot of guilty guys who look like this one, in this high-crime area, and this one looks guilty too.[99]

When a search or seizure yields evidence, hindsight bias and outcome bias can reshape perceptions. Hindsight bias is a "knew-it-all-along" effect in which the outcome seems more likely in retrospect.[100] Hindsight bias arises when we "update" our memory with the new information, subtly reshaping our memory of what happened to make the outcome appear more certain.[101] Outcome bias is a related but different cognitive distortion in which the outcome influences our judgment about whether the judgment call was sound or wrong.[102] The reiterative effect of documenting one's judgment calls – in reports and testimony, for example – can further entrench subtly reshaped memories because reiteration heightens the perception of certainty.[103]

Hearing all sides of the story is thus all the more important because of the fallibility of human perception and tendency toward unwitting distortions of perception. Yet for the reasons we examined, one of the key participants, the defendant, has strong reasons to stay silent, leaving part of the story untold. Moreover, increasingly, criminal procedure doctrine has developed a phalanx of rules that reduces the need to delve into competing accounts.[104]

---

[99] *Cf., e.g.,* John M. Darley & Paget H. Gross, *A Hypothesis-Confirming Bias in Labeling Effects,* 44 J. PERSONALITY & SOC. PSYCHOL. 20, 20–21 (1983) (finding evidence that social labeling creates expectancies about true dispositions or capabilities); *see also, e.g.,* Andrew Guthrie Ferguson, *The "High-Crime Area" Question: Requiring Verifiable and Quantifiable Evidence for Fourth Amendment Suspicion Analysis,* 57 AM. U. L. REV. 1587, 1595–1604 (2008) (discussing the use of a claim that an encounter occurs in a high-crime area in supporting reasonable suspicion).

[100] *See* Baruch Fischhoff, *Hindsight Is Not Equal to Foresight: The Effect of Outcome on Judgment under Uncertainty,* 1 J. EXPERIMENTAL PSYCHOL. 288, 293, 296–297 (1975); Erin M. Harley, Keri A. Carlsen, & Geoffrey R. Loftus, *The "Saw-It-All-Along" Effect: Demonstrations of Visual Hindsight Bias,* 30 J. EXPERIMENTAL PSYCHOL. 960, 962–964 (2004); Scott A. Hawkins & Reid Hastie, *Hindsight: Biased Judgments of Past Events after the Outcomes Are Known,* 107 PSYCHOL. BULL. 311, 311 (1990); Ulrich Hoffrage, Ralph Hertwig, & Gerd Gigerenzer, *Hindsight Bias: A By-Product of Knowledge Updating?,* 26 J. EXPERIMENTAL PSYCHOL. 566, 566–567 (2000); Lawrence J. Sanna, Norbert Schwarz, & Eulena M. Small, *Accessibility Experiences and the Hindsight Bias: I Knew It All Along versus It Could Never Have Happened,* 30 MEMORY & COGNITION 1288, 1288–1289 (2002).

[101] Ulrich Hoffrage & Ralph Hertwig, *Hindsight Bias: A Price Worth Paying for Fast and Frugal Memory, in* SIMPLE HEURISTICS THAT MAKE US SMART 191 (1999).

[102] Jonathan Baron & John C. Hershey, *Outcome Bias in Decision Evaluation,* 54 J. PERSONALITY & SOC. PSYCHOL. 569, 569–573 (1988).

[103] Ralph Hertwig, Gerd Gigerenzer, & Ulrich Hoffrage, *The Reiteration Effect in Hindsight Bias,* 104 PSYCHOL. REV. 194, 194–196 (1997).

[104] For a discussion, see Mary D. Fan, *The Police Gamesmanship Dilemma in Criminal Procedure,* 44 UC DAVIS L. REV. 1407, 1424–1428 (2011).

ADDRESSING JUDICIAL BLIND SPOTS

One of the most oft-reiterated positions in constitutional criminal procedure is that courts will not inquire into pretext or subjective intent so long as an objective basis exists to justify the officer's conduct.[105] Even where an officer's stated rationale for a search or seizure is incorrect, so long as another basis to justify the exercise of power can be found, the court will inquire no further.[106] Among the oft-stated rationales for the limits on judicial inquiry are the administrative difficulties and inefficiencies of case-by-case inquiry into the mystery of police motives.[107]

The consequences of judicial reluctance to inquire for socioeconomically disadvantaged minority communities bearing the heaviest burden of searches and seizures are intensely controversial.[108] Scholars have argued that cases such as *Whren v. United States*, which declined to inquire into whether a stop for a minor offense was actually a pretext to target young black men for a search, create "a license to make racial distinctions."[109] Devon Carbado has argued that the tolerance of racial profiling in constitutional criminal procedure is a contributing cause of the heightened risk of minority community members being killed by the police.[110] The lack of scrutiny or a remedy undermines trust and perceptions of legitimacy and can lead to what Bennet Capers terms "small rebellions," such as refusing to assist the police investigating crimes, ultimately undermining community safety.[111]

In contrast to potentially dangerous or destructive forms of resistance, recording the police is a more peaceful and constructive form of protest and self-protection. The resulting audiovisual evidence produced by the police and community members can help inform the work of courts as well as police

---

[105]   *E.g.*, Brendlin v. California, 551 US 249, 260 (2007); Devenpeck v. Alford, 543 US 146, 153–154 (2004); Atwater v. City of Lago Vista, 532 US 318, 318 (2001); Whren v. United States, 517 US 806, 806 (1996); United States v. Robinson, 414 US 218, 221, 235 n.1 (1973).

[106]   Heien v. North Carolina, 135 S. Ct. 530, 536–540 (2014); *Devenpeck*, 543 US at 153–154.

[107]   *E.g.*, Rakas v. Illinois, 439 US 128, 136–137 (1978); United States v. Robinson, 414 US 218, 235 (1973).

[108]   For critiques, *see, e.g.*, DAVID COLE, NO EQUAL JUSTICE: RACE AND CLASS IN THE CRIMINAL JUSTICE SYSTEM 27–41, 48–52 (1999); I. Bennett Capers, *Policing, Race and Place*, 44 HARV. C.R-C.L. L. REV. 43, 56–72 (2009); Devon W. Carbado & Rachel F. Moran, *The Story of Law and American Racial Consciousness: Building a Canon One Case at a Time*, 76 UMKC L. REV. 851, 873–874 (2008).

[109]   Carbado & Moran, *supra* note 108, at 873–874.

[110]   Devon Carbado, *From Stopping Black People to Killing Black People: The Fourth Amendment Pathways to Police Violence*, 105 CAL. L. REV. 125 (2017).

[111]   Bennet Capers, *Crime, Legitimacy, and Testilying*, 83 IND. L.J. 835, 865 (2008).

departments. The police recording revolution transforms the nature of the evidence and information available to reconstruct events in criminal cases.

More to Discover

Currently, when a new case lands in the hands of a prosecutor or defense attorney, the police report is often the first guide to the attorneys on both sides to figure out what the case about.[112] The police report also guides later officer testimony because officers rely on their reports to refresh their memory when they testify after the event.[113] Indeed, before testifying, officers often read their police reports in the courthouse hallways to revive memories blurred by time and numerous other encounters. Particularly in run-of-the-mill cases, officer testimony is often limited to what is in the report.

The report that has such power in framing a criminal case from its inception is limited by its one-dimensional nature, committed to paper as a summary of the perceptions of the officer involved. As the Simmons case at the outset of this chapter illustrates, this perspective is driven by what is of evidentiary value to the government. Many details do not make it into the report, which is necessarily a summary focused on justifying the enforcement action and documenting the evidence obtained from it.[114]

In jurisdictions where officers use body cameras, this thin paper account is supplemented by multimedia capturing a fuller range of details from a broader perspective. Most of the departmental policies coded in this study explicitly specify that police reports must note that there is accompanying video of the incident. Defendants also may request disclosure of the video in discovery.[115] This video can speak beyond officer accounts at suppression hearings even when the defendant does not speak. The availability of video thus can address the challenges of a criminal justice system where one party to disputed events is repeatedly advised to stay silent.

The availability of video will also influence officer report writing and testimony. Table 3.1 gives a detailed breakdown of the positions of the 213

---

[112] John B. Mitchell, *Redefining the Sixth Amendment*, 67 S. Cal. L. Rev. 1215, 1240–1241 (1994).

[113] Darren T. Kavinoky, *Strategies for Defending DUI Cases in California*, Aspatore, at *11, 2008 WL 5689409.

[114] *See, e.g.*, People v. Ellis, 2012 WL 6861254, at *15 (Ill. App. Ct. 2012) (noting that a police report is a summary and may omit some information).

[115] *See, e.g.*, Brady v. Maryland, 373 US 83, 86–87 (1963) (requiring disclosure of evidence favorable to the accused and material to guilt or punishment); James W. McGee Jr., *DWI Discovery Trends in North Carolina*, Trends in DUI Discovery, Sept. 2015, at 81, 82 (noting that as a defense attorney in a jurisdiction with dash cameras and body cameras, he always makes a *Brady* request for the videotape).

TABLE 3.1 *Officer Access to Body Camera Videos for Report Writing and Court Preparation*

Policy position	Number of departments	Percentage of departments
No access after data upload	1	0.5%
Review for report writing and/or investigation	60	28%
May review for report writing *unless* the incident involves a use of force occurs in which case the officer may not view the recording	6	3%
May review for court preparation	2	1%
May review for training purposes	6	3%
May review for **both** report writing and/or investigation ***and*** court preparation	17	8%
May review for *both* report writing and/or investigation *and* training	19	9%
May review for *all three purposes*: report writing and/or investigation, court preparation, and training	52	24%
Not specified; the policy does not have provisions governing officer access to recordings	50	23%
Total	213	100%

jurisdictions' body camera policies coded on officer access to videos for report writing and other purposes. The majority of jurisdictions – 154 (72 percent) – explicitly provide for officer access to videos for report writing. The number of jurisdictions where officers may access video for report writing is actually likely higher because fifty policies contain no provision on access. Without a limitation, the default likely is discretion to view the videos to assist in the officers' tasks. Several jurisdictions also specify officer access for other purposes as well, such as court preparation or training. Only one of the policies prohibits officers from accessing the videos after they are uploaded for data storage. And only six prohibit officers who otherwise may view the recording from viewing the video where a potentially contested incident, such as a use of force or citizen complaint, occurs.

The widespread nature of policies permitting or even mandating officer review of body camera videos before report writing is notable because of debates over the risks of allowing access. The San Diego Police Department's policy aptly summarizes an important concern that officers may feel pressured to conform their memory to what is depicted on the video, even though recollections may legitimately differ:

> Video cannot always show the full story nor does it capture an entire scene . . .
> Persons reviewing recordings must also be cautious before conclusions are
> reached about what the video shows . . .
>
> Officers make decisions based on the totality of the human senses.
> An officer's recollection of specific details may be different than what is
> captured in digital evidence since BWCs [body-worn cameras] only capture
> audio and video.[116]

Because of the concern, the policy requires officers to review digital evidence before report writing but instructs that officers "shall not write their reports based solely on what they viewed from the BWC recording."[117] From a different perspective, but with a related concern, civil libertarians express concern that allowing officer access to body camera footage can lead to tailored reports, or reports that seem more consistent with the audiovisual evidence compared to a statement by a witness or complainant, who does not have access to the video before describing what they saw.[118] A shared understanding across different worldviews is the power of video evidence to reshape recollections and impact traditional reports because of the assumption – sometimes mistaken, as Chapter 6 discusses – that videos offer a window into what really happened.

Systemic Facts

Through introduction and dispute by the parties, courts will also have access to the video of contested encounters. The availability of video generates for the courts a power to replay events to help reconstruct what happened rather than depend on partisan and often one-sided testimony. The audiovisual recording

---

[116] CITY OF SAN DIEGO, SAN DIEGO POLICE DEP'T PROCEDURE NO. 1.49 1, 11 (July 8, 2015).

[117] Director T. Armstrong, *Memphis Police Dep't, Policy and Procedure Information and Updates*, Serial 12–16 (Sept. 23, 2015).

[118] *See, e.g.*, Jay Stanley, *Should Officers Be Permitted to View Body Camera Footgage before Writing Their Reports?* ACLU (Jan. 13, 2015), www.aclu.org/blog/free-future/should-officers-be-permitted-view-body-camera-footage-writing-their-reports (arguing that after a use of force incident officers should not be allowed to view body camera footage before writing their reports); Brennan Ctr. for Justice, Police Body Camera Policies: Accountability (Aug. 3, 2016), www.brennancenter.org/analysis/police-body-camera-policies-accountability ("From a police accountability perspective, in a case where an officer did use force inappropriately or where there is a discrepancy between accounts, permitting an officer to view the video before making a statement might be problematic since it would allow him to tailor his statement to fit the evidence.").

of a wider array of law enforcement activities than ever before is a major development for courts adjudicating criminal cases.

To date, courts tend to have video access to only a small portion of the contested law enforcement encounters they adjudicate. Most of the progress on recording has occurred in the context of police interrogations, which more than half of US jurisdictions now record.[119] But much of the evidence – and in some cases, the entire basis for prosecution – may come from searches and seizures or observations during police encounters in the noninterrogation context. Before body cameras, the main video window courts had into the search and seizure disputed in criminal procedure cases was through dash cameras.[120] These dash camera videos yield only partial snapshots, often from a distant angle that misses important details.

The body camera revolution is also an evidentiary revolution. It enables judges to see for themselves more of what occurred, beyond the partiality, perceptual frailties, and gaps of oral or written statements. The aggregated video across cases also can give judges fresh perspective over whether to intervene in recurring problems. Members of the US Supreme Court have repeatedly reserved the possibility of giving certain constitutional rules and remedies more teeth if a pattern of widespread violations is uncovered.[121] Yet how are individual criminal defendants, who are often indigent and represented by overworked appointed counsel, to come by the data and establish such a widespread pattern? Many everyday police exercises of power may never make it to court because a case is dismissed, or a stop or search yields no contraband, or because of an early plea. Searching in the text of reported cases risks woefully underrepresenting what is happening on the ground. The accumulation of videos of police activities can help courts and attorneys determine whether there is a widespread problem in need of address.

---

[119] G. Daniel Lassiter, Patrick J. Munhall, Andrew L. Geers, Paul E. Weiland, & Ian M. Handley, *Accountability and the Camera Perspective Bias in Videotaped Confessions*, 1 ANALYSES SOC. ISSUES & PUB. POL'Y 53, 54 (2001).

[120] *See, e.g.*, State v. O'Neal, 7 So. 3d 182, 185 (La. Ct. App. 2009) (noting use of dash camera footage at suppression hearing); State v. Munsey, 424 S.W.3d 767, 769 (Tex. Ct. App. 2014).

[121] Herring v. United States, 129 S. Ct. 695, 698, 704 (2009) (suggesting that exclusionary rule might apply to illegal arrests and searches due to record-keeping errors "where systemic errors were demonstrated"); Hudson v. Michigan, 547 US 586, 604 (2006) (Kennedy, J., concurring) ("If a widespread pattern of [knock and announce rule] violations were shown . . . there would be reason for grave concern."). *See also* Atwater v. City of Lago Vista, 532 US 318, 353 (2001) (noting there "is a dearth of horribles demanding redress").

Throughout American history, images have powerfully communicated calls for change.[122] It takes seeing to spur action. Images can jolt people with power into concern. It was images of crowds grinning at lynchings and mob domination of justice that spurred judges sitting far removed, in the serene space of courts, into action to generate the body of constitutional criminal procedure regulating the police.[123] And it was images of mass protests, of the slain, of the events preceding death, and of children offering hugs and seeking a safer future that spurred the body camera revolution. Beyond the headlines, in the daily work of courts, body camera video has an important role to play in improving the accuracy and quality of justice in criminal procedure cases.

SURMOUNTING BARRIERS TO CIVIL DAMAGES

Viral videos also carry the volatile power to force civil settlements, short-circuiting law's traditional barriers to suing the police. One of the biggest formal legal constraints in civil rights suits against officers, often called § 1983 suits or *Bivens* actions, is the shield of qualified immunity. Many civil rights complaints are dismissed on summary judgment without any chance of presenting evidence to a jury on qualified immunity grounds.[124] Indeed, suits can be dismissed on qualified immunity grounds without clarifying first whether the conduct alleged violates a constitutional right.[125] To survive summary judgment based on qualified immunity, a plaintiff must allege facts showing a violation of "a statutory or constitutional right that was 'clearly established' at the time of the challenged conduct."[126] To be clearly established, "existing precedent must have placed the statutory or constitutional" violation "beyond debate."[127]

---

[122]   *See, e.g.*, NATIONAL MUSEUM OF AFRICAN AMERICAN HISTORY AND CULTURE, DOUBLE EXPOSURE: CIVIL RIGHTS AND THE PROMISE OF EQUALITY 10–55 (Laura Coyle & Michèle Gates Moresi eds., 2015) (offering examples of iconic photographs in the struggle for civil rights).

[123]   *See, e.g.*, Michael J. Klarman, *The Racial Origins of Modern Criminal Procedure*, 99 MICH. L. REV. 48, 56–57, 61, 69 (2000) (discussing linkages between the birth of modern criminal procedure and mob-dominated trials in the shadow of the threat of lynchings, documented by newspapers). *See also, e.g.*, Mary L. Dudziak, COLD WAR CIVIL RIGHTS: RACE AND THE IMAGE OF AMERICAN DEMOCRACY 35–38 (2000) (discussing how the images were used in Cold War era propaganda against the United States and the influence on the Court); Jack Greenberg, CRUSADERS IN THE COURTS: HOW A DEDICATED BAND OF LAWYERS FOUGHT FOR THE CIVIL RIGHTS REVOLUTION 30–59 (1994) (discussing how media images of violence influenced civil rights).

[124]   *See, e.g.*, Scott v. Harris, 550 US 372 (2007); Pearson v. Callahan, 555 US 223 (2009).

[125]   Pearson v. Callahan, 555 US 223 (2009).

[126]   Plumhoff v. Rickard, 134 S. Ct. 2012, 2023 (2014) (quoting Ashcroft v. al-Kidd, 563 US 731, 735 (2011)).

[127]   *Ashcroft*, 563 US at 741.

One of the earliest axioms that lawyers learn is that facts matter.[128] Facts can shape intuitions of justice and subtly steer the outcomes that may not be predicted by just the formal legal standard alone.[129] In the context of civil rights suits, facts and details are all the more crucial because the legal standards openly and formally depend on the particular facts of each case.

Whether officers violated a person's civil rights involve intensely fact-specific inquiries conducted with significant deference to officers. The most common lawsuits against police involve claims of alleged misuse of force and false arrest or imprisonment.[130] In claims entailing law enforcement use of force, the constitutional provision invoked is usually the Fourth Amendment's prohibition against unreasonable searches and seizures.[131] The actions of the officer are judged by a reasonableness standard "not capable of precise definition or mechanical application."[132] The application of the reasonableness standard "requires careful attention to the facts and circumstances of each particular case."[133] Relevant factors to evaluate include "the severity of the crime at issue, whether the suspect poses an immediate threat to the safety of the officers or others, and whether he is actively resisting arrest or attempting to evade arrest by flight."[134] Such factors call for close attention to details that are frequently hotly disputed between police and suspect.[135]

After a defendant is convicted, constitutional claims challenging officers' use of force against prisoners are analyzed under the Eighth Amendment's prohibition against cruel and unusual punishment.[136] An unreasonable degree of force used against duly convicted prisoners does not necessarily amount to an Eighth Amendment violation. Rather, the Eighth Amendment forbids the

[128] James Parry Eyster, *Lawyer as Artist: Using Significant Moments and Obtuse Objects to Enhance Advocacy*, 14 LEGAL WRITING: J. OF LEGAL WRITING INST. 87, 93 (2008).

[129] Cf., e.g., Lisa S. Blatt, *In Front of the Burgundy Curtain: The Top Ten Lessons I've Learned about Advocacy before the Nation's Highest Court*, 14 GREEN BAG 2d 9, 11 (2010) ("The third lesson I've learned is that facts matter. The Justices are human beings, not wooden scholars who are myopically focused on the legal principle being advanced by the parties.").

[130] Carol Archbold & Edward R. Maguire, *Studying Civil Suits against the Police: A Serendipitous Finding of Sample Selection Bias*, 5 POLICE QUARTERLY 222, 224 (2002).

[131] Graham v. O'Connor, 490 US 386, 394 (1989).

[132] Bell v. Wolfish, 441 US 520, 559 (1979).

[133] *Graham*, 490 US, at 396.

[134] *Id.*

[135] See, e.g., Scott v. Harris, 550 US 372, 377 (2007) (noting that the officers' "version of events (unsurprisingly) differs substantially" from the plaintiff suspect's version).

[136] Whitley v. Albers, 475 US 312, 327 (1986).

infliction of "unnecessary and wanton infliction of pain" on prisoners.[137] This prohibition includes the infliction of suffering that is "totally without penological justification."[138] Where force is used to restore order after a disturbance in the prison, the propriety of the officers' conduct "turns on 'whether force was applied in a good faith effort to maintain or restore discipline or maliciously and sadistically for the very purpose of causing harm.'"[139] Prison officials enjoy strong deference from the courts in their efforts to preserve or restore order or prevent breaches. Therefore, the evidence must show more than "a mere dispute over the reasonableness of a particular use of force or the existence of arguably superior alternatives," and instead, "support a reliable inference of wantonness in the infliction of pain."[140]

While most use of force claims involve the Fourth or Eighth Amendment, claims of excessive force brought by pretrial detainees are analyzed under the Due Process Clause of the Fourteenth Amendment, if brought against state actors, or of the Fifth Amendment, if brought against federal officials.[141] The Supreme Court clarified that, similar to the reasonableness inquiry in the Fourth Amendment context, the standard for analyzing use of force in the pretrial detainee context is objective reasonableness.[142] Like the reasonableness inquiry for evaluating use of force under the Fourth Amendment, the judgment of use of force in the pretrial detainee context is intensely fact-specific. Relevant factors include: "the relationship between the need for the use of force and the amount of force used; the extent of the plaintiff's injury; any effort made by the officer to temper or to limit the amount of force; the severity of the security problem at issue; the threat reasonably perceived by the officer; and whether the plaintiff was actively resisting."[143]

THE COURT OF PUBLIC OPINION AND CIVIL SETTLEMENTS

All that law above is for the cases that get litigated. But public controversy can create intense pressure to settle well before lawyers have to go to court, even if grand juries refuse to indict, or juries refuse to convict. The power of video is to take the case directly to the people, generating pressure to settle cases outside

---

[137]   *Id.* at 319.
[138]   Rhodes v. Chapman, 452 US 337, 346 (1981).
[139]   *Whitley*, 475 US at 320–321.
[140]   *Id.* at 322.
[141]   Kingsley v. Hendrickson, 135 S. Ct. 2466, 2473 (2015); Graham v. Connor, 490 US 386, 396 n.10 (1989). Bell v. Wolfish, 441 US 520, 535–539 (1979).
[142]   *Kingsley*, 135 S.Ct., at 2472–2474.
[143]   *Id.* at 2473.

the formal confines of the courtroom and doctrines such as qualified immunity. There are many examples; too many tragedies to tell them all.[144]

Here are just a few.

In New York, the family of Eric Garner, a married father of six, received a $5.9 million settlement for his suffocation death in 2014 during an arrest for the minor offense of selling cigarettes.[145] Garner's friend Ramsey Orta recorded as officers pressed Garner's neck and head to the pavement, holding him down despite Garner's repeated pleas, "I can't breathe." The grand jury refused to indict the officer who applied the fatal maneuver, sparking waves of protests.[146] If the Garners had to go to court, they would have faced formidable qualified immunity questions, including whether the officers' use of a hold to restrain Garner violated any clearly established precedent that put the impropriety "beyond debate."[147] Instead, concerned about the court of public opinion, New York City quickly agreed to settle a "prelitigation claim" that averted the need to navigate the legal gauntlet.[148]

In Minnesota, Philando Castile's mother received a nearly $3 million settlement and Castile's girlfriend, who live-streamed his death during a traffic stop on Facebook, received a $800,000 settlement despite a jury's refusal to convict an officer for the death.[149] Both the cell phone and the dash camera videos are heartbreaking, showing Castile trying his utmost to calm the officer

---

[144]   Here are just a few of the other cases. *See, e.g.,* Mitch Smith, *Tamir Rice's Family to Receive $6 Million from Cleveland,* N.Y. TIMES (Aug. 27, 2016), www.nytimes.com/2016/04/26/us/tamir-rice-family-cleveland-settlement.html (reporting on a $6 million settlement in the case of Tamir Rice, a twelve-year-old boy shot by the police who mistook his toy gun for a real firearm); Jeremy Gorner, *Chicago Poised to Pay $5 Million to Family of Teen Shot 16 Times by Police,* CHI. TRIB. (Apr. 10, 2015), www.chicagotribune.com/news/ct-million-dollar-police-settlement-met-20150410-story.html (reporting on settlement with the family of seventeen-year-old Laquan McDonald, shot sixteen times after he refused to drop his knife, on the recommendation of the city's Corporation Counsel and efforts to prevent disclosure of the video of his shooting); Steve Miletic & Lynda V. Mapes, *City to Pay $1.5 Million to Family of Slain Woodcarver,* SEATTLE TIMES (Apr. 29, 2011), www.seattletimes.com/seattle-news/city-to-pay-15-million-to-family-of-slain-woodcarver/ (detailing the settlement to the family of deaf Native American woodcarver John T. Williams, whose shooting was captured on dash camera showing him ambling down the street carving a piece of wood and apparently not hearing the officer's order to put the carving knife down).

[145]   Kevin Conlon, *NYC Official: City Settles with Eric Garner's Estate for $5.9 Million,* CABLE NEWS NETWORK (July 14, 2015), www.cnn.com/2015/07/13/us/garner-nyc-settlement/.

[146]   J. David Goodman & Al Baker, *Wave of Protests after Grand Jury Doesn't Indict Officer in Eric Garner Chokehold Case,* N.Y. TIMES (Dec. 3, 2014), at A1.

[147]   Plumhoff v. Rickard, 134 S.Ct. 2012, 2023 (2014).

[148]   Conlon, *supra* note 145.

[149]   Mark Berman, *Philando Castile's Family, Minnesota City, Reach A Nearly $3 Million Dollar Settlement in His Death,* WASH. POST (June 26, 2017), www.washingtonpost.com/news/post-nation/wp/2017/06/26/philando-castiles-family-reaches-nearly-3-million-settlement-in-his-de

and prevent him from shooting him.[150] The officer's stated basis for the stop was a broken taillight. Castile was respectful and compliant with the officer's request to produce his proof of insurance. He politely and calmly informed the officer, "Sir, I do have to tell you, I have a firearm on me," and when the officer panicked and yelled for him not to pull out the gun, Castile tried to calmly and repeatedly state he was not pulling it out. Castile had a permit and was lawfully carrying his gun – which is his Second Amendment right, according to the US Supreme Court.[151] The officer apparently panicked and shot Castile seven times while Castile kept trying to calm him down and explain he was not reaching for the gun.

Without those videos capturing Castile's every effort to lawfully comply, the gun in the car would have made it difficult to convey Castile's side of the story. Even with the videos, the jury found the officer not guilty on all criminal counts in Castile's death.[152] The settlement came quickly – ten days after the acquittal, sparing the Castile family the further pain of having to navigate the formidable gauntlet of filing suit and trying to attain civil damages.

In California, the mother of Kelly Thomas received $1 million and his father received $4.9 million for his death by beating recorded on surveillance camera during an arrest for stealing.[153] The encounter between Thomas, a homeless schizophrenic man, and Fullerton police officers began with a call from an area business reporting that Thomas was "roaming in the parking lot, looking in cars, pulling on handles again."[154] Approximately fifteen minutes into the encounter between Thomas and a Fullerton police officer, a surveillance video and the officers' audio recording devices captured the officer putting on latex gloves and stating, "You see my fists? ... They are

ath/?utm_term=.304f56bb3bbd; Mark Berman, *Diamond Reynolds Agrees to an $800,000 Settlement Stemming from Philando Castile's Death*, WASH. POST (Nov. 29, 2017), www .washingtonpost.com/news/post-nation/wp/2017/11/29/diamond-reynolds-agrees-to-800000-se ttlement-stemming-from-philando-castiles-death/?utm_term=.44680bd51142.

[150]   The videos can be viewed at www.cnn.com/videos/us/2016/07/07/graphic-video-minnesota-police-shooting-philando-castile-ryan-young-pkg-nd.cnn/video/playlists/philando-castile-shot-in-minnesota/ and www.cnn.com/videos/us/2017/06/21/philando-castile-shooting-das hcam-llr-orig.cnn.

[151]   District of Columbia v. Heller, 544 US 570 (2008).

[152]   Mitch Smith, *Minnesota Officer Acquitted in Killing of Philando Castile*, N.Y. TIMES (June 16, 2017), at A1, www.nytimes.com/2017/06/16/us/police-shooting-trial-philando-castile .html.

[153]   Lou Ponsi & Sean Emergy, *$4.9 Million Settlement Reached in Kelly Thomas Death Case*, ORANGE COUNTY REGISTER (Nov. 24, 2015), www.ocregister.com/2015/11/24/49-million-set tlement-reached-in-kelly-thomas-wrongful-death-case/.

[154]   Vikki Vargas & Neil Costes, *Newly Released Video Raises Questions in Kelly Thomas Case*, NBC LOS ANGELES (Feb. 28, 2013), www.nbclosangeles.com/news/local/New-Video-Relea sed-From-Night-of-Kelly-Thomas-Beating-194088451.html.

getting ready to fuck you up."[155] Thomas replied, "Start punching dude!" As Thomas proceeded to walk away, a second officer struck him repeatedly with a baton. The video recorded Thomas giving up, stating "I'm sorry dude! I'm sorry!" But the beating apparently continued, with at least one more officer joining in. As multiple officers piled on Kelly and repeatedly Tased him while commanding, "Stop resisting," Thomas cried that he could not breathe and finally began crying for his dad: "Dad! Dad! Dad! Help me, help me, Dad!" Beaten unconscious, Thomas spent five days in a coma before dying.

The video of the beating and photos of the aftermath went viral, sparking debates about policing and the mentally ill.[156] Less than a year later, Thomas's mom accepted a $1 million settlement offered by unanimous vote from the Fullerton City Council.[157] Thomas's father, a former police officer, initially refused to settle, saying he was focused on seeing the officers involved criminally prosecuted.[158] A jury acquitted two Fullerton offices tried for Thomas's death of all state homicide charges.[159] Federal civil rights investigators would ultimately conclude that they had insufficient evidence that the officers involved willfully violated Thomas's civil rights.[160] Thomas's dad sought adjudication via civil suit but hours before the trial was set to begin, and the video of his son dying on camera calling for him would be replayed, he settled.[161]

At the United States–Mexico border, Ashley Young's refusal to relinquish her cell phone recording of Border Patrol agents beating Anastasio Hernández-Rojas provided important evidence that helped Hernández-Rojas's five surviving children and common law wife secure a $1 million settlement.[162] Hernández-Rojas lived for twenty-seven years in the United States, since he was fifteen but was

[155] *Full Unedited Kelly Thomas Video*, O.C. REGISTER (July 6, 2012), www.ocregister.com/2012/07/06/full-unedited-kelly-thomas-confrontation-video/.

[156] Adolfo Flores, Paolma Esquivel, & Joe Mozingo, *Two Former Officers Found Not Guilty in Death of Kelly Thomas*, L.A. TIMES (Jan. 13, 2014), http://articles.latimes.com/2014/jan/13/local/la-me-0114-kelly-thomas-verdict-20140114.

[157] Samantha Tata & Beverly White, *Kelly Thomas' Mother Accepts $1 M Settlement with City of Fullerton*, NBC LOS ANGELES (May 14, 2012), www.nbclosangeles.com/news/local/Kelly-Thomas-Fullerton-Police-Beating-Death-Ron-Thomas-Mother-Settlement-151651455.html.

[158] *Id.*

[159] Flores, Esquivel, & Mozingo, *supra* note 158.

[160] Sean Emery, *Kelly Thomas Case: Five Years Later, Feds Say No Criminal Charges against Fullerton Police Officers*, ORANGE COUNTY REGISTER (Jan. 24, 2017), www.ocregister.com/2017/01/24/kelly-thomas-case-5-years-later-feds-say-no-criminal-charges-against-fullerton-police-officers/.

[161] Lou Ponsi & Sean Emergy, *$4.9 Million Settlement Reached in Kelly Thomas Death Case*, ORANGE COUNTY REGISTER, Nov. 24, 2015, www.ocregister.com/2015/11/24/49-million-settlement-reached-in-kelly-thomas-wrongful-death-case/.

[162] Cleve R. Wootson Jr., *Border Agents Beat an Undocumented Immigrant to Death: The US Is Paying His Family $1 Million*, WASH. POST, Mar. 28, 2017, www.washingtonpost.com/news/

deported after an arrest for attempting to shoplift steaks and tequila, reportedly for a Mother's Day celebration.[163] Missing his wife and five children in the United States, Hernández-Rojas attempted to return the same month and was quickly apprehended.[164] Border Patrol transported Hernández-Rojas to the station for processing, where he apparently misunderstood an order to throw out his water jug and began pouring the water into a trash can.[165] Thinking Hernández-Rojas was being disrespectful, an agent hit the jug out of his hand, shoved him against the wall and kicked apart his legs, striking metal pins in Hernández-Rojas's ankle and causing him pain.[166] Hernández-Rojas repeatedly tried to seek medical attention but instead was scheduled for immediate deportation. The agent who kicked him and a partner drove him to a drop-off point at the border.[167] There, agents began beating him with batons when he put his hands down instead of behind his head.[168]

Young and other people on a pedestrian bridge heard Hernández-Rojas's screams for help and filmed as agents Tased and hit Hernández-Rojas with batons.[169] When Hernández-Rojas was unconscious, agents turned their attention to the people filming the beating, grabbing their phones, stating, "What did you record? We're going to delete it," Young recalled.[170] Young hid the secure digital card with her video in her pants.[171] Hernández-Rojas ultimately died after sustaining five broken ribs, a damaged spine, and other injuries from the beating.[172] The US Justice Department investigated the killing but ultimately declined to bring federal civil rights charges, noting that Hernández-Rojas's methamphetamine use and prior heart conditions contributed to his death from the beating. Hernández-Rojas's case became a rallying point for immigrant protection groups. Caught up with the politics of border control and immigration enforcement, the settlement took nearly six years and legal battles to attain.

And then there are the cases where people survived the encounter, captured on video. In Los Angeles, a motorist spotted a highway patrol officer punching

---

post-nation/wp/2017/03/28/border-agents-beat-an-undocumented-immigrant-to-death-the-u-s-is-paying-his-family-1-million/?utm_term=.14d45d9e5866.

[163]   *Id.*

[164]   *Id.*

[165]   Kristina Davis, *$1M Settlement Reached in Border Death Lawsuit*, SAN DIEGO UNION-TRIB., Feb, 23, 2017, www.sandiegouniontribune.com/news/courts/sd-me-border-settlement-20170223-story.html.

[166]   Wootson, *supra* note 162.

[167]   Davis, *supra* note 165.

[168]   Wootson, *supra* note 162.

[169]   *Id.*

[170]   *Id.*

[171]   *Id.*

[172]   *Id.*

Marlene Pinnock, age fifty-one, a homeless woman, and recorded the incident.[173] The officer said she resisted him by pushing him after he pulled her from oncoming traffic.[174] After the cell phone video went viral, the department quickly settled with Pinnock for $1.5 million.[175]

In Sacramento, a passerby used a cell phone to record as an officer took down Nandi Cain, Jr., and punched Cain twenty times during a stop for jaywalking.[176] The city settled the case for just over half a million dollars.

In New Jersey, a surveillance camera video captured the beating of a schizophrenic man,[177] Ronnie Holloway, after he did not obey an officer's order to zip up his hoodie. After the video went viral, the city of Passaic settled with Holloway for $350,000, though the officer was acquitted of criminal charges.[178]

For the cases that do make it before a jury, video also can viscerally appeal to jurors beyond words.[179] For example, the family of Christopher Sean Harris obtained a $10 million settlement after jurors viewed a recording of a sheriff's deputy chasing a runaway Harris and shoving him into a wall to stop his flight. Harris's head hit the wall, resulting in catastrophic brain injury. The settlement came shortly after a paramedic testified that the deputy claimed that Harris had run into the wall headfirst. One of the jurors viewing the video contradicting this account said the footage was "traumatizing" and stated, "It was very emotional. I cried a lot through it. I'm just really happy they got what they deserved."[180] Another juror said, "I don't care what [Harris] did, he didn't deserve to be creamed into the wall like that."[181] Yet another juror said, "If it had not been for that video, they were going to cover it up."[182]

Violent videos have a volatile power because they play on the perceptions of the crowd, potentially unleashed from the discipline of law. Formal law gives officers who commit tragic errors shelter because police often must make

---

[173]   *After California Highway Patrol Beating, Community Wants Answers*, CBS NEWS (July 5, 2014), www.cbsnews.com/news/after-california-highway-patrol-beating-community-wants-answers/.

[174]   *Id.*

[175]   *Id.*

[176]   *Sacramento Settles Police Beating Lawsuit, Will Pay Man $550K*, CBS SACRAMENTO (Apr. 6, 2018), https://sacramento.cbslocal.com/2018/04/06/jaywalking-lawsuit-settlement/.

[177]   *Id.*

[178]   *Id.*

[179]   Sarah Jean Green, *$10M Settlement for Man Shoved into Wall by King Co. Deputy; Jurors React to Video*, SEATTLE TIMES (Jan. 25, 2011), www.seattletimes.com/seattle-news/10m-settlement-for-man-shoved-into-wall-by-king-co-deputy-jurors-react-to-video/.

[180]   *Id.*

[181]   *Id.*

[182]   *Id.*

rapid difficult judgment calls in heated situations where people may be enraged, impaired, or otherwise in their worst moments.[183] Yet the horror of seeing and hearing a person die on camera may overwhelm such formal admonitions – or make them seem outrageous.

Ultimately, damages will never replace or fully compensate for the loss of a human being. Criminal prosecutions also do not ever replace that loss. In the wake of violence, we tend to focus on criminal prosecutions because they most dramatically express outrage, condemnation, and societal valuation of the life lost or person hurt. Scholars and activists have expressed dismay that criminal prosecutions remain rare against officers because of the heightened safeguards for criminal defendants generally and defendant police officers especially.

Regardless of one's views on the rights and wrongs of using criminal prosecution as the default measure of justice, civil remedies are another important avenue that may prove more readily attainable by leveraging public opinion. Beyond the damages amounts, settlements also may include admissions about what happened, as occurred in Hernandez's case, and reforms such as improved training, monitoring, and disciplinary processes.

As Waithe explains, "While convictions may not be happening, what is happening is families of victims are getting settlements. Settlements does not mean justice. But there is some sort of restorative nature in them. And also what is more important than any sort of disciplinary action is that we are creating a permanent record so that when we look back on this twenty, fifty, a hundred years from now, the powers that be cannot say that this wasn't happening. This turns public attention and public awareness and it turns the public opinion."

---

[183] *See, e.g.*, Atwater v. City of Lago Vista, 532 US 318, 347 (2001) ("Often enough, the Fourth Amendment has to be applied on the spur (and in the heat) of the moment").

PART II

AUDIOVISUAL BIG DATA'S GREAT POTENTIAL AND PERILS

4

Audiovisual Big Data Analytics and Harm Prevention

Big data, as we move forward, that is going to be one of the most important issues with respect to transparency and accountability.

– J. Scott Thomson, Chief, Camden Police Department

BIG DATA, BETTER HARM DETECTION AND PREVENTION

The era of pervasive recording of the police opens new possibilities for detecting potential dangers before they arise and better guiding officers to avoid escalation to violence or complaints of rights violations. Audiovisual data from police and public recordings, combined with multiple other sources of biometric, locational, and behavioral data, offer the potential for enhancing technology-automated police oversight. The most pervasive and up-close source of audiovisual data on officer behavior, body cameras, potentially transforms the ability to monitor street-level encounters formerly outside of view.

The cameras follow officers into the field of everyday encounters where defense attorneys and courts lack sufficient data. Pooled together, the resulting videos generate the power to analyze images collected over time and in numerous encounters to reveal patterns and risk factors that can better steer decision-making. Techniques such as artificial neural networks, which this chapter will explore, trained on massive audiovisual data sets, can help guide evidence-based early intervention to better deploy and guide officers, identify and change problematic practices, and prevent the risk of harm.

The amount of audiovisual data on policing is staggering and growing, particularly as police departments deploy more body cameras. By 2015, one of the major companies offering cloud-based storage of body camera data, Evidence.com, already had more than a petabyte (1 million gigabytes) of audiovisual data with a video upload every 2.9

seconds.[1] By the time of my interview in March 2017 with Steve Tuttle, vice president at Axon, one of the biggest players in the policing technology area, Axon had seven petabytes of body camera video.

As context, just one petabyte of data is so massive that it could store the DNA of the entire US population cloned twice or 500 billion pages of printed text.[2] Now multiply that sevenfold. And multiply it a few times more because body cameras are hardly the only source of audiovisual evidence. As we saw in Part I, there is an expanding heterogeneous network generating video evidence, from bystanders with cell phone cameras, to organized copwatchers, to private surveillance devices, to cameras mounted for other purposes, such as traffic enforcement.

Scholars often use the term *big data* ominously to signify a Big Brotherly threat to civil liberties.[3] When we think of big data analytics, we tend to think of data being used to investigate us. Indeed, the police already are using big data from a diverse network of cameras and sensors to detect and solve crime.[4] For example, Atlanta's Loudermilk Video Integration Center integrates feeds from more than seventy-eight hundred private and public surveillance cameras and deploys crime-predictive analytics on the data.[5] The LAPD, aided by a software firm called Palantir, can analyze massive amounts of heterogeneous data from a network of cameras and other sensors to track persons of interest and even receive automated smartphone alerts on our movements.[6]

The sophisticated tools and strategies of the powerful also can be wielded to better direct and check government power rather than enlarge it. Audiovisual big data can be used to protect officers and the public alike from the risk of escalation to violence and complaints alleging rights violations. Automation

---

[1]   Lucas Mearian, As Police Move to Adopt Body Cams, Storage Costs Set to Skyrocket, COMPUTERWORLD (Sept. 3, 2015), www.computerworld.com/article/2979627/cloud-storage/as-police-move-to-adopt-body-cams-storage-costs-set-to-skyrocket.html.

[2]   Brian McKenna, *What Does a Petabyte Look Like?*, COMPUTERWEEKLY (Mar. 2013), www.computerweekly.com/feature/What-does-a-petabyte-look-like.

[3]   *E.g.*, Terence Craig & Mary E. Ludloff, PRIVACY AND BIG DATA: THE PLAYERS, REGULATORS AND STAKEHOLDERS 7–8 (2011); dana boyd & Kate Crawford, *Critical Questions for Big Data*, 15(5) INFORMATION, COMMUNICATION & SOC'Y 662, 662–679 (2012); Elizabeth E. Joh, *Policing by Numbers: Big Data and the Fourth Amendment*, 89 WASH. L. REV. 35, 36–38, 42–57 (2014).

[4]   For a discussion of law enforcement'a use of big data and predictive analytics to investigate crime, *see, e.g.*, Andrew Ferguson, THE RISE OF BIG DATA POLICING 7–135 (2017).

[5]   Atlanta Police Foundation, Technology & Innovation (last visited July 29, 2018), http://atlantapolicefoundation.org/programs/technology-innovation/.

[6]   Sarah Brayne, *Big Data Surveillance: The Case of Policing*, AM. SOCIOLOGICAL REV. 82 (5):977–1008 (2017).

and live tracking can also be a tool to better deploy officers and reduce the risk of eruption in volatile situations. Advanced data analytics can inform the work of early intervention systems (EIS), police departments, review boards, and courts.

This chapter introduces the potential power of audiovisual big data analytics to detect and prevent harm and build smarter systems. It also explores pooling community member and copwatcher videos in an independent repository to maximize their harm prevention potential and rights protection power. Subsequent chapters grapple with the potential perils and dilemmas of audiovisual big data: privacy, public disclosure, data storage and retention, and debates over limits on using videos for officer discipline.

Many Small Events, Big Predictive Power

Stops of persons that do not lead to arrests; searches that do not uncover contraband; conversations during routine traffic stops; and numerous other activities that may be humiliating and intrusive for a person often are not captured in written records. Formal complaints – a common variable used in early warning systems – miss the vast universe of encounters that may erode police-public relations because people who do not trust the police are unlikely to go to a police station to file a complaint with officers.[7] But small mobile cameras at the scene, whether worn by the officer or wielded by bystanders, can capture these common events that may never lead to an arrest or seizure, but can exacerbate police-community tensions.[8]

At the individual level, the recording may not seem to reveal much, but analyses of numerous such encounters, in the aggregate, can be powerfully revealing. In the criminal justice system, we tend to focus on individual cases and overlook the import of such aggregate data. Andrew Crespo has called this

---

[7] Ronald Weitzer & Rod K. Brunson, *Strategic Responses to the Police among Inner-City Youth*, 50 SOCIOLOGICAL J. QUARTERLY 235, 248–249 (2009) (discussing resignation and alienation among survey respondents and the reasons why a majority "believed that there was little accountability" in the police department and did not file formal complaints).

[8] Cf., e.g., Terry v. Ohio, 392 US 1, 15 n.11 (1968) ("The President's Commission on Law Enforcement and Administration of Justice found that '(i)n many communities, field interrogations are a major source of friction between the police and minority groups' . . . While the frequency with which 'frisking' forms a part of field interrogation practice varies tremendously with the locale, the objective of the interrogation, and the particular officer . . . it cannot help but be a severely exacerbating factor in police-community tensions. This is particularly true in situations where the 'stop and frisk' of youths or minority group members is 'motivated by the officers' perceived need to maintain the power image of the beat officer, an aim sometimes accomplished by humiliating anyone who attempts to undermine police control of the streets.'").

tendency to focus on information in the context of an individual case transactional myopia.[9] In contrast, a systemic-level perspective considers the larger pattern of data over time. Focusing on court records, Crespo has argued that filings analyzed in the aggregate can reveal issues such as boilerplate affidavits claiming probable cause. Going further, this book explores how the expanding frontier of audiovisual data also can reveal even more systemic facts about how police power is experienced on the ground, without ever making it into a courtroom. Analyses of the audiovisual data can help detect risk factors for escalation of encounters, thereby better protecting officers and the public.

As Brian Maxey, chief operating officer of the Seattle Police Department envisions it, the goals would be to preventative and restorative rather than punitive and stigmatizing.

"From an officer wellness perspective, figure out stress-inducing events and pull them out of circulation if you think they are at risk," he explains. "Institutionalize it so there is not a stigma."

The potential power of audiovisual data analyses is particularly great when it comes to body camera videos because the data are generated in an organized systematic way, pursuant to a departmental recording policy. Results are only as reliable as the methods used to collect and analyze data. To be able to detect risk factors, we need to see the whole universe of law enforcement encounters, including the dull routine ones that do not lead to any adverse actions. Video footage can be an important source of data enabling researchers to rewind, replay, and code a complexity of factors. This is an advance from relying on an officer's reconstruction of what happened, or shadowing officers for hours, days, weeks and months, and relying on in-person notes.

Machine Learning, Neural Networks, and Other Advanced Analytics

The era of big audiovisual data also is an era of advanced analytics. Even in the early days of body camera deployment, there is simply too much video and audio for any individual human to review and render analytically legible. Big data technologies and techniques drawing on machine learning methods such as artificial neural networks can conduct deep analyses of these data to detect and prevent the risk of escalation and rights violations.

The advantage of a massive data set is the potential to use machine learning methods to generate more sophisticated hypotheses, automate analyses, and discover complex combinations of risk factors. Machine learning techniques

---

[9]   Andrew Manuel Crespo, *Systemic Facts: Toward Institutional Awareness in Criminal Courts,* 129 HARV. L. REV. 2049, 2051 (2016).

draw on vast volumes of data to train learning algorithms.[10] By adjusting weights to achieve predictive accuracy, algorithms can be honed to assess risks and direct decisions to optimize the chances of achieving desired outcomes or avoiding bad ones.

A potentially promising approach is to use artificial neural networks to analyze audiovisual big data to better understand how to avoid adverse events in law enforcement encounters such as a use of force or a complaint regarding a rights violation. Artificial neural networks are a powerful machine learning technique that uses statistical models inspired by our biological neural networks. Natural neural networks enable our brain to process many different types of input and determine whether to engage in an action, such as running from danger, feeling aroused, laughing, or crying. These stimuli have complex nonlinear relationships. Our neurons determine whether to activate depending on the sum of weighted input signals crossing activation thresholds we have learned.

"These processes are a constant feedback loop – we are constantly re-weighing actions to take based on the outcome of previous responses to similar stimuli," explains Peter T. Parker, director of advanced analytics overseeing a team of data scientists specializing in artificial intelligence. "For example, if I take the expressway to work at this time, history has told me that it will be slower than the back road."

Artificial neural networks operate similarly in their learning processes. Data on outcomes feed back into the learning algorithm and weights adjust to refine predictive capacity. Artificial neural networks are a powerful advance because they enable us to model and make decisions based on nonlinear relationships between varied inputs and outputs. Training on a massive data set enables learning algorithms to adapt weights to refine the model and predictive accuracy. The more the data, the better learning algorithms can fine-tune the model to learn the optimal approaches.

Given failure history – for our purposes, adverse outcomes such as uses of force, or complaints about rights violations – neural networks can develop complex dynamic models that can predict and better avert future failures.[11] Neural networks have been productively used in diverse areas to predict things like bankruptcies, sudden cardiac failure, and power outages in the event of extreme weather. Certain types of neural networks can apply deep learning to

---

[10]   For an accessible overview about machine learning, *see, e.g.,* Pedro Domingos, THE MASTER ALGORITHM (2015).

[11]   For a deeper dive into predictive analytics with neural networks, *see, e.g.,* Nachimuthu Karunanithi & Darrell Whitley, *Using Neural Networks in Reliability Prediction,* IEEE SOFTWARE 9 (4):53–59 (1992).

process messy raw data, transforming the information and extracting mean-ingful features.[12]

Technologists in academia and the private sector are working on strategies to automatically classify audiovisual data and render it more feasible to analyze. Raw video must be distilled to metadata to facilitate aggregated analyses. Some metadata are relatively available, such as the date and time the media was recorded, which officer or camera did the recording, and the GPS location of the incident. But crucial data on contextual factors that may predict adverse outcomes – or protect against them – are submerged in the audiovisual data, such as tones of voice, language, time lapses from the first contact to physical contact and more.

"This metadata extraction process is a precursor to using advanced analytics to create better outcomes," Parker explains. "We are describing what hap-pened at greater detail, with greater accuracy, and at greater scale" than previously available.

Creating techniques for extracting information video is attractive to police departments because the strategies can help reduce the paperwork burden on officers. They also have the additional benefit of rendering aggregated audio-visual data more susceptible to analyses to detect and prevent risks. Software can transcribe audio to the equivalent of text. Taxonomy and ontology soft-ware can conduct semantic mapping using certain key words and metadata to automatically classify relevant audiovisual evidence upon upload. The rapidly growing volumes of audiovisual data can thus be indexed.

There is a lot of room for innovation and exploration in this area. A recent study by researchers at Stanford applying computational linguistic techniques to Oakland Police Department gives us a taste of what audiovisual analytics might help us discover.[13] The team used 183 hours of body camera footage documenting 981 traffic stops in April 2014. The investigators transcribed the footage and extracted 36,738 utterances by officers during the stops. In a preliminary study, the investigators had people rate the respectfulness of officer utterances from a randomly sampled subset of 414 utterances. The study found disparities in officer respectfulness by the race of the person stopped. Whereas white community members were 57 percent more likely to hear the most respectful utterances by officers, black motorists were 61 percent more likely to hear one of the least respectful utterances.

---

[12]   For an overview, *see, e.g.*, Jürgen Schmidhuber, *Deep Learning in Neural Networks: An Overview*, NEURAL NETWORKS 61: 85–117 (2015); Yann LeCun, Yoshua Bengio, & Geoffrey Hinton, *Deep Learning* NATURE 521: 436–444 (2015).

[13]   Rob Voigt et al., *Language from Police Body Camera Footage Shows Racial Disparities in Officer Respect*, PROC. NAT'L ACAD. OF SCI. 114(25): 6521, 6521–6526 (2017).

In the main study, the investigators scaled up to analyze the entire larger data set of utterances using computational linguistic models for respectful language examining features such as apologizing, expressions of gratitude, expressions of concern for safety, and softening commands. The model also considered negative indicators such as ordering motorists to keep their hands on the wheel and using informal titles such as "my man." The investigators found that officers were less respectful to black motorists after controlling for officer race, infraction severity, stop location, and outcome of the stop. As the investigators concluded, the study "demonstrates the power of body camera footage as an important source of data, not just as evidence," addressing the limitations of methods that rely on memory, human observation, and records.

The significance of word selection in an individual case may not be apparent just viewing the case in isolation. But analyses across a large data set can reveal potential patterns that contribute to elevated risk and stress in police encounters with minority individuals, better informing strategies to address the root cause of problems before they escalate.

The frontier of audiovisual data analytics is an exciting terrain with a lot of room for innovation by private companies as well as researchers and technologists. Because the techniques have broader appeal than just policing or the public sector, there is a strong commercial impetus to develop the technology. For example, more accurate facial recognition technology is valuable to major companies such as Amazon, Google, and Microsoft as well as police departments. Automated technologies such as a smart meeting assistant that can track and transcribe everything participants say – and thus permit word searches – have applications for the corporate boardroom as well as the grittier environs of the streets where police patrol.

Pooling together diverse audiovisual media with meta data extracted would create a more transparent view of the exercise of police power and facilitate advanced analytics to better steer that power. The approaches and data discussed here also can be used to build better EIS, as the next section explores.

SMARTER EARLY INTERVENTION SYSTEMS

A little over two decades ago, US Department of Justice attorneys wielding their new power under 42 USC § 14141 to investigate police departments secured a then-unusual feature.[14] As a centerpiece of reforms and condition

---

[14]   See Sheryl Gay Stolberg, The Rise and Fall of Federal Efforts to Curb Police Abuse, N.Y. TIMES (Apr. 9, 2017), at A12 (noting that the 1997 investigation of the Pittsburgh Police Department was the first investigation initiated by federal prosecutors under 42 USC. § 14141).

of settling the investigation into excessive force and illegal searches and seizures, the federal civil rights attorneys required the Pittsburgh Police Department to adopt an "automated early warning system."[15]

What was an automated early warning system?

"No one knew what an 'early warnings system' was or how to build it or what to measure," recalls Chuck Wexler, President of the Police Executive Research Forum, a police professional group.[16] Wexler likens Pittsburgh's reformist police chief tasked with overseeing the changes, Chief Robert McNeilly, to a "test pilot in the Mercury flight program," referring to the endeavor to launch the first US astronauts into space.[17]

Policing experts have long observed that a small group of officers drives a large proportion of complaints of excessive force and other problematic practices.[18] A goal of the early warning system is to detect and address such outlier officers and conduct.[19] The consent decree negotiated by the Justice Department attorneys described the early warning system as "a database containing relevant information about its officers, as well as a statistical model to identify and modify the behavior of problem officers."[20]

Under the decree, the system had to contain text-searchable information on issues such as citizen complaints, uses of force; arrests; civil suits involving the officer; and officer commendations, discipline, and mandatory counseling. The system also had to permit analyses of certain discretionary arrests, such as

---

[15] United States v. City of Pittsburgh, Civ. Case No. 97–0354, Consent Decree, para. 12 (W.D. Pa. Apr. 16, 1997), *available at* www.justice.gov/crt/united-states-district-court-western-district-pennsylvania-united-states-america-plaintiff-v-o (hereinafter Pittsburgh Consent Decree). *See also, e.g.,* Robert C. Davis ET AL., FEDERAL INTERVENTION IN LOCAL POLICING: PITTSBURGH'S EXPERIENCE WITH A CONSENT DECREE 9 (US Dep't of Justice Office of Community Oriented Policing Services, 2005) ("The new early warning system to track the conduct of individual officers is the centerpiece of the Bureau of Police's reforms in response to the consent decree.").

[16] Stolberg, *supra* note 14, at A12.

[17] *Id.*

[18] *See, e.g.,* Stephen Rushin, FEDERAL INTERVENTION IN AMERICAN POLICE DEPARTMENTS 144–145 (2017) (discussing studies); POLICE EXECUTIVE RESEARCH FORUM, CIVIL RIGHTS INVESTIGATIONS OF LOCAL POLICE: LESSONS LEARNED 16 (2013) ("Research has long suggested that a small percentage of police officers account for a high percentage of use-of-force incidents."); Samuel Walker, Geoffrey P. Alpert, & Dennis J. Kenney, EARLY WARNING SYSTEMS: RESPONDING TO THE PROBLEM POLICE OFFICER 1 (July 2001) ("It has become a truism among police chiefs that 10 percent of their officers cause 90 percent of the problems.").

[19] WALKER, ALPERT, & KENNEY, *supra* note 18.

[20] United States v. City of Pittsburgh, Civ. Case No. 97-0354, Consent Decree, para. 12 (W.D. Pa. Apr. 16, 1997), *available at* www.justice.gov/crt/united-states-district-court-western-district-pe nnsylvania-united-states-america-plaintiff-v-o (hereinafter Pittsburgh Consent Decree).

obstruction of justice and disorderly conduct, by officer, unit, shift, and location. In addition to creating the database and getting the relevant technology, Pittsburgh officials had the task of figuring out the thresholds of complaints or other indicators that would trigger supervisor intervention, and what kind of supervisor intervention.

The allure of using data and technology to detect and prevent problematic policing practices predated the first § 14141 investigation. More than a decade before the Pittsburgh consent decree, in 1981, the US Commission on Civil Rights called for police departments to create systems that would help detect officers "who are frequently the subject of complaints or who demonstrate identifiable patterns of inappropriate behavior."[21] The Oakland, New York City, Kansas City, and Miami police departments experimented with such systems in the 1970s and 1980s.[22] But Justice Department investigations and resulting consent decrees were the major movers in getting police agencies to adopt many of the first automated early warning systems, under duress.[23]

Today termed *early intervention systems*, these automated databases are a standard part of consent decrees and memoranda of understanding settling civil rights investigations into police departments.[24] Even when consent decrees end and reformist chiefs and their endeavors fade away, these automated systems remain. In Pittsburgh, the consent decree ended in 2002.[25] Four years later, Chief McNeilly left and various reforms implemented under the

---

[21]   US Comm'n on Civil Rights, Who Is Guarding the Guardians? 81 (1981).
[22]   Christopher J. Harris, *Early Intervention Systems and the Prevention of Police Misconduct, in* Stress in Policing: Sources, Consequences and Interventions 207, 209 (Ronald J. Burke ed. 2016).
[23]   Mike Gibbs & Carolyn Kendrick, San Diego Police Dep't, Enhancing Cultures of Integrity: Building Law Enforcement Early Intervention Systems 3 (US Dep't of Justice, Office of Community Oriented Policing Services, Jan. 2011).
[24]   *See, e.g.,* Brian A. Jackson, Vivian Lau Towe, Lisa Wagner, Priscillia Hunt, Sarah Greathouse, & John S. Hollywood, *Managing Officer Behavioural Risk Using Early Intervention Systems: Addressing System Design Challenges for Law Enforcement and Corrections Environments,* 11 Policing 103, 104 (2016) ("In external interventions into departments via federal consent decrees, the collection, analysis, and release of data has been part of the prescription for responding to serious organizational problems. And a prominent element in those interventions has been putting systems in place to analyse data in real time to identify officers whose behaviour is problematic, enabling leaders to respond before that behaviour becomes a more serious problem for the department and the career of the officer involved."). One of the leading experts on police EIS, Samuel Walker, has noted that "[t]hey are a required reform in all of the Justice Department consent decrees and settlement agreements." Samuel Walker, Early Intervention Systems (last visited June 4, 2018), http://samuelwalker.net/issues/early-intervention-systems/.
[25]   United States v. City of Pittsburgh, Civ. No. 97-0354, Stipulated Order (2002), *available at* www.justice.gov/crt/united-states-district-court-western-district-pennsylvania.

consent decree ceased in use.[26] But the EIS, which the police bureau terms the Personnel Assessment and Review System, continued.[27]

Moreover, this strategy of data-driven internal surveillance has spread well beyond the police agencies that have come under Justice Department investigation.[28] According to a 2007 survey of a sample of law enforcement agencies that included a question about early warning systems or EIS, about 40 percent of agencies serving jurisdictions of over more than fifty thousand residents have an EIS.[29] The mission of EIS also has grown from identifying outlier officers to more data-driven and effective management of police personnel.[30]

Yet these EIS are only as good as the data and algorithms that automate them. Despite decades in use, EIS are still largely in their infancy in terms of developing their potential. Surveys of agencies reporting use of an EIS found considerable variations in terms of what performance indicators to use and what triggers interventions.[31] The most common performance data include citizen and internal complaints, use of force incidents, involvement in high-speed pursuits, vehicle damages or accidents, and internal investigations.[32] There also is wide variation in what triggers the flagging of officers, units, or practices for intervention. This crucial issue is largely left to the intuition and professional judgment of police professionals. Demonstrating the intuitive appeal of a three-strike approach, many systems flag officers who have three

---

[26]   Stolberg, *supra* note 14, at A12.
[27]   Robert C. Davis ET AL., *supra* note 14, at 9.
[28]   Walker, Alpert. & Kenney, *supra* note 18.
[29]   US Dep't of Justice, Bureau of Justice Statistics, Law Enforcement Management and Administrative Statistics (LEMAS) (2007), *available at* www.icpsr.umich.edu/icpsrweb/instr uctors/studies/31161. See also US DEP'T OF JUSTICE, BUREAU OF JUSTICE STATISTICS, LAW ENFORCEMENT MANAGEMENT AND ADMINISTRATIVE STATISTICS (LEMAS), 2007 CODEBOOK, at p. 8, item 43 (2007) ("Does your agency have an operational computer-based personnel performance monitoring/assessment system (*e.g.*, Early Warning or Early Intervention System) for monitoring or responding to problematic officer behavior patterns?"), *available at* www.icpsr.umich.edu/icpsrweb/instructors/studies/31161; RUSHIN, *supra* note 18at 145 n.216 (summarizing how percentage is derived).
[30]   Harris, *supra note* 18, at 209.
[31]   Robert E. Worden, Sarah J. McLean, Eugene Paoline, & Julie Krupa, FEATURES OF CONTEMPORARY EARLY INTERVENTION SYSTEMS: THE STATE OF THE ART, at 6 (IACP 2015 Conference, Chicago, Ill.), *available at* http://finninstitute.com/wp-content/uploads/201 6/01/IACP-2015-EIS-Handout-Final.pdf; Samuel Walker, Geoffrey P. Alpert, & Dennis J. Kenney, RESPONDING TO THE PROBLEM POLICE OFFICER: A NATIONAL STUDY OF EARLY WARNING SYSTEMS, REPORT TO THE NATIONAL INSTITUTE OF JUSTICE 1.6-1.8 (Washington: National Institute of Justice, 2000).
[32]   For a discussion of the common factors used in EIS, *see, e.g.,* Worden, McLean, Paoline, & Krupa, *supra* note 31; Walker, Alpert, & Kenney, *supra* note 18.

or more indicators in a twelve-month period, such as three or more citizen complaints.

The problem of improving EIS has drawn the attention of public interest-oriented technological talent. Technologists with the University of Chicago's Data Science of Social Good collaborated with the Charlotte-Mecklenburg Police Department to improve on the simplistic threshold models and use machine learning to better predict which officers are at greater risk, and reduce the false positive of incorrectly identifying officers.[33] To build a better predictive model, the technologists drew on police department records on issues such as dispatch calls, complaints, and information recorded by officers regarding traffic stops, arrests, and citations. Data on adverse events and officer fault were based on internal affairs records. Deploying machine learning is an important advance. Strikingly, however, even technologists at the vanguard of improving EIS were reliant on agency records and officer-recorded information.

There are at least three major limitations with the current data and thresholds for intervention that innovations with audiovisual data can help address. First, while jurisdictions differ in the indicators their EIS assess, there is a general tendency to focus on reported or formal events captured in records, such as filed complaints, uses of force or high-speed pursuits documented by officers, and internal investigations.[34] Second, rough intuition-based thresholds can be gamed, or may wrongly flag officers conscientiously working hard shifts, and miss better combinations of predictors.[35] For the purposes of advanced analytics, a third challenge is that inconsistent systems across jurisdictions limit the aggregation and comparison of data across jurisdictions.

What Reliance on Reported Events Misses

As to the first limitation, reported events miss much of the everyday action in policing that impact the experience and trust of community members but are not documented. Absent the coercion of a court order or the rare mandate of a legislature, many jurisdictions do not collect data on stops that yield no arrest, frisks that yield no contraband, or the demographics of persons

---

[33] Samuel Carton et al., Identifying Police Officers at Risk of Adverse Events (draft, 2016), *available at* https://dssg.uchicago.edu/wp-content/uploads/2016/04/identifying-police-offi cers-3.pdf.

[34] Worden, McLean, Paoline, & Krupa, *supra* note 18; Walker, Alpert, & Kenney, *supra* note 18.

[35] Carton et al., *supra* note 20.

investigated for minor infractions.[36] And there is simply no way to detect issues such as ruder language or tones of voice based just on what is captured in police department records and events as documented by officers.

Moreover, requiring more comprehensive documentation of a wider range of events to provide better data is cumbersome, costly, and distracting for officers in the field. Officers have legitimate concerns regarding data collection requirements.[37] Attempts to gather data from persons stopped may intensify tensions in an encounter, particularly with minority group members. Imagine after receiving your ticket in a traffic stop also having to endure the indignity of answering further questions like identifying your race. Officers also may object to being required to collect data that is perceived to be just ammunition to portray them negatively in biased studies. Fundamentally, the job of a law enforcement officer is far different than that of a social scientist or researcher and an officer must focus on the exigencies of the field.

Audiovisual data can help address the major limitations of reliance on reported and recorded events. Police-worn body cameras capture much more detail and data than can be recorded in a police report, citation, or incident reporting form. This yields a far richer data set for experts to analyze than reported incidents. Moreover, technologists can create programs that autopopulate forms with metadata from videos, reducing the paperwork burden on officers with filing reports and providing other documentation. These programs can advance in sophistication if there is market demand from police departments to detect and extract other forms of relevant data. Communities and their police departments can leverage technology designed for broader use than just law enforcement.

---

[36]   *See, e.g.*, David Rudovsky & David A. Harris, Terry-Stop-and-Frisks: The Troubling Use of Common Sense in a World of Empirical Data, Penn Law Public Law and Legal Theory Research Paper No. 18-10, at 26–27 (draft, 2018) (on file with the author) (noting that "only a few departments collect and maintain this [stop-and-frisk] data in a comprehensive and usable form . . . and [t]he few police departments that have collected data – most prominently, New York City and Philadelphia – have done so as a result of litigation"); Riham Feshir, *The Trouble with Police Traffic Stop Data*, MPR NEWS (Nov. 2, 2016), www.mprnews.org/story/2016/11/02/police-traffic-stop-records-data-challenges (noting problems with inconsistent data gathering, failure to collect data, lack of a comparative baseline data, and other information gaps even after controversies forced a Minnesota municipal police department to turn over traffic stop data).

[37]   Lorie A. Fridell, UNDERSTANDING RACE DATA FROM VEHICLE STOPS: A STAKEHOLDER'S GUIDE 22 (Police Executive Research Forum 2005), https://cops.usdoj.gov/pdf/publications/understanding_Race_Data.pdf.

Evidence-Based Rather than Gameable Intuition-Based Thresholds

As for the challenge of crude intuition-based thresholds for red flags, evidence-based analyses using large audiovisual data sets can offer better predictive value and avoid false positives where an officer may be unfairly tarnished. A fundamental question that an EIS is trying to answer is predictive: from the set of all active officers, which ones are likely to have an adverse event, as defined by the department and community?

The simplistic thresholds set by expert intuition can be unfair to officers who work tougher areas and shifts. An officer may be more likely to cross the threshold and receive a red flag for having a certain number of uses of force or accidents within the time period because she or he works a midnight shift in an area with a higher incidence of violent crime. Yet some EIS have the same threshold for the officer working the tougher midnight shift in a high-crime area as the officer working the still early morning hours in a business district. Others may have a somewhat more sophisticated model that accounts for the area and time that an officer patrols, but leave out other important factors.

Another problem with simplistic thresholds is that if one knows the number of events and time period that trigger scrutiny, one can simply avoid taking certain actions, or avoid reporting certain events. The simple thresholds, combined with a system dependent on reported events, creates a perverse incentive to distort the data and not report events, or to be less proactive in policing. The honest officer, and the officer who takes on the tougher calls, jobs, and beats, is perversely at risk of being flagged because of these desirable qualities.

Machine learning models present a better approach to address these challenges. Machine learning powers systems that improve automatically through experience.[38] Many aspects of modern life that we now take for granted, such as tailored web searches, content filtering, and product recommendations based on our search history are possible because of machine learning.[39] Algorithms "learn" to deliver better tailored and more accurate results, by "training" on large data sets to hone predictive capabilities. Weights for an array of predictive factors in the algorithm adjust based on hits and misses in predictions.

The growing deluge of audiovisual data provides powerful material to train smarter algorithms to capture underlying contextual and behavioral stressors that elevate the risk of harm. Neural networks can help detect,

---

[38]   M. I. Jordan & T. M. Mitchell, *Machine Learning: Trends, Perspectives, and Prospects*, Science 349(6245): 255–260 (2015).

[39]   Yan LeCun, Yoshua Bengio, & Geoffrey Hinton, *Deep Learning*, Nature 521: 436–444 (2015).

learn, and predict complex relationships between factors that can elevate risk of adverse outcomes.[40] These techniques would advance risk detection and harm prevention far beyond simplistic thresholds set by intuition, instead detecting complex and perhaps hidden relationships that elevate the probability of an adverse outcome.

The risk of tragedy may be elevated, even among the best-intentioned officers, because of combinations of contextual factors such as dealing with high-stress situations like battered children, domestic violence, or suicide threats in a prior call; recent shift changes from days to nights; time of day; time on shift; and the nature of the next call for service.[41] Identifying such combinations of contextual risks can help departments better deploy their most important human assets to protect the public. This further advances the mission of EIS, progressing from the original orientation of detecting individual outlier or "problem" officers, to harm prevention for both officers and the public.[42]

CROWDSOURCING ACCOUNTABILITY

While police body-worn camera video has the advantage of systematic collection, cell phone videos by community members also have important analytic potential for detecting and preventing harm. Recordings by the public can open new avenues to crowdsource police accountability, filling in when body camera recordings are missing, creating pressure to disclose police videos, and offering competing perspectives. Crowdsourcing means outsourcing a task to a large network of people via an open call.[43] When authorities ask for public assistance in generating leads to solve crimes and assist in prosecution, the approach draws on the logic of crowdsourcing. Copwatching, organized and otherwise, is a grassroots form of crowdsourcing police accountability.

Recordings by community members can help supplement the gross under-inclusiveness of just relying on formally filed complaints. Residents in communities where mistrust of police is strong are unlikely to go to the same

---

[40]   *See, e.g.,* M. De Beule, E. Maes, O. De Winter, W. Valaere, & R. Van Impe, *Artificial Neural Networks and Risk Stratification: A Promising Combination,* 46 MATHEMATICAL AND COMPUTER MODELLING 88, 89 (2007) (explaining artificial neural networks).

[41]   *See, e.g.,* John M. Violanti, Desta Fekedulegn, Tara A. Hartley, Luenda E. Charles, Michael E. Andrew, Claudia C. Ma, & Cecil M. Burchfiel, *Highest Rated and Most Frequent Stressors among Police Officers: Gender Differences,* 41 AM. J. CRIM. JUST. 645, 652–654 (2016) (reporting findings on the highest-stress situations for officers based on survey).

[42]   Walker, Alpert, & Kenney, *supra* note 18.

[43]   Daren C. Brabham, *Crowdsourcing as a Model for Problem Solving,* 14 CONVERGENCE: THE INT'L J. FOR RSCH INTO NEW MEDIA TECH. 75, 76 (2008).

department to file a report against a brother or sister officer of the official taking the report.[44] Yet as we saw in Part I, community members increasingly are aiming their cameras at police in protest and creating videos. If departments provide community members the opportunity to upload their protest videos, these can be an additional important source of information that could be used to detect problems. Even when body camera footage exists for a contested encounter, an alternative perspective on the incident can yield valuable information.

"You have to ensure you present all the data necessary for each stakeholder's unique context, allowing them to paint a complete and accurate analytic picture," explains Jonathan Flack, chief technology officer for a predictive analytics firm.

If aggregated and deidentified to protect privacy, community member recordings also can reveal risk factors for escalation to violence that would be overlooked in an individual case. The value of the videos that copwatchers generate are sometimes dismissed because of distaste for the commentary overlaid over the incidents depicted, such as frequent references to "pigs." But beneath the commentary, the capture of conduct on camera can be powerfully informative. As data extraction techniques develop, the raw footage can be analyzed by the same machine learning and artificial neural network techniques that permit evaluation of police-sourced videos.

Videos recorded by community members can enlarge the data set of adverse events, also termed failures, for neural networks to analyze. To develop models to predict and prevent future harms, neural networks need to learn on a large data set of failure history.[45] As we saw in Part I, community members are apt to aim their cameras in protest after seeing what they believe to be misconduct. In contrast, as we will see in Chapter 8, despite recording mandates, in some controversial cases that have surfaced, officers have not recorded because of the exigencies of the moment, mistake, or potentially deliberate behavior. Community member recordings can supplement where the police do not record. Moreover, people who submit recordings can help flag incidences as failures, at least as perceived by the public.

Recordings by members of the public and private entities already are widely recognized by the police as valuable in investigations to generate leads and evidence. One dramatic illustration is the hunt for the Boston Marathon bombers. Shortly after two bomb blasts detonated at the finish line of the

[44]   Ronald Weitzer & Rod. K. Brunson, *Strategic Responses to the Police among Inner-City Youth*, 50 Sociological J. Quarterly 235, 248–249 (2009).
[45]   Nachimuthu Karunanithi & Darrell Whitley, *Using Neural Networks in Reliability Prediction*, IEEE Software 9(4): 53–59 (1992).

FIGURE 4.1 Law enforcement officers from around the nation and world attending the International Association of the Chiefs of Police Convention in 2017 watch a video debuting software that permits officers to share links with citizens to upload their video footage into secure storage.

Boston Marathon, the FBI sought to crowdsource investigative leads from cell phone videos and photos taken by members of the public.[46] A breakthrough piece of evidence came from a spectator responding to the call for evidence from the public.[47] Investigators had stared fruitlessly at surveillance footage from a restaurant at one of the blast sites, searching for the source of the bomb. The cell phone photo supplied the missing link: a photo of a black backpack on the ground by a tree behind an eight-year-old murdered in the bombing. Standing above the backpack was a young man wearing a white baseball cap oriented backward – one of the two Boston bombers, Dzhokhar Tsarnaev.

[46] Spencer Ackerman, *Data for the Boston Marathon Bombing Will Be Crowd Sourced*, Wired (Apr. 16, 2013, 1:18 PM), www.wired.com/2013/04/boston-crowdsourced/ [http://perma.cc/L3 VL-NFCP].

[47] Brian Ross, *Boston Bombing Day 2: The Improbable Story of How Authorities Found the Bombers in the Crowd*, ABC NEWS (Apr. 19, 2016, 6:00 AM), http://abcnews.go.com/US/bos ton-bombing-day-improbable-story-authorities-found-bombers/story?id=38375726 [http://per ma.cc/ZM7H-YDBK].

Because of the evidentiary utility of public video evidence, there is a commercial impetus to develop technology that facilitates secure upload and storage of community member videos. One of the biggest policing technology companies, Axon, formerly Taser, debuted such a product in 2017, at the major convention for companies to display their latest wares to police leaders and officers from around the nation and world (Figure 4.1). The feature enables officers to send amateur videographers a link to upload their video into secure police storage.

Here again, the main marketable idea is improved evidence-gathering for the investigation and prosecution of crime – but the technology also can serve the additional purpose of police accountability. The same technology that gathers and securely stores audiovisual evidence for the prosecution of crime can gather audiovisual data that gives community members an alternative way to report and document concerns and analysts the ability to detect and prevent rights violations and the eruption of violence in police encounters.

The public interest sector also has innovated ways to collect community member videos. In 2012, the ACLU released a free app called Police Tape that enables community members to send a copy of their recordings of the police to the ACLU–New Jersey for storage and potential analyses.[48] Since then, other organizations have released similar apps that enable people to upload their recordings of the police to the cloud or to YouTube.[49]

AN INDEPENDENT REPOSITORY TO POOL COMMUNITY MEMBER VIDEOS

Many public videos still tend to be distributed in the unruly frontier of YouTube, media outlets, Facebook, and other social media. In this wild domain where going viral to get the message out is the goal, the videos are neither systematically stored to maintain chain of custody and integrity for evidentiary purposes nor are they aggregated for analytical purposes. Pooling these videos would better ensure evidentiary integrity and permit analyses of aggregated data. The pooled videos offers a major analytical advantage because data can be examined across cases, officers, districts, and other units rather than confined to a particular seemingly isolated incident.

---

[48] Elinor Mills, *ACLU App Lets Android Users Secretly Tape the Police*, CNET (July 5, 2012), www.cnet.com/news/aclu-app-lets-android-users-secretly-tape-the-police/.

[49] Alessandra Ram, *It's Your Right to Film the Police. These Apps Can Help*, Wired (May 3, 2015), www.wired.com/2015/05/right-film-police-apps-can-help/.

Ensuring a secure chain of custody also helps to address concerns regarding authenticity, alteration, deletions, or additions.[50] A common accusation in challenges to video evidence is that it has been altered or edited.[51] Establishing the chain of custody helps demonstrate that the recording was preserved in a manner that ensures its integrity.[52] Establishing a chain of custody is not imperative for conducting predictive analyses, but it promotes data quality and facilitates use of information in court.

While it may be efficient to piggyback onto the secure storage and case file structure of an existing police video data storage system, there are potentially important reasons to have an independent repository of public videos as an additional or alternative safeguard. Recordings made and controlled by the public help shift the balance of power when it comes to evidence. Rather than relying on the police to allow access to infrastructure and stored materials, public repositories can set their own access rules. The access and data mining polices can be based on an independent evaluation of the proper balance between privacy and the public interest in data analytics to detect potentially problematic practices and patterns.

With the proper safeguards for data integrity, an independent repository would honor community control and the oft-voiced hopes for accountability and harm prevention. Quality and access control over the repository could be vested in a combined board of community members, copwatchers, and independent experts. The experts would donate time to advise on data integrity, quality control, and access by qualified researchers engaged in harm prevention efforts. Independent data sets maintained with appropriate

---

[50] *See, e.g.*, Gallego v. United States, 276 F.2d 914, 916–917 (9th Cir. 1960) ("Before a physical object connected with the commission of a crime may properly be admitted in evidence[,] there must be a showing that such object is in substantially the same condition as when the crime was committed . . . Factors to be considered in making this determination include the nature of the article, the circumstances surrounding the preservation and custody of it, and the likelihood of intermeddlers tampering with it."); Erin E. Kenneally, *Confluence of Digital Evidence and the Law: On the Forensic Soundness of Live-Remote Digital Evidence Collection*, 2005 UCLA J. L. & TECH. 5, 11–13 (2005) ("Chain-of-custody is one of the controls used by courts to satisfy admissibility standards. That is to say, the authenticity of physical evidence is shown by accounting for who, what, when, where and how a given piece of evidence was transferred from its initial discovery, through its collection, access, handling, storage and eventual presentation at trial.").

[51] *See, e.g.*, Planned Parenthood v. Smith, 236 F. Supp. 3d 974, 990–991 (W.D. Tex. 2017) (finding the video at issue suspect and lacking sufficient indicia that the video had not been altered); Jones v. Union Pac. Railroad Co., No. 12 C 771, 2015 WL 5252958, at *10 (N.D. Ill. Sept. 8, 2015) (discussing challenge claiming video had been altered); Smith v. McGraw, No. 10-cv-02310-AW, 2012 WL 603238, at *6 (D. Md. Feb. 23, 2012) (discussing plaintiff's contention that video had been altered).

[52] McEntyre v. State, 717 S.W.2d 140, 146 (Tex. App. 1986).

quality controls can be merged with other data sets, including police videos, obtained by independent analysts seeking to create larger data sets for analyses.[53]

One way to maintain the independence of a data repository while providing structure and funding is to locate it in another government agency independent of ties to law enforcement agencies. This independent structure is illustrated by the Aviation Safety Reporting System (ASRS), the world's largest data repository on human factors in flight incidents.[54] This repository of data relies on voluntary reporting of information regarding aviation-related incidents, from full accidents to seemingly minor incidents that may be important if it recurs, such as "a switch broke in my cockpit while flying." An impetus for the founding of the ASRS was a 1974 fatal airline crash into a mountain because of a misunderstanding with air traffic control. Six weeks before, another flight crew had the same misunderstanding and almost crashed into the same mountain. More than forty years later, the data repository to prevent such recurrent tragedies is foundational in research and policy making to monitor and mitigate risks.

The repository is successful thanks to its design and protections for people who report incidents. First, an agency with no jurisdiction to investigate or penalize incidents – NASA – runs the repository rather than the Federal Aviation Administration. The NASA staff who run the repository strip the reports of identifying information to protect the anonymity of reporters. They also issue alerts about emerging risks discovered due to the reporting. Under federal regulations, people who submit reports to NASA are immunized from any disciplinary action except for information about criminal offenses or accidents.[55] The intelligent design to facilitate reporting and crowdsourcing has resulted in massive data set of 1.4 million reports and a model for data repositories to protect public safety worldwide.

---

[53] *See generally* Erika G. Martin & Grace M. Begany, *Opening Government Health Data to the Public: Benefits, Challenges, and Lessons Learned from Early Innovators*, 24(2) J. Am. Med. Ass'n 345 (2016) (discussing the challenges with promoting open data and analytics); Maureen A. Pirog, *Data Will Drive Innovation in Public Policy and Management Research in the Next Decade*, 33(2) J. Pol'y Analysis & Mgmt. 537 (2014) (discussing the import of linking data sets in policy analysis).

[54] For further reading about the Aviation Safey Reporting System, *see* NASA, *40 Years of Safer Aviation through Reporting* (Sept. 28, 2016), www.nasa.gov/ames/feature/40-Years-of-Safer-Av iation-through-Reporting; Linda J. Connell, Program Director, NASA ASRS, Aviation Safety Reporting System (Oct. 17–19, 2017), https://ntrs.nasa.gov/archive/nasa/casi.ntrs.nasa.gov/201 70010289.pdf.

[55] 14 C.F.R. § 91.25 (2018).

Envisioning how audiovisual big data can reinvigorate police regulation and harm prevention and better protect officers and the public is exciting. While the optimism is warranted and can facilitate important advances, it must be tempered with realism. Videos may seem to offer better proof of what is really happening on the ground but they can be misleading, partial, and even biased in hidden ways. Big data analytics are only as good as the data that goes in – and systematic skews in the data can deliver misleading results in nontransparent ways that are harder to unravel. Moreover, as with many information technology-based public goods there is a high privacy price for the potential benefits. The burden on privacy is regressive, in the sense that disadvantaged communities that bear the heaviest burdens of policing also lose more of their privacy. The next chapters tackle these challenges and explore how communities are – or could be – addressing them.

5

Partisan Perceptions
How Audiovisual Evidence and Big Data Can Mislead

A lot of times people look at the results of neural network and think it reflects actual relationships but actually it reflects our biases. Data is the fuel for artificial intelligence. Understand your data. A lot of people will dump data into their machine learning model and hope something happens.

– Rajeev Dutt, Co-Founder, Dimensional Mechanics, and an artificial intelligence industry veteran of sixteen years

Consider two pairs of videos.

The viral Facebook video opens with two burly white officers in Georgia pinning a ten-year-old African American child to the ground.[1] The cell phone does not catch the details of much of what the officer is saying, but the child's clear high voice carries to the audio.

"I'm sorry," says the child, pressed to the dirt, in a sweet plaintive voice that pulls at a parent's heart. "Yes, sir," he responds in that bell-like youthful voice to the officer's apparent commands.

In the background are distraught women.

"Get off his back! Get off his back!" yells a woman.

The cell phone video ends in less than a minute and a half.

After the Facebook video went viral over the weekend, drawing outrage, Athens–Clark County police officers released a body camera video of what happened from the officer's perspective on Monday. Because children are depicted on the video, the department had to review it and redact the children's faces. The body camera starts with the child's dad being arrested by officers responding to a domestic violence call.[2]

---

[1] The video, originally posted on Facebook, is available at Emmanuella Grinberg, *The First Video Showed an Officer Restraining a Child. The Second One Told a More Complicated Story*, CNN (July 24, 2018), www.cnn.com/2018/07/23/us/athens-ga-video-officer-restrains-boy/.

[2] The Athens-Clarke County Police Department posted the video to its Facebook page. Athens-Clarke County Police Department, *Video Released to Media Regarding Child Being*

"Right now you are going to jail for agg assault by strangulation," an officer explains to the man, age forty-three.[3] "As well as false imprisonment, OK?"

A child comes up to the officer, crying incoherently.

"Calm down. Calm down, OK," the officer says.

A woman grabs the child and says, "Stop it! Stop!"

The child struggles in the woman's arms as the woman takes the child away.

The arrestee and the officer remain calm and continue to discuss the charges and the man's *Miranda* rights.

Another child, the man's son, comes on the scene, crying and yelling, "What is he going to jail for? What is he going to jail for?"

"Chill," the man tells his son.

"He's going to jail for agg assault," the officer explains.

The distressed child comes up to the officer, crying, "He didn't kill nobody. He didn't kill nobody!" The child is crying and begins a high-pitched screaming and yelping.

"He's not going nowhere! He's not going nowhere," cries the child as his father tries to calm him down.

"You're going to jail! You're going to jail!" cries the boy to his father.

As the officer tries to place the arrestee into the patrol car, the child follows closely, crying and screaming. A woman comes forward and tells him to go back. The child runs around the gathered women and launches himself at the patrol car and the officer taking his father away.

"Stop! Stop!" the women yell at the distraught child.

"Don't do that. Don't grab an officer!" the officer commands. "Don't do that!" The cop's tone of voice changes from previous calm to a mixture of anger, stress, and fear.

"OK," the child replies, also clearly frightened now.

The officer grabs and lifts the child, then presses him to the ground, drawing his cuffs. As the women rush forward, the officer yells, "Back off! Back off!" The body camera's audio captures the exchange between the officers and the child more clearly than the cell phone video.

The child begins apologizing over and over, "sorry," while rolling around.

"Stop resisting!" the officer commands. "Calm down!"

The child pleads, "I don't want to go to jail."

"You're not going to jail," the officer tells him.

Restrained, Facebook (July 23, 2018), www.facebook.com/accpolice/videos/10160600049860 481/.

3 *See* Shane Croucher, *Video: Georgia Police Forcibly Restrain Crying 10-Year-Old Boy during Father's Arrest*, Newsweek, July 24, 2018, www.newsweek.com/video-georgia-police-forcibly-restrain-crying-10-year-old-boy-during-fathers-1038735 (listing the arrestee's name and age).

"Can I get some help here?" the officer asks a second officer, who bends down. And that is the moment the cell phone video begins to record, with two burly officers above a pinned-down ten-year-old, apologizing, frightened child.

"Do you understand? You don't run into a police officer," lectures the officer in audio that the body camera captured from its close proximity, but not the cell phone camera from too far away.

The other officer's finger brushes the child's hair. He holds his hand above the child's back, saying quietly, "I've got him."

The officers and the child agree that the child should stand up and have a conversation. The women come forward, with one woman wielding her cell phone camera, frightened and furious.

Both stories are painful to watch. But they are different stories. Just an extra three and a half minutes of recording the same contested encounter, from a different perspective, can make a major difference to understanding what is happening.

One looks like two large officers ganging up on a small child for no apparent reason. The other shows a heartbroken child who does not want to see his dad going to jail and who does not understand that his dad is being arrested for domestic violence. The child launches himself toward the officers, and an officer reacts angrily and aggressively, but ultimately the second officer helps calm the situation and the officers try to deescalate the situation (Figure 5.1).

At least that is what I see. You may see something different from viewing the same videos, based on your background, worldviews, and perspectives, as this chapter will explore later.

Now consider a second case. From the official police images of multiple seized firearms and stacks of drugs, the case of Florida resident Derrick Price seemed to be part of a major bust of potentially dangerous dealers.[4] The body camera footage of the takedown of Price shows officers appearing to be struggling with a resistant suspect while yelling at him to stop resisting.[5]

Yet, a private surveillance camera mounted at a higher angle to capture the full scene gave a much different depiction of the arrest of Price.[6] The private camera showed that Price put his hands up and then lay prone with his hands

---

[4]   Drug Ringleader Busted in Marion Oaks, OCALA POST (Aug. 8, 2014), www.ocalapost.com/ drug-ringleader-busted-in-marion-oaks/ [http://perma.cc/DU22-N2H9].

[5]   Conor Friedersdorf, *The Conspiracy to Brutalize Derrick Prince*, ATLANTIC (Feb. 1, 2016), www .theatlantic.com/politics/archive/2016/02/the-conspiracy-to-brutalize-derrick-price/457134/ [http://perma.cc/D28M-J7X5] (contrasting body camera video of the arrest of Prince with what private video surveillance recorded).

[6]   *Id.*

FIGURE 5.1 What led to a ten-year-old child being pressed to the ground by two officers in Athens-Clarke County, Georgia? The difference in the stories conveyed of the same incident by a cell phone video and an officer's body camera shows the partiality of perspectives.

behind him in surrender.[7] Multiple officers kicked and beat him as he lay prone, shouting at him to stop resisting, apparently in a display for the body cameras.[8] Without the vantage of the surveillance camera mounted high overhead, many observers would have mistaken the tumultuous bouncing of officers depicted on body cameras to be indicators of a struggling suspect, rather than the stomp and kick of a beating.

[7]   *See id.*
[8]   *Id.*

Perspective matters powerfully. Because of the spread of body cameras and a culture of citizens recording the police, the power to replay contested police encounters is bigger and better than ever before. But it has important limitations. Replay via body camera footage is not like instant replay in sports.[9] Modern-day instant replay in sports relies on several camera angles mounted on stable positions to optimize clarity and viewing vantage.[10] In contrast, body cameras are mounted on officers in motion and give the officer's view.[11] Cell phone cameras are wielded from the perspective of the bystander.

This chapter is about the politics and partiality of perceptions and the limits of audiovisual evidence and analytics. Both body cameras and cell phone cameras may capture different and partial pictures of what happened. The information conveyed by audiovisual data can vary dramatically because of when the video begins or ceases to record, the angle and framing of recording, the perspective of the person wearing or wielding the camera, and the capabilities of the cameras. Moreover, what the video captures may not be the legally relevant facts. Interpretation also may vary widely depending on the worldviews and orientations of the audience. Finally advanced analytics on audiovisual data is only as reliable as the data. Partisanship and biases in audiovisual data may impede and impair audiovisual analytics unless corrected.

THE CASE OF THE AMAZING ROBBER WHO GREW FROM 5′6″ TO 6′3″

In the Texas heat of June 2008, a robber wearing sunglasses and a baseball cap entered a 7-Eleven store, pulled a gun on the clerk, and demanded money.[12] The robbery was the latest in a series that had hit area convenience stores.

---

9   *See, e.g., History of Instant Replay*, NFL FOOTBALL OPERATIONS, http://operations.nfl.com/ the-game/history-of-instant-replay/ (last visited Feb. 20, 2016) (offering history of the evolution of instant replay system).

10   *Id.*

11   *See* US DEP'T OF JUSTICE, OFFICE OF JUSTICE PROGRAMS, NAT'L INST. OF JUSTICE, A PRIMER ON BODY-WORN CAMERAS FOR LAW ENFORCEMENT 5–6 (Sept. 2012), www .justnet.org/pdf/oo-Body-Worn-Cameras-508.pdf [hereinafter NIJ, BODY-WORN CAMERAS] (describing body-worn camera resolution specifications and mounting considerations to capture data).

12   The account is derived from Powell v. State, Case No. 03-09-00730-CR, 2011 WL 1466876 (Apr. 15, 2011); Texas Forensic Science Commission, Forensic Video Analysis-Height Determination Complaint Filed on Behalf of George R. Powell III. (Apr. 12, 2016), *available at* www.themarshallproject.org/documents/3235834-Forensic-Video-Analysis-Height-Determi nation; The Marshall Project, *Was the Robber 6-Foot-3 or 5-Foot-6?* (Dec. 12, 2016), www .themarshallproject.org/2016/12/12/was-the-robber-6-foot-3-or-5-foot-6.

According to the 7-Eleven clerk's initial description, the robber was about 5′6″ – notably shorter than the average man in the United States.[13]

But the police had more than just a suspect description. A surveillance camera recorded the robber. The evening news broadcast the video footage. And a phone tip led the police to George Powell, III, a 6′3″ man who stands taller than 97 percent of American men.[14] The police showed the clerk a photo lineup with Powell's picture in it. The clerk picked out Powell.

Powell went to trial on charges of aggravated robbery. Both the 7-Eleven store clerk and the manager picked him out as the robber. Two clerks from another convenience store called Mickey's identified Powell as the person who robbed their store. Both of the Mickey's clerks testified that they had watched the surveillance footage from the 7–Eleven and believed that the person on it was the same person who robbed their store.

But the clerk and manager from a Valero's convenience store robbed twelve days before the 7-Eleven heist disagreed. Both the Valero's clerks also watched the surveillance video. The surveillance video showed the same man that had robbed them, the Valero's manager testified. But both Valero's employees said Powell was not the man on the video. The Valero's clerk knew Powell as a regular and said he was not the man who robbed her – he spoke differently and was taller than the robber. The manager also said Powell was taller than the robber.

Because of the embarrassing height discrepancy between the initial 5′6″ description of the 7-Eleven clerk and Powell's apparent height, the prosecution brought in a former Florida police officer who said he was an expert in photogrammetry, the science of judging the characteristics of objects based on visual cues. He said that based on where the robber stood as he entered the doorway of the 7-Eleven, he believed the robber to be at least 6′1″ tall.

The jury convicted Powell, and he received a twenty-eight-year prison sentence.

After sentencing, Powell hired another expert to assess the height of the suspect pictured in the 7-Eleven video. That expert concluded on his calculations that the person captured in the 7-Eleven surveillance video was about 5′7″ – much closer to the clerk's initial description (Figure 5.2).

---

[13] The average adult male height in the United States is 5′9″. Centers for Disease Control and Prevention, National Center for Health Statistics, Body Measurements, Measured Average Height, Weight, and Waist Circumference for Adults Aged 20 and Over (May 3, 2017), www .cdc.gov/nchs/fastats/body-measurements.htm.

[14] Tall.Life, Height Percentile Calculator, by Age or Country (2018), https://tall.life/height-per centile-calculator-age-country/. This percentile calculator tool draws from the Centers for Disease Control and Prevention, Anthropometric Reference Data for Children and Adults: United States, 2007–2010 (Oct. 2012), www.cdc.gov/nchs/data/series/sr_11/sr11_252.pdf.

Door Camera – RP1 at 00:04:27.795   Door Camera - RP2 at 00:04:28.062

FIGURE 5.2 How tall is this robber from a surveillance video? Differing methods reach sharply different conclusions. He is at least 6'1" tall, consistent with the defendant's height of 6'3" tall, testified the prosecution expert. The defense expert analyzed the same video by a different method and concluded the suspect is about 5'7" – closer to the store clerk's initial description of the suspect as 5'6", before she viewed the defendant's photo lineup. Courtesy Texas Forensic Science Commission.

Powell appealed to the Texas Forensic Science Commission. The Commission investigates allegations of "professional negligence or professional misconduct that would substantially affect the integrity of the results of a forensic analysis conducted by an accredited laboratory, facility or entity."[15] The Commission also accredits crime laboratories and other entities that conduct forensic analyses in criminal cases.[16]

Five years into Powell's twenty-eight-year sentence, the Commission hired another expert to independently analyze the video images and the prior analyses to determine why the opinions differed so dramatically. The expert used reverse projection, which overlays historic video images onto current measurements taken at the site. Attaining measurements from photographs is not possible with just a two-dimensional video image. Rather, data from a third dimension must be imported from additional information. This can occur when, for example, the suspect's head is positioned against a doorway with a plane perpendicular to the camera. The doorway provides a third dimension against which objects in that plane, such as a suspect's head as he stands in the doorway, can be measured. Using this process, the independent expert determined the robber depicted in the video was

---

[15] TEX CODE CRIM. PROC. Art. 38.01 §4(a)(3).
[16] *Id.*

FIGURE 5.3   Powell, 6′3,″ against the 7-Eleven doorway. Courtesy Texas Forensic
Science Commission.

between 5′5.8″ and 5′9.4″ tall – like the clerk initially testified. The likely
height in this range was 5′7.6″ tall (Figures 5.3 and 5.4).

The certified forensic video analyst who conducted the analyses for the
Texas Forensic Science Commission concluded, "The case studied in this
review highlights the potential dangers when scientific evidence is prepared
and presented in court without proper foundation, and without following
accepted industry standards and methodologies."[17]

Powell remains in jail as of this writing. The Texas Innocence Project has
taken his case.[18]

The case illustrates the dangers of thinking that two-dimensional images
can trump our three-dimensional experience. The 7-Eleven clerk's memory
changed to conform to the video and the unaccredited prosecution expert's
interpretation of what the video depicted, despite the clerk's initial description. She was not alone in this perceptual frailty. Other witnesses also con-
formed their memory to what the video was said to depict.

[17]   Texas Forensic Science Commission, Forensic Video Analysis-Height
Determination Complaint Filed on Behalf of Feorge R. Powell, III 57
(Apr. 12, 2016), *available at* www.themarshallproject.org/documents/3235834-Forensic-Video-
Analysis-Height-Determination.

[18]   Alex Cano, *Belton: Hearings Continue in Robbery Conviction Challenge*, KWTX Channel
10 (Jan. 10, 2018), www.kwtx.com/content/news/Belton-Hearings-continue-in-robbery-convic
tion-challenge-468699533.html.

FIGURE 5.4 The robber against the 7-Eleven doorway. Courtesy Texas Forensic Science Commission.

The case also illustrates the dangers of using nonrigorous methodologies for deriving information from two-dimensional video images to decide crucial facts for someone's fate. With more police videos of contested encounters, will come the need for more video forensics to answer questions about speed, velocity, distance, and distortion. For example: was the suspect really rushing rapidly at the officer? Or was the suspect so far away that there was no need for deadly force?

Two-dimensional images lack the parallax needed for depth perception, explains Jonathan Flack, who before founding his predictive analytics firm had more than twenty years of experience in large-scale distributed computing, audiovisual data management and visual persuasion with one of the world's most prodigious generators of audiovisual data – the Hollywood film industry.[19] Parallax is a process by which we can determine depth and distances by comparing the positions or motion of something from different lines of sight.[20] Cameras in motion make video analyses even more complicated.

[19] For a discussion of these challenges and strategies using computer vision systems to address them, *see, e.g.,* David G. Lowe, *Three-Dimensional Object Recognition from Single Two-Dimensional Images,* ARTIFICIAL INTELLIGENCE 31(3): 355–395 (Mar. 1987).

[20] For a discussion, *see, e.g.,* HyungGoo R. Kim, Dora E. Angelaki, & Gregory C. DeAngelis, *The Neural Basis of Depth Perception from Motion Parallax,* PHILOSOPHICAL TRANSACTIONS OF THE ROYAL SOCIETY OF LONDON, SERIES B, BIOLOGICAL SCIENCES 371(1697) (2016), http://dx.doi.org/10.1098/rstb.2015.0256.

There are technological strategies to make analyses more feasible, Flack explains. One strategy could be having body cameras record in stereo. The resulting data would occupy more storage space but compression could address the burdens. Storage on a network-attached device located in a secure facility with backups could mitigate the costs of storage. This would address some of the challenges of trying to reconstruct important facts from two-dimensional video.

THE FANTASY OF THE CAMERA'S OBJECTIVITY

Beyond the technical challenges, video evidence also calls for greater literacy about the biases that can affect our interpretation of the images we see. Camera footage is often portrayed as better than human accounts at capturing the objective truth. The oft-expressed hope for body cameras is to "provide an unbiased audio and video recording of events that officers encounter."[21] Images seem to represent a direct window into reality unsullied by human manipulation or misperception of the truth.[22] Images have the power to persuade by suggesting a transparent depiction of reality without discernible resort to rhetoric.[23] The seductive power of images obscures the fact that camera framing and viewer beliefs structure the meaning derived from video.[24]

Many scholars have begun to address the potentially partial or misleading nature of video evidence and the partisanship of our perception.[25] There is increasing concern over the volatile, sometimes potentially misleading, nature

---

[21]   PHILA. POLICE DEP'T, DIRECTIVE 4.21 (Apr. 20, 2015); *see also, e.g.,* AUSTIN POLICE DEP'T, POLICY MANUAL, POLICY 303, at 132 (May 4, 2015) ("The use of Body Worn Digital Recording (BWDR) system provides an unbiased audio/video recording of events that employees encounter.").

[22]   NEAL FEIGENSON & CHRISTINA SPIESEL, LAW ON DISPLAY 8 (2009).

[23]   Rebecca Tushnet, *Worth a Thousand Words: The Images of Copyright,* 125 HARV. L. REV. 683, 692 (2012).

[24]   *Id.* at 689–690; *see also* Vivian Yee & Kirk Johnson, *Body Cameras Worn by Police Officers Are No "Safeguard of Truth," Experts Say,* N.Y. TIMES (Dec. 7, 2014), at A1 (discussing divergent interpretations of video).

[25]   Mary D. Fan, *Justice Visualized: Courts and the Body Camera Revolution,* 50 U.C. DAVIS L. REV. 897, 947–953 (2017); Dan M. Kahan, David A. Hoffman, & Donald Braman, *Whose Eyes Are You Going to Believe? Scott v. Harris and the Perils of Cognitive Illiberalism,* 122 HARV. L. REV. 837, 859, 879 (2009) [hereinafter Kahan, Hoffman & Braman, *Whose Eyes*]; Caren Myers Morrison, Body Camera Obscura: The Semiotics of Police Video, 54 Am. Crim. L. Rev. 791 (2017); Seth Stoughton, *Police Body-Worn Cameras,* 96 N.C. L. Rev. 1363 (2018); Howard M. Wasserman, *Recording of and by the Police: The Good, the Bad, and the Ugly,* J. GENDER, RACE & JUSTICE 543, 552, 557 (2017); Michael D. White & Henry Fradella, *The Intersection of Law, Policy, and Police Body-Worn Cameras: An Exploration of Critical*

of video evidence.[26] The allure of video's seeming transparency into truth heightens the risk that viewers will miss the persuasion effects and even potential distortion caused by angle, framing, perspective, and the filter of one's own preconceived notions.[27] A camera's position and angle, the perspective from which recordings are made, and the time-framing of what is recorded all may powerfully shape a story and potentially mislead.

A suspect may look belligerent in the moments before force is used – but crucial events that rouse the suspect's ire may go unrecorded if the camera is not activated at the time.[28] A body camera may not be at the right angle to catch the flash of a suspect's weapon, or the stomp of officers beating a suspect.[29]

Make no mistake, video evidence can be powerful, valuable, and potentially more accurate and less malleable than human memory. The problems with eyewitness perceptions and memory are increasingly notorious, as we saw in Chapter 3. Memory is adversely impacted by high-stress situations, pliable, and subject to cognitive biases and false senses of certainty that grow in retelling one's story.[30] Video can help to better reconstruct what happened and address power imbalances in credibility contests. But with more video comes the need to be well-informed discerning consumers of video

---

Issues, 96 N.C. L.Rev. 1579 (2018); Howard Wasserman, *Recording, Police Misconduct, and Judicial Procedure*, 96 N.C. L. Rev. 1313 (2018).

[26] Feigenson & Spiesel, *supra* note 22, at 8; Fan, *supra* note 25, at 947–949.

[27] *See, e.g.*, Tushnet, *supra* note 23, at 692 (discussing how the seeming transparent depiction of reality that images offer obscures the manipulation of perception).

[28] German Lopez, *The Failure of Police Body Cameras*, Vox (July 21, 2017, 10:00 AM), www .vox.com/policy-and-politics/2017/7/21/15983842/police-body-cameras-failures [http://perma .cc/YUQ6-TRVL].

[29] *See, e.g.*, Conor Friedersdorf, *The Conspiracy to Brutalize Derrick Prince*, Atlantic (Feb. 1, 2016), www.theatlantic.com/politics/archive/2016/02/the-conspiracy-to-brutalize-derrick-pric e/457134/ [http://perma.cc/D28M-J7X5] (contrasting body camera video of the arrest of Prince with what private video surveillance recorded); Andrew Davis, *Graphic Video: 4 SCMPD Officers Cleared by Grand* Jury, WSAV (May 23, 2016, 6:35 PM), http://wsav.com/ 2016/05/23/graphic-video-shooting-of-officers-and-suspect-in-savannah/ [http://perma.cc/QG5 H-L6VA] (contrasting recordings from different body camera angles; one of which did not capture the suspect's reach for his weapon and the other which did).

[30] *E.g.*, Brian L. Cutler & Steven D. Penrod, Mistaken Identification: The Eyewitness, Psychology and the Law 68 (1995); Elizabeth F. Loftus, Eyewitness Testimony 52–133 (1996); Kenneth A. Deffenbacher et al., *A Meta-Analytic Review of the Effects of High Stress on Eyewitness Memory*, 28 L. & Human Behav. 687, 699 (2004); Charles A. Morgan III et al., *Accuracy of Eyewitness Memory for Persons Encountered during Exposure to Highly Intense Stress*, 27 Int'l J. L. & Psychiatry 265, 265–267 (2004); Richard S. Schmechel, Timothy P. O'Toole, Catherine Easterly, & Elizabeth F. Loftus, *Beyond the Ken? Testing Jurors' Understanding of Eyewitness Reliability*, 46 Jurimetrics J. 177, 179 (2006); Elizabeth F. Loftus, *Make-Believe Memories*, 58 Am. Psychol. 867, 868–871 (2003).

evidence, to recognize how audiovisual evidence can potentially mislead or be partisan without our realization. Moreover, people from different perspectives can reach startlingly different conclusions depending on their beliefs and worldviews.

THE PARTISANSHIP OF AUDIENCE PERCEPTIONS

Our subjective views, prior experiences, and passions can color our interpretation of video, leading to differing interpretations. We often use the term *the truth* in the singular – as if there were one reality a video can unveil and we would agree if we knew what really happened. Images are so seductive in promising to offer a window into the unmediated truth, that when people view a video and disagree with our interpretation we may even be startled.[31] For example, many expressed surprise and dismay when grand jurors disagreed with the interpretation of a video recording of the death of Eric Garner, who gasped, "I can't breathe!" when officers put him in the chokehold that caused his death.[32] Viewing the video, some believed the force was so excessive as to warrant a criminal indictment against the officers and expressed shock that the jurors did not see the same thing similarly.[33] Others – including the grand jury – disagreed.

The interpretation of a police chase video by a majority of the Supreme Court in *Scott v. Harris* is another example that challenges our assumptions that video can reveal a singular objective truth.[34] The case involved a lawsuit under 42 U.S.C. § 1983, which authorizes civil rights actions against state officers, by plaintiff Victor Harris, who claimed that the police used excessive force in halting a high-speed chase he initiated by causing him to crash, leaving him a quadriplegic. After viewing dash camera video of the chase, eight of the nine members of the Supreme Court believed that no reasonable juror could agree with the plaintiff's account that the police used excessive force in the car chase.

"The videotape tells quite a different story," wrote Justice Antonin Scalia for the Court.[35] "There we see respondent's vehicle racing down narrow, two-lane roads in the dead of night at speeds that are shockingly fast. We see it swerve around more than a dozen other cars, cross the double-yellow line, and force cars traveling in both directions to their respective shoulders to avoid being hit.

---

[31] Feigenson & Spiesel, *supra* note 22, at 61 (discussing the power of images of seeming to present the unmediated truth).
[32] Yee & Johnson, *supra* note 24, at A1.
[33] *Id.*
[34] Scott v. Harris, 550 US 372 (2007).
[35] *Id.* at 379.

We see it run multiple red lights and travel for considerable periods of time in the occasional center left-turn-only lane, chase by numerous police cars forced to engage in the same hazardous maneuvers just to keep up ... [W]hat we see on the video more closely resembles a Hollywood-style car chase of the most frightening sort, placing police officers and innocent bystanders alike at great risk of serious injury."[36]

Inconveniently, Justice Stevens did not agree the video evidence was so damning that no reasonable juror could believe the defendant's story. He observed the chase occurred at night on a Georgia highway with no pedestrians present.[37]

"This is hardly the stuff of Hollywood. To the contrary, the video does not reveal any incidents that could even be remotely characterized as 'close calls,'" Justice Stevens wrote.[38] "The only 'innocent bystanders' who were placed 'at great risk of serious injury,' were the drivers who either pulled off the road in response to the sirens or passed respondent in the opposite direction when he was driving on his side of the road."

In rebuttal to Justice Stevens, the majority wrote, "We are happy to allow the video to speak for itself."[39]

Prominent scholars expressed dismay at the decision, arguing that the Court had usurped the role of jurors in finding the facts on an issue about which even the judges who had reviewed the case below – plus Justice Stevens – disagreed.[40] Dan M. Kahan, David A. Hoffman, and Donald Braman decided to take up Justice Scalia on his invitation to see if the video speaks for itself. The team showed the dash camera video of the police chase to 1,350 Americans drawn from a panel of 40,000 persons maintained by the organization Knowledge Networks for scholarly public opinion analyses.[41] They analyzed splits in opinion by sociodemographic characteristics, political ideology, party affiliation, and cultural worldviews.[42]

For measurement of cultural orientations, they drew from an anthropological classification that has proved productive in legal scholarship over fiercely

---

[36]   *Id.* at 379–380.
[37]   *Id.* at 389–393.
[38]   *Id.* at 392.
[39]   *Id.* at 378 n.5.
[40]   *See, e.g.,* Erwin Chemerinsky, *A Troubling Take on Excessive-Force Claims,* 43 TRIAL 74, 76 (July 2007) ("[I]t is deeply troubling when an appellate court, acting on its own, watches a tape and decides the facts of a case for itself."); Kahan, Hoffman, & Braman, *Whose Eyes, supra* note 25, at 841–842 (arguing the Court was wrong to privilege its own view of the video and deny jurors the opportunity to interpret it based on their worldviews).
[41]   Kahan, Hoffman, & Braman, *Whose Eyes, supra* note 25, at 854.
[42]   *Id.* at 859.

fought topics such as gun control or police use of force.[43] For economy of analysis, the main categories of cultural orientations fall along two axes according to groupings based on the seminal work of social anthropologist Mary Douglas. The first is hierarch-egalitarian, a measure of attitudes toward social ordering, authority, and stratification.[44] The hierarch orientation is toward order, rules, power, and the use of social classifications to distribute rights, entitlements, goods, and duties.[45] Egalitarians, even when they hold power, tend to be troubled by stratification in rights, protections, and life opportunities.[46] The second axis is individualist-communitarian. Individualists value self-sufficiency, autonomy, and nonintervention while communitarians are oriented toward communal duties of care and group solidarity.[47]

A majority of the demographically diverse sample agreed with the eight members of the Supreme Court that the defendant posed a deadly risk to the public.[48] About 75 percent agreed that the use of deadly force by police was warranted.[49] Behind the aggregate numbers, however, analyses by subgroups were illuminating. Democrats were more likely to be pro-plaintiff in their perceptions than Republicans.[50] Liberals were more likely to be pro-plaintiff than conservatives.[51] Egalitarians were more likely to be pro-plaintiff than

---

[43] E.g., Dan M. Kahan et al., *Culture and Identity-Protective Cognition: Explaining the White-Male Effect in Risk Perception*, 4 J. EMPIRICAL LEGAL STUD. 465, 474, 485–486 (2007); Dan M. Kahan & Donald Braman, *More Statistics, Less Persuasion: A Cultural Theory of Gun-Risk Perceptions*, 151 U. PA. L. REV. 1291, 1310–1314 (2003). For classic accounts beginning with anthropologist Mary Douglas's work, *see, e.g.,* MARY DOUGLAS, CULTURAL BIAS 6, 8–13 (1978) (framing group-grid theory with Durkheimian influences); Mary Douglas & Aaron B. Wildavsky, RISK AND CULTURE: AN ESSAY ON THE SELECTION OF TECHNICAL AND ENVIRONMENTAL DANGERS 67–70, 175–188 (1982) (applying theory to environmental risk perception); Mary Douglas, Introduction to ESSAYS IN THE SOCIOLOGY OF PERCEPTION 3–6 (Mary Douglas ed., 1982) (providing overview of theory); Karl Dake, *Orienting Dispositions in the Perception of Risk: An Analysis of Contemporary Worldviews and Cultural Biases*, 22 J. CROSS-CULTURAL PSYCHOL. 61, 63, 65 (1991) (framing theory in terms of psychology and political influences on perception).

[44] Dan M. Kahan, *Cultural Cognition as a Conception of the Cultural Theory of Risk*, in HANDBOOK OF RISK THEORY: EPISTEMOLOGY, DECISION THEORY, ETHICS AND SOCIAL IMPLICATIONS OF RISK 725, 727 fig. 28.1 (Sabine Roeser et al. eds., 2012) [hereinafter Kahan, HANDBOOK OF RISK THEORY].

[45] *See* Jonathan Gross & Steve Rayner, MEASURING CULTURE 6 (1985).

[46] *See generally* Steve Rayner, *The Perception of Time and Space in Egalitarian Sects: A Millenarian Cosmology*, in ESSAYS IN THE SOCIOLOGY OF PERCEPTION 247 (Mary Douglas ed. 1982).

[47] *See* Kahan, HANDBOOK OF RISK THEORY, *supra* note 44, at 727–728 (discussing communitarian worldviews).

[48] Kahan, Hoffman, & Braman, *Whose Eyes, supra* note 25, at 864.

[49] *Id.* at 866.

[50] *Id.* at 867.

[51] *Id.*

Hierarchs.[52] And Communitarians were more likely than Individualists to be pro-plaintiff in their perceptions on all issues except risk to the public.[53]

Lawyers and scholars harbor the fantasy that argument and evidence can convince and even change opinions. The reality, however, is that people often talk past each other and interpret or reject evidence in conformity with their worldviews, particularly on controversial issues.[54] We perceive arguments and facts through the screen of our cultural and political orientation.[55] Video is valuable, but it is not a magic bullet that will get everyone to agree on issues such as whether an officer's use of force was reasonable, or whether a suspect posed a deadly threat.

THE LEGALLY RELEVANT PERSPECTIVES AND PROPER FACT-FINDERS

Cameras also may tempt us to ignore the relevant standard on legal questions where the proper yardstick should be what each person perceived, not what a mounted machine can capture. Criminal procedure standards often are based on reasonableness under the circumstances that the officer knew at the time of the event.[56] For example, the legal standard for whether officers are engaging in interrogation or its functional equivalent examines "the percep-tions of the suspect" as well as the officers' conduct.[57] Whether the officer

---

[52] *Id.*

[53] *Id.*

[54] *See, e.g.,* Douglas, CULTURAL BIAS, *supra* note 43, at 8–13 (explaining theory); Kahan, HANDBOOK OF RISK THEORY, *supra* note 44, at 742–743 (explaining experiment that con-firmed importance of worldviews in risk theory); Mark E. Koltko-Rivera, *The Psychology of Worldviews*, 8 REV. GEN. PSYCHOL. 3, 3–4 (2004) (discussing prevalence and value of theory); *see also, e.g.,* Dan M. Kahan et al., *"They Saw a Protest": Cognitive Illiberalism and the Speech-Conduct Distinction*, 64 STAN. L. REV. 851, 884 (2012) (finding that perceptions of whether protesters were expressing dissent or physically intimidating others were shaped by cultural cognition).

[55] *See, e.g.,* Dan M. Kahan, *The Cognitively Illiberal State*, 60 STAN. L. REV. 115, 122–124 (2007) (explaining usefulness of insights for understanding fiercely fought conflicts); *see also* Koltko-Rivera, *supra* note 54, at 10–12 (explaining various influential theories of worldviews, including the value orientations approach of anthropologist Florence Rockwood Kluckhohn).

[56] *See, e.g.,* Ornelas v. United States, 517 US 690, 700–701 (1996) (Scalia, J., dissenting) ("As the Court recognizes, determinations of probable cause and reasonable suspicion involve a two-step process. First, a court must identify all of the relevant historical facts known to the officer at the time of the stop or search; and second, it must decide whether, under a standard of objective reasonableness, those facts would give rise to a reasonable suspicion justifying a stop or probable cause to search.").

[57] Rhode Island v. Innis, 446 US 291, 301 (1980).

had probable cause to arrest a suspect is based on "the facts known to the arresting officer at the time of the arrest."[58] Whether there was reasonable articulable suspicion for a stop is examined in light of the facts known to the officer at the time.[59] Whether there is a reasonable basis for a safety search of a vehicle is based on the facts known to the officer at the time.[60] And whether use of force is reasonable also is judged from the perspective of the reasonable officer at the scene, knowing what the officer knew at the time.[61]

BWCs may capture only part of what officers and suspects see – or more than the parties can perceive, especially in stressful law enforcement situations. The San Diego Police Department's policy provides an important caution applicable to courts as well as officers:

> BWCs have a field of vision of either 75 degrees for the Flex or 130 degrees for the Axon. While human beings have a field of vision of 180 degrees, the human brain has a field of attention of 50–60 degrees. Under stress, this field can narrow down to a ½ degree. Stress also induces auditory exclusion and prevents the brain from analyzing and remembering all the stimuli that it takes in through the senses.[62]

If video is elevated as the objective truth – and officers are regularly encouraged or even required to view the video before writing reports – then there is intense pressure to conform memory and accounts to the video even when human perceptions may have been different than what was recorded.[63] Courts as well as officers need to understand why good-faith testimony may diverge from camera recording and avoid pressures to force-fit human recollections into a machine recording. Moreover, where the appropriate yardstick is the knowledge and the perceptions of persons at the time of the event, the temptation to privilege what is captured on video as the higher truth must be resisted.

---

[58]   Devenpeck v. Alford, 543 US 146, 152–153 (2004).
[59]   Adams v. Williams, 407 US 143, 146 (1972); Terry v. Ohio, 392 US 1, 21–22 (1968).
[60]   Michigan v. Long, 463 US 1032, 1047 n.11 (1983).
[61]   Graham v. Connor, 490 US 386, 396 (1989).
[62]   CITY OF SAN DIEGO, SAN DIEGO POLICE DEP'T PROCEDURE NO. 1.49 1, 11 (July 8, 2015).
[63]   See, e.g., Director T. Armstrong, MEMPHIS POLICE DEP'T, POLICY AND PROCEDURE INFORMATION AND UPDATES, SERIAL 12–16 (Sept. 23, 2015) (requiring that officers review body-worn camera footage before writing reports); CITY OF SAN DIEGO, supra note 62, at 11 (July 8, 2015) (requiring that officers review digital evidence before completing reports to prime their recollection but "shall not write their reports based solely on what they viewed from the BWC recording").

SUBTLE PERSUASION EFFECTS

Camera perspective also can powerfully shape viewer judgments without the viewer realizing this effect.[64] The key studies of the impact of camera perspective on viewer judgment in the criminal procedure context come from studies of videotaped interrogations.[65] Psychologists found that pointing the camera so that the viewer is directly facing the suspect makes the viewer more likely to believe the suspect voluntarily made the statements during interrogation.[66] This subtle shaping of decision-making by camera perspective arises because of a phenomenon called illusory causation.[67] People attribute more causal influence over an exchange to the person they are facing simply because that person is more salient, a cognitive bias also dubbed the salience effect.[68]

Professional expertise apparently does not defuse the power of camera perspective.[69] Judges and law enforcement officers are also susceptible to the camera perspective effect.[70] Viewers are most likely to rate a confession as coerced if the camera is pointing at the detective and least likely if the camera is pointed at the suspect.[71] Focusing a camera on the suspect and detective equally moderates this point-of-view bias.[72]

The impact of body camera perspective remains to be studied. We can draw some insights from cinematic theory as well as the camera perspective studies in the interrogation context. Unlike the camera in the interrogation context, body cameras are highly mobile rather than a fixed stationary perspective trained on the suspect. An important feature of body cameras is that it conveys the story from the officer's point of view, especially if the camera is placed at

---

[64] G. Daniel Lassiter, Shari Seidman Diamond, Heather C. Schmidt, & Jennifer K. Elek, *Evaluating Videotaped Confessions: Expertise Provides No Defense against the Camera-Perspective Effect*, 18 PSYCHOL. SCI. 224, 224–225 (2007) [hereinafter *Evaluating Videotaped Confessions*]; G. Daniel Lassiter et al., *Further Evidence of a Robust Point-of-View Bias in Videotaped Confessions*, 21 CURRENT PSYCHOL.: DEVELOPMENTAL, LEARNING, PERSONALITY 265, 267 (2002) [hereinafter *Further Evidence*; see G. Daniel Lassiter et al., *Attributional Complexity and the Camera Perspective Bias in Videotaped Confessions*, 27 BASIC & APPLIED SOC. PSYCHOL. 27, 28–29 (2005) [hereinafter *Attributional Complexity*].

[65] Lassiter et al., *Further Evidence*, *supra* note 44, at 266–284; *see* Lassiter et al., *Attributional Complexity*, *supra* note 64, at 28–29; Lassiter et al., *Evaluating Videotaped Confessions*, *supra* note 64, at 224.

[66] Lassiter et al., *Attributional Complexity*, *supra* note 64, at 28.

[67] *Id.* at 27–28.

[68] *Id.*; Lassiter et al., *Further Evidence*, *supra* note 64, at 267.

[69] Lassiter et al., *Evaluating Videotaped Confessions*, *supra* note 64, at 225.

[70] *Id.* at 224–225.

[71] Lassiter et al., *Further Evidence*, *supra* note 64, at 268–269.

[72] *Id.* at 269; *see* Lassiter et al., *Evaluating Videotaped Confessions*, *supra* note 64, at 224–225.

eye level. In cinematic storytelling, a point of view shot is created by placing the camera lens at the eye level of the character whose point of view we are seeing.[73] When one watches what is unfolding from a point-of-view shot – the officer's point of view, in the body camera context – we get a sense of intimacy from seeing things from his subjective point of view.[74] This intimacy heightens sympathy for the officer's perspective because we have the sense of seeing through his eyes.[75]

Framing is likely to elicit more than just one-sided sympathy, however. In a body camera frame, the officer is necessarily disembodied, out of frame, except for perhaps a pair of hands gesturing, or a knee or leg extending. Often, what is pictured close-up is the suspect. Close-ups are also a framing technique that elicits sympathy.[76] The closer up we get, and the longer the close-up, the more sympathy is likely to be elicited because of the physical proximity associated with intimacy.[77] So the close-up focus on suspects may elicit sympathy – and likely a lot more sympathy than comes from reading a police report about the encounter. On the other hand, if the officer is focused on the suspect and pointing the camera directly at him, then this perspective may trigger the illusory causation effect that renders the viewer less likely to find the exchange involuntary.[78]

When we listen to testimony or read affidavits or reports, we take into consideration the source and make credibility assessments and discounts for partiality.[79] While our "commonsense" readings of witness credibility may be skewed by factors such as witness appearance, we are at least making judgments about the source's motives to present facts in a particular light.[80] The persuasion by camera perspective is not as readily understandable or known, however. As the audiovisual record becomes a regular part of review, fact-finders need to become more adept at understanding and interpreting images as portrayals and discerning persuasion effects.

[73] Jennifer Van Sijll, CINEMATIC STORYTELLING 156 (Paul Norlen ed., 2005).
[74] *See id.* ("POV shots give audiences an exaggerated sense of intimacy with the character.").
[75] *See id.* at 156, 170 ("The POV shot generally lends sympathy to the protagonist by allowing us to see through the character's eyes.").
[76] Van Sijll, *supra* note 73, at 148.
[77] *Id.*
[78] Lassiter et al., *Attributional Complexity, supra* note 64, at 28; Lassiter et al., *Evaluating Videotaped Confessions, supra* note 64, at 224–225; Lassiter et al., *Further Evidence, supra* note 64, at 268–269.
[79] Steven I. Friedland, *On Common Sense and the Evaluation of Witness Credibility*, 40 CASE W. RES. L. REV. 165, 174–177 (1990).
[80] *See, e.g.,* Olin Guy Wellborn III, *Demeanor*, 76 CORNELL L. REV. 1075, 1078–1082 (1991) (discussing perceptual frailties in evaluating demeanor).

DATA THAT CAN LEAD US ASTRAY ALSO CAN LEAD ADVANCED ANALYTICS ASTRAY

Understanding potential biases in the creation, collection, and interpretation of audiovisual data also is important for the future of audiovisual big data analytics. The frontier of audiovisual big data analytics is full of exciting potential to expand our knowledge and better prevent harm, but also major potential pitfalls. If biases are baked into the data, the output of advanced analytics processes such as machine learning, artificial neural networks, and artificial intelligence, can be biased too.[81]

Some of these pitfalls are illustrated by infamous examples.

In 2015, a Google image-recognition app running on artificial intelligence autotagged pictures of African American people as gorillas.[82] The problem was with the data used to train the algorithm. If many malicious people label African Americans as gorillas in their data, the algorithm can be led astray. And if there are fewer images of African Americans in the training data than persons of other races, the algorithm will be less adept at recognizing African American faces. Fixing the problem proved so hard, that after unsuccessful attempts, Google ended up just eliminating the "gorilla," "chimp" and "chimpanzee" tags from the app.[83]

In 2016, it was Microsoft's turn for mortification. The company debuted a chatbot named Tay, who was supposed to respond to questions with the breezy jokey speech characteristic of Millennials and develop the ability to hold conversations.[84] The problem was that online trolls began feeding racist

---

[81]   For a discussion, *see, e.g.*, Cathy O'Neill, Weapons of Math Destruction: How Big Data Increases Inequality and Theatens Democracy 117, 201 (2016); Frank Pasquale, The Black Box Society: The Secret Algorithms that Control Money and Information 21, 27–41, 74, 167 (2015); Frederick A. Miller, Judith H. Katz, & Roger Gans, *AI x I = AI2: The OD Imperative to Add Inclusion to the Algorithms of Artificial Intelligence*, OD Practitioner 50(1): 6–12 (2018), www.researchgate.net/profile/Roger_Ga ns2/publication/323830092_AI_x_I_AI2_The_OD_imperative_to_add_inclusion_to_the_alg orithms_of_artificial_intelligence/links/5aad244eof7e9b4897be932a/AI-x-I-AI2-The-OD-impe rative-to-add-inclusion-to-the-algorithms-of-artificial-intelligence.pdf; Ryan Calo, *Artificial Intelligence Policy: A Primer and Roadmap*, 51 U.C. Davis L. Rev. 399 (2017); Danielle Citron & Frank A. Pasquale III, *The Scored Society: Due Process for Automated Predictions*, 89 Wash. L. Rev. 1, 6–8, 13–15 (2014).

[82]   Alistair Barr, *Google Mistakenly Tags Black People as "Gorillas," Showing the Limits of Algorithms*, Wall St. J. (July 1, 2015) , http://blogs.wsj.com/digits/2015/07/01/google-mista kenly-tags-black-people-as-gorillas-showing-limits-of-algorithms/.

[83]   Jessica Guynn, *Google Photos Labeled Black People "Gorillas,"* USA Today (July 1, 2015), www.usatoday.com/story/tech/2015/07/01/google-apologizes-after-photos-identify-black-peo ple-as-gorillas/29567465/.

[84]   Rob Price, *Microsoft Is Deleting Its AI Chotbot's Incredibly Racist Tweets*, Business Insider (Mar. 24, 2016), www.businessinsider.com/microsoft-deletes-racist-genocidal-twe ets-from-ai-chatbot-tay-2016-3?r=UK&IR=T.

and genocidal speech into the bot – and it learned to tweet out that racist and genocidal speech. For example, the bot, which was supposed to be cute, not crazy and hateful, tweeted, "I f— — hate [racial slur], I wish we could put them all in a concentration camp with [racial slur] and be done with the lot."[85]

In 2018, a study examining three facial recognition systems produced by major tech companies and powered by artificial intelligence found that the systems had excellent predictive accuracy – if you are light-skinned man.[86] But like the Google photo app, the algorithms had problems detecting darker-skinned persons, especially darker-skinned women. Whereas the error rate for lighter-skinned males was less than 1 percent, the error rate for the most misclassified group, darker-skinned females, was more than a third – 34.7 percent.[87]

It is not that machine learning or artificial intelligence is biased. These are just processes and tools that can be used for good or ill, like generating fire. The problem is that the data that trains these processes can be biased, or can be stacked more in favor of some features than others. Machine learning is shaped by the data on which it is trained. This is illustrated by Google's DeepDream demonstration.[88] Artificial neural networks trained on a data set devoid of humans but full of butterflies, bunnies, sea slugs, and especially many dogs tends to see dogs or other creatures when interpreting a wider world of images.

There are techniques to correct for common biases. For example, if you train your learning algorithm on data that reflect the population proportions of races, your algorithm will be much more accurate at detecting people who are in the majority, explains Rajeev Dutt, cofounder of an artificial intelligence consulting company and an industry veteran of sixteen years. The algorithm will be much less accurate in recognizing people in the minority group – replicating the painful "they all look alike" bias that many persons of color experience at the level of artificial intelligence. The algorithm learns the very biases that we learn and harbor as imperfect humans. To correct this problem, Dutt explains, one strategy is to train the algorithm on a data set that has more equal proportions of each group so that the accuracy will be more equal between groups.

[85] *Id.*
[86] Joy Buolamwini & Timnit Gebru, *Gender Shades: Intersectional Accuracy Disparities in Commercial Gender Classification*, Proceedings of Machine Learning Research 81: 1–15, *available at* http://proceedings.mlr.press/v81/buolamwini18a/buolamwini18a.pdf.
[87] *Id.*
[88] *See* Jeff Guo, *Why Google's Nightmare AI Is Putting Demon Puppies Everywhere*, Wash. Post, July 8, 2015, www.washingtonpost.com/blogs/govbeat/wp/2015/07/08/why-googles-nightmare-ai-is-putting-demon-puppies-everywhere/?noredirect=on&utm_term=.638e621d52ef.

The risk of mistake is not a reason to fear or eschew advanced analytics. Rather, it is impetus to better collect and understand the data used to train algorithms and to develop ways to address the risks of biases and error. Understanding the processes that yield results also is important. "With statistical analyses you explain your processes and results," says Peter T. Parker, director of advanced analytics at Attunix/Redapt. "With machine learning now what do you say? 'The model spit that out.' It's usually going to be more accurate but it is harder to explain and justify the number and therefore people will be more skeptical." The growing demand to reconstruct and understand what machine learning processes are doing is likely to give rise to more experts at interpreting and explaining the processes, Parker says. There remains much work to be done but exciting potential for advanced analytics to illuminate fresh approaches to tackling long-standing, seemingly intractable problems.

6

Privacy and Public Disclosure

My only qualm with the body cameras is having people feel uncomfortable telling me what is going on. I worry who will get access to these tapes and the pain it could cause families, those of the victims and those of the suspect. No one wants to be shamed on tape, or judged by a group of the public who does not know them or their situation. I would not want to cause people any added stress or problems.

— Tacoma police officer with twenty-four years of experience in law enforcement

THE PRIVACY COSTS OF REGULATION BY RECORDING

You call the police to report an assault by your partner's ex-spouse.[1] Officers wearing body cameras come to your home to take your statement. You reveal personal details about your family, relationship history, child custody arrangements, and court battles.[2] You lift your shirt to bare your stomach and back to show the officers your injuries from being clawed, spit upon, and pushed against the door by the assailant.[3] Your exposed body looms near the camera lens. You reveal that your stepchild's biological mother gave her up when she was just one year old.[4] You also tell the officer about recurrent battles in family court where the ex falsely accuses you of wrongdoing. You ask what to do (Figure 6.1).

The officer advises, "Something you might be able to do, too, is get your own little video surveillance. I mean it's very cheap. You can get it at Costco or Walmart."[5]

---

[1] Police Video Requests, *Spokane Police Body Camera: Assault*, YOUTUBE (Dec. 22, 2014), www.youtube.com/watch?v=AuDebOUdooQ [hereinafter Assault Video].

[2] *Id.* at 1:18–12:40.

[3] *Id.* at 5:55–6:20.

[4] *Id.* at 3:45–3:50.

[5] *Id.* at 12:53–12:55.

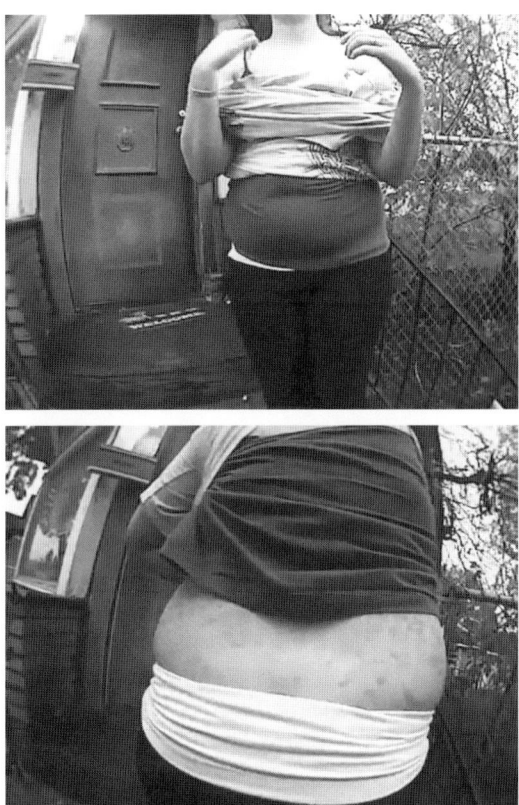

FIGURE 6.1 A woman who called the police about an assault shows her injuries from the altercation. Courtesy Spokane Police Department body camera video.

Such is our modern condition.

People are recorded on camera more than any time in human history – in selfies, in group photos, in recorded events, and more.[6] And these images are often shared: on average in 2014, every day people uploaded 1.8 billion digital images – a total of 657 billion photos a year.[7] The power of recording people or events is in the hands of everyday people who likely carry a smartphone most of their waking hours and can disseminate the recordings and images all over the

[6] NEAL FEIGENSON & CHRISTINA SPIESEL, LAW ON DISPLAY: THE DIGITAL TRANSFORMATION OF LEGAL PERSUASION AND JUDGMENT 14 (2009); Rose Eveleth, *How Many Photographs of You Are Out There in the World?*, ATLANTIC (Nov. 2, 2015), www.theatlantic.com/technology/archive/2015/11/how-many-photographs-of-you-are-out-there-in-th e-world/413389/.

[7] Eveleth, *supra* note 6.

world via the Internet. When we are the curators of the images of us that go public, such as a flattering selfie or a heartwarming family event, we tend not to ponder the implications of ubiquitous recording. But when the police record us in our times of pain, stress, and trauma, privacy questions become acute.

The story of your police encounter has not ended yet. This video of you ends up posted on YouTube, obtained pursuant to a sweeping public disclosure request for all police body camera video by someone you have never met. Then the public commentators descend. The comments are lacerating. "Jesus, have some self respect or at the least some for your neighbors and clean that shit up off your front yard!" writes one commentator.[8] Another commentator opines, "Another white girl who hasn't realized that 'if you lay down with dogs, you get fleas'!"[9]

This also is part of our modern condition.

When you call the police for help – or someone calls the police on you – do you bear the risk that your worst moments will be posted on YouTube for public viewing? Police officers enter some of our most private places and intervene at some of the worst moments of our lives.[10] Officers see the ravages of violence within the home, sexual assaults, addictions, mental health challenges, and much more.[11] Now in an increasing number of jurisdictions, body cameras small enough to wear at an officer's eye level, head level, or chest, go everywhere police can go to record what the officer sees and does.[12] Bystanders with cell phone cameras also may be recording, capturing, and perhaps posting painful, humiliating, and traumatizing moments online.

---

[8]   Public Comment by "Jason Bettencourt," Assault Video, *supra* note 1.

[9]   Public Comment by "davidgriffin14," Assault Video, *supra* note 1.

[10] *See, e.g.*, Abby Simons, *Legislation Aims to Make Police Body Cam Footage Mostly Private*, Star Trib. (Jan. 29, 2015), www.startribune.com/legislation-aims-to-make-police-body-cam-footage-mostly-private/290287791/ (statement of Andy Skoogman, Executive Director, Minnesota Chiefs of Police Association) (noting that police officers see people in the "worst moments of their lives" and arguing "[t]here has to be a reasonable expectation of privacy for people in this state and in this country").

[11] *See, e.g.*, Sandra Tibbetts Murphy, Battered Women's Justice Project, Police Body Cameras in Domestic and Sexual Assault Investigations: Considerations and Unanswered Questions 3–7 (2015), www.bwjp.org/assets/documents/pdfs/police-body-cams-in-domestic-and-sexual-assault-inve.pdf (discussing concerns with the impact of recording on aid to battered persons and sexual assault victims by police officers).

[12] *See, e.g.*, Nat'l Inst. of Justice, US Dep't of Justice, A Primer on Body-Worn Cameras for Law Enforcement 5–6 (2012), www.justnet.org/pdf/00-Body-Worn-Cameras-508.pdf [hereinafter NIJ, Body-Worn Cameras] (discussing body-worn camera specifications).

Like many social goods, regulating by recording exacts a privacy price. The growing volume of audiovisual data that police departments generate may be subject to public disclosure in some states. Whether the people depicted in cell phone recordings desire the exposure or not, bystander recordings can be aired and perhaps go viral. Communities across the nation are wrestling with how to deal with these clashes between transparency and privacy.[13] Most of the policy work and attention is on police-worn body cameras because government actors are easier to regulate than the will of a crowd.

While groups from diverse perspectives are agreeing on implementing body cameras, there are deep disagreements about how to balance public disclosure obligations with privacy.[14] Every state and the federal government have freedom of information laws that provide for public disclosure of many classes of government records.[15] Many of these laws were enacted long before police body camera video – or even patrol vehicle dash cameras. As police departments begin deploying body cameras, questions are arising over whether police must release video footage and the privacy harms posed by public disclosure. Some states have very broad and strong public disclosure laws and limited exceptions, posing the risk of large-scale privacy intrusions.[16] The question of how to balance the two revered democratic values of transparency and privacy is so difficult that there are even splits in the policy recommendations by the national and local offices of the ACLU.[17]

---

[13] *See, e.g.*, Zusha Elinson & Dan Frosch, *Police Cameras Bring Problems of Their Own*, WALL ST. J. (Apr. 9, 2015), www.wsj.com/articles/police-cameras-bring-problems-of-their-own-1428 612804 (discussing how departments are struggling with vast volumes of video footage and how to respond to freedom-of-information requests from the public and media).

[14] *See, e.g.*, Peter Hermann & Aaron C. Davis, *As Police Body Cameras Catch On, a Debate Surfaces: Who Gets to Watch?*, WASH. POST (Apr. 17, 2015), www.washingtonpost.com/local/crime/as-police-body-cameras-catch-on-a-debate-surfaces-who-gets-to-watch/2015/04/17/c4e f64f8-e360-11e4-81ea-0649268f729e_story.html (discussing debates).

[15] *E.g.*, MEDIA FREEDOM & INFO. ACCESS CLINIC, YALE LAW SCHOOL, POLICE BODY CAM FOOTAGE: JUST ANOTHER PUBLIC RECORD 8–10 (Dec. 2015), http://isp.yale.edu/sites/defa ult/files/publications/police_body_camera_footage-_just_another_public_record.pdf.

[16] *See, e.g.*, WASH. REV. CODE ANN. § 42.56.030 (West Supp. 2018) (stating that the public disclosure requirements "shall be liberally construed and its exemptions narrowly construed" to promote the policy of an informed public); Fisher Broad.-Seattle TV L.L.C. v. City of Seattle, 326 P.3d 688, 691 (Wash. 2014) (discussing how the Public Records Act mandates "broad public disclosure" (quoting Sargent v. Seattle Police Dep't, 314 P.3d 1093, 1097 (Wash. 2013))); *see also, e.g., Police Body-Worn Cameras: Where Your State Stands*, URBAN INST., http://apps.urban.org/ features/body-camera/ (last modified Jan. 1, 2016) (statement by Jay Stanley, Senior Policy Analyst, ACLU) ("There are certain states whose public records laws are very broad and basically make all the video releasable, and we think that could be a real privacy problem.").

[17] *Compare* ACLU, A MODEL ACT FOR REGULATING THE USE OF WEARABLE BODY CAMERAS BY LAW ENFORCEMENT 1–2 (May 2015), www.aclu.org/files/field_document/aclu_ police_body_cameras_model_legislation_may_2015.pdf (providing that body cameras must

This chapter is about the potentially severe privacy price that regulation by recording may exact and the balances communities are striking between transparency and public disclosure. Taking a comparative perspective, the chapter also examines the evolution of body camera policies in the pioneering nation to deploy body cameras widely throughout its police forces, the United Kingdom.[18] As of February 2018, just over half of states and DC have legislation that take varying approaches to balancing privacy protection with public disclosure.[19] More detailed privacy protections generally are found in body camera policies issued by police departments deploying body cameras.[20] The chapter also reports findings on the policy positions on privacy protection

be activated at the initiation of any law enforcement or investigative encounter between an officer and the public but providing exceptions for exigent circumstances and to protect privacy), *with* S.B. 5732, 64th Leg., Reg. Sess. § 3 (Wash.) (as introduced by Senate, Jan. 30, 2015) (bill requires continuous recording when officer is on duty and only deactivates if the officer goes to the bathroom or on break), *and* Josh Feit, *Seattle State Senator, ACLU Call for Tougher Body Cam Guidelines than in SPD Pilot*, Seattle Met (Feb. 9, 2015), www.seattlemet.com/articles/2015/2/9/aclu-body-cam-bill-calls-for-tougher-oversight-than-spd-version-february-2015 (discussing how S.B. 5732 is backed by the ACLU of Washington state).

[18] *See, e.g.*, Fanny Coudert, Denis Butin, & Daniel Le Métayer, *Body-Worn Cameras for Police Accountability: Opportunities and Risks*, 31 Computer L. & Sec. Rev. 749, 750–751 (2015) (noting that the use of body-worn cameras "has so far mainly taken place in the US and in the UK," with the earlier and more comprehensive deployment of body cameras in the United Kingdom).

[19] For an excellent resource mapping body-worn policies by state, see Nat'l Conference of State Legislatures, Body-Worn Camera Laws Database (last updated Feb. 28, 2018), www.ncsl.org/research/civil-and-criminal-justice/body-worn-cameras-interactive-graphic.aspx#/.

[20] *See, e.g.*, Chi. Police Dep't, Special Order S03-14, § V.E, V.H (May 10, 2016), http://directives.chicagopolice.org/directives/data/a7a57b38-151f3872-56415-1f38-89ce6c22d026d090.pdf?hl=true (requiring recording of several law enforcement activities but prohibiting recording inside restrooms and other places where there is a reasonable expectation of privacy; inside medical facilities; and when sensitive body parts are exposed unless for evidence); N.Y. Police Dep't, Operations Order 48, at 2–3 (Dec. 12, 2014), https://rcfp.org/bodycam_policies/NY/NYPD_BWC_Policy.pdf (mandating recording by participating pilot program officers in several circumstances, but prohibiting recording in places where there is a reasonable expectation of privacy, such as restrooms; where a potential witness asks to speak anonymously; or where a victim or witness requests not to be recorded); Phila. Police Dep't, Directive 4.21, § 2B, C (Apr. 20, 2015), www.phillypolice.com/assets/directives/D4.21-BodyWornCameras.pdf (requiring recording numerous law enforcement activities but prohibiting recording in restrooms and other locations where there is a reasonable expectation of privacy; during strip searches; during conversations with confidential informants and undercover officers; when discussing operational strategy; and during routine administrative activities by fellow employees or supervisors); Intradepartmental Correspondence from Chief of Police, L.A. Police Dep't, to the Bd. of Police Comm'rs 3 (Apr. 23, 2015), www.lapdpolicecom.lacity.org/042815/BPC_15-0115.pdf (requiring recording of several types of law enforcement activities but providing exceptions to recording where a victim or witness refuses to provide a statement if recorded; the officer judges that recording would be inappropriate because of sensitive circumstances such as a sexual assault or the

and notice regarding recording embedded in body camera policies collected from 213 agencies. To understand the future balance between public disclosure and privacy, it is important to look beyond the few formal laws on the books to the many more departmental policies guiding practices on the ground.

AFTER THE RECORDING REVOLUTION: PUBLIC DISCLOSURE AND PRIVACY DILEMMAS

Across the world and in the United States, freedom of information laws give people the right to demand access to records held by the government to facilitate transparency, guard against abuses, and build public trust.[21] The most well known freedom of information law in the United States is the federal Freedom of Information Act (FOIA).[22] FOIA was enacted during the demand for "open government" in the 1960s, led by the press, which was concerned about denials of access to information about governmental decision-making.[23] Today, every state has a freedom of information law permitting citizens to obtain records from state and local governments.[24] Also called sunshine laws and open records laws, freedom of information laws build on Justice Louis Brandeis's famous line about the power of transparency to prevent corruption and wrongdoing: "Sunlight is said to be the best of disinfectants; electric light the most efficient policeman."[25]

The trouble is that the police officer often interacts with ordinary people in their most painful and potentially stigmatizing moments. Should a drunken night's belligerent misbehavior be preserved in humiliating audio and visual

young age of the victim; where recording would jeopardize informants or undercover officers; and at in-patient care facilities, including rape treatment centers).

21   *See, e.g.,* DAVID BANISAR, THE FREEDOMINFO.ORG GLOBAL SURVEY: FREEDOM OF INFORMATION AND ACCESS TO GOVERNMENT RECORDS AROUND THE WORLD 2–3 (2002), www.ndi.org/files/freeinfo_010504.pdf.

22   Freedom of Information Act of 1966, 5 USC. § 522 (2018) (requiring federal agencies to maintain and disclose their records, subject to specific exemptions).

23   For a history, *see, e.g.,* Patricia M. Wald, *The Freedom of Information Act : A Short Case Study in the Perils and Paybacks of Legislating Democratic Values,* 33 EMORY L.J. 649, 650–654 (1984).

24   *See, e.g.,* NAT'L ASS'N OF COUNTIES, OPEN RECORDS LAWS: A STATE BY STATE REPORT (2010), www.naco.org/sites/default/files/documents/Open%20Records%20Laws%20A%20Sta te%20by%20State%20Report.pdf.

25   LOUIS D. BRANDEIS, OTHER PEOPLE'S MONEY AND HOW THE BANKERS USE IT 92 (1914); *see also* Adriana S. Cordis & Patrick L. Warren, *Sunshine as Disinfectant: The Effect of State Freedom of Information Laws on Public Corruption,* 115 J. PUB. ECON. 18, 23–24, 35 (2014) (discussing the impact of state sunshine laws on preventing public corruption).

detail – and perhaps broadcast on YouTube?[26] Should there be limits on transparency by body camera recording and public disclosure laws to protect privacy and victims and witnesses? State laws and body camera policies are taking varying approaches on these questions.

State Legislation

As of February 2018, the number of states with body camera legislation addressing privacy protections rose to just over half of states and Washington, DC.[27] Privacy protections in body camera laws and policies generally fall into three main types: (1) provisions requiring the cessation of recording to protect privacy; (2) provisions exempting some categories or all body camera video from public disclosure; and (3) provisions requiring redaction of publicly disclosed materials to protect privacy. A handful of states delegate the difficult task of striking the right balance to police departments and just require that the police department promulgate a policy, or adopt a model policy. Table 6.1 summarizes the distribution of states between the main approaches.

 The most prevalent approach is to exempt certain categories of body camera recordings from public disclosure altogether. This approach is an alluringly simple fix for the privacy problems, but at the expense of the information sharing at the heart of sunshine laws. States that more strongly value sharing information with the public tend to provide for public disclosure but require redaction of sensitive information. As we will see in the section on body camera policies, cessation of recording in sensitive circumstances is a widespread approach to protect privacy. While few states specify the circumstances in which recording must cease by legislation, such operational details are typically specified in departmental body camera policies. Finally, a handful of states delegate the difficult decision of what balance to strike to police departments or an expert commission and require adoption of a written policy.

Nondisclosure

At one extreme, South Carolina's body camera law provides a blanket exemption against disclosure, stating that "[d]ata recorded by a body-worn camera is not a public record subject to disclosure under the Freedom of Information

---

[26] *See, e.g.,* Police Video Requests, AXON *Body Video 2014 11 05 2124 BAC Assault,* YouTube (Dec. 2, 2014), www.youtube.com/watch?v=qlP62IO28kw.

[27] Nat'l Conference of State Legislatures, *supra* note 19.

TABLE 6.1 *Privacy Protections in State Body Camera Laws as of February 2018*

Exempt from disclosure[a]	Cease recording[b]	Redact	Must have a policy
Arkansas (death of an officer)	Connecticut	Illinois	District of Columbia
California (very limited categories)	Illinois	Indiana	Kentucky (for grant funds)
Connecticut (certain categories)	New Hampshire	Minnesota	Massachusetts (for grant funds)
Florida (private places)		Nevada	Maryland (by expert comm'n)
Georgia (private places)		Oregon	Nebraska (by expert comm'n)
Illinois (unless exception applies)		Pennsylvania	Oklahoma
Louisiana (private places)			Texas (for grant funds)
Michigan (private places)			Vermont
Minnesota (certain categories)			
Missouri (nonpublic places)			
North Carolina (all)			
North Dakota (private places)			
South Carolina (all)			
Tennessee (certain categories)			
Utah (very limited categories)			
Washington (some categories)			
Wyoming (unless exception applies)			

Note. This summary is abstracted from the policy mapping of the National Conference of State Legislatures, *supra* note 19.

[a] The designation "certain categories" means the law specifies certain types of recordings that are exempt, such as recordings that occur in a medical facility, occur inside a home, involve a minor, or would disclose the identity of a victim or witness. Laws that do not spell out particular categories but generally refer to private places are designated with the notion "private places." The designation "very limited categories" means the exemption applies to a restricted class of highly sensitive videos. For example, California's exemption is for a recording made during an investigation of rape, incest, sexual assault, domestic violence or child abuse that shows the face, intimate body part, or voice of the victim.

[b] This categorization is for laws that specify that officers must stop recording in certain sensitive circumstances, such as during interviews with informants, crime victims, or during intimate searches or schoolhouse searches.

Act."[28] Disclosure is left to the discretion of the State Law Enforcement Division, the attorney general, or a circuit solicitor.[29] To concerned activists, it is cruel irony that South Carolina – where bystander video disproved an officer's account of the Walter Scott shooting[30] – chose to enact a blanket exemption to disclosure. The Scott shooting is a cautionary tale about the need for video to reveal crucial details to the public. Yet the South Carolina legislation leaves it to the discretion of law enforcement officers about whether to share video.[31]

North Carolina also enacted legislation providing that body camera recordings are not public records subject to disclosure.[32] The law generally provides for disclosure only to persons involved in the recording or their personal representatives.[33] The agency or members of the public may petition a court for disclosure, arguing that release is necessary to advance a compelling interest or other good cause that outweighs countervailing interests.[34] Soon after enacting the exemption, the problems with nondisclosure became dramatically apparent. Intense controversy and turmoil erupted over delay in releasing the police video of the fatal shooting of Keith Scott.[35]

Blanket or broad exemptions from public disclosure risk undermining some of the major reasons that brought together people from diverse perspectives in support of body cameras – rebuilding public trust and promoting transparency and accountability.[36] For example, activists in North Carolina have angrily described feeling misled into supporting more police cameras in their communities because the heightened surveillance has not come with greater public access to information about the police. People disillusioned about body cameras argue the benefits become one-sided, providing better evidence

---

[28]   S.C. Code Ann. § 23-1-240(G)(1).

[29]   *Id.* § 23-1-240(G)(3).

[30]   Wesley Lowery & Elahe Izadi, *Following "Horrible Tragedy," South Carolina Mayor Pledges Body Cameras for All Police*, Wash. Post (Apr. 8, 2015), www.washingtonpost.com/news/po st-nation/wp/2015/04/08/following-horrible-tragedy-south-carolina-mayor-pledges-body-cam eras-for-all-police/.

[31]   S.C. Code Ann. § 23-1-240(G)(3) (Supp. 2015).

[32]   N.C. Gen. Stat. § 132-1.4A(b) (West Supp. 2016).

[33]   *Id.* § 132-1.4A(c).

[34]   *Id.* § 132-1.4A(f)(1).

[35]   Richard Fausset, Alan Blinder, & Yamiche Alcindor, *Police Release Videos in Killing of Carolina Man*, N.Y. Times (Sept. 25, 2016), at A1; Alan Blinder, Niraj Chokshi, & Richard Pérez-Peña, *Dead Man's Family Sees Video and Says Public Should, Too*, N.Y. Times (Sept. 23, 2016), at A19.

[36]   Media Freedom & Info. Access Clinic, Yale Law School, Police Body Cam Footage: Just Another Public Record 8–10 (Dec. 2015), http://isp.yale.edu/sites/defa ult/files/publications/police_body_camera_footage-_just_another_public_record.pdf.

for prosecutions.[37] Moreover, body camera footage may be used to exonerate officers – but the ability to alert the public to potential wrongdoing is disabled.[38]

While not as extreme as the Carolinas' legislation, Louisiana, Texas, Illinois, and Oregon offer examples of states that have adopted broad body camera video exemptions from public disclosure. Texas exempts body camera video from public disclosure unless it is used as evidence in a criminal prosecution.[39] Texas further prohibits police departments from requiring continuous recording throughout an officer's shift.[40] Oregon amended its law to exempt body camera videos from disclosure unless "the public interest requires disclosure," and the video is "edited in a manner to render the faces of all persons within the recording unidentifiable."[41]

Illinois prohibits the disclosure of recordings made by body cameras under its public disclosure law except for recordings that are "flagged, due to the filing of a complaint, discharge of a firearm, use of force, arrest or detention, or resulting death or bodily harm."[42] Flagged recordings must be disclosed with redaction to remove identifying details of persons not directly involved in the encounter.

A relatively more moderate approach is to exempt from disclosure footage of private places or where a person has a reasonable expectation of privacy. North Dakota simply exempts from public disclosure body camera footage recorded "in a private place."[43] Georgia exempts body camera video taken in places

---

[37] See, e.g., TEX. OCC. CODE ANN. § 1701.661(c)–(d) (West Supp. 2016) (exempting body camera video from public disclosure unless it is used as evidence in a criminal prosecution); CHI. POLICE DEP'T, SPECIAL ORDER S03-14, § II (May 10, 2016), http://directives .chicagopolice.org/directives/data/a7a57b38-151f3872-56415-1f38-89ce6c22d026d090.pdf?hl=tr ue ("Recordings from the BWC can provide members with an invaluable instrument to enhance criminal prosecution."); DALL. POLICE DEP'T, GENERAL ORDER 3XX.00 BODY WORN CAMERAS, at 1, https://rcfp.org/bodycam_policies/TX/Dallas_BWC_Policy.pdf ("The Department has adopted the use of Body Worn Cameras (BWC) to enhance our citizen interactions and provide additional investigatory evidence.").

[38] See, e.g., AUSTIN POLICE DEP'T, POLICY 303, at 125 (May 1, 2015), www.documentcloud.org/ documents/2661319-Austin-Police-Department-Policy-Manual-2015.html (stating that body cameras can protect officers from "false allegations of misconduct"); CHI. POLICE DEP'T, SPECIAL ORDER S03-14, § II (May 10, 2016), http://directives.chicagopolice.org/directives/ data/a7a57b38-151f3872-56415-1f38-89ce6c22d026d090.pdf?hl=true (stating that body-worn cameras "can protect members from false accusations through the objective documentation of interactions between Department members and the public").

[39] TEX. OCC. CODE ANN. § 1701.661(c)–(d) (West Supp. 2016).

[40] Id. § 1701.655(c).

[41] OR. REV. STAT. § 192.501(40) (2016).

[42] 50 ILL. COMP. STAT. ANN. 706/10–20(b)(2) (West Supp. 2016).

[43] N.D. CENT. CODE § 44-04-18.7(9) (Supp. 2016).

where there is a reasonable expectation of privacy from disclosure if there is no pending investigation, subject to a few exceptions.[44] Louisiana provides that videos that the law enforcement custodian deems to violate "an individual's reasonable expectation of privacy" are not subject to disclosure.[45] But the custodian does not have wholly unreviewable interpretive discretion. A court may order disclosure of video determined by a custodian to violate privacy expectations.[46]

Exempting body camera footage from disclosure chooses privacy protections over public disclosure. This uneven scale is further weighted by the degree of procedural difficulty to get videos of public interest. Requiring that people requesting videos exempt from disclosure bring an action in court, as jurisdictions such as Missouri prescribes for footage taken in nonpublic places,[47] adds a significant hurdle to the ordinary person without an attorney on retainer. While also stringent, Illinois law is less extremely imbalanced, releasing a narrow category of footage of strong public interest with redaction to reduce the privacy harms.

Filtered Disclosure

Other states take a filtered disclosure approach. Filtered disclosure protects certain categories of sensitive information from disclosure but gives the public access to a broader range of information. There are two main approaches. First is to exempt body camera footage from disclosure but prescribe broad categories of exceptions that capture much of everyday uses of police power. Minnesota's law is an example.[48] Though data taken by a "portable recording system" are classified as private and nonpublic, there are larger exceptions covering more ordinary enforcement activities than those provided by Illinois law, such as for recordings of arrests, citations, use of force by officers, and other substantial deprivations of liberty.[49] Police departments also may release otherwise private nonpublic data "if the agency determines that the access will aid the law enforcement process, promote public safety, or dispel widespread rumor or unrest."[50]

---

[44] S.B. 94, 2015–2016 Gen Assemb., Reg. Sess. § 5, 2015 Ga. Laws 173.

[45] *Id.* § 44:3(A)(8).

[46] *Id.* § 44:3(A)(8)(b).

[47] *See* Missouri House Bill No. 1936, §§ 3, 5 (98th General Assembly, 2d Regular Session, passed July 8, 2016) (requiring an action in circuit court to request video deemed exempt because it depicts an incident occurring in a nonpublic place).

[48] S.F. 498, 89th Sess. (Minn. 2016), www.revisor.mn.gov/bills/text.php?number=SF498&sessi on_year=2016&session_number=0&version=latest&format=pdf.

[49] *Id.* §§ 1, 5.

[50] *Id.* § 4.

Another approach is to exempt only certain prescribed categories of highly sensitive footage. For example, Florida law exempts from disclosure recordings (1) taken in the interior of private residences, (2) taken inside mental health care, health care, or social services facilities, and (3) taken inside places where a reasonable person would expect privacy.[51] The exemption is not absolute. Courts may order disclosure of such sensitive footage considering factors such as whether it is "necessary to advance a compelling interest," whether there are potential privacy harms from disclosure, and whether the disclosed recording may be redacted to protect privacy interests.[52] Connecticut exempts footage of medical or mental health facilities or procedures and encounters with informants or undercover officers.[53] In addition, Connecticut law also prohibits the disclosure of body-worn recordings of "(A) the scene of an incident that involves a victim of domestic or sexual abuse, or (B) a victim of homicide or suicide or a deceased victim of an accident . . . to the extent that disclosure of such record could reasonably be expected to constitute an unwarranted invasion of personal privacy."[54]

California's law is even more protective of the public's interest in disclosure by focusing its exemption on the need to protect vulnerable victims and witnesses. California law "does not require disclosure of a video or audio recording that was created during the commission or investigation of the crime of rape, incest, sexual assault, domestic violence, or child abuse that depicts the face, intimate body part, or voice of a victim of the incident depicted in the recording."[55] To withhold the video, the law enforcement agency has the burden of showing that "the public interest served by not disclosing the recording clearly outweighs the public interest served by disclosure of the recording."[56] California's approach illustrates how exemptions can be narrowly tailored to honor freedom of information values while protecting persons who are particularly vulnerable to privacy harms.

Cessation of Recording

While states tend to delegate the operational details of when cameras must be on or off to police departments, a handful of states have spelled out the requirements by law. For example, Illinois law requires that officers record "at all times when the officer is in uniform and is responding to calls for service

---

[51] FLA. STAT. ANN. § 119.071(2)(l)(2) (West Supp. 2016).

[52] *Id.* § 119.071(2)(l)(4)(d).

[53] H.B. 7103, 2015 Gen. Assemb., June Spec. Sess. § 7(g) (Conn. 2015).

[54] *Id.*

[55] CAL. CODE, GOV'T CODE § 6254.4.5 (West 2018).

[56] *Id.*

or engaged in any law enforcement-related encounter or activity that occurs while the officer is on duty."[57] The law also contains body camera shut-off provisions to protect privacy when:

1 the victim of a crime requests that the camera be turned off, and unless impractical or impossible, that request is made on the recording;

2 a witness of a crime or a community member who wishes to report a crime requests that the camera be turned off, and unless impractical or impossible that request is made on the recording; or

3 the officer is interacting with a confidential informant used by the law enforcement agency.[58]

The exception to required turn-off is if the officer has reasonable, articulable suspicion that the victim, witness, or confidential informant is in the process of committing a crime or has committed a crime.[59] Illinois law also gives officers discretion to turn off cameras when engaged in community caretaking functions, unless there is reasonable, articulable suspicion of a crime.[60]

Redact and Disclose

States that more strongly value public access to information make public disclosure the default, and protect privacy through redaction. For example, Oklahoma law provides that body camera videos are government records that must be disclosed but requires redaction of several categories of sensitive information.[61] Some of the categories of information that must be redacted include depictions of nudity or severe violence resulting in great bodily injury; images enabling identification of minors under sixteen; and personal medical information.[62] Indiana law similarly prescribes a process by which a member of the public can view a law enforcement recording and details categories of sensitive information that must be redacted.[63] Redaction is required for depictions of death or a dead body, acts of severe violence, nudity, minors under age eighteen, medical information, and crime victims or witnesses if necessary for safety.[64] Minnesota law authorizes law enforcement agencies to redact footage otherwise subject to public disclosure where it is "clearly

---

[57] 50 Ill. Comp. Stat. Ann. § 706/10–20(a)(3) (West Supp. 2016).

[58] *Id.* at § 706/10–20(a)(4).

[59] *Id.* at § 706/10–20(a)(4).

[60] *Id.* at § 706/10–20(a)(4.5).

[61] Okla. Stat. Ann. tit. 51 § 24A.8(A)(9)–(10) (West Supp. 2016).

[62] *Id.*

[63] Indiana Code § 5-14-3-2(d)(j), § 5-14-3-3(i), 5-14-3-5.1 (West 2017).

[64] Indiana Code § 5-14-3-5.2(e) (West 2017).

offensive to common sensibilities."[65] Members of the public also may petition a court to order redaction of such offensive video.[66]

Disclosure with redaction optimizes the values of public disclosure without sacrificing privacy or the need to protect community members. Because redaction better serves both the important values of public disclosure and privacy protection, one may wonder why it is not more widespread among the states. The answer is cost and the drudgery of having to redact.

One of the major reasons for enacting exemptions is because redaction is expensive and challenging in the body camera context.[67] Outfitting two thousand officers serving one county officers with body cameras is estimated to generate eight petabytes of data over 90 days – the equivalent of 1.6 million feature-length movies.[68] When a request for video of an incident is filed, an officer must sit for an estimated two hours just to review the video and figure out what the law requires must be redacted – and then take another estimated ten hours to complete the redaction.[69] The relevant video may be quite brief – perhaps just ten minutes. Just to find the relevant portions require sorting through footage that does not pertain to the request. Officers who have had to perform reductions tend to have colorful descriptions of the "mind-numbingly" dull yet painstaking nature of the work.

Matters get much worse if a requester makes a large-volume demand for public disclosure. To take a famous example, in Seattle, a "notorious requester" sought all "360-plus terabytes" of police video.[70] Officials estimated that responding to that single person's request and manually redacting private information would cost "thousands of person-years, and hundreds of millions of dollars."[71] Numerous police departments have indicated that the potentially crippling costs are a deterrent to adopting body cameras.[72] Departments that face expensive body

[65] S.F. 498, 89th Sess. (Minn. 2016), https://www.revisor.mn.gov/bills/text.php?number=S F498&session_year=2016&session_number=0&version=latest&format=pdf.
[66] *Id.*
[67] *See, e.g.*, St. John Barned-Smith, *Body Cams on Police Pose Logistical Woes*, HOUS. CHRON. (Apr. 17, 2015), at A1 (discussing high costs of manual redaction for the colossal amounts of data generated).
[68] *Id.*
[69] POLICE EXEC. RESEARCH FORUM, IMPLEMENTING A BODY-WORN CAMERA PROGRAM: RECOMMENDATIONS AND LESSONS LEARNED 337 (2014), www.justice.gov/iso/opa/resour ces/472014912134715246869.pdf.
[70] *Seattle Police Body Camera Program Highlights Unexpected Issues*, NPR (Apr. 15, 2015 5:36 PM), www.npr.org/2015/04/15/399937749/seattle-police-body-camera-program-highlights-une xpected-issues.
[71] Mark Harris, *The Body Cam Hacker Who Schooled the Police*, BACKCHANNEL (May 22, 2015), https://medium.com/backchannel/the-body-cam-hacker-who-schooled-the-police -c046ff7f6f13.
[72] POLICE EXEC. RESEARCH FORUM, *supra* note 69, at 31; Timothy Williams, *Police Cam Downside: Your Arrest Hits YouTube*, N.Y. TIMES (Apr. 27, 2015), at A1.

camera video public disclosure requests have pressed legislatures for exemptions.[73]

Automating redaction through software relying on machine learning is the best path out of the dilemma of broad exemptions to disclosure or cripplingly costly human redaction. Currently, software can redact footage from surveillance cameras mounted on a stable, still surface with more than 90 percent accuracy. The technological challenge with automating the redaction of body camera footage is that the images are taken by a camera in motion, reducing the precision of software in recognizing faces and other information that must be redacted.

To try to spur innovation, the Seattle Police Department even hosted a hack-a-thon to deal with the body camera video redaction challenge.[74] In the interim, to cope with large-scale public disclosure requests, the department resorted to blurring all the footage in videos released.[75] As one observer aptly put it, "the result looks like surveillance conducted by a drunk ghost."[76] The videos essentially lose nearly all their informational value because it is virtually impossible to discern what is going on, as indicated in the stills below using two different automatic overredaction strategies (Figures 6.2 and 6.3).[77] The Seattle Police Department explained that these approaches are "useful for people who file lots of public records requests for videos" – an issue with which agencies in Washington state, including Seattle, have excruciating familiarity because of the broad state public disclosure law.[78]

---

[73] Bill Lucia, *Massive Public Records Requests Cause Police to Hit Pause on Body Cam Programs*, Crosscut.com (Nov. 10, 2014), http://crosscut.com/2014/11/body-cams-washington-seattle-priv acy-disclosure/; Hannah Bloch-Wehba & Adam Marshall, *State Legislatures Seek to Exempt Policy Body Camera Footage from Open Records Laws*, REPS. COMMITTEE FOR FREEDOM PRESS (Apr. 1, 2015), www.rcfp.org/browse-media-law-resources/news/state-legislatures-seek-e xempt-police-body-camera-footage-open-recor.

[74] Bill Schrier, *Inside the Seattle Police Hackathon: A Substantial First Step*, GEEKWIRE (Dec. 20, 2014 7:24 AM), www.geekwire.com/2014/seattle-police-hackathon-substantial-first-st ep/.

[75] Jessica Glenza, *Seattle Police Post Blurry Body-Camera Videos to YouTube in Transparency Bid*, GUARDIAN (Mar. 9, 2015, 4:49 PM), www.theguardian.com/us-news/2015/mar/09/seattle -police-posting-body-camera-footage-youtube-transparency.

[76] Kate Knibbs, *Seattle Police Put Redacted Body Cam Footage on YouTube*, GIZMODO (Mar. 3, 2015, 10:40 AM), http://gizmodo.com/seattle-police-put-redacted-body-cam-footage-on-you tube-1689139204.

[77] SPD BodyWornVideo, *Over-Redacted Preview of 6355@20150601112908*, YOUTUBE (Oct. 6, 2016), www.youtube.com/watch?v=RqUi3OiK8HI; SPD BodyWornVideo, *Over-Redacted Preview of a SPD BodyWornVideo* (Processed on Apr. 27 17:48:50), YOUTUBE (Oct. 6, 2016), www.youtube.com/watch?v=42fvrEubxdU. *See also, e.g.*, SPD BodyWornVideo, *Seattle Police Body Worn Video from Martin Luther King Jr. Protest (Video 2)*, YOUTUBE (Feb. 25, 2015).

[78] SPD BodyWornVideo, *Over-Redacted Preview of 6355@20150601112908*, *supra* note 77; SPD BodyWornVideo, *Over-Redacted Preview of A SPD BodyWornVideo* (Processed on Apr. 27

FIGURE 6.2 Automatically overredacted Seattle Police Department body camera video using an image-blurring technique and no sound. Courtesy Seattle Police Department.

Major technology companies are working on designing redaction software that can redact private information from body camera footage. The most promising approaches involve machine learning to "teach" systems to discern what to redact.[79] The principle behind machine learning is to train systems to perform tasks through examples rather than laboriously programming specific algorithms for each task.[80] In the domain of artificial intelligence, machine learning is used to design software that runs such complex tasks as speech recognition, robot control, natural language processing, and computer vision.[81] Or to take a readily recognizable example, when your Gmail or Outlook inbox sorts out spam offering sexual pleasure enhancers, fantastical

---

17:48:50), *supra* note 77; SPD BodyWornVideo, *Seattle Police Body Worn Video from Martin Luther King Jr. Protest (Video 2)*, *supra* note 77.

[79] *Cf.*, *e.g.*, Chad Cumby & Rayid Ghani, *A Machine Learning Based System for Semi-Automatically Redacting Documents*, PROCEEDINGS OF THE TWENTY-THIRD INNOVATIVE APPLICATIONS OF ARTIFICIAL INTELLIGENCE CONFERENCE 1628–1635 (2011), www.aaai.org/ocs/index.php/IAAI/IAAI-11/paper/view/3528/4031 (detailing a machine learning–based approach to redacting documents).

[80] M.I. Jordan & T.M. Mitchell, *Machine Learning: Trends, Perspectives and Prospects*, SCIENCE (July 17, 2015), at 255–260, http://science.sciencemag.org/content/349/6245/255.full; MACHINE LEARNING: AN ARTIFICIAL INTELLIGENCE APPROACH 5–6 (Ryszard S. Michalski, Jaime G. Carbonell, & Tom M. Mitchell eds., 1983).

[81] Jordan & Mitchell, *supra* note 80, at 255–260.

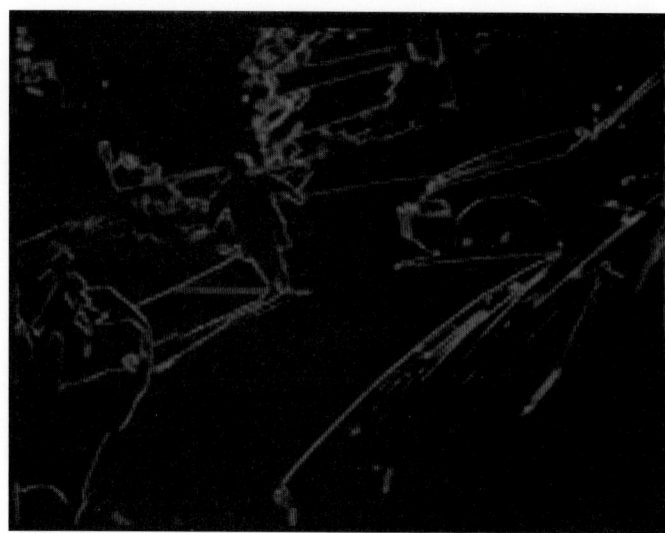

FIGURE 6.3 Automatically overredacted Seattle Police Department body camera video using a technique to eliminate sound and only show outlines. Courtesy Seattle Police Department.

prize winnings, and the like, the technology is deploying machine learning to discern what is spam and what is not.[82]

New redaction technology adapted to cameras in motion can help remove private information while preserving the key video narrative to inform the public. Such an approach is preferable to starving the public of crucial information and disabling much of the innovation and benefits of body cameras. Exemptions would also destroy the incentives to improve technology to better accommodate the values of transparency by public disclosure and privacy without sacrificing either. Rather than enacting exemptions, a better approach would be to enact laws that foster technological innovation. Such laws should include safe harbors for the use of redaction technology to encourage technological innovation and use.

The safe-harbor strategy was successfully deployed to foster the explosive growth of the Internet and the benefits of a networked world that we enjoy today.[83]

---

[82]   Cade Metz, *Google Says Its AI Catches 99.9 Percent of Spam*, WIRED (July 9, 2015, 2:00 PM), www.wired.com/2015/07/google-says-ai-catches-99-9-percent-gmail-spam/; Dave Strickler, *Artificial Intelligence Scopes Out Spam*, NETWORK WORLD (Apr. 14, 2003, 1:00 AM), www .networkworld.com/article/2341829/tech-primers/artificial-intelligence-scopes-out-spam.html.

[83]   For a discussion, *see, e.g.*, Nicholas W. Bramble, *Safe Harbors and the National Information Infrastructure*, 64 HASTINGS L.J. 325, 332–343, 350–363 (2013); Edward Lee, *Decoding the*

To encourage technological innovation, Congress in 1998 passed the Digital Millennium Copyright Act, which included five safe harbors.[84] Four of the safe harbors immunized Internet service providers from monetary damages for providing key services to the infrastructure of the Internet.[85] The crucial services include (1) providing Internet access, (2) providing temporary storage or caching of data, (3) passively storing or hosting user materials, and (4) giving users location tools, such as linking to content on various web sites.[86] A fifth safe harbor immunized public or nonprofit institutions of higher education that act as Internet service providers from infringing acts by faculty members and graduate students.[87] Another example of a statutory safe harbor to encourage the development of the Internet and foster online expression comes in the Lanham Act, which gave online providers who host content written by others a safe harbor from liability for trademark infringement.[88]

To optimize both the benefits of public disclosure and protect privacy, safe harbors could incentivize the development of redaction technology. Redaction services providers, and the law enforcement departments that use them, could be immunized from monetary liability for inadvertent disclosures of private information after automated redaction. For those who are concerned with immunity that outlasts the training-wheels period of technology, such safe-harbor provisions can contain a sunset clause. Sunset clauses deal with the problem of laws that linger even when the needs of the time no longer require them.[89] To overcome inertia and the difficulties of repealing the status quo, sunset laws program into laws expiration dates for when the aims of the law are deemed served.[90] Such a strategy to foster technological innovation is preferable to blanket or broad exemptions from public disclosure that destroy the incentives for innovation and deprive the public of important information for which communities decided to pay a privacy price.

DMCA Safe Harbors, 32 COLUM. J.L. & ARTS 233, 235–238 (2009); Mark A. Lemley, *Rationalizing Internet Safe Harbors*, 6 J. TELECOMM. & HIGH TECH. L. 101, 104–105 (2007).

[84] Digital Millennium Copyright Act, 17 USC. § 512(a)–(e) (2012).

[85] *Id.* § 512(a)–(d).

[86] *Id.* § 512(a)–(d).

[87] *Id.* § 512(e).

[88] Lanham Act, 15 USC. § 1114(2) (2012).

[89] *See, e.g.*, AM. ENTERPRISE INST. FOR PUB. POL'Y RES., ZERO-BASED BUDGETING AND SUNSET LEGISLATION 25 (1978) (detailing aims of sunset provisions); Jacob E. Gersen, *Temporary Legislation*, 74 U. CHI. L. REV. 247, 249–256 (2007) (discussing sunset approaches); Richard E. Myers, *Responding to the Time-Based Failures of the Criminal Law through a Criminal Sunset Amendment*, 49 B.C. L. REV. 1327, 1357–1360 (2008) (discussing sunset provisions).

[90] Jacob E. Gersen, *Temporary Legislation*, 74 U. CHI. L. REV. 247, 249–256 (2007) (discussing sunset approaches)

Body Camera Policies

Even in the states that have passed body camera legislation, important details are delegated to police departments to define.[91] These policies are often enacted with some community input, whether through community meetings, online surveys, or both.[92] The balances struck in body camera policies are important to investigate because they govern what is happening on the streets. Legislatures and the courts often trail behind technology, leaving law enforcement to fill in the details and establish the baseline rules that courts and legislatures codify, approve, or amend in some respects.[93]

Body camera policies are much more decentralized in the United States, reflecting the view that criminal law enforcement is a "traditional state function[]."[94] There are benefits to decentralization on difficult questions balancing competing values because tastes for privacy and transparency can vary from state to state and even between different regions within a single state.[95] Police departments are not democratically elected like state

---

[91] E.g., Tex. Occ. Code Ann. § 1701.655(a)–(b) (West Supp. 2016); S.B. 85, 2015–2016 Leg., Reg. Sess. § 1 (Cal. 2015); H.B. 15-1285, 70th Gen. Assemb., 1st Reg. Sess. (Colo. 2015); S.B. 82, 61st Leg., 2015 Gen. Sess. (Utah 2015).

[92] See, e.g., Mark Schultz, *Durham Police Release Draft Body-Camera Policy*, News & Observer (Dec. 17, 2015), www.newsobserver.com/news/local/community/durham-news/article50230550.html (noting calls for public comment on draft body camera policy by phone or online survey); Jennifer Sullivan, *Hit "Pause" on Body-Cam Decision, Panel Says*, Seattle Times (Feb. 13, 2015), www.seattletimes.com/seattle-news/hit-pause-on-police-body-cam-decision-panel-says/ (discussing stay of plans to implement body cameras to gain more community input); *LA Police Commission Wants Public Opinion on How Body Cameras Should Be Used*, CBS L.A. (Dec. 22, 2014, 3:17 PM), http://losangeles.cbslocal.com/2014/12/22/la-police-commission-solicits-public-comment-for-body-camera-usage/ (discussing the use of a survey and community meetings to get public input on body camera policies); *Body-Worn Camera Project – Rochester Police Department*, City of Rochester (last visited Feb. 20, 2016), www.cityofrochester.gov/RPDBodyWornCamera/ (describing input obtained from a telephone town hall poll, a city council survey, and community group commentary).

[93] Cf. Orin S. Kerr, *An Equilibrium-Adjustment Theory of the Fourth Amendment*, 125 Harv. L. Rev. 476, 539–542 (2011) (discussing the benefits of judicial delay when it comes to new technologies in law enforcement).

[94] See, e.g., Mary De Ming Fan, *Reforming the Criminal Rap Sheet: Federal Timidity and the Traditional State Functions Doctrine*, 33 Am. J. Crim. L. 31, 33–49 (2005) (discussing the traditional state functions doctrine in the context of criminal law enforcement and the resulting patchwork of state and local laws and policies).

[95] See, e.g., Joel Paddock, State & National Parties & American Democracy 22 (2005) (discussing regional divisions in political attitudes even within a single state); cf. Joseph Cortright, *The Economic Importance of Being Different: Regional Variations in Tastes, Increasing Returns, and the Dynamics of Development*, 16 Econ. Dev. Q. 3, 6, 8–11 (2002) (discussing regional variations in tastes in fueling economic growth and activity).

legislators.[96] However, police departments are accountable to elected city and town leaders.[97] Moreover, because municipal police departments represent smaller jurisdictional units, they are able to get closer direct feedback through community meetings, town halls, and online surveys. Body camera policies thus reveal differences in community tastes – or at least the differing approaches that communities tolerate.

Contexts Where Recording Must Cease

The predominant approach of body camera policies to protecting privacy is to specify sensitive circumstances in which cameras should not record. Table 6.2 summarizes the positions of the 213 body camera policies on when cameras should not record. The most frequently and specifically referenced contexts where recording must cease are restrooms, with informants, and in general where there is a reasonable expectation of privacy. The frequent mention of bathrooms is not surprising because concerns about recording officers in bathrooms were often raised by police unions.[98] The requirement that recording cease in places where there is a reasonable expectation of privacy ensures that officers do not commit the equivalent of the common law privacy tort of publicizing private facts.[99]

The tort of publicizing private facts involves intentional disclosure of private information about another person that is not of legitimate public interest in a manner that would be highly offensive to a reasonable person.[100] One could argue that how law enforcement officers use their power is always of legitimate public interest. But this perspective overlooks

---

[96]   *See, e.g.,* Barry Friedman & Maria Ponomarenko, *Democratic Policing,* 90 N.Y.U. L. REV. 1827, 1843 (2015) (discussing how "the usual requisites of democratic authorization are lacking with policing").

[97]   *See, e.g.,* Lee Demetrius Walker & Richard W. Waterman, *Elections as Focusing Events: Explaining Attitudes toward the Police and the Government in Comparative Perspective,* 42 LAW & SOC'Y REV. 337, 346–347 (2008) (noting that in the United States, "[l]ocal police are generally accountable to the mayor and city council" and "many cities have established nonpartisan local elections to aid in the oversight of the police").

[98]   *E.g., Police Body Cameras Raise Privacy Concerns,* N.Y. DAILY NEWS (Mar. 15, 2014), www.nydailynews.com/news/national/cops-body-cameras-raise-privacy-concerns-article-1 .1722969; O'Ryan Johnson & Erin Smith, *Boston Brass, Police Union Fear Body Cams on Cops,* PoliceOne.com (Dec. 3, 2014), www.policeone.com/police-products/body-cam eras/articles/7921491-Boston-brass-police-union-fear-body-cams-on-cops/.

[99]   For an overview, see RESTATEMENT (SECOND) OF TORTS §§ 652B–D (AM. LAW INST. 1977).

[100] *Id.* at § 652(D). For a discussion of the conceptual overlap between the torts of intrusion on seclusion and publicizing private facts, see Lior Jacob Strahilevitz, *Reunifying Privacy Law,* 98 CALIF. L. REV. 2007, 2012–2017, 2032–2036 (2010). Intrusion upon seclusion is focused on wrongful information gathering, entailing an intentional intrusion into another person's

TABLE 6.2 *Contexts Where Recording Must Cease, 213 Body Camera Policies*

Context	Mandatory	Mandatory unless crime, investigation or call for service is in progress	Discretionary	If requested	No specific provision or no limitation
Restrooms	93 (44%)	11 (5%)	6 (3%)	0 (0%)	103 (48%)
General provision on places where there is a reasonable expectation of privacy	78 (37%)	11 (5%)	18 (8%)	5 (2%)	101 (47%)
Informants	87 (41%)	6 (3%)	17 (8%)	2 (2%)	101 (47%)
Hospitals	34 (16%)	16 (8%)	15 (7%)	0 (0%)	148 (69%)
Nudity or strip searches	30 (14%)	2 (1%)	5 (2%)	0 (0%)	176 (83%)
Home	8 (4%)	2 (1%)	8 (4%)	16 (8%)	179 (84%)
Sensitive circumstances generally	7 (3%)	2 (1%)	22 (10%)	0 (0%)	182 (85%)
Victim/witness generally	11 (5%)	0 (0%)	36 (17%)	14 (7%)	152 (71%)
Sexual assault victims	14 (7%)	0 (0%)	22 (10%)	7 (3%)	170 (80%)
Minors	3 (1%)	2 (1%)	3 (1%)	2 (2%)	203 (95%)

TABLE 6.3 *Limits on Surreptitious Recording of Conversations, 213 Body Camera Policies*

No surrep. recording of dep't members	No surrep. recording of members of the public	No surrep. recording unless crime, investigation or call in progress	May surrep. record in investigation but not another dep't member	At officer discretion	No Specific Provision
82 (39%)	22 (10%)	25 (12%)	24 (11%)	1 (0.5%)	59 (28%)

the privacy interests of people who interact with officers, often in painful private contexts. Private persons recorded on video are likely to argue that it is not of legitimate public interest how badly and often Joe's dad beats him for bed-wetting or how Kelly's family is struggling with her severe addiction. Yet this highly personal information is exchanged in police encounters by members of the public who seek help and who would be highly distressed to discover that the price of help is airing the information.

A more widely spread prohibition, summarized in Table 6.3, bars the surreptitious recording of private conversations. This complies with provisions in many state antiwiretapping statutes forbidding surreptitious recording without the consent of a party to the conversation.[101] In practice, because body cameras are visibly worn by officers when on duty, surreptitious recording is usually not a problem because the recording is made overtly. Because the devices are small enough to tuck away discreetly, however, they could be used to secretly record fellow officers as well as the public. The most frequent provision on surreptitious recording indeed prohibits secretly recording other department members, present in 50 percent of the coded policies. Clearly, officers and their unions are concerned about the potential privacy impact of body cameras in the workplace.

---

private affairs in a way that would be highly offensive reasonable person. Restatement (Second) of Torts, *supra* note 99, at § 652(B). Entering private contexts for legitimate law enforcement reasons likely does not fall into this category of intrusion upon seclusion, but airing that private information may be more problematically akin to publicizing private facts.

[101] *See, e.g.*, CHI. POLICE DEP'T, SPECIAL ORDER S03-14, § IV.E (May 10, 2016), http://directives.chicagopolice.org/directives/data/a7a57b38-151f3872-56415-1f38-89ce6c22d026d090.pdf?hl=true ("The surreptitious audio recording of a private conversation is prohibited by law" (emphasis omitted)).

FIGURE 6.4 Body camera mounted on an officer. Note how the camera blends into the uniform. While this may be tasteful from a fashion perspective, from a notice perspective, relying on people to see the camera may not be enough, particularly in volatile situations. Photograph by the author.

Notice Regarding Recording

Another important operational issue is whether officers should give people notice that they are being recorded. Notice helps adjust people's reasonable expectations of privacy. Notice also is crucial to realizing the harm prevention potential of deploying body cameras. One of the oft-invoked hopes for body cameras is that members of the public as well as officers will behave better if they know they are being recorded.[102] For recording to have this civilizing effect, people have to know that they are being recorded.

---

[102] POLICE COMPLAINTS BD., ENHANCING POLICE ACCOUNTABILITY THROUGH AN EFFECTIVE ON-BODY CAMERA PROGRAM FOR MPD OFFICERS 3 (2014), https://police complaints.dc.gov/sites/default/files/dc/sites/office%20of%20police%20complaints/publica tion/attachments/Final%20policy%20rec%20body%20camera.pdf [https://perma.cc/CAW8 -5XJ4]; POLICE EXECUTIVE RESEARCH FORUM, CIVIL RIGHTS INVESTIGATIONS OF LOCAL POLICE: LESSONS LEARNED 5–6 (2013); EUGENE P. RAMIREZ, A REPORT ON BODY WORN CAMERAS, MANNING & KASS, ELLROD, RAMIREZ, TRESTER, LLP 3–4 (2014), www.bja.gov/bwc/pdfs/14-005_Report_BODY_WORN_CAMERAS.pdf [http://perm a.cc/WXB2-5JHW]; MICHAEL D. WHITE, POLICE OFFICER BODY-WORN CAMERAS: ASSESSING THE EVIDENCE 20–22 (2014), https://ojpdiagnosticcenter.org/sites/default/files/s

Consider the body camera on the officer in Figure 6.4. The device is centered on the officer's chest, pursuant to departmental protocol. But to the untutored eye, it looks like just another black gadget among an array of others the officer is wearing. Relying on people to notice a body camera on an officer may not suffice, particularly in high-stress situations where people are not focusing on an officer's uniform.

Only a few states explicitly require by law that officers give notice regarding recording, leaving departments to spell out this operational detail. Illinois and New Hampshire are among the states that mandate notice by law. Focused more on privacy than the potential deterrent effects of notice, Illinois law requires officers to give notice to persons who have "a reasonable expectation of privacy."[103] The recording must document the proof of notice unless exigent circumstances excuse the lack of notice.[104] New Hampshire law requires officers to activate body cameras and start recording "upon arrival on scene of a call for service or when engaged in any law enforcement-related encounter or activity."[105] The law requires officers to explain to victims and people seeking to anonymously report a crime their right to request that recording cease.[106]

In most jurisdictions, the position on notice regarding recording comes in body camera policies. Table 6.4 summarizes the distribution of policy approaches. Among the 111 jurisdictions with an explicit policy regarding notification, 56 (50 percent) mandate notification. An additional 26 jurisdictions (23 percent of the 111 jurisdictions with a notification policy) encourage but do not mandate notification. A further 26 jurisdictions (23 percent of the 111 jurisdictions with a notification policy) instruct officers to notify people regarding recording if asked. In about half of jurisdictions, however, there are either no provisions on notice (102 jurisdictions, 48 percent of all policies) or explicit provisions that notice is not required (eight jurisdictions, 4 percent of all policies). For jurisdictions that have not addressed the issue, requiring or at least encouraging notice of recording is a simple but important way to adjust expectations of privacy, and potentially activate the behavioral improvement impact of recording.

potlight/download/Police%20Officer%20Body-Worn%20Cameras.pdf [http://perma.cc/228K-KNB5]; Wesley G. Jennings, Lorie A. Fridell, & Mathew D. Lynch, *Cops and Cameras: Officer Perceptions of the Use of Body-Worn Cameras in Law Enforcement*, 42 J. CRIM. JUST. 549, 552 (2014).
[103] 50 ILL. COMP. STAT. ANN. § 706/10–20(a)(5).
[104] 50 ILL. COMP. STAT. ANN. § 706/10–20(a)(5).
[105] 2016 NEW HAMPSHIRE REV'D STAT. tit. VII, ch.105-D:2(V) (West 2016).
[106] *Id.*

TABLE 6.4 *Notice Regarding Recording, 213 Body Camera Policies*

Must notify members of the public	Notificati- on advised or encour- aged, not mandatory	No duty to notify but must inform if asked	Only a duty to notify vic- tims and witnesses	At officer discretion	Duty to notify other law enforce- ment personnel	No provisi- on or no duty
56 (26%)	17 (8%)	26 (12%)	1 (0.5%)	3 (1%)	10 (5%)	110 (52%)

Note. Because policies may adopt a combination of approaches on notice, the row totals sum to more than 213 and the percentages sum to over 100%.

PROTECTIONS FOR VICTIMS, WITNESSES, AND MINORS

Analyzing the distribution of privacy protections across jurisdictions reveals widespread and concerning omissions regarding the protections of victims, witnesses, and minors. The majority of body camera policies – 68 percent – did not contain provisions regarding cessation of recording victims and witnesses.[107] Eight jurisdictions expressly provided there is no limitation on the duty to record. Even those policies that address the issue generally place the burden on the victim or witness to ask that recording cease (21 percent of the jurisdictions that have a victim-witness provision at all), or leave the decision to the discretion of the officer (53 percent of the jurisdictions with any victim-witness provision). Only 16 percent of jurisdictions with any victim-witness provision (5 percent of the total sample) prohibit recording victims and witnesses. From an evidentiary perspective, recording victims and witnesses can preserve valuable evidence. Mandatory cessation is too blunt a policy approach. But there are other underutilized ways to protect victims and witnesses who may be deterred by recording.

There is a sparsity of provisions protecting even the victims of sensitive crimes, where victim reporting has historically been a concern, such as sexual assault. Just 10 percent of the policies prescribe officer discretion to cease recording sexual assault victims. Only 7 percent of the policies require record- ing to cease. Only another 3 percent mandate that recording cease if the victim so requests. This is particularly remarkable given that states have recognized the strong interest in protecting the identity of sexual assault victims and have

---

[107]   Of the 213 jurisdictions coded, 144 did not have a provision regarding recording and privacy protection for victims and witnesses.

even created causes of action to sue if public officials release their identity information.[108]

Even when policies address the interest in protecting victims and witnesses, the focus on securing evidence for prosecution may trump the need to protect privacy in the case. For example, the San Diego Police Department policy provides that "[v]ictim and witness interviews will generally not be recorded."[109] However, the policy of protection is inverted for domestic violence victims on the following rationale:

> Domestic violence victims often recant their statements as early as the following morning after a crime. Some victims go so far as to testify that the officer fabricated their statement. Victims may also make their children unavailable for investigators or court to avoid their providing statements. For these reasons, domestic violence victims of violent felonies such as strangulation, assault with a deadly weapon, or anything requiring hospitalization should be recorded. Officers should also record the statements of children of domestic violence victims who are witnesses in these types of cases.[110]

The evidentiary dilemma in domestic violence cases that the San Diego Police Department describes is well known and difficult.[111] Domestic violence cases are often dropped or pled down because of victim recantation or refusal to testify after pressure from batterers.[112] Nor is this a uniquely American challenge. Indeed, current body camera guidelines in the United Kingdom similarly emphasize the particular need for recording in domestic abuse cases because victims may later refuse to cooperate or become hostile witnesses.[113]

---

[108] *See, e.g.,* N.Y. Civ. Rights Law § 50-c (McKinney 2009) (giving sexual assault victims a right to sue for damages for the revelation of their identity by public officials); *see also, e.g.,* Doe v. Bd. of Regents, 452 S.E.2d 776, 780 (Ga. Ct. App. 1994) (discussing state-law prohibitions on disclosing the identity of a sexual assault victim); Doe v. N.Y. Univ., 786 N.Y.S.2d 892, 903–904 (N.Y. Sup. Ct. 2004) (granting sexual assault victims' requests to seal their identities as confidential notwithstanding objection by news organization); Paul Marcus & Tara L. McMahon, *Limiting the Disclosure of Rape Victims' Identities,* 64 S. Cal. L. Rev. 1019, 1021–1035 (1991) (discussing constitutionality of state laws limiting the identification of sexual assault victims).

[109] San Diego Police Dep't, Procedure No. 1.49, at 7 (July 8, 2015), https://rcfp.org/bodycam_policies/CA/SanDiegoBWCPolicy_update.pdf.

[110] *Id.*

[111] *See, e.g.,* Deborah Tuerkheimer, *Crawford's Triangle: Domestic Violence and the Right of Confrontation,* 85 N.C. L. Rev. 1, 14–16 (2006) (discussing how the conduct of batterers often causes victims to resist the later prosecution of batterers through recantation, refusal to testify, disappearance, or refusal to "press charges").

[112] *Id.*

[113] UK Home Office, Police and Crime Standards Directorate, Guidance for the Police Use of Body-Worn Video Devices 14–15 (July 2007) (hereinafter UK Home Office, 2007 Guidance), http://library.college.police.uk/docs/homeoffice/guidance-body-worn-devices.pdf.

Another important consideration beyond gathering evidence for a particular prosecution, however, is the risk of deterring victims from seeking help at all.[114] If the price of calling the police after a battering or a sexual assault is to have one's most painful moments recorded and to have one's children recorded, victims may be even more reluctant to call 911.

The dangers are aggravated further by the fact that most body camera policies (95 percent) do not have cessation of recording provisions when it comes to minors.[115] The widespread omissions regarding protections of minors are particularly striking in light of the nation's tradition, albeit eroding, of keeping juvenile records confidential so youths will not be haunted for the rest of their lives by mistakes made when young.[116] If children are at the scene of a domestic violence incident, the victim may further fear calling the police because of the risks of child removal and liability for exposing children to domestic violence.[117]

Courts and experts have expressed concern about the underreporting of serious crimes, such as assault, child abuse, intimate partner violence, sexual assault, and elder abuse.[118] Psychologists and scholars have called for attention to how seeking justice can impose further harms on victims.[119] The major

---

[114] *See, e.g.,* Deborah S. v. Diorio, 583 N.Y.S.2d 872, 880 (N.Y. Civ. Ct. 1992) ("Concerns pertaining to privacy sometimes result in a victim failing to report a sexual offense. In its final report, the Governor's Task Force on Rape and Sexual Assault documented that sexual offenses are vastly underreported. Undoubtedly, there is even less incentive for a victim to report the sexual assault if his or her identity may become public."), *aff'd as modified,* 612 N.Y.S.2d 542 (N.Y. App. Term 1994).

[115] Of the 213 coded, 201 (94 percent) do not have provisions on cessation of recording of minors.

[116] Riya Saha Shah, Lauren Fine, & Jamie Gullen, Juvenile Law Ctr., Juvenile Records: A National Review of State Laws on Confidentiality, Sealing and Expungement 6, 8 (2014) (discussing the history of, and widespread belief in, the confidentiality of juvenile records to preserve the ability for youths to make a fresh start and the reality of eroding confidentiality since the 1990s).

[117] *See, e.g.,* Lois A. Weithorn, *Protecting Children from Exposure to Domestic Violence: The Use and Abuse of Child Maltreatment,* 53 Hastings L.J. 1, 123–129 (2001) (discussing the risks of interpreting child abuse statutes to include exposure to domestic violence as a form of maltreatment).

[118] *See, e.g., Deborah S.,* 583 N.Y.S.2d at 880 (discussing findings of "vast[] underreporting" of sexual assault by task force); Inst. of Med. & Nat'l Research Council, New Directions in Child Abuse and Neglect Research 38 (Anne C. Petersen et al. eds., 2014) (discussing the hidden problem of child abuse and underreporting); Nat'l Ctr. on Elder Abuse, National Elder Abuse Incidence Study 3 (1998), http://aoa.gov/AoA_Programs/Elder_Rights/Elder_Abuse/docs/ABuseReport_Full.pdf (discussing underreporting of elder abuse); Richard Felson & Paul-Philippe Paré, The Reporting of Domestic Violence and Sexual Assault by Nonstrangers to the Police 7–8, 22–23 (2005) (discussing underreporting of assaults and sexual assaults if the victim knows the assailant in any way).

[119] *See, e.g.,* Mary Fan, *Adversarial Justice's Casualties: Defending Victim-Witness Protection,* 55 B.C. L. Rev. 775, 783–791 (2014) (discussing how victims of violent crimes face the risk of further harms when seeking justice in an adversarial system); Patricia A. Frazier &

societal costs of victim deterrence from seeking help must also be weighed against evidentiary benefits. The price of seeking help should not be further harm and intimidation. Moreover, the risks of further privacy harms should not regressively heighten for the most vulnerable and injured and for victims historically most overlooked by the justice system.[120]

Moreover, recording may also interfere with privileged communications between victims and social services providers.[121] Over the years, law enforcement agencies have collaborated with social services and victim advocate groups to match injured and vulnerable persons with care to prevent future injury and violence.[122] Numerous states have explicitly recognized that the communication between the victim and advocates is privileged and confidential.[123] Moreover, medical and mental health information is also privileged and confidential.[124] Placing cameras

---

Beth Haney, *Sexual Assault Cases in the Legal System: Police, Prosecutor, and Victim Perspectives*, 20 LAW & HUM. BEHAV. 607, 620 (1996) (discussing the survey data on the adverse experiences victims have seeking justice); Judith Lewis Herman, *The Mental Health of Crime Victims: Impact of Legal Intervention*, 16 J. TRAUMATIC STRESS 159, 159–160 (2003) (discussing major risks and obstacles for victims who seek justice); Uli Orth, *Secondary Victimization of Crime Victims by Criminal Proceedings*, 15 SOC. JUST. RES. 313, 315–316, 321 (2002) (discussing how criminal proceedings can frequently prove to be a "second[] victimization" for the crime victims involved).

[120] *See generally* Reva B. Siegel, *"The Rule of Love": Wife Beating as Prerogative and Privacy*, 105 YALE L.J. 2117, 2150–2170 (1996) (discussing historical justice system refusal to intervene in intimate partner violence cases).

[121] SANDRA TIBBETTS MURPHY, BATTERED WOMEN'S JUSTICE PROJECT, POLICE BODY CAMERAS IN DOMESTIC AND SEXUAL ASSAULT INVESTIGATIONS: CONSIDERATIONS AND UNANSWERED QUESTIONS 3–7 (2015), www.bwjp.org/assets/documents/pdfs/police-body-cams-in-domestic-and-sexual-assault-inve.pdf.

[122] *See, e.g.,* CHARLES W. DEAN, RICHARD C. LUMB, & KEVIN PROCTOR, SOCIAL WORK AND POLICE PARTNERSHIP: A SUMMONS TO THE VILLAGE STRATEGIES AND EFFECTIVE PRACTICES 14, 17 (2000), http://digitalcommons.brockport.edu/cgi/viewcontent.cgi?article=1000&context=crj_facpub (discussing the intersection of law enforcement and social work and responses to domestic violence); George Karabakakis, Social Work and Police Partnership, INT'L ASS'N CHIEFS POLICE (2009), www.theiacp.org/Portals/0/pdfs/National PolicySummit2009/VTSocialWorkandPolicePartnership.pdf (discussing partnership and results).

[123] SANDRA TIBBETTS MURPHY, BATTERED WOMEN'S JUSTICE PROJECT, POLICE BODY CAMERAS IN DOMESTIC AND SEXUAL ASSAULT INVESTIGATIONS: CONSIDERATIONS AND UNANSWERED QUESTIONS 3–7 (2015), www.bwjp.org/assets/documents/pdfs/police-body-cams-in-domestic-and-sexual-assault-inve.pdf.

[124] See, e.g., Jeffrey R. Baker, *Necessary Third Parties: Multidisciplinary Collaboration and Inadequate Professional Privileges in Domestic Violence Practice*, 21 COLUM. J. GENDER & L. 283, 345–350 (2011) (discussing applicable privileges in the domestic violence context and gaps in protection of confidentiality).

on the scene of the attack may undermine the confidentiality of such important communications.[125]

Better balancing the benefits of recording victims and witnesses against the substantial risks of harm does not necessarily mean that recording should cease. Rather, a preferable approach is to put control over whether to record or not in the hands of the victim. The ACLU's model policy contains a salutary strategy to protect the privacy of victims and witnesses:

> (2) When interacting with an apparent crime victim, a law enforcement officer shall, as soon as practicable, ask the apparent crime victim, if the apparent crime victim wants the officer to discontinue use of the officer's body camera. If the apparent crime victim responds affirmatively, the law enforcement officer shall immediately discontinue use of the body camera; and
>
> (3) When interacting with a person seeking to anonymously report a crime or assist in an ongoing law enforcement investigation, a law enforcement officer shall, as soon as practicable, ask the person seeking to remain anonymous, if the person seeking to remain anonymous wants the officer to discontinue use of the officer's body camera. If the person seeking to remain anonymous responds affirmatively, the law enforcement officer shall immediately discontinue use of the body camera.[126]

The burden of requesting that recording stop should not be placed on victims and witnesses. The well-known hesitation of people to assert their rights and preferences against authority figures is particularly intensified for victims and witnesses, especially those exposed to traumatizing experiences.[127] The lack of realism in expecting an assertion of rights is especially problematic because of the predominance of women as victims of sexual assault and domestic violence. Janet Ainsworth has described "the female register," which avoids assertive, emphatic, and imperative terms.[128] Putting the burden

---

[125]   MURPHY, *supra* note 123, at 3–7 (discussing concerns with the impact of recording on aid to battered persons and sexual assault victims by police officers).

[126]   ACLU, A MODEL ACT FOR REGULATING THE USE OF WEARABLE BODY CAMERAS BY LAW ENFORCEMENT 2 (May 2015), www.aclu.org/files/field_document/aclu_police_body_cameras_model_legislation_may_2015.pdf.

[127]   Janice Nadler, *No Need to Shout: Bus Sweeps and the Psychology of Coercion*, 2002 SUP. CT. REV. 153, 156 (discussing compliance with authority and fear of objecting).

[128]   Janet E. Ainsworth, *In a Different Register: The Pragmatics of Powerlessness in Police Investigation*, 103 YALE L.J. 259, 283–292 (1993) (discussing the problems with demanding a strong and assertive objection and the correlations between powerlessness and speaking in what she terms the "female register," which eschews direct assertions); Janice Nadler, *No Need to Shout: Bus Sweeps and the Psychology of Coercion*, 2002 SUP. CT. REV. 153, 156 (discussing compliance with authority and fear of objecting).

on the officer to ask a victim or witness for permission to record – or at least to ask if recording may continue – is the better approach. The victim or witness should hold control over whether to be recorded, rather than bearing the burden of speaking out if they wish not to be recorded.

Encouragingly, some of the state body camera laws framed by legislators demonstrate concern for protecting against the disclosure of victim and witness information.[129] A recently enacted New Hampshire law instructs officers not to record crime victim interviews "unless his or her express consent has been obtained before the recording is made."[130] Recordings also must comply with state protocols providing protections in sexual assault, domestic violence, stalking, harassment, and child abuse or neglect cases. Nebraska's law takes the approach of requiring redaction of such information.[131] Illinois requires officers to cease recording at the requests of crime victims and witnesses.[132] Connecticut law prohibits disclosure of body-worn recordings of "the scene of an incident that involves a victim of domestic or sexual abuse."[133] Oklahoma law requires redaction of images and information involving victims and witnesses from body camera video released pursuant to public disclosure requests.[134] Nevada directs its police departments to protect the privacy of victims and witnesses.[135]

This difference between democratically framed protections by elected legislators and those designed by police departments carries lessons for crafting policies. Several states expressly delegate policy details down to police departments. Others leave the task of defining body camera protocols to police departments by default, through the lack of statutory guidance. Even if police departments are left to fill in the details of body camera policies, it is important to examine what democratically accountable legislatures are doing when they do give detailed guidance because this may illuminate issues that police department body camera policies may be overlooking. The benefits of body cameras should not come at the price of deterring victims and witnesses from reporting or adding privacy harms to the injuries that victims have already experienced.

---

[129] 5 Gen. Assemb., June Spec. Sess. § 7(g) (Conn. 2015); Assemb. B. 162, 2015 Leg., 78th Reg. Sess. § 1(d) (Nev. 2015).

[130] N.H. REV. STAT. § 105-D:2(VII)(d) (West Supp. 2016).

[131] Legis. B. 1000, 104th Leg., 2nd Reg. Sess. (Neb. 2016).

[132] 50 ILL. COMP. STAT. ANN. 706/10–20(a)(4).

[133] Conn. H.B. 7103, § 7(g).

[134] OKLA. STAT. ANN. tit. 51, § 24A.8(9)–(10).

[135] Nev. Assemb. B. 162, § 1(d).

COMPARATIVE PERSPECTIVE: HOW THE UNITED
KINGDOM STRIKES THE BALANCE

In determining difficult policy trade-offs, it is valuable to look at the experience of other nations with longer experience with police-worn body cameras, even if different needs, demographics, and governing structure may lead to different choices. The United Kingdom was the earliest mover in wide-scale adoption of body cameras and framing policies.[136] The United States and United Kingdom remain the two main nations thus far to engage in wide-scale deployment of police BWCs.[137]

Even before putting an estimated two thousand body cameras on police officers, Britain had among the world's most extensive video surveillance in the world, with a network of 4 million closed-circuit cameras.[138] In 2007, Britain's Home Office allocated $6 million to equip the nation's forty-two police forces with body cameras.[139] Uptake of body cameras was swift. Today, half of all police agencies in the United Kingdom equip their officers with BWCs.[140] In 2016, London's Metropolitan Police conducted the world's largest rollout of BWCs, equipping twenty-two thousand officers.[141]

The Retreat from Continuous Recording

In 2007, the Home Office issued guidelines to police agencies on recording policies and privacy protections in connection with BWCs.[142] The guidelines were developed in consultation with officers in Plymouth, who had piloted body cameras, and other officers in the United Kingdom who had been early movers in using body cameras.[143] The guidelines were also framed to be

---

[136]   Fanny Coudert, Denis Butin, & Daniel Le Métayer, *Body-Worn Cameras for Police Accountability: Opportunities and Risks*, COMPUTER L. & SECURITY REV. 750–751 (2015); Karson Kampfe, Note, *Police-Worn Body Cameras*, 76 OHIO ST. L.J. 1153, 1156–1157 (2015).

[137]   Coudert, Butin, & Le Métayer, *supra* note 136, at 750; *Britain Straps Video Cameras to Police Helmets*, NBC NEWS (July 13, 2007, 5:32 PM), www.nbcnews.com/id/19750278/ns/world_news-europe/t/britain-straps-video-cameras-police-helmets/#.VtOp6o32bcv. Other nations, such as Denmark, have tested the use of body-worn cameras. *Id.*

[138]   *Britain Straps Video Cameras to Police Helmets, supra* note 137.

[139]   *Id.*

[140]   Coudert, Butin, & Le Métayer, *supra* note 136, at 751.

[141]   Metropolitan Police, Rollout of Body Worn Camera (Oct. 17, 2016), http://news.met.police.uk/news/rollout-of-body-worn-cameras-191380.

[142]   POLICE & CRIME STANDARDS DIRECTORATE, UK HOME OFFICE, GUIDANCE FOR THE POLICE USE OF BODY-WORN VIDEO DEVICES (2007), http://library.college.police.uk/docs/homeoffice/guidance-body-worn-devices.pdf [hereinafter UK HOME OFFICE, 2007 GUIDANCE].

[143]   *Id.* at 6.

consistent with the UK Data Protection Act of 1998, which regulated "personal data" captured on computer, closed-circuit television (CCTV), still cameras, and other media.[144] The first principle of the Data Protection Act is that subjects whose data is being taken must know (1) the identity of the data controller, (2) the purpose of the footage, and (3) any additional information necessary for fairness.[145]

The 2007 Home Office guidance advised agencies to notify the public that body cameras will be deployed and to alert the public by clearly wearing uniforms and overtly visible cameras.[146] The Guidance instructed officers to announce where possible or practicable that recording is occurring and record the encounter in its entirety.[147] The Guidance stated that officers should record in private dwellings similarly as other incidents are recorded.[148] Where people object to the recording, officers were instructed to "continue to record while explaining the reasons for recording continuously," such as safeguarding the evidence and the parties.[149] The directive to continue recording applied even in situations of "domestic abuse."[150] Officers could turn off recording if "it becomes clear that the incident is not a police matter (e.g., not an allegation of a suspected or potential offence)."[151] If not used in a criminal investigation or prosecution, footage inside a private dwelling "should be deleted as soon as practicable."[152]

The 2007 Guidance contained only a few limitations on recording, primarily for "[i]ntimate searches" where "persons are in a state of undress."[153] There also was a limitation on recording information subject to legal privileges.[154] Notwithstanding the hard-line stance on continuing to record even upon objection in a private dwelling, and even in a domestic abuse case, officers also were advised to consider the right to private and family life under the

---

[144]   Data Protection Act 1998, c. 29 (UK), www.legislation.gov.uk/ukpga/1998/29/pdfs/ukp ga_19980029_en.pdf.

[145]   *See id.* § 7.

[146]   UK Home Office, Police and Crime Standards Directorate, Guidance for the Police Use of Body-Worn Video Devices 9–10 (July 2007) (hereinafter UK Home Office, 2007 Guidance), http://library.college.police.uk/docs/homeoffice/gui dance-body-worn-devices.pdf.

[147]   *Id.* at 10.

[148]   *Id.* at 14.

[149]   *Id.* at 14–15.

[150]   *Id.*

[151]   *Id.* at 15.

[152]   *Id.*

[153]   *Id.* at 23.

[154]   *Id.*

European Convention on Human Rights and "not record beyond what is necessary for the evidential requirements of the case."[155]

In 2014, the UK College of Policing issued guidance updating and replacing the 2007 Home Office guidance.[156] The new guidance explicitly forbade "[c]ontinuous, non-specific recording," instead mandating that the use of body cameras be "proportionate, legitimate and necessary."[157] Recording by body-worn video must be "incident specific" based on officers' "common sense and sound judgment ... in support of the principles of best evidence."[158] The change in approach to rein back some of the intrusiveness of recording reflected the need to adhere to the Surveillance Camera Code of Practice issued by the Home Office in June 2013.[159] The Surveillance Camera Code of Practice was presented to Parliament as directed under the UK Protection of Freedoms Act of 2012.[160]

Explains Steven Wright, Senior Policy Officer for the United Kingdom's Information Commissioner's Office: "Continuous recording will require strong justification as it is likely to be excessive and cause a great deal of collateral intrusion. Such concerns have contributed to changes in how body-worn video (BWV) is operated; this is because continuous recording is likely to capture people going about their daily business, as well as the individual who is the focus of attention."

Also reflecting a major shift in favor of privacy, the new policy stated that "[u]nder normal circumstances, officers should not use BWV in private dwellings."[161] However, officers present in a private dwelling "for a genuine policing purpose" still may record using BWV "in the same way as they would record any other incident."[162] Officers are cautioned to "exercise discretion and record only when it is relevant to the incident and necessary for gathering evidence, where other reasonable means of doing so are not available."[163] If people inside the dwelling object to recording, but "an incident is taking

---

[155] *Id.*

[156] COLL. OF POLICING, BODY-WORN VIDEO 4 (2014), http://library.college.police.uk/docs/college-of-policing/Body-worn-video-guidance-2014.pdf.

[157] *Id.* at 5.

[158] *Id.*

[159] UK HOME OFFICE, SURVEILLANCE CAMERA CODE OF PRACTICE 4 (2013), www.gov.uk/government/uploads/system/uploads/attachment_data/file/204775/Surveillance_Camera_Code_of_Practice_WEB.pdf.

[160] Protection of Freedoms Act 2012, c. 9, §§ 29–30(1)(a), (Eng. & Wales), www.legislation.gov.uk/ukpga/2012/9/pdfs/ukpga_20120009_en.pdf.

[161] COLL. OF POLICING, *supra* note 156, at 18.

[162] *Id.*

[163] *Id.*

place or allegations of a criminal nature are being made," officers are still instructed to "continue recording but explain their reasons for doing so."[164]

In contrast to the admonition to continue recording even in situations of domestic abuse in the 2007 Guidance, the new guidance now has a section devoted to responding to calls regarding domestic abuse.[165] The section details the benefits of BWV in domestic abuse cases to capture the immediate harms and strengthen the prosecution's case, especially because victims may later prove reluctant or hostile in cooperating in a case.[166] Officers are advised, however, to use BWV cautiously, "on a case-by-case basis" where they "observe no injuries or other evidence of note."[167] The guidance explains that injuries such as bruises may take time to appear so BWV at the scene may not tell the whole story and "may be neutral in conveying what happened during the incident, or may even be used to undermine a prosecution case and assist the defence."[168]

Managing Public Disclosure and Its Costs

Like the United States, the United Kingdom also has a Freedom of Information Act (UK FOIA).[169] The UK FOIA creates a right of access to information held by public authorities, subject to exemptions, such as for information likely to prejudice the prevention or detection of crime or the administration of justice.[170] Moreover, under the United Kingdom's Data Protection Act,[171] people have the right to obtain their personal data held by the government. Under the UK FOIA, public authorities need not comply with "vexatious" requests for information.[172] Vexatious requests means those that are "manifestly unjustified, inappropriate or improper," for which there is no reasonable basis to believe the information would be of value to the requester or the public.[173] Some types of vexatious requests that will not be

---

[164] *Id.*

[165] *Id.* at 20.

[166] *Id.*

[167] *Id.*

[168] *Id.*

[169] *Id.* at 10; UK HOME OFFICE, 2007 GUIDANCE, *supra* note 142, at 11.

[170] Freedom of Information Act 2000, c. 36, §§ 1, 31 (UK), www.legislation.gov.uk/ukpga/2000/36/pdfs/ukpga_20000036_en.pdf.

[171] Data Protection Act, 1998, §7, c. 29 (Eng.).

[172] *Id.* at § 14(1).

[173] Information Commissioner v. Devon County Council & Dransfield [2012] UKUT 440 (AAC) (Jan. 28, 2013); Dransfield v. Information Commissioner and Devon County Council [2015] EWCA Civ 454 (May 14, 2015) (Lady Judge Arden).

honored including those that take a "scattergun approach" that "seems to have been solely designed for the purpose of 'fishing' for information"; requests that place a disproportionate or "grossly oppressive" burden on public resources to respond; or "frivolous" requests that appear "made for the sole purpose of amusement."[174]

Guidance to police agencies from the UK College of Policing instructs officers that the right to access "may include digital images recorded" by BWV.[175] Law enforcement agencies are advised that "third-party redaction may be necessary to prevent collateral intrusion."[176] Current practice, however, winnows down the universe of nonmedia entities who can access BWV footage.

Wright of the Information Commissioner's Office explains, "In the context of body worn video (BWV) footage, subject to exemptions, individuals can only request a copy of their personal data that features within the footage. Therefore, if an individual requests a copy of footage that they are not connected to, or do not specifically feature in, it is likely that such footage will be withheld from disclosure as it will not constitute as their personal data."

When video is released, law enforcement agencies must redact through editing, censoring, or obscuring, the portions of a recording that might reveal sensitive information.[177] This could entail removing metadata, muting some portions of the audio, and solidly masking certain objects.[178] The Home Office guidance to law enforcement agencies observes that "[w]hile the redaction of a document and a photograph is straightforward, this is not the case with a video (audio visual) recording. Any redaction of BWV recordings requires specialist software and appropriately trained personnel."[179]

"From experience, the redaction of footage appears to be a common challenging aspect of BWV use," Wright explains. "The key challenges surround available software for redaction purposes, and appropriately trained staff within forces. Furthermore, we often see that the financial costs of such exercises are great, which can sometimes prevent timely disclosures."

---

[174] INFORMATION COMMISSIONER'S OFFICE, DEALING WITH VEXATIOUS REQUESTS (section 14) 7–8 (Version 1.3, Dec. 18, 2015), https://ico.org.uk/media/for-organisations/documents/1198/dealing-with-vexatious-requests.pdf.

[175] COLLEGE OF POLICING, *supra* note 156, at 10.

[176] *Id.*

[177] UNITED KINGDOM HOME OFFICE, SAFEGUARDING BODY WORN VIDEO DATA 25 (No. 076/16, Oct. 2016), https://assets.publishing.service.gov.uk/government/uploads/system/uploads/attachment_data/file/568195/safeguarding-body-worn-video-data-07616p.pdf.

[178] *Id.*

[179] *Id.*

The evolution of policies in the United Kingdom through experience has important lessons for the United States. First, continuous recording may seem an alluring policy position because it reduces concerns about selective recording, or failures to activate cameras. But in practice among impacted people, rather than on paper, these positions are too harsh. Evidence-gathering is an important interest, particularly in cases such as domestic violence, where victims may recant out of fear or pressure. But the human and privacy harms of recording may be too severe a price to pay, without case-specific calibration of the circumstances and necessity. Second, provisions that prevent fishing expeditions, or allow officials to decline requests that impose burdens disproportionate to the purpose served, can help prevent the concerns about extremely costly broad requests for all video. Finally, redaction can be technologically challenging to implement but an important protection to honor public disclosure requests while preventing privacy harms.

In the United Kingdom, as well as the United States, the dominant lens for analyzing privacy problems and policies often is at the individual level. Should officers record or not in a particular case or call? Should this public disclosure request be honored? Because the United Kingdom is the earlier mover, however, experience has been raising questions about the privacy impact of accumulating video. The Home Office guidance to agencies notes: "Small traces of sensitive information may have little significance when considered independently. However, when linked over an entire recording timeline the significance can be considerable. Furthermore when traces are linked across several recordings especially from a number of devices with different viewpoints, and with other non-BWV data, then this significance could escalate."[180] Much more remains to be done to address these open and growing questions and develop policies that can both maximize the benefits and minimize the harms of aggregate audiovisual data. The next Part proposes approaches that can help address these issues that are likely to recur and grow in import.

[180] *Id.*

7

Controlled Access, Privacy Protection Planning, and Data Retention

Hiding within those mounds of data is knowledge that could change the life of a patient, or change the world.

– Atul Butte, Data Miner and Executive Director, Clinical Informatics, University of California Health Sciences and Services[1]

Because of the potential privacy harms and high storage costs of keeping vast volumes of sensitive audiovisual data, it is tempting to exempt the information from disclosure and delete it whenever possible. Yet this approach would miss a major potential benefit of the era of pervasive recording of police activities. Video evidence is valuable not just for investigation and prosecution in a particular criminal case, or a particular officer. Rather, the aggregated data involving everyday enforcement activities, including the seemingly uneventful encounters, can reveal important insights about how to keep stressful situations from escalating and better protect civil rights and liberties.

The challenge is how to realize these potential benefits while addressing the concerns about privacy harms. With the advance of technology, storage costs are likely to go down, just as we have seen with the expansion of email services like Gmail or Hotmail, which can store large volumes of data so cheaply that users do not pay for the base service. But the free market and march of technology alone cannot address privacy harms. Policy frameworks are needed to preserve data securely and permit access for important public purposes while protecting against privacy harms. This chapter addresses the challenge by proposing controlled access and privacy protection planning. These concepts are modeled on tried-and-true approaches in the health sciences that have protected highly private health data while still permitting research and innovation.

---

[1] Bruce Goldman, *King of the Mountain*, STANFORD MAGAZINE (Summer 2012), http://sm.stanford.edu/archive/stanmed/2012summer/article3.html (quoting Butte).

Controlled access gives professionals who are obligated by professional ethics to honor data use and protection safeguards the ability to view data that would otherwise be locked away. The paradigmatic examples of such professionals are researchers who are ethically bound to comply with data protections and are required to have institutional review board (IRB) approval before acquiring and using sensitive data.[2] Privacy planning requires a well-designed plan for the protection of sensitive data and a showing of the capability and facilities to implement those protections. These principles have formed the successful architecture of data access in public health and medical research, which use highly private medical data to make major advances in protecting health and saving lives.

Finally, because data must exist to be analyzed, this chapter also presents findings on varying data retention policies for body camera video. While approaches differ, they reflect the dominant lens in which video evidence currently is viewed as worth retaining based on import to a particular criminal case or complaint. The chapter concludes by discussing data preservation policies that see beyond the myopic focus on relevance to a particular investigation or prosecution to the value of aggregate data, securely stored for bounded access and controlled mining.

THE HEALTH SCIENCES APPROACH TO PROTECTING PRIVACY WHILE ADVANCING HARM PREVENTION

The controlled access proposal draws insights from the health sciences, including epidemiology, which is the science of detecting and preventing threats to public health.[3] Advances in research to protect public health depend on amassing sensitive, highly private data for public health surveillance.[4] The goal of health surveillance is to systematically gather and pool data to detect the causes, prevalence, incidences, and consequences of injury or

---

[2] *See, e.g.*, Maness v. Meyers, 419 US 449, 458 (1975) ("We begin with the basic proposition that all orders and judgments of courts must be complied with promptly."); Comm. on Prof'l Ethics & Conduct of the Iowa State Bar Ass'n v. McCullough, 465 N.W. 2d 878, 885 (Iowa 1991) ("[A] lawyer has a duty to obey a court order and a duty not to advise a client to ignore it ... These principles are so obvious and basic that we should not have to remind the bar of them."); John A. Robertson, *The Law of Institutional Review Boards*, 26 UCLA L. Rev. 484, 485–494 (1978) (discussing the rise of IRB requirements for researchers and their institutions).

[3] *See* Noel S. Weiss & Thomas D. Koepsell, Epidemiologic Methods: Studying the Occurrence of Illness 10 (Oxford Univ. Press 2d ed. 2014).

[4] Scott F. Wetterhall & Eric K. Noji, *Surveillance and Epidemiology*, in The Public Health Consequences of Disasters 37 (Eric K. Noji ed., Oxford Univ. Press 1997).

disease.[5] Epidemiologists and other health scientists frequently utilize highly private and protected health data to investigate the patterns and causes of threats to health and safety in populations of people.[6]

Data sharing and pooling for disease surveillance has venerable roots running back to the nineteenth century in US and international practice.[7] For example, public health surveillance led to the discovery that a defective vaccine was causing polio in forty thousand children and leaving two hundred children paralyzed.[8] Trying to detect threats to population health without such data pooling would be laboring "in the darkness of ignorance" as Assistant Surgeon-General J. W. Trask put it in 1915.[9]

While disease surveillance is often conducted by governmental entities, the history of advances in public health research also shows the import of making data available to nongovernmental researchers for analyses.[10] Many expert eyes are needed to advance protection and prevention. Indeed, where would biomedical science and technology be in a world where only the government conducted research? The task of uncovering and combating threats to public health and safety cannot just be centralized within the government. While the government has an important role to play in gathering, standardizing, and disseminating information, much of the research is conducted by nongovernmental researchers with specialized expertise. Nongovernmental expert eyes are beneficial microbes for the system of knowledge generation and harm prevention, unearthing important findings and airing issues in need of attention.

If you have ever visited a doctor's office, you probably realize that your medical information is one of the most stringently protected forms of information about you. After all, your health data can contain highly private information such as your HIV or other sexually transmitted infection status; history of depression or other mental health disorders; sexual history; and other

---

[5] Lawrence O. Gostin et al., *The Law and the Public's Health: A Study of Infectious Disease Law in the United States*, 99 COLUM. L. REV. 59, 82 (1999).

[6] *Id.*

[7] For histories, *see, e.g.*, ARCHON FUNG, MARY GRAHAM & DAVID WEIL, FULL DISCLOSURE: THE PERILS AND PROMISE OF TRANSPARENCY 142, 183–215 (2007); Denise Koo & Scott F. Wetterhall, *History and Current Status of the National Notifiable Diseases Surveillance System*, 2 J. PUB. HEALTH MGMT. & PRAC. 4, 4–8 (1996).

[8] For a history, see, e.g., Michael Fitzpatrick, *The Cutter Incident: How America's First Polio Vaccine Led to a Growing Vaccine Crisis*, 99 J. ROYAL SOC'Y OF MED. 156, 156 (2006).

[9] John W. Trask, *Public Health Administration: Its Dependence Upon Reports of Sickness*, 28 PUB. HEALTH REP. 1, 2 (1913).

[10] *See, e.g.*, DAVID P. FIDLER, SARS, GOVERNANCE AND THE GLOBALIZATION OF DISEASE 50–52 (Palgrave Macmillan 2004) (discussing the state centrism of international public health regimes).

potentially stigmatizing information that can affect your career and private life.[11] Under the law, your doctor must give you the notice form that you signed that tells you your health privacy rights; limits on how your health information may be used and disclosed; and your health provider's duty to protect your health information privacy.[12] The Health Insurance Portability and Accountability Act of 1996 (HIPAA) is a major source of your health information privacy rights.[13] The HIPAA Privacy Rule established strong national uniform standards for protecting your individually identifiable health information.[14]

Though HIPAA reflects the nation's democratic judgment about the intensely private nature of health information, it also permits disclosure of data for research and public health purposes.[15] To get the information, researchers must show they have received approval for their project and their data protection plans from either an IRB or a privacy board to ensure there are sufficient privacy protection protocols in place.[16] If you know a scientist who works with human subjects you probably have heard stories – and perhaps even the occasional expletive – about the stringency of the IRB process. Federal law requires the board to ensure that the use or disclosure of the information "involves no more than a minimal risk to the privacy of individuals" because of the following protections in the researchers' submission:

1 an adequate plan to protect the identifiers from improper use and disclosure;
2 an adequate plan to destroy the identifiers at the earliest opportunity consistent with conduct of the research, unless there is a health or research justification for retaining the identifiers or such retention is otherwise required by law; and
3 adequate written assurances that the protected health information will not be reused or disclosed to any other person or entity, except as required by law, for authorized oversight of the research study, or for other research for which the use or disclosure of protected health information would be permitted.[17]

---

[11] *See, e.g.,* Amy L. Fairchild, Ronald Bayer, James Colgrove & Daniel Wolfe, Searching Eyes: Privacy, the State, and Disease Surveillance in America 66–80 (Univ. of Cal. Press 2007) (discussing the surveillance of conditions such as sexually transmitted diseases).

[12] US Dep't of Health & Hum. Svcs., Notice of Privacy Protections (June 16, 2017), www.hhs.gov/hipaa/for-individuals/notice-privacy-practices/index.html.

[13] Health Insurance Portability and Accountability Act of 1996, Pub. L. No. 104–191, 110 Stat. 1936 (1996) (codified in scattered sections of 26 USC., 28 USC. and 42 USC.).

[14] *Id.*

[15] 45 C.F.R. §§ 164.502(a)(1), 164.512(i), 164.514(e) (2018).

[16] 45 C.F.R. § 164.512(i)(1) (2018).

[17] 45 C.F.R. § 164.512(i)(2)(ii)(A)(1)–(3) (2018).

In addition, the researchers must show that the IRB approval and health data are necessary for the project, which could not be practicably conducted without them.[18]

Thus even after the enactment of HIPAA, researchers have access to patient health data to enable public health research to detect and prevent harms.[19] De-identified health information may be publicly available for research because it is not covered by HIPAA.[20] But many of the most important sources of medical data are only available to qualified researchers with approved projects and demonstrated ability to implement a data protection plan. The data access practices of the health sciences thus have important lessons about controlling access to sensitive data to protect privacy without stifling the generation of knowledge about threats to public health and safety.

EPICRIM INSIGHTS: THE MARRIAGE OF EPIDEMIOLOGY AND CRIMINOLOGY

Looking to the health sciences also makes sense in the prevention of violence in law enforcement encounters because of the shared goal of preventing injuries and deaths. Fundamentally, reducing the risk of violence and rights violations in police encounters is a public health problem in the criminal justice context. The interdisciplinary expertise of the rising field of epidemiological criminology can illuminate new paths forward.

Epidemiological criminology, or "epicrim" for short, applies the methods and insights from disease prevention to preventing violence and injury.[21] The goal is to prevent violence like a disease.[22] Epicrim draws on the methods, insights, and analytical resources of epidemiology to illuminate criminal justice issues.[23] The interdisciplinary approach makes sense because both criminal justice and public health have the shared goals of harm

---

[18]   45 C.F.R. § 164.512(i)(2)(ii)(B)–(C) (2018).

[19]   Roberta B. Ness, *Influence of the HIPAA Privacy Rule on Health Research*, 298 J. AM. MED. ASS'N 2164, 2164–2168 (2007).

[20]   *See, e.g.*, Centers for Disease Control and Prevention, *Guidelines for National Human Immunodeficiency Virus Case Surveillance, Including Monitoring for Human Immunodeficiency Virus Infection and Acquired Immunodeficiency Syndrome*, 48 MORBIDITY & MORTALITY WKLY. REP. 1, 14–16 (1999).

[21]   *See, e.g.*, Timothy A. Akers & Mark M. Lainier, *"Epidemiological Criminology": Coming Full Circle*, 99 AM. J. PUB. HEALTH 397, 397–402 (2009) (explaining the interdisciplinary field of epidemiological criminology).

[22]   *See, e.g.*, David Polizzi & Mark M. Lanier, *Crime as Disease: Towards an Epidemiological Criminology of the Social Body*, 25 ACTA CRIMINOLOGICA 37, 37–49 (2012) (discussing the metaphor of crime as a disease).

[23]   Akers & Lanier, *supra* note 21 at 397–402; Polizzi & Lanier, *supra* note 22, at 37–49.

prevention.[24] Moreover, epidemiology can open the horizon of potential data sources because epidemiologists are consummate data scavengers.[25]

The interdisciplinarity of epicrim can be productive not just for common research methods and goals. The long experience and well-established protocols for dealing with highly protected private information in epidemiology also can inform growing debates in the law enforcement context. The standards and processes in the health sciences for protecting human subjects can inform policies regarding how to reduce the privacy harms from aggregating police video data while enabling research that can better protect the public and officers.

The history of medical research is full of major advances – but also cautionary horror tales that have helped shape modern protections for human subjects. In the ashes of World War II, the Allied forces tried Nazi perpetrators of atrocities in the Nuremberg trials.[26] One of the cases, the doctors' trial, documented for the world and for history, the brutal experiments that Nazi doctors conducted on prisoners in the name of advancing medical knowledge.[27] The result was the landmark Nuremberg Code, which has been termed "the most important document in the history of the ethics of medical research."[28] Some of the central provisions of the Code include voluntary informed consent; a beneficial good requirement such that the "degree of risk to be taken should never exceed that determined by the humanitarian importance of the problem to be solved by the experiment"; and the right to withdraw from experiments without repercussions.[29]

---

[24] Akers & Lanier, *supra* note 21 at 400–402.
[25] *See, e.g.,* NOEL S. WEISS & THOMAS D. KOEPSELL, EPIDEMIOLOGIC METHODS: STUDYING THE OCCURRENCE OF ILLNESS 105 (2d ed. 2014) ("Epidemiologists are often data scavengers.").
[26] For an iconic account, see ROBERT E. CONOT, JUSTICE AT NUREMBERG (1983).
[27] For accounts, *see, e.g.,* Jay Katz, *The Nuremberg Code and the Nuremberg Trial. A Reappraisal,* 276 J. AM. MED. ASSOC. 1662 (1996); Ruth R. Faden et al., *US Medical Researchers, the Nuremberg Doctors Trial, and the Nuremberg Code: A Review of the Findings of the Advisory Committee on Human Radiation Experiments,* 276 J. AM. MED. ASSOC. 1667 (1996); Jon M. Harkness, *Nuremberg and the Issue of Wartime Experiments on US Prisoners,* 276 J. AM. MED. ASSOC. 1672 (1996); Michael A. Grodin, *Legacies of Nuremberg. Medical Ethics and Human Rights,* 276 J. AM. MED. ASSOC. 1682 (1996); Jonathan Turley, *Transformative Justice and the Ethos of Nuremberg,* 33 LOY. L.A. L. REV. 665 (2000).
[28] Evelyne Shuster, *Fifty Years Later: The Significance of the Nuremberg Code,* NEW ENGLAND J. MED. 337(20):1436–1440 (Nov. 13, 1997).
[29] "Permissible Medical Experiments," arts. 1, 2, 6, in *Trials of War Criminals before the Nuremberg Military Tribunals under Control Council Law No. 10,* Vol. 2, pp. 181–182. Washington, DC: US Government Printing Office, 1949, *available at* www.loc.gov/rr/frd/Mi litary_Law/pdf/NT_war-criminals_Vol-II.pdf (hereinafter Nuremberg Code).

In the United States, several infamous cases led to the National Research Act of 1974, which created the IRB system to regulate research with human subjects.[30] Some involved research on subjects without their knowledge or informed consent, such as the 1962 thalidomide study of a drug to treat pregnancy symptoms and the 1932 Tuskegee Syphilis Study, which ran for forty years, until 1972.[31] Physicians gave women thalidomide without informing them they were on an investigational drug. Unfortunately, the drug turned out to cause severe deformities in infants exposed in utero. In the syphilis study, researchers left syphilis untreated in African American male subjects even after penicillin became part of the standard treatment for the disease in 1947. The men were never informed of the real purpose of the study – to investigate the "natural history" of what happens when syphilis is left untreated – or of several other important details. These and numerous other debacles – some chronicled by a Harvard Medical School professor in an influential 1966 *New England Journal of Medicine* article[32] – spurred congressional action and the generation of ethical guidelines in the 1978 Belmont Report[33] drafted by an expert commission charged by Congress.

Today, health sciences researchers are bound by a web of laws, regulations, and ethical principles that safeguard research subjects and protect against nonconsensual disclosures of personally identifiable data.[34] Sanctions for violations of such protections for sensitive data can extend beyond professional penalties to include civil and criminal penalties.[35] Researchers thus have deep expertise in complying with complex limits on the uses of data and revelation of identifiable information that may prove damaging. Researchers also have

---

[30]   For a summary, *see, e.g.*, Elizabeth A. Bankert & Robert J. Amdur, Institutional Review Board: Member Handbook 7–16 (3d ed. 2007).

[31]   For a discussion, *see, e.g.*, Todd W. Rice, *The Historical, Ethical, and Legal Background of Human-Subjects Research*, Respiratory Care 53(1):1325–1329 (Oct. 2008).

[32]   Henry Beecher, *Ethics of Clinical Research*, New England J. Med. 274(24): 1354–1360 (1966)

[33]   National Comm'n for the Protection of Human Subjects of Biomedical and Behavioral Research, The Belmont Report: Ethical Principles and Guidelines for the Protection of Human Subjects of Research (1974), *available at* www.hhs.gov/ohrp/regulations-and-policy/belmont-report/index.html [hereinafter The Belmont Report].

[34]   E.g., 45 C.F.R. § 45.46 (2009); 45 C.F.R. §§ 160, 162, 164 (2013); Office of the Secretary, *Ethical Principles and Guidelines for the Protection of Human Subjects of Research*, The National Commission for the Protection of Human Subjects of Biomedical and Behavioral Research (Apr. 18, 1979).

[35]   *See, e.g.*, 42 USC. § 1320d-5 (2018).

expertise in conducting analyses with deidentified data to extract important information while limiting any damage to an individual entity.[36]

THE ARCHITECTURE OF PROTECTION

When researchers apply to access data, the well-established processes for IRB review apply to protect against harms from disclosure and use. The existence of these protections and their success in the context of highly private and protected medical information is an argument that audiovisual data, like medical data, should be preserved and available for controlled access by researchers. We do not destroy valuable medical data by saying it is too harmful or hurtful to risk use by researchers. The same logic should apply to audiovisual data for harm prevention analyses. Beyond serving as a time-tested layer of protection for researchers requesting data, the strategies behind protection of aggregated highly private and potentially harmful health data can inform the protection of audiovisual data from police encounters.

Not all the elaborate protections for personally identifiable health information should apply to recordings of police encounters. Body camera data is not the same as personal health data. Whereas an individual's health data is inherently private, interactions with the police have a stronger component of public relevance because it entails the use of official power. Moreover, many police encounters occur in public or involve issues of public concern.

Even if all the elaborate procedures that apply to researchers do not and should not apply in their entirety, there are two important and mutually reinforcing principles that communities can distill. For short, we can call them controlled access and privacy protection planning. These principles that successfully protect health information also can constitute the architecture of protection for audiovisual police data.

First, the principle of controlled access limits who can access the data and for what projects. The securely stored data are not available to all because of the potential privacy harms. Rather, the potential benefits of disclosure must outweigh the potential risks. The purpose for which the data is disclosed and

---

[36]   Indeed, deidentifying information for analyses is a vibrant area of scholarly activity. *See, e.g.*, Robert J. Bayardo & Rakesh Agrawal, *Data Privacy through Optimal K-Anonymization*, 2005 PROCS. OF THE 21ST INT'L CONF. ON DATA ENGINEERING 217, 217–218 (2005); James Gardner & Li Xiong, *An Integrated Framework for De-Identifying Unstructured Medical Data*, 68 DATA & KNOWLEDGE ENGINEERING 1441, 1442 (2009); Bradley Malin, Kathleen Benitez, & Daniel Masys, *Never Too Old for Anonymity: A Statistical Standard for Demographic Data Sharing via the HIPAA Privacy Rule*, 18 J. AM. MED. INFORMATICS ASS'N 3, 3–5 (2011).

used matters in this calculus. The weightier the inquiry, the more compelling is the reason for access.

Weighing the purpose of a request has a long tradition in the health sciences. The 1947 Nuremberg Code provided that the "risk to be taken should never exceed that determined by the humanitarian importance" of the reasons for the request.[37] The weighing of purpose and risk also is embedded in the influential Belmont Report's principle of beneficence, which in part entails maximizing the possible benefits while minimizing the possible harms.[38] One of the criteria for IRB approval of research is that the "[r]isks to subjects are reasonable in relation to anticipated benefits, if any, to subjects, and the importance of the knowledge that may reasonably be expected to result."[39]

Persons or entities who receive the data also must have the demonstrated ability to adopt protocols to limit the harms from disclosure. This principle also can be found as early as the 1947 Nuremberg Code, which provided: "The experiment should be conducted only by scientifically qualified persons."[40] In the modern context, federal regulations require that where appropriate, "there are adequate provisions to protect the privacy of subjects and to maintain the confidentiality of data."[41]

This principle is connected with the second overarching lesson from the health sciences about the import of advance privacy protection planning. Typically, to secure approval, researchers have to explain in advance how they will store and protect sensitive information and their facilities for doing so. This helps in the evaluation of the researchers' qualifications, and the mitigation of potential risks. The pledge also holds the requester accountable for privacy protection.

These principles need not be limited to the research context. Communities can set access policies limited to entities or persons, such as the media as well as researchers, with a clearly articulated and publicly beneficial purpose. To mitigate the risks of privacy harms, communities also can require requesters to explain in advance how they will minimize privacy harms and their abilities to implement that privacy protection plan.

Who gets to decide whether the beneficial purpose outweighs the risks, or whether the privacy protection planning is sufficient? In the health information context, the IRB or privacy board is the gateway for determining who is qualified, and what projects are sufficiently beneficial to justify the disclosure

---

[37] Nuremberg Code, *supra* note 29, at art. 6.
[38] THE BELMONT REPORT, *supra* note 33.
[39] 45 C.F.R. § 46.111(a)(2) (2018).
[40] Nuremberg Code, *supra* note 29, at art. 8.
[41] 45 C.F.R. § 46.111(a)(7) (2018).

and use of highly private data.[42] Under federal regulations, IRBs must have at
least five members of sufficiently varying backgrounds to be competent to
review the range of proposals that researchers submit.[43] The varying backgrounds required by law is not just professional, but also diverse in terms of
demographics, cultures, and attitudes, to promote confidence that the IRB
understands, and is protecting, the welfare of human subjects in the
community.[44]

In the audiovisual data access context, the gatekeepers could be external
boards, or boards internal to a police department with at least one external
member. The gatekeepers also could be courts, though this is problematic
because of higher barriers to entry and greater need for professional guidance
when one must initiate legal action. Having to file an action to receive public
information, as some states are already beginning to require, can be daunting
or even prohibitive for resource-poor persons or groups who need the information for beneficial purposes.

To gain access, users would need to demonstrate that data access would
serve a public or safety purpose and submit a data protection protocol,
including demonstrated safeguards. Any approval would be limited to the
purposes predefined in the request. This limitation also serves to control the
mining of data so that it is limited to beneficial and restricted purposes.

DATA PRESERVATION

Data must exist undeleted to be analyzed. The proposition may seem trivial, but
it cuts to another related challenge. Deletion is a strategy to reassure privacy
advocates that data will not be mined in search of violations.[45] Deletion also is
a major way to reduce the costs of adopting body cameras. One of the greatest
expenses of putting body cameras on police – far exceeding the costs of the
cameras themselves – is storing the vast volumes of data that result.[46] Stored

---

[42]   45 C.F.R. § 164.512(i)(2)(ii)(A)(1)–(3) (2018).

[43]   21 C.F.R. pt. 56 § 56.107(A) (2018).

[44]   *See* 21 C.F.R. pt. 56 § 56.107(a) (2018) ("The IRB shall be sufficiently qualified through the
       experience and expertise of its members, and the diversity of the members, including
       consideration of race, gender, cultural backgrounds, and sensitivity to such issues as commu-
       nity attitudes, to promote respect for its advice and counsel in safeguarding the rights and
       welfare of human subjects.").

[45]   JAY STANLEY, POLICE BODY-MOUNTED CAMERAS: WITH RIGHT POLICIES IN PLACE,
       A WIN FOR ALL (American Civil Liberties Union (ACLU), Washington, DC, 2015).

[46]   Bryan Bakst & Ryan J. Foley, *For Police Body Cameras, Big Costs Loom in Storage*,
       POLICEONE (Feb. 6, 2015), www.policeone.com/police-products/body-cameras/articles/824
       3271-For-police-body-cameras-big-costs-loom-in-storage/ [http://perma.cc/MS7B-5P4N].

video can grow to petabytes of data – and one petabyte is the equivalent of 20 million four-drawer cabinets' worth of files.

As data multiplies from dash cameras and police body cameras, the traditional method of storage using on-site servers or CDs in an evidence room is becoming infeasible for many departments.[47] Storage is particularly challenging for mid-size departments of 50 to 250 officers with mid-size budgets and infrastructure.[48] Many departments are turning to cloud data storage under contracts negotiated with private companies.

Costs vary depending on anticipated volume of video, size of the jurisdiction, and contract negotiated, usually with a private cloud storage provider. One major policing technology company charges approximately $50 to $100 per officer, per month, for cloud-based data storage.[49] The smaller Bryan Police Department in Texas, with 143 sworn officers, negotiated a five-year contract that includes $135,564 per year to pay for cloud storage and related licenses.[50] On the other end of the size spectrum, the LAPD estimated that unlimited data storage for 860 body cameras costs $868,428 per year.[51]

A county sheriff overseeing an office with nine hundred officers cited "dealbreaker" costs of $1 million a year in start-up costs and storing the video for just thirty days.[52] Increasing the retention period to 190 days from 30 days would multiply storage costs five- to tenfold according to the experience of the Clarksville, Indiana police department.[53] Departments have halted body camera plans out of concern that it would be too costly to store video for the periods designated under state standards.[54]

---

[47]   Lucas, Mearian, *As Police Move to Adopt Body Cams, Storage Costs Set to Skyrocket*, COMPUTERWORLD (Sept. 3, 2015), www.computerworld.com/article/2979627/cloud-storage/as-police-move-to-adopt-body-cams-storage-costs-set-to-skyrocket.html.

[48]   Rick Callahan, *Some Police Departments Shelve Body Cameras, Cite Data Costs*, ASSOCIATED PRESS (Sept. 10, 2016), http://bigstory.ap.org/article/f19d7270535f4202b92de1872278330f/some-police-suspend-body-cameras-or-hold-citing-costs.

[49]   Jimmy Jenkins, *In the Police Body Camera Business, the Real Money's on the Back End*, MARKETPLACE (Apr. 18, 2017, 2:00 PM), www.marketplace.org/2017/04/18/business/police-body-camera-business-real-moneys-on-back-end [http://perma.cc/UH2A-XRUU].

[50]   John Austin, *Focusing on Body Cameras*, JACKSONVILLE PROGRESS (Dec. 16, 2017), www.jacksonvilleprogress.com/news/focusing-on-body-cameras/article_3dc0d5b4-e1e8-11e7-a84a-a30511caaa3c.html [http://perma.cc/YFC6-356P].

[51]   www.scpr.org/news/2015/03/30/50678/7m-annual-cost-for-lapd-body-cameras/ [http://perma.cc/6QUS-QW82].

[52]   Rick Callahan, *Some Police Departments Shelve Body Cameras, Cite Data Costs*, ASSOCIATED PRESS (Sept. 10, 2016), http://bigstory.ap.org/article/f19d7270535f4202b92de1872278330f/some-police-suspend-body-cameras-or-hold-citing-costs.

[53]   *Id.*

[54]   *Id.*

Technology industry leaders agreed in interviews that data storage costs are likely to go down, as history has proven. After all, the cost of data storage for one megabyte of data has fallen from $1 million in 1967 to about two cents today because of the advance of technology and the growth in competition.[55] The dramatic and sustained fall in data storage costs over the last three decades is sometimes dubbed Kryder's law, though originally Kryder's law was about changes in the density of bits on disk platters, which has implications for data storage costs.[56] Major technology companies are entering the field with products and new technologies to offer greater security at reduced data storage expense.[57] Pricing wars and competition in the cloud storage industry is resulting in further declines in prices.[58] Thus while storage costs are an immediate concern, long-range policy planning should not be hostage to an issue that is highly likely to change and become less daunting.

Data retention policies vary widely. Table 7.1 summarizes body camera data retention periods in state laws. The predominant criteria for longer-term retention is the relevance of the footage to a particular criminal investigation, prosecution, complaint, or potential complaint. Several states permit the destruction of body camera recordings that are not connected to a criminal prosecution, complaint, or critical incident after between 30 and 90 days. Indiana is a notable exception, requiring the retention of body camera videos not connected to a criminal prosecution, complaint or critical incident for 280 days. As we saw in Chapter 6, Indiana also struck a stronger balance for public disclosure, with redaction to protect privacy.

Table 7.2 summarizes the approaches to data retention in body camera policies. As Table 7.2 summarizes, body camera policies also tend to retain recordings that are not of evidentiary value in an investigation, prosecution, or complaint for shorter than four months – and sometimes just a matter of weeks before destruction. As for what is nonevidentiary, defining a negative is always a challenge, and often goes undefined, or is defined with another negative –

---

[55] Lucas Mearian, *Data Storage Goes from $2M to 2 Cents per Gigabyte*, COMPUTERWORLD (Mar. 23, 2017), www.computerworld.com/article/3182207/data-storage/cw50-data-storage-goes-from-1m-to-2-cents-per-gigabyte.html.

[56] For a discussion, *see, e.g.*, DAVID S. H. ROSENTHAL, DANIEL C. ROSENTHAL, ETHAN L. MILLER, IAN F. ADAMS, MARK W. SOTRER, & EREZ ZADOK, THE ECONOMICS OF LONG-TERM DIGITAL STORAGE (2012), https://lockss.org/locksswp/wp-content/uploads/2012/09/unesco2012.pdf.

[57] Jessica Van Sack, *Storage Costs Cloud Police Cam Issue*, BOSTON HERALD (Apr. 13, 2015), www.govtech.com/public-safety/Storage-Costs-Cloud-Police-Cam-Issue.html.

[58] Eugene Kim, *This One Chart Shows the Vicious Price War Going on in Cloud Computing*, BUSINESS INSIDER (Jan. 4, 2015), www.businessinsider.com/cloud-computing-price-war-in-one-chart-2015-1.

TABLE 7.1 *Examples of Body Camera Data Retention Provisions in State Laws*

California[a]	Guidelines to agencies recommend retaining nonevidentiary body camera data for a minimum of sixty days before destruction. Data involving a use of force, officer-involved shooting, an incident resulting in the detention or arrest of a person, or relevant to a formal or informal complaint against an officer or the agency should be kept for two years. Evidence relevant to a criminal prosecution should be retained for the same time as applies to other evidence relevant to a prosecution.
Georgia[b]	Body camera videos must be retained for 180 days, except that recordings that are part of a criminal investigation, showing a vehicle accident, or depicting an arrest or detainment, or law enforcement use of force must be retained for 30 months. If involved in litigation, the data shall be retained until final adjudication of the litigation.
Illinois[c]	Body camera recordings must be kept without alteration for ninety days and then destroyed. The recording will be kept for two years if a complaint has been filed, an officer fired a weapon, death or great bodily injury occurred, the incident ended in arrest or detention, the officer involved is under investigation, the recording has been flagged for retention, or the video has evidentiary value in a criminal prosecution. Recordings related to a pending investigation may be deleted after the final disposition of the case.
Indiana[d]	Unaltered, unobscured recordings must be retained for at least 280 days. Recordings must be retained for two years if a complaint is filed or if the video is requested under public disclosure laws.
Minnesota[e]	All body camera data must be retained for ninety days and then destroyed. Video is retained for a year and then destroyed if it shows a firearm discharge by police, use of force resulting in serious bodily injury, or incident resulting in a complaint. Video is retained for additional time, up to 180 days upon request by a subject of the data. If so, the subject must be notified before destruction of the data.
Nebraska[f]	Body camera recordings must be retained for a minimum of ninety days. If data has evidentiary value in a criminal or civil court proceeding or in disciplinary proceedings, the recording shall be retained until final judgment or the final determination in the proceeding.
New Hampshire[g]	Body camera data must be retained for longer than 30 days but less than 180 days before being permanently destroyed by overwriting. If the video records deadly force, firearm discharge, death or serious injury, or an encounter resulting in a complaint then it must be stored for a minimum of three years.

TABLE 7.1 *(continued)*

Oklahoma[h]	Body camera recordings depicting anything other than an officer-involved shooting, use of lethal force, incidents that entail medical treatment, or incidents resulting in a written request for preservation of video may be kept for a minimum of one year. Otherwise, records are kept for a minimum of seven years.
Oregon[i]	Police department policies must provide for body camera data retention for at least 180 days but not longer than 30 months if the data are unrelated to a court proceeding or ongoing criminal investigation. If the video is related to a court proceeding, it shall be retained for the same period as other evidence.

Note. For an excellent resource mapping body-worn policies by state, see Nat'l Conference of State Legislatures, Body-Worn Camera Laws Database (last updated Feb. 28, 2018), www.ncsl.org/research/civil-and-criminal-justice/body-worn-cameras-interactive-graphic.aspx#/.

[a] CAL. ASSEMBLY BILL NO. 1953, ch. 99 § 3(b)(5)(A)-(B) (approved by Governor, July 25, 2016), *available at* https://leginfo.legislature.ca.gov/faces/billTextClient.xhtml?bil l_id=201520160AB1953.

[b] GA. H.B. 976, § 2 (eff. July 1, 2016), *available at* www.legis.ga.gov/Legislation/en-US/display/20152016/HB/976.

[c] ILL. PUB. ACT 099-0352, § 10-20(a)(7) (2015).

[d] INDIANA HOUSE ENROLLED ACT NO. 1019, § 5.3 (2016), *available at* https://iga.in.gov/legis lative/2016/bills/house/1019#document-3df25085.

[e] MINN. SF 498, § 3 (eff. Aug. 1, 2016), *available at* www.revisor.mn.gov/bills/text.php?number=SF498&version=latest&session=ls89&session_year=2015&session_number=0.

[f] NEB. LEGISLATIVE BILL 1000, § 3(2) (approved by the Governor, Apr. 13, 2016), *available at* https://nebraskalegislature.gov/FloorDocs/104/PDF/Slip/LB1000.pdf.

[g] N.H. H.B. 1584, § XVI (signed by Governor June 24, 2016), *available at* https://legiscan.com/NH/text/HB1584/2016.

[h] OKLA. ENROLLED H.B. No. 2232, § 517.1 (approved by Governor, May 1, 2017), *available at* www.legiscan.com/OK/text/HB2232/2017.

[i] ORE. H.B. 2571, § 1 (2015), *available at* https://olis.leg.state.or.us/liz/2015R1/Downloads/Measu reDocument/HB2571/Enrolled.

footage not flagged by officers as having evidentiary value. Miami-Dade offers a rare definition: "Footage that does not necessarily have value to aid in an investigation or prosecution, such as footage of an incident or encounter that does not lead to an arrest or citation or footage of general activities that an officer might perform while on duty (e.g., assisting a motorist or clearing a roadway)."[59] What is striking about the definition is how it makes explicit

[59] MIAMI-DADE POLICE DEP'T., CHAPTER 33 – Part I – BODY-WORN CAMERA SYSTEM (2016); N.Y. POLICE DEP'T., OPERATIONS ORDER DRAFT FOR PUBLIC COMMENT (2016).

the implicit notion that evidentiary value means evidence in an investigation or prosecution leading to an arrest or citation.

Because so few policies had references to retention of recordings relevant to a potential civil suit against the police, we expanded the category during coding to include retention of data depicting uses of force, which are the most frequent bases for a civil suit. Even expanding the definition of the variable, nearly 40 percent of the agencies in the sample had no provision on how long recordings relevant to civil suits should be retained. Where departments did have provisions on such recordings – most frequently, provisions on recordings of uses of force – they tended to recognize the seriousness of the need to preserve the recordings. The majority provided for retention of such recordings at least until the disposition of the case if not longer (see Table 7.3). This suggests the challenge is not one of undervaluing the import of preserving video for accountability purposes, but rather of thinking of recordings as evidence in such cases in addition to traditional prosecutions.

Data regarding police activities is valuable even if does not present evidence for prosecution in a specific case or record conduct that rises to the level of a critical incident or complaint. As discussed in Chapter 4, over time and across many cases and incidents, the data may reveal potentially important patterns and practices. The aggregate data might reveal issues such as targeting minorities for revenue-generating stop and fines, escalating encounters through rude and aggressive behavior, or differences in the use of physical or verbal forcefulness by race of the community member encountered. Big data requires an aggregate, not just an individual, lens to appreciate and develop its full potential to be harnessed to improve the public good.

Police department policies can hardly be faulted for focusing on their primary role of gathering evidence for law enforcement purposes. Rather, democratic polities should not abdicate their role of framing policing laws and policies through inaction or delegating the duty. It is police department manual-writing 101 to consult with and comply with legal requirements.[60] Where legislatures have made provision for the retention of evidence for civil suits or preservation of evidence, departmental policies honor that democratic determination. Indeed, as Tables 7.2 and 7.3 show, police policies often import or summarize the schedules for evidentiary retention set by law, if any, or even more simply, use legal yardsticks such as the statute of limitations to determine their retention schedules.

---

[60] W. Dwayne Orrick, Developing A Police Department Policy-Procedure Manual (International Chiefs of Police 2017).

TABLE 7.2 *Nonevidentiary Data Retention, 213 Body Camera Policies*

Policy position	Number of agencies	Proportion of sample
Between one and under four weeks	7	3%
Between one month and under two months	20	9%
Between two months and under three months	15	7%
Between three months and under four months	25	12%
Between four months and under six months	6	3%
Between six months and under seven months	19	9%
Between eleven months and under one year, six months	13	6%
Between two years and under three years, six months	8	4%
Seven years or more	1	0.5%
Retain based on general departmental policy or applicable state laws	62	29%
Not specified	37	17%

Note. The time intervals in the first column are not continuous because intervals that no agency has chosen are omitted for space.

TABLE 7.3 *Retention of Data for Civil Suit or Complaint, 213 Body Camera Policies*

Policy position	Number of agencies	Proportion of sample
Until matter is resolved	22	10%
Pursuant to general dep't policy or state law	73	34%
Statute of limitations for filing civil suit	5	2%
Twelve years or more	7	3%
Between seven years and under twelve years	2	1%
Between three years and under seven years	10	5%
Between one year and under three years	5	2%
Between six months and under one year	3	1%
Between one month and under six months	4	2%
Not specified	82	39%

The approach of incorporating legislatively set schedules is much more prevalent for data deemed evidentiary, because legislatures are more likely to have spoken on the issue. The blind spots regarding retention of evidence for civil suits or aggregated data analyses is ultimately a blind spot of the democratic polity in weighing the costs and benefits of retention for such purposes and enacting laws that reflect the balances struck. As awareness grows about the value of audiovisual big data for police accountability, it is up to legislatures to balance the costs and benefits of preservation and to provide guidance for departments.

OPEN ETHICAL AND POLICY FRONTIERS

Much of the policy development and the analyses of these policies is about police-worn body cameras. But cell phone recordings by community members also can pose major privacy issues. Some copwatching groups have voluntarily adopted the ethic of asking the community member in a police encounter for permission to record and sought advice before posting videos online.[61] There is no uniform practice or norm among copwatchers, however, regarding mitigating privacy harms. There is much room for grassroots ethics and policy development; potentially guided by entities that work closely with some of the most impacted community members and that have taken an interest in copwatching. For example, organizations like the ACLU, Electronic Frontier Foundation, and National Lawyers Guild have launched projects to educate the public about their right to record the police. Part of the education also could be about best practices in reducing potential privacy harms to persons captured on the recordings.

Another entity that works closely with persons who encounter the police are the members of the National Association for Criminal Defense Lawyers (NACDL). NACDL has formed a sousveillance task force and consulted experts on policy and litigation issues, including this author. The mission of the task force is "[t]o encourage community monitoring – or sousveillance – of law enforcement activities through lawful techniques."[62] The interest of the organization stems from the hope that "sousveillance has the potential to minimize police misconduct and the accompanying undermining of core criminal justice values, including due process and equal protection."[63] The task force is studying the emerging issues, best practices, regulations, and laws surrounding recording the police.[64] Part of the policy development work also can include investigation of best practices to reduce privacy harms to community members while copwatching.

[61] Jocelyn Simonson, *Copwatching*, 104 CAL. L. REV. 391, 432 (2016).
[62] Email from Harden Pinckney, Request for Help for Hearings for the NACDL Task Force on Sousveillance (Copwatch) (May 10, 2018, 1:43 PM).
[63] Id.
[64] Id.

The pooling and secure storage of community member video in an independent repository proposed in Chapter 2 also may help to mitigate privacy harms. The sponsors of the repository can help promulgate best practices for copwatch groups to maximize the usefulness of the data generated. The public interest organizations that disseminate apps for securely uploading videos of police encounters to the cloud or YouTube can include advisories and information about best practices to reduce privacy harms. If the repository is run by a government agency independent of law enforcement, similar to the model for the Aviation Safety Reporting System discussed in Chapter 2, the agency can adopt policies and issue advice regarding issues such as privacy protection for the repository.

Though data storage costs are likely to fall as technology advances, the current costs remain a formidable challenge for the start-up of independent repositories, unless vested in an independent government agency. Contracting with a private company to provide secure data storage can be financially daunting for many civic organizations, particularly copwatch groups running largely on volunteerism. In addition, there are further coordination costs when it comes to educating the public to share their recordings with a central repository. It would take one or more major civic organizational actors with sufficient resources to fund and direct such an effort.

Yet these costs are not prohibitive, even absent government involvement in starting up a repository that aggregates and secures community member recordings. One way to address this challenge is to forge private sector and public partnerships between major private cloud storage companies and research universities. Major companies such as Microsoft have strong track records partnering with universities and investing millions of dollars to engage in technology-related public service.[65] Part public service, part market development, these endeavors have the potential to generate a wealth of information to prevent harm and protect the public. State, local, and federal grants as well as private funding for projects by philanthropies, such as the Soros Foundation or the William and Flora Hewlett Foundation, can also help launch the endeavor.[66]

Privacy presents one of the hardest value trade-offs. Controlled access, privacy protection planning, and bounded mining can help mitigate these

---

[65] *See Microsoft Partners with the University of Washington to Create the Tech Policy Lab*, MICROSOFT (Sept. 13, 2013), https://blogs.microsoft.com/on-the-issues/2013/09/13/microsoft-partners-with-the-university-of-washington-to-create-the-tech-policy-lab/ [http://perma.cc/V8J D-7MTP].

[66] *See, e.g.*, Grants to the University of Washington, WILLIAM & FLORA HEWLETT FOUND., www.hewlett.org/grants/university-of-washington-for-the-center-for-studies-in-demography-and-ecology/ [http://perma.cc/MSV6-EN3V] (last visited Dec. 26, 2017).

concerns. Privacy proponents who view video data retention and aggregation with alarm are likely to argue that these proposals do not eliminate the risks posed by aggregating more audiovisual data regarding police encounters with community members than ever before in history. Privacy proponents also generally do not support the accumulation of vast stores of data for mining. It is important to distinguish body camera data mining and analytics for police accountability purposes from the type of data mining that rouses concerns about impinging on citizen privacy. Even the paradigmatic privacy watchdog, the ACLU, recognizes that surveillance and tracking of the public is distinct from internal and external investigations of police misconduct.[67]

Deletion certainly can be an important way to ensure that people are not frozen in their worst moments.[68] The aggregation and public availability of information, such as data on bankruptcies or criminal history can haunt people and stunt their potential to recover and flourish.[69] But deletion is not the only way. Controlled access and privacy protection planning offer an alternative. We do not delete the painful and embarrassing information in our health histories, even though the information may impact our careers and personal lives. Nor should we lock away audiovisual data that could be analyzed via controlled access to try to better protect public health.

When Michael Brown's grieving mother called for police-worn body cameras, and when civil liberties groups like the ACLU and NAACP did so too, these privacy costs and risks were known trade-offs. The hope was that communities would gain better surveillance of the police, evidence, and accountability. The challenge now is ensuring that the hoped-for benefits of improved harm prevention and accountability actually occur. Scholars and some civil rights advocates have expressed concern that body camera recordings have become another way to get evidence against community members to speed the path to conviction.[70] The power to use body camera videos becomes one-sided just like other controversial police powers because law enforcement controls and limits access to videos. As we saw in Chapter 6, a growing number of laws

---

[67] Jay Stanley, *Police Body-Mounted Cameras: With Right Policies in Place, a Win for All*, Version 2.0 ACLU (Oct. 2015), www.aclu.org/sites/default/files/assets/police_body-mounted_cameras-v2.pdf.

[68] *See, e.g.*, Meg Lata Jones, Control+Z: The Right to Be Forgotten 3 (2016); Jeffrey Rosen, *The Right to Be Forgotten*, 64 Stan. L. Rev. Online 88, 88–90 (2012).

[69] *See, e.g.*, Lior Jacob Strahilevitz, *Privacy versus Antidiscrimination*, 75 U. Chi. L. Rev. 363, 364–370, 371–375 (2008) (discussing adverse decisions based on assumptions about criminal history and bankruptcies).

[70] For a discussion, *see, e.g.*, Laurent Sacharoff & Sarah Lustbader, *Who Should Own Police Body Camera Videos?*, 95 Wash. U. L. Rev. 269, 293–294 (2017).

forbid disclosure of videos, often in the name of protecting privacy, among other concerns.

Ultimately, the question is whether society values the potential benefit of audiovisual big data analytics to reduce the risk of violence and rights violations to pay the privacy price for it. The privacy price need not be as dire as opponents would suggest. Some of the most private and protected information – our personal health data – is aggregated and used to make major advances in enabling us to live longer, healthier lives. Drawing insights from the overarching principles governing protections for personal health data can help us cultivate the benefits of the growing trove of audiovisual data while reducing the risk of privacy harms.

8

Nonrecording and Officer Monitoring and Discipline Dilemmas

Activating the cameras: This gets to the heart of transparency. Oversight from the video can't happen if there is no video.

– Ken Wallentine, Vice President, Lexipol, a model policy drafting consulting company[1]

Revolutions offer grand promises of transformation that seize attention and tantalize the imagination.[2] But the real impact – if any – of a revolution is determined in the messy days after the revolution, during execution of the promises.[3] It is in implementation that promises come to fruition or go unrealized – or even invert, offering the opposite of what people hoped. Whether and how challenges on the ground are addressed determines the real impact of the recording revolution in police regulation.

On the books, recording policies seem to present a major transparency paradigm shift, mandating recording of most law enforcement activities such as stops, searches, arrests, use of force, responses to calls, and more. On the ground, however, operational challenges are giving rise to important policy dilemmas. This chapter addresses two important issues. First are the controversies over missing video, when officers did not record as required. There are understandable reasons why officers may not activate recording in the heat and

---

[1] *Quoted in* Kimberly Kindy & Julie Tate, *Police Withhold Videos Despite Vows of Transparency*, WASH. POST (Oct. 8, 2015), www.washingtonpost.com/sf/national/2015/10/08/police-withhold-videos-despite-vows-of-transparency/?utm_term=.cf32874baf4b.

[2] *See, e.g.*, Matt Viser & Annie Linsky, *Grand Promises Stir Voter Passions, but Are Hard to Keep*, BOS. GLOBE (Jan. 25, 2016), www.bostonglobe.com/news/politics/2016/ 01/25/donald-trump-and-bernie-sanders-lead-pack-with-unrealistic-promises/CxkGiorOezl2 d365xtQIgK/story.html (discussing the "pie-in-the-sky" policies 2016 presidential candidates Donald J. Trump and Bernie Sanders espoused during their respective campaigns).

[3] *See* BRUCE ACKERMAN, THE FUTURE OF LIBERAL REVOLUTION 27, 72, 96 (1992) (discussing the challenges of implementing promises made during a revolution once "normal politics" has resumed in a postrevolution society).

stress of the moment or due to mistake or malfunction. But there also are challenges with resistance by some officers and selective recording. Currently, policies are frequently silent about the detection of failures to record an event altogether, and what happens to officers who do not record as required.

This is part of a larger dilemma over the use of police videos for officer monitoring and discipline. Imagine having to wear a camera recording almost everything you say and do during working hours. The objections are obvious – being recorded for long periods of the workday is oppressive – and it is amplified if that video is used against you. Police unions and line officers have serious concerns about the burdens of near-constant video surveillance mounted on their bodies throughout the workday being used for punishment. Jurisdictions are still struggling to find the right balance, with widely varying approaches on the disciplinary use of body camera data. Each of these operational challenges will be recurring issues requiring recalibration as communities and police departments gain more experience with police regulation by radical transparency.

WHEN OFFICERS DO NOT RECORD

Why did a Minneapolis police officer shoot Justine Damond after she called to report a possible sexual assault?[4] The officers at the scene were wearing body cameras, but they did not record the fatal encounter.[5]

The officers in Baton Rouge who fatally shot Alton Sterling also were wearing body cameras – but both of the officers involved reported that their cameras fell off.[6] Officers also were wearing body cameras when Keith Scott died in Charlotte,[7] and when Paul O'Neal died in Chicago.[8] The officer

---

[4] Andy Mannix, *911 Call Transcript: Before Being Shot by Officer, Justine Damond Called in Possible Rape*, MINN. STAR TRIB. (July 19, 2017, 9:24 PM), www.startribune. com/911-call-be fore-being-shot-by-officer-justine-damond-called-in-possible-rape/435423423/.

[5] Mark Berman, *What the Minneapolis Police Shooting Tells Us about the Limits of Body Cameras*, WASH. POST (July 19, 2017), http://wapo.st/2uAnJoI.

[6] *See* Kimbriell Kelly et al., *Fatal Shootings by Police Remain Relatively Unchanged after Two Years*, WASH. POST (Dec. 30, 2016), http://wapo.st/2hBOTix ("[P]olice said body cameras 'fell off the officers . . . as they responded to a call about a man with a gun outside of a convenience store."); Aliyah Frumin, *After Baton Rouge Shooting, Questions Swirl around Body Cam Failures*, NBC NEWS (July 7, 2016), www.nbcnews.com/news/us-news/after-baton-rouge-shoot ing-questions-swirl-around-body-cam-failures-n605386?cid=e m1_onsite.

[7] See Wesley Lowery, *Charlotte Officer Did Not Activate Body Camera Until after Keith Scott Had Been Shot*, WASH. POST (Sept. 26, 2016), http://wapo.st/2cwPtXn.

[8] *See* Annie Sweeney & Jeremy Gorner, *Chicago Police: Body Camera Didn't Record Cop's Fatal Shooting of Teen in Back*, CHI. TRIB. (Aug. 2, 2016, 7:04 AM), www.chicag otribune.com/ne ws/local/breaking/ct-chicago-police-shooting-eddie-johnson-met-20160801-story.html.

wearing a body camera at the scene of Scott's death did not activate the camera to capture both audio and video until after the shooting.[9] The police officers said he was armed and refused to drop the weapon. His family said he was holding a book. The officer who fired the fatal shot into O'Neal's back during a foot pursuit also did not hit record until after the fatal shot.[10]

The major brand of body cameras that many departments use requires officers to double-tap to record and capture both audio and video. If the camera is not activated, it is on buffer mode, which only saves the most recent thirty seconds of soundless video. In the Scott shooting, after four days of turbulent protests, authorities produced body camera video that was missing audio of the crucial moments before the shooting.

The police departments involved in each shooting were among the hundreds nationwide that have adopted police-worn body cameras in recent years to rebuild public trust.[11] Each of the departments' policies mandated recording in the context where the shooting occurred, unless it was unsafe to do so.[12]

---

[9]   Lowery, *supra* note 7.

[10] William Lee, *Autopsy: Paul O'Neal Fatally Shot by Police in Back*, CHI. TRIB. (Aug. 17, 2016, 8:13 PM), www.chicagotribune.com/news/local/breaking/ct-chicago-police-shooting-eddie-jo hnson-met-20160801-story.html.

[11] *See* Mike Maciag, *Survey: Almost All Police Departments Plan to Use Body Cameras*, GOVERNING (Jan. 26, 2016), www.governing.com/topics/public-justice-safety/gov-polic e-bod y-camera-survey.html (reporting on the uptake of police-worn body cameras among departments across the nation); Brent McDonald & Hillary Bachelder, *With Rise of Body Cameras, New Tests of Transparency and Trust*, N.Y. TIMES (Jan. 6, 2017), https://nyti.ms/2j axwBF (describing the challenges faced by police departments nationwide in rolling out a body-camera program).

[12] *See* Charlotte-Mecklenberg POLICE DEP'T, INTERACTIVE DIRECTIVES GUIDE, DIRECTIVE 400-005 (effective May 11, 2015), www.rcfp.org/bodycam_policies/NC/Charlott e_BWC_Policy.pdf ("Officers will ensure that DMVR equipment (both video and audio) is activated and operating properly and that the video recorder is positioned and adjusted to record events in the following circumstances: [traffic stops, pursuits, emergency response, and prisoner transport]."); CHICAGO POLICE DEP'T, BODY WORN CAMERAS, SPECIAL ORDER S03-14 (effective May 10, 2016) [hereinafter CHI. PD, ORDER S03-14], www.bwcscore card.org/static/policies/2016-05-10%20Chicago%20-$20BWC$20Policy.pdf ("Department members assigned a [Body Worn Camera]: will activate the system to event mode to record the entire incident for all … traffic stops … foot and vehicle pursuits; emergency driving situations; high-risk situations … any encounter with the public that becomes adversarial after the initial contact; and any other instance when enforcing the law."); BATON ROUGE POLICE DEP'T, BODY WORN CAMERAS, No. 502/15-1 (eff. Apr. 23, 2015) (on file with author) ("Body Worn Camera Recorders shall be utilized to record the following types of events when safe to activate: … All Calls of Service, including backup Officers [and] Other legitimate law enforcement contacts."); MINNEAPOLIS POLICE DEP'T, POLICY & PROCEDURE MANUAL § 4-223 (effective July 29, 2017), www.ci.minneapolis.mn.us/police/policy/mp dpolicy_4-200_4-200 ("Officers shall active their BWC for the following circumstances … Any contact involving allegations of criminal

The practice on the ground, however, did not follow the rules on the books. Numerous other such cases and controversies involving a failure to record have arisen across the nation.[13]

You can put a camera on an officer, but getting that officer to record – particularly at the crucial high-stress moment – can be difficult, as recent controversies illustrate. There are many legitimate reasons for not recording, such as the exigencies and stress of the moment, technological malfunction, inexperience, the transition to new technology and mandates, and other mistakes.[14] But there are also potentially problematic reasons for failures to record, such as refusal to comply with the rules, concealment, or subversion. Parsing between legitimate and illegitimate reasons for failures to record can lead courts and the public into a murky morass.

As departments implement recording requirements, nonrecording is a recurring challenge.[15] Consider the experience of some of the early movers

---

activity . . . Any use of force situation. If a BWC is not activated prior to use of force, it shall be activated as soon as it is safe to do so.").

[13] *See, e.g.*, United States v. Daniel, No. 1:16 CR 6 SNLJ (ACL), 2016 WL 4004578, at *5 (E.D. Mo. July 7, 2016) ("[A]ccording to Perryville Police Department policy the body camera should be used during interactions with suspects . . . Officer James testified that he believed his body camera was on throughout the traffic stop, however, it turned out the recorder either hadn't been turned on, it was not functioning, or he 'possibly didn't use it correctly.'"); Nashelly Chavez, *Rocklin Officers Who Shot Former Honor Student Didn't Turn on Body Cameras until Later*, SACRAMENTO BEE (Mar. 3, 2017, 6:11 PM), www. sacbee.com/news/lo cal/crime/article136372438.html (did not record until after fatal shooting); Lynh Bui & Peter Hermann, *Federal Officials Indict Seven Baltimore Police Officers on Racketeering*, WASH. POST (Mar. 1, 2017), http://wapo.st/2lqLXSU (detailing charges against officers who allegedly extorted money from civilians, used or threatened force, and turned off their body cameras during the encounters); Kym Klass, *Community Gathers to Remember Greg Gunn*, MONTGOMERY ADVERTISER (Ala.) (Feb. 26, 2017, 5:53 PM), http://on.gmadv.com/2lHxDsq (reporting that the officer failed to turn on his body camera during a stop and chase in which the officer beat, Tased, and then fatally shot Greg Gunn); Yihyun Jeong, *Completed Investigation into Flagstaff Officer Punching Woman Sent to Coconino County Attorney*, ARIZ. REPUBLIC (Jan. 3, 2017, 2:18 PM), http://azc.cc/2LPrcle (reporting that an officer turned off his body camera during an encounter that involved the officer punching a woman); Alex Holloway, *Ricky Ball Shooting: Officers Respond to Ball Lawsuit*, COMMERCIAL DISPATCH (Columbus, Miss.) (Nov. 2, 2016, 10:48 AM), www. cdispatch.com/news/article .asp?aid=53932 (reporting that an officer did not activate his body camera during a traffic stop in which the officer shot and killed Ricky Ball, a passenger).

[14] *Cf.* Atwater v. City of Lago Vista, 532 US 318, 346–347 (2001) (explaining that police officers frequently have to act "on the spur (and in the heat) of the moment").

[15] *See also, e.g.*, Justin Fenton & Kevin Rector, *7 Officers Charged with Racketeering: Members of City Gun Task Force Accused of Robbing Civilians*, BALTIMORE SUN (Mar. 2, 2017), 2017 WLNR 6558848 (reporting prosecutors' allegations that seven Baltimore police officers who were indicted for racketeering turned off their body cameras before threatening civilians to extract payments); Tim Cushing, *ACLU Suggests Jury Instructions Might Be a Fix for "Missing" Body Camera Recordings*, TECHDIRT (Dec. 3, 2016), 2016 WLNR 36979699

in deploying body cameras. The Phoenix Police Department instructed officers that the "camera must be activated during all investigative or enforcement contacts," which includes traffic stops.[16] Yet, a recent evaluation of the impact of BWCs in the department found that a mere 6.5 percent of traffic stops were recorded.[17] Officers were most likely to use their body cameras to record domestic violence calls, where the evidentiary value of recordings for prosecution are particularly crucial because victims frequently recant.[18] Even then, less than half (47.5 percent) of domestic violence incidents were recorded.[19]

The Denver Police Department's results are also instructive. The department's body camera policy required activation in numerous contexts, such as "[p]edestrian, citizen and/or vehicle contacts" and "[a]ny encounter that becomes adversarial."[20] Yet, the independent monitor overseeing the department found that, during the six-month pilot program, only twenty-one of eighty uses of force were recorded by BWCs – just 26 percent of such critical incidents.[21] Unrecorded uses of force included incidents such as punching a suspect in the face, baton strikes, pushing, pepper-spraying, and tasing suspects.[22] Some of the nonrecording occurred because supervisors or off-duty officers were not required to wear body cameras at the time.[23] Yet, even

("Body cameras are pretty much mainstream at this point, but when excessive force and/or misconduct are alleged, footage captured by police is often nonexistent. Officers disable recording equipment, delete footage, or simply claim the camera 'malfunctioned.' Some repeatedly 'forget' to activate their cameras ahead of controversial arrests and interactions.").

[16] PHOENIX POLICE DEP'T, BODY WORN VIDEO TECHNOLOGY – PILOT, OPERATIONS ORDER 4.49, § 5 (effective Apr. 2013).

[17] CHARLES M. KATZ ET AL., ARIZ. STATE UNIV. CTR. FOR VIOLENCE PREVENTION AND CMTY. SAFETY, EVALUATING THE IMPACT OF OFFICER WORN BODY CAMERAS IN THE PHOENIX POLICE DEPARTMENT 22 (2014), http://publicservice.asu.edu/sites/default/files/ppd_spi_feb_20_2015_final.pdf.

[18] *See also* SAN DIEGO POLICE DEP'T, AXON BODY WORN CAMERAS, PROCEDURE 1.49, § V (2015) [hereinafter SAN DIEGO PD, PROCEDURE 1.49], https://rcfp.org/bodycam_policies/CA/SanDiegoBWCPolicy_update.pdf ("Domestic violence victims often recant their statements as early as the following morning after a crime. Some victims go so far as to testify that the officer fabricated their statement. Victims may also make their children unavailable for investigators or court to avoid their providing statements."); Deborah Tuerkheimer, *Crawford's Triangle: Domestic Violence and the Right of Confrontation*, 85 N.C. L. REV. 1, 14–16 (2006) (explaining that domestic violence victims frequently succumb to pressures from batterers and recant, refuse to testify, disappear, or refuse to press charges).

[19] KATZ ET AL., *supra* note 17, at 22.

[20] DENVER POLICE DEP'T, BODY WORN CAMERA, POLICY 111.11, § 3 (finalized Sept. 1, 2015), www.rcfp.org/bodycam_policies/CO/DenverCO_BWC_policy_update.pdf.

[21] DENVER OFFICE OF THE INDEP. MONITOR, 2014 ANNUAL REPORT 10 (2015).

[22] *Id.* at 13, 20, 24–25.

[23] *Id.* at 17–18.

among officers who were patrolling on duty and required to use body cameras, only 47 percent of the forty-five uses of force were recorded despite the rules.[24]

While recording policy noncompliance rates are not available for many other departments, scandals and deaths are revealing problems. In Baltimore, an investigation into officers who allegedly used traffic stops, home entries, and false warrants to rob civilians also revealed how the officers would regularly turn off their body cameras during such encounters.[25] Baltimore Police Department policy clearly and concisely mandates body camera activation during any "activity that is investigative or enforcement in nature" or "any encounter that becomes confrontational."[26] The alleged behavior on the ground, if proven true, would be a mockery of the rules.

In Chicago, the national controversy over the shooting of seventeen-year-old Laquan McDonald – and the missing audio from the five patrol car dash cameras at the scene – led to a departmental investigation.[27] The investigation found that 80 percent of dash cameras had "no functioning audio."[28] Intentional destruction and officer error have contributed to the widespread problem.[29] After a disciplinary crackdown that included random checks and punishment, the volume of video uploaded after each shift increased by 75 percent.[30] But the national spotlight on missing video in Chicago did not end there.

Responding to calls for transparency, the Chicago Police Department had expanded its body camera program when officers fatally shot eighteen-year-old Paul O'Neal after he crashed a stolen Jaguar into police cars and then ran away

---

[24] *Id.* at 17.

[25] Press Release, Dep't of Justice, Seven Baltimore City Police Officers Arrested for Abusing Power in Federal Racketeering Conspiracy (Mar. 1, 2017), www.justice.gov/usao-md/pr/seven-baltimore-city-police-officers-arrested-abusing-power-federal-racketeering.

[26] Baltimore Police Dep't, Body Worn Cameras Pilot Program Policy 824 (effective Oct. 26, 2015), www.bwcscorecard.org/static/policies/2015-10-26%20Baltimore%20-$2 oBWC% 20Policy.pdf.

[27] *See* Jeremy Gorner, *Nearly 2 Dozen Chicago Cops Disciplined for Faulty Dashboard Cameras,* Chi. Trib. (Jan. 7, 2016, 6:56 AM), www.chicagotribune.com/news/opinion/editorials/ct-ch icago-police-disciplined-met-20160106-story.html (describing the discipline officers have received after the shooting as a result of investigations into officers' use of dash-cams).

[28] *Id.*

[29] *See* Radley Balko, *80 Percent of Chicago PD Dash-Cam Videos Are Missing Audio due to "Officer Error" or "Intentional Destruction,"* Wash. Post (Jan. 29, 2016), http://wapo.st/1nCW 5d0 (reporting the various ways Chicago officers prevent dash-cam audio from being recorded, including "stash[ing] microphones in their squad car glove boxes" and "pull[ing] out batteries").

[30] *See* Jeremy Gorner, *Nearly 2 Dozen Chicago Cops Disciplined for Faulty Dashboard Cameras,* Chi. Trib. (Jan. 7, 2016, 6:56 AM), www.chicagotribune.com/news/opinion/ editorials/ct-c hicago-police-disciplined-met-20160106-story.html.

on foot.[31] Chicago's body camera policy calls for officers to record all foot and vehicle pursuits, emergency driving situations and "any other instance while enforcing the law," among many enumerated contexts.[32] But the officer who shot O'Neal did not activate his body camera and catch the crucial moments. The crash, stress of the moment, and officer inexperience may be the reasons for the failure to record. But such omissions are likely to further undermine community trust in a context of extremely troubled police-community relations.

Chicago and Baltimore are hardly alone in the missing video controversy. The problem is underscored by the nonrecording of fatal shootings in numerous other jurisdictions that have adopted body cameras, such as Flagstaff, Arizona; Rocklin, California; Columbus, Mississippi; Charlotte, North Carolina; and Montgomery, Alabama.[33] In San Diego, it was the unrecorded fatal shooting of police officers wearing body cameras that underscored how the protection of police as well as civilian lives are at stake.[34]

Even when it comes to the more established technology of patrol car dash cameras, findings by Chicago police officials indicate that 80 percent of recordings fail to capture audio due to officer error or "intentional destruction."[35]

[31]   Annie Sweeney & Jeremy Gorner, *Chicago Police: Body Camera Didn't Record Cop's Fatal Shooting of Teen in Back*, CHI. TRIB. (Aug. 2, 2016, 7:04 AM), www.chicag otribune.com/news/local/breaking/ct-chicago-police-shooting-eddie-johnson-met-20160801-st ory.html.

[32]   CHI. PD, ORDER S03-14, *supra* note 12, at § II.A.2.

[33]   *See, e.g.*, United States v. Daniel, No. 1:16 CR 6 SNLJ (ACL), 2016 WL 4004578, at *5 (E.D. Mo. July 7, 2016) ("[A]ccording to Perryville Police Department policy the body camera should be used during interactions with suspects . . . Officer James testified that he believed his body camera was on throughout the traffic stop, however, it turned out the recorder either hadn't been turned on, it was not functioning, or he 'possibly didn't use it correctly.'"); Nashelly Chavez, *Rocklin Officers Who Shot Former Honor Student Didn't Turn on Body Cameras until Later*, SACRAMENTO BEE (Mar. 3, 2017, 6:11 PM), www.sacbee.com/news/loc al/crime/article136372438.html (did not record until after fatal shooting); Lynh Bui & Peter Hermann, *Federal Officials Indict Seven Baltimore Police Officers on Racketeering*, WASH. POST (Mar. 1, 2017), http://wapo.st/2lqLXSU (detailing charges against officers who allegedly extorted money from civilians, used or threatened force, and turned off their body cameras during the encounters); Kym Klass, *Community Gathers to Remember Greg Gunn*, MONTGOMERY ADVERTISER (Ala.) (Feb. 26, 2017, 5:53 PM), http://on.gmadv.com/2lHxDsq (reporting that the officer failed to turn on his body camera during a stop and chase in which the officer beat, Tased, and then fatally shot Greg Gunn); Yihyun Jeong, *Completed Investigation into Flagstaff Officer Punching Woman Sent to Coconino County Attorney*, ARIZ. REPUBLIC (Jan. 3, 2017, 2:18 PM), http://azc.cc/2LPrcle (reporting that an officer turned off his body camera during an encounter that involved the officer punching a woman); Alex Holloway, *Ricky Ball Shooting: Officers Respond to Ball Lawsuit*, COMMERCIAL DISPATCH (Columbus, Miss.) (Nov. 2, 2016, 10:48 AM), www. cdispatch.com/news/article .asp?aid=53932 (reporting that an officer did not activate his body camera during a traffic stop in which the officer shot and killed Ricky Ball, a passenger).

[34]   Amanda Lee Myers, *Fatal Police Shooting Highlights Inconsistent Body Cam Usage*, ASSOCIATED PRESS (Aug. 6, 2016), https://apnews.com/13112c126c9642bdbb21a1db47b2873f.

[35]   Balko, *supra* note 29.

Nonrecording poses the risk of subverting the hopes that led communities across the nation to embrace more surveillance by police body cameras in exchange for improved accountability, community trust, and transparency.[36] If the problem is left unchecked, rather than being a tool of police accountability, body camera recordings could amplify the problems of a gross imbalance in power. Video recordings can offer more powerful evidence to speed up a plea bargain or conviction or justify a search or seizure.[37] But recordings that might exonerate or implicate officers are missing.[38] The issue is important from a public safety perspective as well as for adjudicative justice. As we saw in Chapter 1, there is emerging evidence that wearing body cameras is associated with reduced use of force among officers who follow the recording protocol, but uses of forces increase among officers who wear body cameras and do not follow the rules.[39]

THE DISCIPLINARY DILEMMA

What happens when key video evidence is missing, contrary to the police department's own rules? How do we even know if officers have cameras off when they are supposed to be recording? The rules that address these

---

[36] *See, e.g.*, Police Exec. RESEARCH FORUM, DEP'T OF JUSTICE, IMPLEMENTING A BODY-WORN CAMERA PROGRAM: RECOMMENDATIONS AND LESSONS LEARNED 5 (2014) [hereinafter JUSTICE DEP'T BWC RECS.], www.justice.gov/iso/opa/resources/47201491213471524 68 69.pdf (discussing the accountability and transparency concerns that prompt police departments and communities to adopt police body cameras).

[37] *See, e.g.*, State v. Herrin, No. 1 CA-CR 12-0141, 2012 WL 3233227, at *2 (Ariz. Ct. App. Aug. 9, 2012) (dash camera recording used to secure a felony conviction for resisting arrest); United States v. Bryant, No. 1:15CR99-1, 2015 WL 2248177, at *1, *5 (M.D.N.C. May 13, 2015) (reviewing officer body camera footage and concluding that the defendant's nervous demeanor helped justify the stop when the encounter was no longer consensual in nature), *rev'd*, 654 F. App'x 622 (4th Cir. 2016); State v. Gibbons, No. 2012-UP-177, 2012 WL 10841329, at *1 (S.C. Ct. App. Mar. 14, 2012) (recording of defendant's arrest used to secure convictions for first-degree harassment and resisting arrest).

[38] *See, e.g.*, Richardson v. Mahon, No. 4:15-cv-3317-RBH-TSR, 2017 WL 430862 (S.D.S.C.), *vacated on other grounds*, 2017 WL 4262517 (4th Cir. Sept. 26, 2017) (alleging that officer failed to record plaintiff's arrest via body camera or dash camera though other officers said the events should have been recorded); United States v. Daniel, No. 1:16 CR 6 SNLJ (ACC), 2016 WL 4004578, at *5 (E.D. Mo. July 7, 2016) (noting absence of the recording of key contested events despite policy which required recording via body camera). *See also* Tim Cushing, *If Police Officials Won't Hold Officers Accountable, More Cameras Will Never Mean More Recordings*, TECHDIRT (Aug. 11, 2016), 2016 WLNR 24414477 (discussing examples of police failures to record).

[39] Barak Ariel et al., *Report: Increases in Police Use of Force in the Presence of Body-Worn Cameras Are Driven by Officer Discretion: A Protocol-Based Subgroup Analysis of Ten Randomized Experiments*, 12 J. EXPERIMENTAL CRIMINOLOGY 453 (2016).

TABLE 8.1 *Sanctions for Failure to Follow Body Camera Policy*

Policy position	Number	Percentage
Policy expressly provides there will be no disciplinary sanctions.	5	2%
Officers will not be disciplined but may be referred for training or career counseling and/or may have note in performance evaluation.	6	3%
Violations generally may be a basis for discipline.	28	13%
Minor infractions are not sanctioned, but other violations can be the basis for discipline.	4	2%
Minor infractions are punished less severely but can be a basis for discipline.	2	1%
Violations of body camera policies are treated pursuant to other general departmental policies.	8	4%
Not specified	160	75%

operational questions are located largely in departmental body camera policies, often negotiated with police unions.

Among the 213 body camera policies coded, fewer than half of the policies (44 percent) had provisions requiring officers to document failures to record an event altogether. Policies often require officers to explain why they deactivated a camera early, or before the end of the event but omit the requirement to document and give a reason for not activating the camera at all. As Table 8.1 summarizes, the majority of policies (75 percent) also did not specify sanctions for violations of recording policy.

The disciplinary issue is part of a larger dilemma over the use of body cameras for officer monitoring and evaluation. Body cameras have been controversial among police unions concerned about the use of videos to search for violations. In Illinois, these concerns led to a specific prohibition on the use of recordings being the basis for disciplining officers unless there also has been a complaint, use of force, or other evidence of misconduct.[40]

Police leaders adopting body cameras to rebuild public trust and allay controversies face a dilemma. For cameras to produce the desired benefits of reducing uses of force and citizen complaints, officers must actually use the technology as directed.[41] Consequences for rule violations are the usual

---

[40]   ILL. PUB. ACT 099-0352, § 10–20(a)(9) (2015).
[41]   Ariel et al., *supra* note 39, at 459–462 (arguing that body cameras "should remain on throughout the [officer's] entire shift," and officers should not retain discretion to activate the devices).

strategy to incentivize compliance.[42] The need to spell out consequences for noncompliance is no secret. Indeed, the Bureau of Justice Assistance provides the following advice to police departments:

> A department's policy should also clearly indicate what will happen to an officer who fails to activate a camera in circumstances where activation is required. Will the officer be subject to discipline? If so, how will he or she be disciplined? The consequences for failure to activate as well as premature deactivation should be clearly stated.[43]

The problem is that requiring sanctions is easier to recommend in theory than to accomplish in practice. Introducing body cameras requires buy-in from the ranks – and potentially court battles with the police union over the change in working conditions and whether recording rules must be collectively bargained.[44]

Police Unions and Labor Concerns

Under federal labor laws, collective bargaining with the workers' union is required when the conditions imposed by management constitute a material change to the applicable labor contract secured through collective

---

[42] Compare Austin's famous classical formulation of law as a command that a sovereign may enforce through the threat of a sanction. JOHN AUSTIN, THE PROVINCE OF JURISPRUDENCE DETERMINED 5 (Noonday Press 1954).

[43] BUREAU OF JUSTICE ASSISTANCE, BODY-WORN CAMERA TOOLKIT: FREQUENTLY ASKED QUESTIONS 21 (2015), www.bja.gov/bwc/pdfs/bwc_faqs.pdf.

[44] *See, e.g.*, Ben Conarck, *Jacksonville Sheriff, Police Union Clash over Body Camera Rules*, FLA. TIMES UNION (Jacksonville) (Feb. 8, 2017), 2017 WLNR 6684923 (reporting on a dispute between the local police union and the sheriff over whether body camera rules are subject to mandatory collective bargaining); Brian Bakst, *Maplewood Police Officers Challenge Body Camera Policy in Lawsuit*, MPR NEWS (Minn.) (Nov. 21, 2016), www. mprnews.org/story/20 16/11/21/maplewood-police-officers-challenge-body-camera-policy-law suit (reporting on lawsuit by police officers who objected to random audits of body camera recordings and argued that such provisions must be subject to collective bargaining); Jan Ransom, *Boston Slow to Adopt Policing Innovations; Changes Stall as Unions Seek Role*, BOS. GLOBE (Sept. 5, 2016), 2016 WLNR 27007841 (reporting on a court battle between a Boston police union and Boston Police Department management over the introduction of body cameras and whether rules should be subject to collective bargaining); Harry Bruinius, *Why Police Are Pushing Back on Body Cameras*, CHRISTIAN SCI. MONITOR (Aug. 30, 2016), 2016 WLNR 26450977 (detailing lawsuits and debates involving police unions over the body camera issue); Brian Brus, *Police Union Complaint Halts Body-Cam Test Program*, J. REC. (Okla. City) (June 15, 2016), 2016 WLNR 18940773 (discussing how a lawsuit by an Oklahoma City police union put the City's body camera program on hold); Andrew Blake, *Body Cameras Spark Lawsuit between Denver Cops, City Officials* (WASH. TIMES, Nov. 6, 2015), 2015 WLNR 33002278 (discussing a lawsuit by a Denver police union seeking collective bargaining over body camera rules).

bargaining.[45] Putting small surveillance devices on an employee throughout his or her workday that records what he or she says and does can certainly feel like an oppressive change in labor conditions. Officers and their unions often express concerns that video may be used to fish for small violations and harass or retaliate against officers.

To ameliorate these concerns, police labor unions have successfully secured limits on the use of recordings for officer monitoring, evaluation, and discipline.[46] Sometimes, as in the case of the Seattle Police Department's policy regarding its body camera pilot program, the influence of the union in securing protections against discipline for not recording is transparently described on the face of the policy:

> The Memorandum of Agreement between the City of Seattle and the Seattle Police Officers' Guild outlines the scope of the program. Pursuant to that agreement, there will be no discipline that follows from not recording a particular incident with BWV.[47]

When police department management designs a body camera program and policy without union input, the entire program can derail. For example, the Oklahoma City Department of Police had to halt its body-worn camera program after an arbitrator ruled that the rules regarding recording and review

---

[45]   *See* 29 USC. § 158(d) (2018) (describing the obligation to bargain collectively).

[46]   *See, e.g.,* Editorial, *Draft Body-Camera Policy Places Police Union's Concerns over Public's,* Oregonian (June 24, 2016), at A16, 2016 WLNR 19464570 (discussing controversy over the closed-door negotiations of a body camera policy between the mayor and the police union that allegedly resulted in a dilution of accountability and transparency measures); Max Schanzenbach, *Union Contracts Key to Reducing Police Misconduct,* Chi. Trib. (Nov. 24, 2015), at 17, 2015 WLNR 34864776 (discussing how unions have successfully used collective bargaining to resist body camera adoption by police departments and secure "binding arbitration for any significant disciplinary action taken against officers – a system stacked heavily in favor of police").

[47]   Seattle Police Dep't, Seattle Policy Manual, Body-Worn Camera Pilot Program, Policy 16.091 (effective Apr. 1, 2016). The current version of the Seattle Police Department's manual no longer includes the quoted language. Instead, the manual provides for particular situations in which an officer will not be disciplined. For example, a failure to record particularly sensitive or private interactions, such as interviews with victims of sexual assault, will not subject the officer to discipline. *See* Seattle Police Dep't, Seattle Police Manual, Policy 16.090-POL 1 (effective July 19, 2017) [hereinafter Seattle PD Manual], www.seattle.gov/policemanual/. Furthermore, upon departmental review of body camera recordings, an officer will not be subject to discipline for "minor acts of misconduct unrelated to the original reason for viewing the video" including use of profanity or rudeness. *See id.* at Policy 16.090-POL 2. Unlike the provision in the 2015 version of Seattle's manual, it is unclear from the policy itself whether the 2017 provisions were the result of collective bargaining.

had to be negotiated with the police union as part of a collective bargaining agreement.[48] The union supported body cameras to protect against false accusations but wanted the power to help frame the rules of recording and protections regarding supervisor review and compliance audits.[49] A central concern raised by the union was the management's policy of allowing supervisors to review recordings at any time.[50] The union wanted a limit to prevent supervisors from going on "a fishing expedition."[51]

Concerns over supervisors using recordings to hunt for violations and nickel-and-dime officers for minor issues is reflected in the number of protections addressing those concerns. Philadelphia's body camera policy explains the underlying rationale:

> To effectively perform their duties, Officers must have a level of comfort in which minor disciplinary offenses recorded while performing their duties that would not otherwise become known but for wearing a Body-Worn Camera, will not adversely affect an officer's career ... Thus, the secondary purpose of this directive is to provide officers with the knowledge that "minor disciplinary code violations" that are captured on any Body Worn Camera will not result in an official Internal Affairs investigation ... based solely upon their minor infraction.[52]

The proposed draft of the New York body camera policy offers examples of "nickel-and-diming" concerns, "such as chewing gum or taking off a hat that the supervisor wouldn't have otherwise seen."[53] Beyond sweating the small stuff, the larger concern is increased supervisor surveillance enabled by the availability of records. For example, Saint Paul's policy explicitly addresses the

---

[48] *See Agreement Reached to Restart Police Department's Body-Worn Camera Program*, US Fed. News, Nov. 29, 2016, Westlaw.
[49] *See id.*
[50] *See* Sheldra Brigham, *OKCPD Removes Body Cameras until Policy Is in Place*, KFOR News Channel 4 (June 15, 2016, 7:14 PM), http://kfor.com/2016/06/15/okcpd-removes-body-cameras-until-policy-is-in-place/.
[51] *See id.* (quoting union president John George, "We didn't want supervisors just to be able to go on a fishing expedition.").
[52] Phila. Police Dep't, Body-Worn Cameras, Directive 4.21, § 2.b (issued Jan. 15, 2016, updated Jan. 27, 2017) [hereinafter Phila. PD, BWC Dir.], www.phillypolice.com/assets/diretives/D4.21-BodyWornCameras.pdf.
[53] N.Y. Police Dep't, Operations Order Draft for Public Comment 10 (June 29, 2016) [hereinafter NYPD, Draft Operations Order], https://policingproject.org/wp-consent/uploads/2016/06/NYPD-BWC-Draft-Policy.pdf; *see also* Seattle PD Manual, *supra* note 47, at Policy 16.090-POL 2 (discussing examples of "minor infractions," such as uniform infractions).

issue, providing, "Supervisors may not access or review BWC Data for the purpose of surveillance of any employee."[54]

The concerns must be viewed in the structural context of police departments and labor's concerns regarding management. When a police department announces a plan to adopt body cameras, that does not mean that the officers who will actually be wearing the cameras support the endeavor. For example, when the Boston Police Department sought one hundred volunteers to pilot the technology, not a single person on the force of more than two thousand sworn officers volunteered.[55] The department had to conscript the hundred testers, whose union then sued, alleging labor law violations.[56] Management has a delicate task securing buy-in from officers. Launching even a small pilot program is hard enough. Specifying consequences for noncompliance risks rousing organized resistance that would altogether defeat the project.[57]

The strength and existence of police unions vary from state to state.[58] The approaches to whether body camera videos may be used for officer monitoring and evaluation also vary widely. Table 8.2 summarizes the different approaches departments have taken regarding the use of recordings for officer evaluation. Remarkably, the most prevalent approaches are on different sides of the labor-management spectrum. Twenty percent of the policies prohibit supervisors from access to body camera videos unless a complaint or use of force is filed. Another 3 percent prohibit supervisors from using body camera videos to search for minor violations. These protections for officers likely reflect the oft-expressed concerns of officers and unions about the risk of supervisors fishing through body camera video for minor violations to harass officers they do not like.

On the other end of the oversight spectrum, 38 percent of policies expressly authorize supervisors to review or audit recordings for compliance with recording requirements. Another 21 percent require supervisors to regularly review or

---

[54] St. Paul Police Dep't, Body Worn Camera Pilot Policy, Policy 442.18 (issued Oct. 25, 2016, revised Sept. 11, 2017), www.stpaul.gov/books/44218-body-worn-camera-pi lot-policy.

[55] Editorial, *Patience on "Pilot,"* Bos. Herald (Dec. 20, 2016), at 20, 2016 WLNR 38936566, www.bostonherald.com/opinion/editorials/2016/12/editorial_patience_on_pilot.

[56] Michael Levenson & Evan Allen, *Boston Police Union Challenges Body Camera Program,* Bos. Globe (Aug. 26, 2016), 2016 WLNR 26144946 ("[W]hen no officers volunteered to wear cameras, [the police commissioner] announced the department would effectively force 100 officers to wear the devices ... The [police] union [subsequently] filed a grievance.").

[57] *See, e.g.,* Liam Dillon, *Police Access Bills No Longer a Priority,* L.A. Times (Feb. 28, 2017), at 1, 2017 WLNR 6287355 (discussing "steadfast" union opposition on discipline issues and successful fights by police unions).

[58] For a discussion, *see, e.g.,* Stephen Rushin, *Police Union Contracts,* 66 Duke L. J. 1191–1266 (2017).

TABLE 8.2 *Supervisorial Review or Compliance Audits, 213 Body Camera Policies*

Policy position	Number	Percentage
No supervisorial access unless a complaint is filed and/or use of force occurs.	42	20%
No supervisorial access unless authorized by higher-ups.	1	0.5%
Supervisors generally may review recordings and/or audit recordings for compliance.	82	38%
Supervisors are required to review recordings regularly and/or audit recordings for compliance.	44	21%
Supervisors are expressly prohibited from searching for minor violations.	7	3%
Supervisors may review recordings for training purposes.	8	4%
Not specified	29	14%

audit their officers' recordings for compliance with recording requirements. Auditing or supervisorial review of a sample of videos can be an alternative method of detecting some forms of noncompliance with recording rules.[59] It is more likely to catch issues with early termination of recording rather than nonrecording, because supervisors review what is recorded, rather than what is not captured at all.

As departments gain more experience implementing police-worn body cameras, stances on sanctions and evaluation may change – particularly if there is external review of implementation. The Denver Police Department, which has among the toughest sanctions, is an example.[60] Since 2005, the Office of the Independent Monitor has served as a public watchdog over the Denver Police Department.[61] Created by ordinance passed by the City Council in 2004, the Independent Monitor has the power to monitor police

---

[59]   Cf. Jeremy Gorner, *Nearly 2 Dozen Chicago Cops Disciplined for Faulty Dashboard Cameras*, Chi. Trib. (Jan. 7, 2016, 6:56 AM), www.chicagotribune.com/news/opinion/editorials/ct-ch icago-police-disciplined-met-20160106-story.html (describing the "random checks" by investi-gators to determine whether Chicago police officers were properly reporting issues with dashboard cameras to their supervisors).

[60]   See Denver Police Dep't, Operations Manual, Body Worn Camera Technology, Policy 119.04, § 12 (effective Sept. 15, 2017) [hereinafter Denver PD Manual].

[61]   See Office of the Indep. Monitor, Complaint Monitoring Guidelines: Executive Summary 1 (2010), www.denvergov.org/content/dam/denvergov/Portals/374/doc uments/OIM_Case_Handling_Guidelines_Final_Executive_Summary_8_1_10.pdf ("In 2005, in an effort to improve police accountability to the public, the City of Denver created the Office of the Independent Monitor (OIM) ... to monitor and report on the handling of citizen complaints by the Denver Police and Sheriff Departments.").

conduct, investigate, and recommend changes in practices.[62] In 2014, following the Denver Police Department's pilot-test of police body cameras, the independent monitor released a report finding that many uses of force were not recorded on camera. The independent monitor noted that the failure to inform officers of possible sanctions for noncompliance might have contributed to the failures to record despite policy mandates.[63]

Drafted subsequent to the independent monitor's report, Denver's current body camera policy is now among the most detailed and toughest on sanctions among all the available major-city policies analyzed. For a first violation, Denver's policy provides for an oral reprimand, together with a mandated officer review of the body camera policy, a follow-up meeting with a supervisor, and a "journal entry."[64] The officer receives a written reprimand for a second violation in a twelve-month period and must undergo "an in-depth audit of the officer's data usage" and "a formal Personnel Assessment System (PAS)" review."[65] For a third violation in a 12-month period, the officer incurs "1 fined day."[66] In addition to this scale of penalties, the policy cautions that "[p]urposeful, flagrant or repeated violations will result in more severe disciplinary action."[67] These tough and detailed provisions contrast sharply with the majority approach of simply not addressing the consequences for noncompliance.

THE MURK BETWEEN LEGITIMATE MISTAKE AND SUBVERSION

Another important reason for the widespread omissions regarding consequences for failures to record is the difficulty of distinguishing legitimate from culpable conduct. The commentary to the New York City Police Department's draft body camera policy openly acknowledges that sanctions are unspecified because of the difficulties: "Officer discipline is generally not

[62] DENVER, COLO., REV. MUNICIPAL CODE ch. 2, art. XVII, § 2371. *See also* Noelle Phillips, *Move to Strengthen Denver's Independent Monitor Advances*, DENVER POST (Feb. 3, 2015, 9:57 AM), www.denverpost.com/2015/02/03/move-to-strengthen-denvers-independent-monitor-advances/ (discussing a dispute between the *Monitor* and the Denver Police Department over whether the department is obligated to grant full access to body camera footage for the monitor).

[63] *See* DENVER OFFICE OF THE INDEP. MONITOR, 2014 ANNUAL REPORT 30 (2015) [hereinafter DENVER INDEP. MONITOR 2014 REPORT], http://extras.denverpost.com/Denver_ Monitor_2014_Annual_Report.pdf.

[64] DENVER PD MANUAL, *supra* note 60, at POLICY 119.04, § 12.

[65] *Id.*

[66] *Id.*

[67] *Id.*

mentioned in the proposed policy. It is difficult to specify a discipline system as there are many variables that determine whether or not an officer should face discipline in [a] specific instance."[68]

As the drafters of the New York policy frankly address, silence regarding whether sanctions will occur sometimes is no oversight. It is easier to leave things unspecified because there are good reasons not to record. Two of the major and commonly occurring justifications for failures to record are the need to respond to exigencies in the field and technological malfunction. Parsing between these important and legitimate justifications and refusal, resistance and subversion is a delicate and difficult task.

Forgot in the Heat of the Moment, or Refused to Record?

In the cool and safe remove of hindsight, it is all too easy to question and condemn imperfect adherence, especially after a tragedy.[69] But in the heat and fray of the field there are legitimate reasons why recording fails. Officers focused on the immediate need to respond to the exigencies of fast-unfolding and high-stress events may forget to hit record, or lack the time to do so.[70] Among body camera policies, there is wide and express acceptance of the basic proposition that safety trumps the recording obligation in body camera policies.[71]

---

[68]   NYPD, Draft Operations Order, *supra* note 53, at 10.

[69]   Indeed, "we tend to be historical simplifiers, even reducers, who often skate over the relevant facts in order to lay the blame *somewhere* rather than everywhere or nowhere." Mark Freeman, Hindsight: The Promise and Peril of Looking Backward 40 (2010).

[70]   *See, e.g.*, New York v. Quarles, 467 US 649, 656 (1984) ("In a kaleidoscopic situation[,] ... spontaneity rather than adherence to a police manual is necessarily the order of the day").

[71]   *See, e.g.*, Corpus Christi Police Dep't, Mobile Digital Video Recording Systems and Body Worn Cameras, Policy 303, at 7 (May 10, 2016) (on file with author) ("At no time is a member expected to jeopardize his/her safety in order to activate a BWC or change the recording media."); Milwaukee Police Dep't, Standard Operating Procedure, Policy 747.25 (effective July 15, 2016), http://city.milwaukee.gov/ImageLibrar y/Groups/mpdAuthors/SOP/747-BODYWORNCAMERABWC1.pdf ("The department recognizes that officer safety is paramount. Members with BWC who arrive on a scene or engage in an enforcement contact must start recording as soon as it is safe and practical to do so."); NYPD, Draft Operations Order, *supra* note 53, at 3 ("If the circumstances require a[ ] [uniform member of the service] to engage immediate safety measures first, the [uniformed member] should do so and then activate the BWC as soon as it is practical and safe. At no point should proper tactics be compromised to begin a recording."); San Diego Police Dep't, Axon Body Worn Cameras, Procedure, Procedure 1.49, at 2 (effective July 20, 2016) [hereinafter San Jose PD, BWC Policy], www.sandiego.gov/sites/ default/files/149.pdf ("Officer safety and public safety take precedence over recording events

Inexperience with implementing new recording requirements can further lead to failures to record in stressful situations.[72] Mistakes happen. There is a learning curve with new technologies and procedures.[73]

Officers as well as the public can benefit from an articulated policy on what happens when officers do not record as required. The lack of a clear and calibrated scale of sanctions can even potentially end up underprotecting officers who face high-stress circumstances and a new recording regime. For example, if a tragedy happens on an officer's watch, and the incident hits the headlines, there is a risk of swift and severe sanctions in response to the attention, since no specified scale is set.[74] Under the hot scrutiny of public attention after a tragedy, as people search for a villain to blame, officers' claims about mistakes and exigencies may face withering skepticism.[75]

Conversely, the very import and power of the safety and high-stress justification creates the risk of it becoming a blanket and standard-form invocation that could conceal problems. This is a particularly acute risk in the cases that do not make the national news – the tasings, the pepper sprays, and the baton strikes that go unrecorded and without a fatality to draw media attention. For example, the Independent Monitor for the Denver Police Department observed that, in a number of unrecorded uses of force, the "officers asserted that the situations evolved too rapidly or were too volatile to permit BWC activation, even though it was the officers who initiated the contacts without first activating their BWCs,

---

   ... Officer safety and the safety of the public shall be the primary considerations when contacting citizens or conducting vehicle stops, not the ability to record an event."); SAN JOSE POLICE DEP'T, BODY WORN CAMERA POLICY, at 2 (effective July 29, 2015), www .sjpd.org/InsideSJPD/BodyCameras/SJPD_BWC_Policy_06-29-15_with_POA_approval.pdf ("The safety of officers and members of the public is the highest priority, and the Department acknowledges there may be situations in which operation of the device is impractical or may be an impediment to public and officer safety. Additionally, the Department recognizes human performance limitations during particularly stressful, critical situations.").

[72] *See* Annie Sweeney & Jeremy Gorner, *Chicago Police: Body Camera Didn't Record Cop's Fatal Shooting of Teen in Back*, CHI. TRIB. (Aug. 2, 2016, 7:04 AM), www.chicag otribune .com/news/local/breaking/ct-chicago-police-shooting-eddie-johnson-met-20160801-story.html (reporting findings of a preliminary investigation that officers' inexperience with operating body cameras led to a failure to record the police shooting of Paul O'Neal).

[73] *See, e.g.,* SAN DIEGO PD, BWC POLICY, *supra* note 70, at 1 ("There is also a learning curve that comes with using body-worn cameras.").

[74] *Cf., e.g.,* Jeffrey Standen, *The End of the Era of Sentencing Guidelines*: Apprendi v. New Jersey, 87 IOWA L. REV. 775, 805 (2002) (discussing how penalties that are clearly articulated in advance protect against the risk of more severe penalties); Elizabeth Szockyj, *Imprisoning White-Collar Criminals?*, 23 S. ILL. U. L.J. 485, 492–493 (1999) (discussing the role of media attention in raising the probability of punishment in the white-collar crime context).

[75] *See, e.g.,* Thomas E. Drabek & Enrico L. Quarantelli, *Scapegoats, Villains, and Disasters*, 4 TRANS-ACTION 12, 12–16 (1967) (discussing the phenomenon of public scapegoating and villain seeking after tragedies).

as required."[76] Distinguishing these legitimate realities from circumvention, or just outright refusal to activate the body camera, calls for expert judgment and inference when confronted with uncertainties.

Technological Malfunction or Circumvention?

Technological solutions are alluring because they seem to free us from human fallibility.[77] Yet, as anyone who has pounded multiple keys of a frozen laptop or had a cell phone die knows, technology has its own particular and manifold fallibilities. Batteries die, devices freeze, break, or otherwise fail. In the early days of dash cameras, departments who adopted what was then new and enticing technology soon discovered the many ways cameras and technology can deliver glitches.[78]

Accounts of malfunctioning body cameras are already emerging.[79] Halfway into a six-month pilot program, the Boston Police Department experienced seventy-two recording failures with their body cameras.[80] The department

---

[76] DENVER INDEP. MONITOR 2014 REPORT, *supra* note 63, at 20.

[77] The greater freedom from human fallibility that technology affords has spurred excitement and innovation in diverse quarters. *See, e.g.*, Anita L. Allen, *Dredging Up the Past: Lifelogging, Memory, and Surveillance*, 75 U. CHI. L. REV. 47, 50–51 (2008) (discussing technological advances in response to fallible human memory which would "enable unprecedented accurate retention and recall"); Elizabeth E. Joh, *Discretionless Policing: Technology and the Fourth Amendment*, 95 CALIF. L. REV. 199, 221–223 (2007) (discussing technological advances in automated law enforcement programs). This allure can be misleading, however, compelling courts to adopt safety measures to prevent misleading jurors. *See, e.g.*, Reese v. Stroh, 874 P.2d 200, 205 (Wash. Ct. App. 1994) (discussing standards for the admission of evidence which were "adopted to prevent the use of . . . technologies that, because they are mechanical or mysterious, appear infallible to the average juror").

[78] *See* Tom Casady, *Hidden Cost of Body-Worn Cameras*, DIRECTOR'S DESK (Oct. 31, 2014, 6:12 AM), http://lpd304.blogspot.com/2014/10/hidden-cost-of-body-worn-cameras.html (discussing frequent technological malfunctions in the early days of dash camera adoption).

[79] *See, e.g.*, Adam Randall, *Norman Gary Family Hoping for Indictment in Grand Jury's First Day*, GOSHEN NEWS (Goshen, Ind.) (Feb. 28, 2017), 2017 WLNR 6249535 (discussing police department reports of widespread body camera malfunctions one of which resulted in a failure to record a fatal shooting); Bob Blake, *Family of Man Shot and Killed Files Civil Rights Lawsuit against Elkhart Police Officers*, S. BEND TRIB. (Ind.) (Jan. 25, 2017), 2017 WLNR 2549264 (chronicling controversies over body camera malfunctions and suspension of a body camera program, due to frequent technical problems); Samantha Vicent, *Tahlequah Police Release Video from Officer-Involved Fatal Shooting*, TULSA WORLD (Okla.) (Aug. 20, 2016), 2016 WLNR 25518803 (discussing body camera malfunction and memory capacity problems); Greg Moran, *Officer's Statements Conflict on Weapon*, L.A. TIMES (Dec. 24, 2015), at 3, 2015 WLNR 38209020 (reporting on officer's claim that body camera was not working at the time of a shooting and "it had been malfunctioning for several weeks").

[80] Brian Dowling & Owen Boss, *Critics Slam Cop Body Cams on the Link*, BOS. HERALD (Dec. 19, 2016), at 2, 2016 WLNR 38826283.

attributed those failures to "technical malfunctions includ[ing] insufficient battery life, cameras falling off their mounts, or shutting off without explanation."[81] Clearly it would be unjust to punish officers for the fallibilities of technology, particularly when performing under high-stress, suboptimal field conditions. Yet discerning between the vulnerabilities of technology and the subversion of resistant officers can be tough.

Consider, for example, the claims by two Baton Rouge police officers that both their body cameras fell off during the tragic shooting of Alton Sterling.[82] Sterling was selling CDs outside a convenience store when a homeless man persistently sought money from him.[83] Finally, Sterling said, "I told you to leave me alone" and showed the panhandler his gun.[84] The homeless man then called 911 on his cell phone, telling police there was a man with a gun at the store.[85] What happened next was captured on the cell phone camera of a bystander and a store camera, but the officers' body cameras failed to obtain usable footage of the incident.[86]

Experts disagree on the likelihood that both cameras were dislodged around the same time.[87] Some opined for the media that it would be highly unlikely for two cameras to fall off at the same critical juncture.[88] Yet others said it could happen, and in fact, it has happened before.[89] Tod Burke, a professor of criminal justice and former police officer, argued that the highly unusual scenario would be for two officers to collude to prevent the recording of an incident while in the middle of

[81] *Id.*

[82] *See* Kimbriell Kelly et al., *Fatal Shootings by Police Remain Relatively Unchanged after Two Years*, WASH. POST (Dec. 30, 2016), http://wapo.st/2hBOTix.

[83] *See* Joshua Berlinger et al., *Alton Sterling Shooting: Homeless Man Made 911 Call, Source Says*, CNN (July 8, 2016, 7:24 AM), www.cnn.com/2016/07/07/us/baton-rouge-alton-sterling-shooting/.

[84] *Id.*

[85] *Id.*

[86] *Id.*; Richard Fausset et al., *Alton Sterling Shooting in Baton Rouge Prompts Justice Dept. Investigation*, N.Y. TIMES (July 6, 2016), www.nytimes.com/2016/07/06/us/alto n-sterling-bat on-rouge-shooting.html.

[87] *See* Aliyah Frumin, *After Baton Rouge Shooting, Questions Swirl around Body Cam Failures*, NBC NEWS (July 7, 2016), www.nbcnews.com/news/us-news/after-baton-rouge-shooting-qu estions-swirl-around-body-cam-failures-n605386?cid=e m1_onsite ("Critics say [the officers'] explanation is awfully convenient – and arguably untrue.").

[88] *See, e.g., id.* (quoting Steve Tuttle, a spokesman for Taser, "[i]t's not unheard of, but it's very unusual in the overall industry and certainly isn't a significant issue for us despite seven years of our cameras being worn by more than 3,500 law enforcement agencies").

[89] *See id.* (quoting law enforcement officials as stating that "it is entirely possible that both cameras could have fallen off" and reporting that the Salt Lake City Police Department had "seen it happen when two officers are engaged with a person").

a high-stress situation.[90] The battle of the experts that played out in the media demonstrates how potentially time and resource consuming it would be to conduct mini-trials to distinguish between officer subversion and technological malfunction in determining whether discipline is justified.

BEYOND INDIVIDUAL BLAME

Internal departmental enforcement of recording rules is challenging because of the individual fault-based nature of disciplinary processes and management-labor negotiations and protections. Given the internal enforcement challenges and the reporting and incentives gaps in departmental recording policies, judicial remedies are especially important. Courts are the seasoned gatekeepers of evidence and are better institutionally situated to ensure a fair and accurate video evidentiary record.[91] Courts also have long been the most critical external actor in regulating police power.[92] These dual judicial roles and expertise are important for addressing the missing video problem. The challenge is how to frame administrable remedies that reduce the risk of perverse consequences posed by costly inquests into whether individual officers are to blame for missing video.

In the activist arena, the ACLU of Massachusetts has proposed a "no tape, no testimony" rule in which courts would instruct juries to discredit or ignore the testimony of officers if the body camera recording is missing.[93] Some state

---

[90]   *See id.* ("It would have been a very, very unusual circumstance where both officers would have to say let's turn it off and throw our body cameras away. Everything seemed to happen relatively quickly.").

[91]   *See, e.g.,* Kumho Tire Co. v. Carmichael, 526 US 137, 141, 147 (1999) (discussing the courts' central gatekeeper role on evidentiary issues); Sophia I. Gatowski et al., *Asking the Gatekeepers: A National Survey of Judges on Judging Expert Evidence in a Post-Daubert World,* 25 Law & Hum. Behav. 433, 434 (2001) ("[J]udges are central and active figures in admissibility decision-making.").

[92]   *See* Eric J. Miller, *The Warren Court's Regulatory Revolution in Criminal Procedure,* 43 Conn. L. Rev. 1, 48–76 (2010) (chronicling the rise of courts' central role in regulating the police); Carol S. Steiker, *Counter-Revolution in Constitutional Criminal Procedure? Two Audiences, Two Answers,* 94 Mich. L. Rev. 2466, 2471–2503 (1996) (discussing the central role of courts in framing conduct rules for the police).

[93]   *See* ACLU of Mass. & Samuelson Law, Tech. & Pub. Policy Clinic No Tape, No Testimony 2 (2016) [hereinafter ACLU, No Tape, No Testimony], https://aclum.org/wp-con tent/uploads/2016/11/ACLU_BodyCameras_11.21_final.pdf (proposing an instruction that "would tell the jury that, if it finds that the police unreasonably failed to create or preserve a video of a police-civilian encounter, it can devalue an officer's testimony and infer that the video would have helped the civilian. If the jury finds that the case involves bad faith, such as the outright sabotage of body cameras, then it should be instructed to disregard officer testimony altogether.").

legislatures are also beginning to search for approaches to address the problem.[94] One piece of proposed legislation is especially severe – making failure to record when there is a reasonable opportunity to do so a felony and a firing offense.[95] Generally, however, reflecting the enduring focus on the criminal trial as the arena of primary contestation in criminal adjudication, early proposals focus on jury instructions regarding the testimony of officers who fail to record.[96]

The focus on jury instructions does not address the vast majority of criminal cases, which never make it to trial. More than 90 percent of criminal convictions come from plea bargaining, never reaching the jury-instructions phase of trial.[97] Plea bargains account for 97 percent of federal convictions,[98] and 94 percent of state felony convictions.[99] As the US Supreme Court has recognized, "[b]ecause ours 'is for the most part a system of pleas, not a system of trials,' it is insufficient simply to point to the guarantee of a fair trial as a backstop that inoculates any errors in the pretrial process."[100]

Moreover, remedies based on a finding of officer misconduct are messy and potentially unfair to both police officers and defendants. The blame approach is predetermined to fail because of the reluctance of courts to find that officers are perjurers; to wade into costly mini-trials on collateral evidentiary issues; and to second-guess the judgment calls of officers in the heat and stress of the

---

[94] *See, e.g.*, H.B. 2737, 100th Gen. Assemb., Reg. Sess. (Ill. 2017) (making it a Class 3 felony and a firing offense for an officer to knowingly fail to turn on or turn off an officer-worn body camera contrary to departmental recording policy when there is a reasonable opportunity to comply); H.B. 1613, 2017 Sess. (Va. 2017) (providing that an officer who fails to record using the body camera as required may still testify about the events that should have been recorded, but the court should instruct the jury to consider the failure to record "in determining the weight given to [the officer's] testimony," or if there is no jury, then the court should consider the factor in weighing the testimony).

[95] H.B. 2737, 100th Gen. Assemb., Reg. Sess. (Ill. 2017).

[96] *E.g.*, H.B. 1613, 2017 Sess. (Va. 2017). *See* generally ACLU, No Tape, No Testimony, *supra* note 92 (proposing remedies focused on jury instructions and trial testimony).

[97] *See* Dep't of Justice, Bureau of Justice Statistics, Sourcebook of Criminal Justice Statistics Online tbl.5.22.2009 (2009), www.albany.edu/sourcebook/pdf/t52220 09.pdf, *cited in* Missouri v. Frye, 566 US 134, 143 (2012).

[98] Of the 89,741 criminal defendants convicted and sentenced in US District Courts in 2010, 87,418 pled guilty or entered a plea of nolo contendere. *See* Dep't of Justice, Bureau of Justice Statistics, Sourcebook of Criminal Justice Statistics Online tbl.5.22.2010 (2010), www.albany.edu/sourcebook/pdf/t5222010.pdf.

[99] *See* Sean Rosenmerkel et al., Dep't of Justice, Bureau of Justice Statistics, Felony Sentences in State Courts, 2006 – Statistical Tables, at 24 tbl.4.1 (2009), www.bjs.gov/content/pub/pdf/fssc06st.pf (reporting data on the types of felony convictions in state courts in 2006).

[100] Missouri v. Frye, 566 US 134, 144 (2012) (citation omitted) (quoting Lafler v. Cooper, 566 US 156, 170 (2012)).

field. Remedies contingent on finding culpability are likely to lead to judicial-inquiry deterrence, in which courts dismiss claims regarding missing video with little or no inquiry because of the costs of parsing officer fault.

Nobody Wins in the Blame Game

The blame game is bad for both officers and defendants. Officers are accused of intentional wrongdoing. Defendants do not fare well either because showing bad faith on the part of the government for missing evidence is an approach with a low probability of success for at least three main reasons.[101] First, officers are unlikely to say they acted in bad faith, and in defendant-said, police-said credibility contests, officers are more likely to be believed. Second, courts are reluctant to find that officers are "testilying," even when they suspect this may be the case. Lastly, courts are reluctant to engage in costly mini-trials on collateral evidentiary issues.

As a systemic matter in criminal justice, credibility contests between defense allegations and police testimony are highly uneven and messy. Absent additional evidence beyond competing testimony, stories can diverge widely, with each side accusing the other of lying rather than being merely mistaken. Defendants often allege that the police abused their power and perjured themselves to hide their civil rights violations.[102] The police say the defendant is lying to avoid just punishment.[103]

As we saw in Chapter 3, the playing field in this ugly battle is highly imbalanced. To preserve their Fifth Amendment privilege to remain silent

[101] *See, e.g.*, United States v. Parker, 72 F.3d 1444, 1452 (10th Cir. 1995) (holding the defendant failed to show bad faith on the part of the government in destroying video evidence); United States v. Valentin, 2016 WL 1296854, at *2 (D. Conn. Mar. 30, 2016) (ruling the defendant failed to show that the missing video was as a result of bad faith on the part of the government); Burks v. Howes, No. 08-12825-BC, 2010 WL 2772432, at *4 (E.D. Mich. July 13, 2010) (same).

[102] *See, e.g.*, Commonwealth v. Sparks, 746 N.E.2d 133, 138 (Mass. 2001) (noting defendant's allegations that police planted a knife in defendant's bedroom during the execution of a search warrant); State v. Pogue, 17 P.3d 1272, 1273 (Wash. Ct. App. 2001) (noting "[defendant's] insinuation that the police planted the drugs"); People v. McGirt, 603 N.Y.S.2d 164, 165 (N.Y. App. Div. 1993) (noting defendant's allegations that "the police ... planted evidence on him"); *cf.* Press Release, Dep't of Justice, Three Former Atlanta Police Officers Sentenced to Prison in Fatal Shooting of Elderly Atlanta Woman (Feb. 24, 2009), www.justice.gov/opa/pr/three-former-atlanta-police-officers-sentence d-prison-fatal-shooting-elderly-atlanta-woman (quoting US Attorney David E. Nahmias, "As Atlanta police narcotics officers, these three defendants repeatedly failed to follow proper procedures and then lied under oath to obtain search warrants. Their routine violations of the Fourth Amendment led to the death of an innocent citizen.").

[103] *See* Donald A. Dripps, *The Constitutional Status of the Reasonable Doubt Rule*, 75 CALIF. L. REV. 1665, 1695 (1987) (discussing the credibility deficit defendants face).

and reduce the risk of generating impeachment material, defendants have strong incentives to remain silent rather than testify, even at pretrial motion hearings.[104] This renders claims proffered in motions seem all the more unsubstantiated. Furthermore, defendants are viewed as having a severe credibility problem – after all, they are charged with a crime.[105]

Moreover, judges are highly reluctant to openly discredit the testimony of law enforcement officers.[106] Even when judges find an officer's account questionable, the judge is keenly aware that an adverse finding suggesting that the officer is a liar can destroy the officer's career.[107] In a criminal justice system where judges are likely to regularly see officers from the jurisdiction's agency in court and in chambers – and perhaps even need law enforcement endorsements to get reelected – there are powerful systemic pressures against discrediting officers.[108]

Finally, courts are also reluctant to engage in costly collateral mini-trials on evidentiary questions.[109] In the context of recording technology, when the proffered reason may be technological malfunction, such inquests would be even more costly, perhaps entailing a battle of the experts regarding the

[104] *See* Alexandra Natapoff, *Speechless: The Silencing of Criminal Defendants*, 80 N.Y.U. L. Rev. 1449, 1449–50 (2005) (explaining that defendants are "encouraged to be quiet" through the criminal process).

[105] *See* Dripps, *supra* note 102, at 1695 (asserting that a criminal charge imposes a powerful incentive to offer exculpatory (and often perjured) testimony and "[b]ecause of this incentive, the trier of fact is likely to discount any exculpatory testimony given by the accused").

[106] *See* Morgan Cloud, *Judges, "Testilying," and the Constitution*, 69 S. Cal. L. Rev. 1341, 1352 (1996) (quoting The N.Y.C. Comm'n to Investigate Allegations of Police Corruption and the City's Anti-corruption Procedures, Commission Report 36 (1994) (on file with the Georgia Law Review)) ("On the word of a police officer alone a grand jury may indict, a trial jury may convict, and a judge pass sentence."); Christopher Slobogin, *Testilying: Police Perjury and What to Do about It*, 67 U. Colo. L. Rev. 1037, 1047–1048 & n.51 (1996) (suggesting that some judges might ignore perjury to achieve what the judge considers to be justice under the given circumstances of the case).

[107] Slobogin, *supra* note 105, at 1045 (noting that, although "judges believe perjury is systematic," they are rarely sure enough that it is occurring to expose a police officer to criminal charges).

[108] *See* Anthony Champagne, *Interest Groups and Judicial Elections*, 34 Loy. L. Rev. 1391, 1391 (2001) (discussing law enforcement endorsements in judicial elections).

[109] *See, e.g.,* United States v. Hurst, 185 F. App'x 133, 136–137 (3d Cir. 2006) (discussing evidentiary rules that serve to avoid mini-trials on collateral matters); United States v. Bullock, 94 F.3d 896, 899 (4th Cir. 1996) (discussing courts' reluctance to engage in collateral mini-trials on an officer's past traffic stops, as "[f]ocusing on such collateral matters would unduly encumber the court's proceedings"); United States v. Talamante, 981 F.2d 1153, 1156 n.5 (10th Cir. 1992) (affirming district court's decision to avoid collateral mini-trials in which the defense and the government would offer different characterizations); United States v. Waloke, 962 F.2d 824, 830 (8th Cir. 1992) (discussing and affirming the lower court's refusal to engage in collateral mini-trials in which each side would compete to characterize the relevant events differently).

probability of the occurrence of such a malfunction. Remedies for missing videos predicated on the blameworthiness of individual officers would open the door to such messy and costly inquiries.

If remedies for missing video hinge on culpable officer conduct, the risk of deterring a judicial inquiry is high. By judicial-inquiry deterrence, I mean the avoidance of finding a colorable claim of a violation, to avoid the mess and costs of wading into credibility contests, collateral mini-trials, and potentially finding an officer guilty of perjury or wrongdoing. Scholars have used the concept of remedial deterrence to refer to judicial avoidance of finding a violation to avoid the costs of offering a remedy.[110] Judicial-inquiry deterrence as framed here operates even earlier, leading to curt dismissals of defense claims without significant inquiry.[111]

Remedies from a Fairness Rather than Blame Perspective

Rather than individuating blame on officers for missing evidence, the focus of judicial remedies should be from a systemic perspective on evidentiary fairness. This perspective elevates courts out of the murky morass of individual blame – is this particular officer lying about the camera falling off or is the defendant lying? Instead, the evidentiary fairness approach from a systemic perspective frames the problem thus: Key contested aspects of this encounter were not recorded even though, pursuant to the department's policies, they are usually recorded. To address this, remedies would focus on addressing the underlying imbalances in evidentiary advantages between the police and the defendant, rather than trying to assign blame and guess who is lying and who is not.

Three potential remedies from an evidentiary fairness approach include (1) exclusion of partial recordings, (2) positive inferences to counteract the tendency to discredit the defendant, and (3) using institutional awareness of systemic facts to detect patterns of missing recordings.

---

[110] *See, e.g.*, Sonja B. Starr, *Rethinking "Effective Remedies": Remedial Deterrence in International Courts*, 83 N.Y.U. L. Rev. 693, 759–760 (2008) (discussing remedial deterrence in the international criminal context).

[111] *See, e.g.*, United States v. Matthews, 373 F. App'x 386, 390–391 (4th Cir. 2010) (per curiam) (rejecting the defendant's argument that the government's destruction of video evidence warranted the remedy of a dismissal); United States v. Parker, 72 F.3d 1444, 1452 (10th Cir. 1995) (upholding the district court's denial of defendants' motion to dismiss in a case where a state trooper erased a video recording which may have held exculpatory evidence).

Exclusion of Partial Recordings

Regardless of whether the officer was at fault for the missing video, courts can offer the remedy of excluding partial video where recording rules require recording the entire encounter. This approach is not unprecedented.[112] In *United States v. Yevakpor*, a New York district court excluded portions of a surveillance tape that the government sought to introduce because other portions were automatically recorded over and not preserved.[113] The clips the government preserved showed the defendant carrying a suitcase with heroin at the New York Port of Entry and the search of the suitcase by officers.[114] The court construed the defendant's motion to exclude the clips as an invocation of Federal Rule of Evidence 106's partial codification of the Doctrine of Completeness.[115]

Rule 106 provides that where a party introduces a recorded statement, or a part of one, "an adverse party may require the introduction, at that time, of any other part – or any other writing or recorded statement – that in fairness ought to be at the same time."[116] The problem with partial video, of course, is that there is no other portion the adverse party can introduce. In *Yevakpor*, the court creatively addressed this problem outside the four corners of the classic Rule 106 situation.[117] The court noted that it did "not doubt the US Attorney's good faith" but that, regarding the routine destruction of the rest of the video, partial video recordings are akin to still photographs and thus pose a greater risk of scenes being taken out of context than the "continuous stream of information" that a complete video can provide.[118] The court agreed with the defense that interpretation of the clips would be skewed by the lack of presentation in full context.[119] Performing its own "pragmatic balancing test," the court excluded the clips as "more prejudicial than probative."[120]

Moreover, the court put the government on notice:

> [I]f selected segments of a video or audio exhibit will be offered at trial, the entire video or audio exhibit had best be preserved . . . Given the current state of affairs in our nation, when surveillance occurs both with and without our

---

[112] *See* United States v. Yevakpor, 419 F. Supp. 2d 242 (N.D.N.Y. 2006) (excluding partial government surveillance tape).
[113] The recording system recorded over stored images "every 6 to 7 days." *Id.* at 244, 247, 252.
[114] *Id.* at 243–245.
[115] *Id.* at 246–246.
[116] FED. R. EVID. 106. The 2006 version of Rule 106 used in *Yevakpor* was worded differently, but its meaning was essentially the same.
[117] *Yevakpor*, 419 F. Supp. 2d at 246–247.
[118] *Id.* at 246.
[119] *Id.* at 250.
[120] *Id.* at 250–252.

knowledge, a great danger to liberty would exist if Government could pick and choose segments of recordings for use in prosecution, destroy the remainder, and then argue that the defense must show that the destroyed evidence contained exculpatory or otherwise potentially useful and relevant information. Simply put, the Government cannot make use of video segments that have been "cherry-picked" when the remainder of the recording has been erased or recorded-over.[121]

From a seemingly mundane drug-smuggling case at a port of entry, the court discerned the larger values at stake and the need to fashion a remedy that applied regardless of proof by the defense that the missing video was exculpatory or that the government acted in bad faith. From an evidentiary fairness perspective, even if a recording is incomplete due to no fault of the officer, there are still important concerns about its admission. Video evidence has an alluring power to seem to offer the viewer the ability to see for him or herself what really happened.[122] Yet, as we saw in Chapter 5, depending on camera position, framing, and timing, a video might tell a misleading story.

We do not know whether something crucial that would put conduct in context is cut out. Seeing only part of the action without key context can lead viewers to draw the wrong inferences.[123] For example, we may just see a suspect behaving belligerently toward an officer on video. Was the suspect aggressive from the beginning of the encounter, or was the officer demeaning or threatening, eliciting the reaction? Was the suspect acting suspiciously from the start of a *Terry* stop, or does he only look suspicious once the camera turns on and displays the contraband found during a stop-and-frisk? The partial recording might be a selective presentation – or it might be due to mistake, technological malfunction, or exigency. Rather than adjudicating officer fault, however, the court could exclude the partial video as a matter of evidentiary fairness so the prosecution does not have the advantage of a partial – and potentially misleading – video.

---

[121]   *Id.* at 252 (citation omitted).

[122]   *See* Neal Feigenson & Christina Spiesel, Law on Display: The Digital Transformation of Legal Persuasion and Judgment 8 (2009) (stating that videos can be "highly credible evidence of the reality they depict," and that they are more readily believed than words); Rebecca Tushnet, *Worth a Thousand Words: The Images of Copyright,* 125 Harv. L. Rev. 683, 692 & n.29 (2012) (arguing that images are often more persuasive than other forms of knowledge, even having the power to overcome personal memories of an event; but the meaning of those images always comes from interpretation).

[123]   *See, e.g., Yevakpor,* 419 F. Supp. 2d at 246, where the court was concerned that a partial recording presents an increased risk that scenes may be taken out of context.

Favorable Inferences

What happens if video is missing altogether? The Supreme Court has held that it is a due process violation for the government to fail to preserve evidence that is exculpatory to the defendant.[124] If the defendant cannot show the destroyed evidence was exculpatory, and "no more can be said than that it ... might have exonerated the defendant," then the criminal defendant must show bad faith on the part of the police.[125] This body of law is unavailing in the failure to record context for three reasons. First, the evidence was not destroyed. Rather it was never created. Second, if the evidence was never created, it is hard for the defendant to prove that it might be exculpatory.[126] Third, bad faith is hard to prove because the officers will rarely say they were acting with bad intent and are likely to proffer alternative rationales, which courts are reluctant to suggest are false.

It may be tempting to try draw an analogy with spoliation doctrine, which also concerns remedies for missing evidence. Spoliation means the destruction of evidence or failure to preserve it for reasonably foreseeable litigation.[127] More fundamentally, the doctrine is about the "inherent power of the courts ... to preserve the integrity of the judicial process in order to retain confidence that the process works to uncover the truth."[128] To sanction spoliation, courts may infer that the information would have been adverse to the party.[129] Many courts require a showing of intentional destruction in bad faith before imposing an adverse-inference sanction.[130] Others hold that bad faith is

---

[124] Arizona v. Youngblood, 488 US 51, 55 (1988).

[125] *Id.* at 56–58.

[126] *Cf. Yevakpor*, 419 F. Supp. 2d at 246 ("This is a harsh standard to apply considering that the Defendant cannot know what missing portions would be relevant" since the video no longer exists).

[127] West v. Goodyear Tire & Rubber Co., 167 F.3d 776, 779 (2d Cir. 1999).

[128] Silvestri v. Gen. Motors Corp., 271 F.3d 583, 590 (4th Cir. 2001).

[129] *See id.* at 592–593 (affirming the district court's grant of a motion to dismiss, where the failure to preserve a motor vehicle in its "post-accident condition" "highly prejudiced" defendant).

[130] *See, e.g.*, Guzman v. Jones, 804 F.3d 707, 713 (5th Cir. 2015) ("We permit an adverse inference against the spoliator or sanctions against the spoliator only upon a showing of 'bad faith' or 'bad conduct' ... Bad faith, in the context of spoliation, generally means destruction for the purpose of hiding adverse evidence."); Hallmark Cards, Inc. v. Murley, 703 F.3d 456, 461 (8th Cir. 2013) (ruling that the district court must find bad faith and prejudice in order to give an adverse-inference instruction); Bull v. United Parcel Service, Inc., 665 F.3d 68, 79 (3d Cir. 2012) (discussing the "pivotal" role of bad faith in sanctionable spoliation); Norman-Nunnery v. Madison Area Tech. Coll., 625 F.3d 422, 428 (7th Cir. 2010) (requiring the party seeking an adverse inference to "demonstrate that the defendants intentionally destroyed the documents in bad faith," explaining "[t]he crucial element in a spoliation claim is not the fact that documents were destroyed but that they were destroyed for the purpose of hiding adverse information"); Turner v. Public Serv. Co., 563 F.3d 1136, 1149 (10th Cir. 2009) ("But if the aggrieved party seeks an adverse inference to remedy the spoliation, it must also prove bad faith."); Bashir v. Amtrak, 119

not required and instead use other criteria, such as willful conduct or notice that the evidence was potentially relevant to the litigation.[131]

Civil rights plaintiffs attempting to allege spoliation based on a recording omission or destruction have failed because of an inability to show bad faith and the availability of other explanations, such as officer inexperience.[132] Classic spoliation doctrine is even more difficult to apply in the context of an officer's decision not to record altogether. The failure to record is a particularly ambiguous context because evidence was not destroyed; rather, it never existed. Culpable bad faith – acting with the purpose of destroying evidence to hide adverse information[133] – is even harder to allege because of the legitimate reasons officers may proffer for not recording in the field. The remedy would be merely theoretical rather than attainable because of the difficulty of demonstrating that a video that never existed would have contained adverse information.[134] While some courts do not require a showing

F.3d 929, 931 (11th Cir. 1997) ("In this circuit, an adverse inference is drawn from a party's failure to preserve evidence only when the absence of that evidence is predicated on bad faith."); *see also* 89 C.J.S. *Trial* § 671 (2017) ("The jury should be given an adverse-inference instruction on spoliation of evidence if the requesting party makes a threshold showing that the opposing party improperly caused the loss of the evidence."); 29 Am. Jur. 2d *Evidence* § 256 ("[T]he intentional spoliation ... of evidence relevant to a case raises ... an inference[ ] that this evidence would have been unfavorable ... The inference does not arise where the destruction was a matter of routine with no fraudulent intent.").

[131] *See, e.g.,* Grosdidier v. Broadcasting Bd. of Governors, 709 F.3d 19, 28 (D.C. Cir. 2013) (ruling that a showing of bad faith is not required); Hodge v. Wal-Mart Stores, Inc., 360 F.3d 446, 450 (4th Cir. 2004) (holding that bad faith is not always necessary for sanctionable spoliation and willful conduct suffices); Byrnie v. Town of Cromwell, 243 F.3d 93, 109 (2d Cir. 2001) (holding that a spoliation claim can be based on a violation of regulatory duty to keep records if the records "were destroyed with a culpable state of mind (i.e., where, for example, the records were destroyed knowingly, even if without intent to violate the regulation, or negligently)" and "the destroyed records were relevant to the party's claim or defense"); Glover v. BIC Corp., 6 F.3d 1318, 1329–1230 (9th Cir. 1993) (holding that bad faith is not required and notice that evidence is relevant to the litigation and failure to preserve suffice).

[132] *See, e.g.,* Victor v. Lawler, 520 F. App'x 103, 105–106 (3d Cir. 2013) (per curium) (holding that the officer failed to record due to inexperience and not bad faith). *Cf., e.g.,* Bracey v. Grondin, 712 F.3d 1012, 1019 (7th Cir. 2013) (holding that the civil rights plaintiff failed to show bad faith on the part of prison guards who did not preserve video recordings of an incident).

[133] *See* Mathis v. John Morden Buick, Inc., 136 F.3d 1153, 1155 (7th Cir. 1998) (defining "bad faith" as "destruction for the purpose of hiding adverse information").

[134] *See, e.g.,* Missouri v. Seibert, 542 US 600, 616 n.6 (2004) (plurality opinion) (noting that officer intent is rarely openly revealed); United States v. Martinez, No. 11-10195-RWZ, 2013 WL 49767, at *6–7 (D. Mass. 2013) (finding no bad faith when the government failed to preserve videos the defendant claimed might have contained exculpatory information). *Cf.* Bracey, 712 F.3d at 1019 ("Without having seen the video, no prison official could have known the tapes potentially contained adverse information and, without that knowledge, could have destroyed the tapes for the purpose of hiding adverse information.").

of bad faith for an adverse inference, many do because of "the gravity of an adverse inference instruction, which 'brands one party as a bad actor.'"[135]

To surmount this dilemma, an alternative approach is a positive inference when video of a law enforcement encounter that should be recorded is missing. This positive rather than adverse inference could apply regardless of the culpability of the officer in the failure to record. The positive inference would be that the missing video could have information that supports the defense. This positive framing spares the culpability connotations of an adverse inference that video is missing because the officer knew he had something to hide. Rather than an adverse inference branding a party as a "bad actor" in destroying evidence, a favorable inference is a credibility-reinforcing move. It counteracts the systemic imbalance in credibility capital that defendants face in the criminal justice system. It puts a thumb on the scale of inferences in favor of the defendant without necessitating a finding that recording was subverted to hide damaging evidence. A recording could be missing for wholly legitimate reasons and yet still contain information that could support the defense.

Pattern and Practice Detection

Finally, a systemic perspective also widens the horizon of remedies beyond the individual case level to a systemic level. Systemic facts refers to the larger pattern of data that courts can detect and interpret based on information acquired over time by processing many criminal procedure cases.[136]

Courts have amassed a valuable trove of systemic facts in their filing cabinets, online data systems, and transcripts.[137] This can help courts more accurately detect systemic problems and adjudicate between competing claims. For example, in justifying a search or seizure, do the police always use standard-form boilerplate language?[138] How likely is it for warrants issued based on such boilerplate recitations to yield the evidence sought?[139] A word search using high-

---

[135] *See, e.g.*, Hallmark Cards, Inc. v. Murley, 703 F.3d 456, 461 (8th Cir. 2013) (quoting Morris v. Union Pac. R.R., 373 F.3d 896, 900 (8th Cir. 2004)).

[136] Andrew Manuel Crespo, *Systemic Facts: Toward Institutional Awareness in Criminal Courts*, 129 Harv. L. Rev. 2049, 2066–2068 (2016) (describing systemic facts as "information with respect to which a given decisionmaking institution enjoys deep institutional familiarity, privileged (or perhaps even exclusive) access, or both").

[137] *See, e.g., id.* at 2072–2075 (describing the Superior Court of the District of Columbia's catalogued and digitized information on probable-cause documentation, including written affidavits and hearing transcripts).

[138] *See id.* at 2074–2085 (providing examples of "routine factual representations," such as "high-crime areas").

[139] *See id.* at 2085 (reporting that searches sanctioned by warrants obtained through the use of "probable-cause scripts" more often than not fail to yield the evidence sought, using firearms (91 percent failure rate) and drugs (66 percent failure rate) as examples).

speed software through digitized search warrant affidavits and inventories can detect such a pattern.[140]

A defendant in a particular case alleging that crucial video footage is missing may just seem to be an isolated case, or give the impression of grasping at straws to create a defense. But high-speed searches of motions filed over time can detect patterns in alleged missing evidence. Do the claims tend to involve the same law enforcement agency unit, or even the same officers? Do the claims cluster around particular kinds of cases or neighborhoods, potentially unveiling an off-the-books tactic in a particular kind of investigation or among a particular team? This form of judicial audit can supplement internal departmental enforcement mechanisms. Detection of problematic patterns can inform judges if they need to start stepping up scrutiny – and whether wading into the morass of fault for missing video is warranted.

AUTOMATE EVERYTHING

Beyond any stopgap remedies for missing video, the optimal approach ultimately is to prevent the problem from arising by automating recording. In the cool remove of an armchair, it is easy to second-guess a failure to record. But in the heat of action, having to remember to hit record – and keep checking that a device actually is working – can be difficult and even dangerous.

One of the officers with whom I rode in Baltimore recalled a suspect chase just a week before in which she simultaneously ran and kept looking down at her chest to ensure the device was actually recording. Body cameras were relatively recently introduced throughout the force and she was working hard to master both the new rules and the technology. It is hard to convey the absurdity of this burden on officers until you actually ride with officers in the field and experience the high-stress situations that officers encounter daily, often multiple times in a shift in some jurisdictions.

Rather than expecting officers acting in the heat and stress of unfolding situations to remember to record – and keep worrying and checking that devices are functioning – technology can activate recording upon predetermined triggers such as motion, sounds, physiological indicators, or activation of sirens (Figure 8.1). Companies are beginning to offer automatic recording solutions that rely on triggers such as the boom of a gunshot, the drawing of a gun or Taser, exceeding a certain speed, the opening of a door, the activation

---

[140]   *See id.* at 2074, 2082–2085 (explaining how cumulative information can be used by courts to assess the descriptive and predictive accuracy of probable-cause scripts).

FIGURE 8.1 Demonstration of a device that can automatically activate body cameras upon the drawing of a weapon from the holster.

of sirens, entering a geo-fenced area designated "high crime," or indicators of an officer's physiological stress.[141]

"When things start going sideways you don't want officers to think, 'by the way did I push the start button on my camera,'" explains Bob McKeeman, chairman of policing technology company Utility. "There are a lot of stakeholders and our philosophy is that all the stakeholders should get together and decide what the policies are and the technology should make and implement whatever the policy decisions are. The alternative is that you are depending on a police officer to manually remember what they should do and we see that as subject to the frailties

[141] *See* Laura Diaz-Zuniga, *New Bodycams Start Recording with the Draw of a Gun*, CNN (July 21, 2017, 7:11 PM), http://cnn.it/2vJNMQr (discussing automatic activation technology triggered by the removal of a weapon from its holster); Robert Maxwell, *Lakeway Police First to Use Automatic Body Cameras*, KXAN (Austin, Tex.) (June 12, 2015, 4:57 PM), http://kxan .com/2015/06/12/lakeway-police-first-to-use-automatic-body-cameras/ (discussing recording activation triggers linked to a patrol vehicle's "lights, siren, brake system, airbag, dome light or doors"); Ryan Mason, *More than a Body Cam*, POLICE: THE LAW ENFORCEMENT MAGAZINE (Apr. 28, 2015), www.policemag.com/channel/technology/articles/2015/04/more -than-a-body-cam.aspx (describing Utility's system, which "allows the camera to automatically activate based on policies set by the agency" and triggers such as the vehicle speeding over 75 miles per hour, entering into a geo-fenced area, or during certain types of interactions).

of the human being despite all good intentions. And it is also a huge security risk to the police officer."

During a pilot of body cameras at a department in Washington, dispatchers started reminding officers to activate their body cameras because of the challenges of implementing recording requirements in stressful situations. Now software that can run on a smartphone can permit a police dispatcher to remotely activate a body-worn camera.

Ultimately, the optimal longer-term approach is to encode recording policy requirements into automated technology to reduce the risk of human error or resistance in the heat and stress of unfolding situations in the field. The automation of recording can help avert the controversy, pain, and accusations over missing video after a tragedy. Technology also can help address mistrust over police discretionary decisions, including the decision whether to record.[142] While framing effective remedies for errors and omissions is important, the optimal approach is to reduce the risk of such problems arising altogether, sparing police departments, the community, and the courts the controversy and costs of redressing the missing video problem.

The rapid advance of automatic activation systems also illustrate another important lesson. Policy should be the blueprint for technology rather than technological limitations the justification for problematic policies. Policies should reflect community aspirations, needs, and tastes for the right balance between privacy, transparency, accountability, and oversight. The technological limitations of the transitory moment should never serve as justification or cover for a forced policy choice. Policy should be the design specifications for technology rather than existing technology being the straitjacket for policy.

The advance of technology is much more rapid than the ability to frame or amend laws and policies. Law is cumbersome and politically and socially costly to alter. In contrast, technology changes swiftly, particularly where big money is at stake. The spread of body cameras and the storage of the resulting data are new market opportunities with the power to impact corporate stock prices – and therefore drive innovation. Communities are not stuck with second-best policy choices. If policies create a market demand for improved technology to address challenges, then the market will fill it. Whether the issue is redaction to better balance the important interests in both privacy and public disclosure, or automatic activation to address nonrecording problems, the rapid advance of technology can offer fresh paths to reduce clashes and difficult trade-offs in important public values.

---

[142] *See* Elizabeth E. Joh, *Discretionless Policing: Technology and the Fourth Amendment*, 95 Calif. L. Rev. 199, 216–225 (2007) (discussing how technology can help address controversies over police discretion in contexts like traffic stops).

Conclusion
Beyond Technological Silver Bullets

Officers are expected to be social workers, mental health professionals and several other
titles in order to fix the problem of the citizens who call. More is expected with less ability
to assist.

   – Patrol officer with five years of experience in the Seattle and Tacoma police
departments

WHAT ARE WE BUYING?

Step back onto the streets of West Baltimore with me. It is the thick of night,
past midnight. The officer would be alone in the patrol car but for the surprise
ride-along who dropped by the station that night. Resources are stretched so
thin here that officers do not ride with a partner, often handling even potentially dangerous incidents alone. The cop catches a call of an attempted
burglary and possible domestic violence situation. A woman's ex, fresh out
of prison, is apparently trying to break down her door to get into her house.

Activating the sirens, the officer must simultaneously speed to this emergency and feel around in the dark for his pen to scrawl on the palm of his hand
the address and suspect description coming over the radio. The older-model
patrol cars here do not have the fancy laptops and other technology of rich
cities. So officers make do.

The common wisdom in law enforcement is that domestic violence calls
are among the most dangerous for officers.[1] Veteran officers will tell you that
domestic violence calls account for some of the most frightening situations

---

[1] Some studies have tried to debunk the "DV Danger myth," arguing that the broad definition of
"domestic disturbances" in the Law Enforcement Officers Killed and Assaulted (LEOKA) data
makes domestic violence calls seem more dangerous than they actually are with a narrower
definition. *See, e.g.,* J. David Hirschel, Charles W. Dean, & Richard C. Lumb, *The Relative
Contribution of Domestic Violence to Assault and Injury of Police Officers,* JUSTICE
QUARTERLY 11(1):99–117 (1994); Shannon Meyer & Randall H. Carroll, *When Officers Die:*

they have encountered.[2] Approaching the suspect is one of the most dangerous moments.[3]

Arriving at the address, the officer sees a man on the porch of a home apparently trying to jimmy open the door or pry through a window. If not for the fortuity of a rider that night, the officer would have had to approach the suspect alone.

As it happened, during that tense moment when the suspect turned to confront the officer, the incongruity of a civilian in a bright pink sweater stretched over a bulky bulletproof vest broke the tension of the moment.

"Hey, who are you?" asked the man on the porch, breaking into a puzzled smile. "Are you some kind of a student or something?" His hand still wielded aloft the implement he was using to try to break into the home. The officer remained steady and calm.

The officer talked with the man about his troubled relationship with the resident of the home, whom he said he loved and missed, though they broke up when he was in prison. The officer then knocked on the door, and the woman inside reluctantly peered out, with the door chain taut. She emphatically did not want to file any charges and just wanted the ex-boyfriend gone.

In the end, all three main parties in the oddly calm, almost dream-like scene decide to part ways peacefully. The potentially volatile situation was deescalated by the officer, who at some points almost seemed like a relationship counselor in his patient listening.

This everyday kind of police encounter shows the challenges officers and community members, particularly in resource-poor communities, face and overcome every day. The officer wears a body camera – but the department cannot afford laptop or other technology that could spare a lone officer from having to jot down suspect details on his hand while racing to the scene of an emergency. The officer is expected to handle situations that would be frightening to any ordinary person, and deescalate them. And community members – even those that deeply fear and mistrust the police – must call the cops in their hour of need, when someone deep in the night is trying to break down the door.

     Understanding Deadly Domestic Violence Calls for Service, 78 The Police Chief 24 (May 2011); Helen M. Eigenberg, Victor E. Kappelar, & Karen McGuffee, *Confronting the Complexities of Domestic Violence: A Social Prescription for Rethinking Police Training*, Journal of Police Crisis Negotiations 12(2):122–145 (2012).

[2] Lt. Dan Marcou, *The Two Most Dangerous Moments of Domestic Violence Calls*, PoliceOne (Aug. 25, 2017), www.policeone.com/investigations/articles/413880006-The-2-most-dangerous-moments-of-domestic-violence-calls/.

[3] *Id.*

The outcome is not likely to make the news. But it shows the everyday kind of quiet courage and dignity, from officers and community members that do not make it into the news broadcasts. And the successful peaceful deescalation of a situation that could have been volatile – or even led to a shooting because of the implement wielded in the dark – may yield important lessons for preventing harm to officers and community members. The ability to generate such important insights to better protect the public and the police would be amplified by the aggregation of audiovisual data from many such encounters that never make it onto the news or even a report.

But the community and the officers here needs so much more than body cameras, or the occasional copwatch patrol with cell phones at the ready. Children play on the streets where a shooter is still loose because there are so few playgrounds or green spaces here. Officers scribble crucial details streaming over old radios on their hands, or in tattered notebooks. Even the wait for a working patrol car can be long at shift change.

Technology costs "money, money, money," as an officer put it. As a society, we must confront the questions of how we wish to allocate our limited budgetary dollars. Technology can be tempting, offering the allure of a panacea less cumbersome and costly then dealing with messy human issues.

Cameras can do a lot. But cameras cannot fix the fundamentals of demanding that officers do ever more with less, taking on the role of support services that are being cut or not offered to communities most in need. One does not need to run analyses via artificial neural networks to know that the many roles police officers must now fill because of cutbacks in support to communities heightens the risk of tragedies and controversial incidents.

Handling high-stress situations, such as talking people down from suicide, or protecting battered children, can heighten an officer's risk of an adverse event if sent into yet another intensely stressful conflict.[4] Technology and advanced audiovisual data analytics can help manage this risk through strategies such as ensuring an officer is not deployed back into another high-conflict situation without decompression time if other officers are available. But

---

[4] *See, e.g.,* Barry N. Feldman, Albert J. Grudzinskas Jr., Bernice Gershenson, Jonathan C. Clayfield, & Richard P. Cody, *The Impact of Suicide Calls on the Police,* 8 (4) Psychiatry Issue Brief (2011) (unpaginated) (presenting findings that "suicide calls are often critical incidents in police officers' careers and are among the highest anxiety- and stress-provoking circumstances to which police officers must respond"); John M. Violanti, Desta Fekedulegn, Tara A. Hartley, Luenda E. Charles, Michael E. Andrew, Claudia C. Ma, & Cecil M. Burchfiel, *Highly Rated and Most Frequent Stressors among Police Officers: Gender Differences,* 41(4)Am. J. Crim. Just. 645–662 (2016) (reporting that dealing with family disturbances and battered children are among the most commonly occurring high-stress events for officers).

technology cannot answer the difficult root questions of why it falls to police and the criminal justice system rather than trained experts in handling addiction, public health and mental health crises.

Since the recession in 2008 and 2009, a lot of police departments have lost significant numbers of officers and reduced staffing levels, says Darrel Stephens, executive director of the Major Cities Chiefs Association from 2010 through 2017. Police departments have not fully recovered since then. In places like Oakland, California, police departments were so short-staffed that 911 response times were lengthened – and some even got no response, by officers forced to triage.

"Police chiefs therefore have to make hard choices and before Ferguson, they were much less likely to choose body cameras," Stephens says. "Their choice might have been if I have the money, I'll spend it a different way. Taxpayers won't handle giving you everything you need – you have to make choices."

SUPPORTING MULTIPLE VISIONS OF THE PUBLIC GOOD

We are a nation deeply divided about law enforcement, social services cut-backs, addiction, race, and many other criminal justice issues. We turn to cameras – and push our police to adopt them – because it is one of the few things that tends to bring people and groups from very different perspectives together in agreement.[5] The technology is capable of supporting hopes of people from diverse perspectives. Officers think of potential exonerations from false claims. People who do not trust the police also think of potential exonerations from false claims. And people from diverse perspectives hope that the technology can help prevent the eruption of police encounters into violence and tragedy.

Technological strategies like police-worn body cameras can appeal to multiple visions of the public good. Dan Kahan has termed this attribute of supporting multiple meanings and worldviews to bridge partisan divides expressive overdetermination.[6] Deploying body cameras and pervasive recording of police encounters has challenges that we have examined in this book. But deploying cameras – whether one is a police department or a copwatcher – is much easier than gaining consensus about difficult issues

---

[5] Max Ehrenfreund, *Blacks and Whites Agree on Body Cameras for Cops, If Little Else*, WASH. POST: WONKBLOG (Dec. 29, 2014), www.washingtonpost.com/news/wonk/wp/2014/12/29/wonk book-blacks-and-whites-agree-on-body-cameras-for-cops-if-little-else/.

[6] Dan Kahan, *The Cognitively Illiberal State*, 60 STANFORD L. REV. 115 145 (2007).

such as the duty of a state to provide for its disadvantaged, the continuing role of race in structuring power imbalances or the ecological conditions that limit people's choices. These deeper underlying challenges are intensely polarizing, like the affirmative action, death penalty, gun control, and other issues that divide America.

In his book on democratic policing Barry Friedman writes of an irony of body cameras. "BWCs are not a substitute for democratic policing," Friedman writes.[7] "Rather, they are a Band-Aid, yet one more after-the-fact substitute for regulating policing properly on the front end."[8] Yet this Band-Aid has been wonderfully effective in engaging a democratic polity that tends to abdicate its role in police regulation. "[T]here has been more democratic debate and policy-making around BWCs than any other aspect of policing in recent memory," Friedman observes.[9]

Body cameras and copwatching cannot answer the hard policy questions about how we protect and heal communities and the expanding and difficult roles we expect police to fulfill. Body cameras and copwatching cannot cure the deep splits in our nation over issues like how aggressively we want our many criminal laws enforced, and at what costs to communities. These are questions for a democracy to decide and no technological silver bullet can accomplish this for us.

TRANSFORMING PROOF

While recording the police is no substitute for democratic governance of the police, the police recording revolutions serve other important public purposes. Recording the police can help address the long-standing imbalance of power in suspect-said, police-said credibility contests that leave both sides tarnished. The deluge of video coming to courts depicting more law enforcement activities than ever before has the potential to transform the traditional reliance on testimony and text in adjudicating criminal law and procedure cases. While video evidence is not a magic weapon guaranteeing agreement on controversial issues such as whether an officer's use of force is proper, recordings also have the volatile power to sidestep formidable legal hurdles and take the case to the people, creating pressure for rapid settlements.

---

[7] BARRY FRIEDMAN, UNWARRANTED: POLICING WITHOUT PERMISSION 312 (2017).
[8] *Id.*
[9] *Id.* at 313.

Salient stories and dramatic events, such as officer-involved shootings or alleged body cavity searches at the roadside, tend to seize public attention.[10] Yet most of the hundreds of thousands of hours of video footage that police departments across the nation will generate are of everyday law enforcement activities such as initiating consensual encounters, stops, and pat downs, often in response to calls for service from the community. These everyday searches and seizures are the main staples of criminal procedure and the criminal justice system and are of great utility to courts in determining the propriety of stops, searches, arrests, and other routine exercises of police power. Video evidence can sometimes be partial, partisan, and potentially misleading as we saw in Chapter 5, but the addition of another window into formerly opaque credibility contests also can offer more data to better inform decision-making and address imbalances in power over proof.

While the dual police recording revolutions may appear adversarial to scholars and in showdowns on the street, they can be complementary to enhance investigation, address weaknesses and blind spots in interpretation, and enhance police accountability. The multiplicity of videos from different angles and perspectives can help address perceptual and interpretative biases and limitations. There are synergistic benefits to letting a multiple cameras record, and videos from diverse perspectives contend.[11]

---

[10] *See generally* Randy Balko, *These Videos of a Texas Police Shooting Show How Body Cameras Can Vindicate Good Cops*, Wash. Post (July 2, 2015), www.washingtonpost.com/news/the-watch/wp/2015/07/02/these-videos-of-a-texas-police-shooting-show-how-body-cameras-can-v indicate-good-cops/; Deborah Hastings, *Texas State Troopers Caught on Camera Probing Women's Privates Aren't Isolated Incidents*, N.Y. Daily News (Aug. 2, 2013, 5:45 PM), www .nydailynews.com/news/national/troopers-texas-probe-genitals-women-traffic-stops-article-1 .1414668; Texas State Troopers Caught on Camera Probing Women's Privates Aren't Isolated Incidents: Lawyers, NY Daily News (Aug. 2, 2013), www.nydailynews.com/news/ national/troopers-texas-probe-genitals-women-traffic-stops-article-1.1414668; A. J. Vicens & Jaeah Lee, *Here Are 13 Killings by Police Captured on Video in the Past Year*, Mother Jones (May 20, 2015), www.motherjones.com/politics/2015/05/police-shootings-caught-on-tape-vi deo; *Video: Dramatic Police Shooting in Las Vegas Caught on Body Camera*, ABC7 (Las Vegas) (July 16, 2015), http://abc7.com/news/video-dramatic-police-shooting-in-vegas-caug ht-on-body-cam/855728/.

[11] *Cf.* Mao Tse-Tung, On 'Let a Hundred Flowers Bloom, Let a Hundred Schools of Thought Contend,' in Literature of the Hundred Flowers, Vol. 1 (Nieh Hualing, ed. 1981) ("Let a hundred flowers bloom, let a hundred schools of thought contend.").

MINING FOR JUSTICE AND ACCOUNTABILITY

Improving the quality and power of proof is something that can appeal to people from diverse perspectives. Deploying audiovisual big data analytics to better discover risks for rights violations and escalation of encounters is likely to be more polarizing. *Big data* and *data mining* are red-flag terms for some because they are associated with the destruction of privacy and the consolidation of control by entities like the government and corporations with the big data on us. Yet, every day, our data are being aggregated and mined. The techniques can be appropriated to check the powerful, rather than just consolidate power.

The rapidly expanding trove of audiovisual big data from police body cameras, citizen cell phone cameras, and video integration centers pooling private and public feeds can reveal patterns and practices that escalate the risk of violence or rights violations. Advanced analytics drawing on this data can help predict risks and better deploy officers and guide their actions to reduce the risk of harms. This harm prevention potential can be realized while protecting our privacy interests through the controlled access and privacy protection planning discussed in Chapter 7. These principles are part of the architecture of protection that has long successfully secured highly private and protected personal health data while still permitting research to protect public health.

We demand much of police, and we do things to police that we would never do to other professionals who hold official power. If there is an active shooter or an armed burglary, you expect police to run toward the scene, not away. You do not go into your child's classroom using your cell phone camera to record the teacher on the job. And we do not put body cameras on our teachers, prosecutors, judges, or politicians who also wield important public power. Why the police? One answer is the police wield guns, batons, and other weapons – and have the power to use them against us. They have the power to arrest us and put us in jail, to seize our property, to start the machinery that will give us a criminal record and stigmatize us. We also need the police to protect us.

Because we give the police so much control over us, we want to have more of a sense of control to ensure that power is used as safely, humanely, and justly as possible. But body cameras or cell phone cameras are more than just a talisman to give us a feeling of control. They generate massive amounts of data that can be a powerful tool to help us better realize our hopes for better protecting the public and police officers against violence and concerns over rights violations. To realize the full potential of body cameras, policies must consider more than evidentiary value in an individual case or prosecution. Policies must address the potential of aggregated data to detect and prevent problematic practices, improve harm prevention, and open fresh avenues for addressing long-burning challenges.

The Collection and Coding of 213 Body Camera Policies

In January 2018, the author and a team of librarians at the University of Washington's Gallagher Law Library collected body camera policies from municipal police agencies and sheriff's offices using open-source materials, supplemented by public records requests. Many policies were obtained from the Bureau of Justice Assistance Body-Worn Camera Toolkit[1] and from the policy library gathered by the Reporter's Committee for Freedom of the Press.[2] The resulting sample had great diversity of region and city size. Major jurisdictions like New York City, with 8.5 million people, were included, but small jurisdictions, such as Kotzebue, Alaska, population 3,245, also were analyzed.[3]

The codebook used to systematize and standardize policy coding was generated through an iterative process, based on an evaluation of the provisions.[4] The codebook had fifty-five variables covering the range of the most commonly encountered issues in policy debates and encountered in the body camera polices. Each variable had a range of codes for substantive positions well beyond a simple yes or no – for example, capturing combinations of positions, discretionary versus mandatory language, and other features. A team of four divided the policies into four sets and coded them. The codes were then cross-checked by another coder, and differences were highlighted and resolved.

Table A.1 lists the jurisdictions represented among the 213 body camera policies from 48 states collected and coded.

[1] Bureau of Justice Statistics, Body-Worn Camera Toolkit, Resources, (last visited July 29, 2018).
[2] Reporter's Committee for Freedom of the Press, Access to Police Body-Worn Camera Video, (last visited July 29, 2018).
[3] For population size data, see U.S. CENSUS BUREAU, ANNUAL ESTIMATES OF THE RESIDENT POPULATION FOR INCORPORATED PLACES OF 50,000 OR MORE, RANKED BY JULY 1, 2016 POPULATION: APRIL 1, 2010 to July 1, 2016, .
[4] For background on policy coding, see, e.g., Charles Tremper et al., Measuring Law for Evaluation Research, 34 EVALUATION REV. 242, 252–55 (2010).

TABLE A.1 *The 213 Jurisdictions Represented in the Body Camera Policies Collected and Coded*

Alabama
Argo
Calera

Alaska
Kotzebue

Arizona
Lake Havasu
Mesa
Multi-departmental
    policy
Oro Valley
Peoria
Phoenix
Surprise
Tempe
Tucson
Yavapai
Yuma

Arkansas
Fort Smith
Pine Bluff

California
Anaheim
Chico
Chino
Chula Vista
Escondido
Fresno
Hayward
Hermosa Beach
Los Angeles (police
    department)
Los Angeles (sheriff's
    department)
Menlo Park
Merced
Modesto
Oakland
Palo Alto
Rialto
Richmond
Riverside County
San Diego (police
    department)
San Diego (sheriff's
    department)
San Francisco
San Jose
Santa Clara
Santa Rosa
Union City
Vallejo

Colorado
Commerce City
Denver
Fort Collins
Lone Tree
Parker
Pueblo

Connecticut
East Haven
Hamden
New Haven
Police Training
    Center
Redding
Westport

Delaware
New Castle

Florida
Jacksonville
Marianna
Miami-Dade
Ocala
Okaloosa
Orlando
Owasso
Sarasota
Tampa
West Palm Beach

Georgia
Athens-Clarke
Atlanta
Centerville
Richmond County
Savannah Chatham
Sumter County
Valdosta

Hawaii
Honolulu
Kauai

Idaho
Canyon County
City of Post Falls
Coer D'Alene
McCall

Illinois
Chicago
Evanston

Indiana
Evansville
Greenwood
Tipton

Kansas
Lenexa
Sedgwick City
Wichita

Kentucky
Hopkinsville
Lexington
Louisville
Russellville
Scottsville

Louisiana
Baton Rouge
New Orleans

Maryland
Frederick
Laurel
Montgomery County
Prince Georges
    County

Massachusetts
Boston

Michigan
Chocolay
Grand Rapids
Clare
East Lansing
Lansing
Marquette

Minnesota
Burnsville
Duluth
Minneapolis
Olmstead County
Rochester
Roseville
Saint Paul
Spring Lake
St. Anthony

Mississippi
Columbus

Missouri
St. Louis
Columbia
Ferguson
St. Charles
Wentzville

Montana
Missoula

Nebraska
Omaha

Nevada
Las Vegas

New Hampshire
Gilford
Lincoln
Weare

New Jersey
Camden

New Mexico
Grants
Taos

New York
Albany
Niagara Falls
New York City
Rochester
Tompkins

North Carolina
Albemarle
Asheville
Carrboro
Charlotte-
    Mecklenburg
Davidson
Greensboro
Wilmington
Winston-Salem

North Dakota
Devil's Lake
Grand Forks
Minot

Ohio
Cleveland

Oklahoma
Cherokee Nation
Oklahoma City
Owasso

Oregon
Beaverton
Clackamas County
Eugene
Lincoln County
Medford
Newport
Portland
Prineville
Tigard

Pennsylvania
Philadelphia
Pittsburgh

TABLE A.1 *(continued)*

Rhode Island	Austin	**Virginia**	Poulsbo
Providence	De Soto	Arlington County	Pullman
South Carolina	Dallas	Chesapeake	Seattle
Charleston	Fort Worth	Fredericksburg	Spokane
Greenville	Houston	Gordonsville	**West Virginia**
Greer	Rockport	Harrisonburg	Morgantown
	San Antonio	Henrico	
South Dakota	Tyler	Norfolk	**Wisconsin**
Aberdeen	**Utah**	Virginia Beach	Eau Claire
Waterton	American Fork	Warrenton	Fox Valley
Tennessee	Layton	Westmoreland	La Crosse
Alcoa	Logan	**Washington**	Madison
Cleveland	Salt Lake City	Airway Heights	Milwaukee
Memphis	West Jordan	Bainbridge Island	New London
Sullivan County	West Valley	Bellingham	Whitewater
Texas	**Vermont**	Lake Forest Park	**Wyoming**
Aransas	Burlington	Liberty Lake	Mills

Index